KV-351-547

THE WORLD'S CLASSICS

32

SELECTED ENGLISH ESSAYS

Oxford University Press, Ely House, London W. 1

GLASGOW NEW YORK TORONTO MELBOURNE WELLINGTON
CAPE TOWN SALISBURY IBADAN NAIROBI DAR ES SALAAM LUSAKA ADDIS ABABA
BOMBAY CALCUTTA MADRAS KARACHI LAHORE DACCA
KUALA LUMPUR SINGAPORE HONG KONG TOKYO

SELECTED ENGLISH ESSAYS

CHOSEN AND ARRANGED BY

W. PEACOCK

LONDON

OXFORD UNIVERSITY PRESS

This Selection of English Essays for The World's Classics *was first published in* 1903, *and reprinted in* 1904, 1906, 1908 (*twice*), 1909, 1910, 1911 (*twice*), 1912, 1915, 1917, 1918, 1919 (*twice*), 1921, 1922, 1923, 1926, 1929, 1930 (*twice*). *Reset in* 1932 *and reprinted in* 1935, 1939, 1943, 1946, 1948, 1954, 1956, 1959, 1961, 1963, 1966, *and* 1970.

SBN 19 250032 5

PRINTED IN GREAT BRITAIN

PREFACE

THE purpose of this book is to provide in a convenient and inexpensive form a selection of some of the best English essays. While it is hoped that the volume will appeal to general readers, it should be observed that it is intended more especially for students who are preparing for examinations in which essay-writing is one of the prescribed subjects, and who are recommended to study the great masters of English prose, particularly the essayists, both for matter and form.

In making the selection a liberal interpretation has been given to the term Essay, as will be seen by the inclusion of certain character sketches, and of one of Carlyle's lectures on 'Heroes'; and it should, perhaps, be added that there has been no attempt to observe any common standard of length in the specimens chosen.

A chronological order of arrangement has been adopted, and the orthography, where necessary, has been conformed to that of the present time. The essayists represented range from Francis Bacon to Robert Louis Stevenson.

I may remark that for the most part the selections given have formed materials for study and discussion in a class in English Literature which I have the privilege to conduct, and I may be permitted to indulge the hope that the volume will be found of some little use in other classes of the same kind.

I need, perhaps, hardly say that my sympathies are with those critical readers who think that this great essayist or that masterpiece should have been included, but I would urge in extenuation of the shortcomings of the selection in this respect, that considerations of space, and, in the case of the more modern essayists, difficulties of copyright, will account for many omissions.

W. P.

CONTENTS

PAGE

FRANCIS BACON

VISCOUNT ST. ALBANS

1561–1626

I. OF TRUTH

WHAT is truth? said jesting Pilate; and would not stay for an answer. Certainly there be that delight in giddiness, and count it a bondage to fix a belief; affecting free-will in thinking, as well as in acting. And though the sects of philosophers of that kind be gone, yet there remain certain discoursing wits, which are of the same veins, though there be not so much blood in them as was in those of the ancients. But it is not only the difficulty and labour which men take in finding out of truth; nor again, that when it is found, it imposeth upon men's thoughts, that doth bring lies in favour; but a natural though corrupt love of the lie itself. One of the later schools of the Grecians examineth the matter, and is at a stand to think what should be in it, that men should love lies; where neither they make for pleasure, as with poets; nor for advantage, as with the merchant, but for the lie's sake. But I cannot tell: this same truth is a naked and open daylight, that doth not show the masks, and mummeries, and triumphs of the world, half so stately and daintily as candle-lights. Truth may perhaps come to the price of a pearl, that showeth best by day, but it will not rise to the price of a diamond or carbuncle, that showeth best in varied lights. A mixture of a lie doth ever add pleasure. Doth any man doubt, that if there were taken out of men's minds vain opinions, flattering hopes, false valuations, imaginations as one would, and the like, but it would leave the minds of a number of men poor shrunken things, full of melancholy and indisposition, and unpleasing to themselves? One of the fathers, in great severity, called poesy 'vinum dæmonum,' because it filleth the imagination, and yet it is but with the shadow of a lie. But it is not the lie that passeth through the mind, but the lie that sinketh in, and settleth in it, that doth the hurt, such as we spake of before. But howsoever these things are thus in men's depraved judgments and affections, yet truth, which only doth judge itself, teacheth, that the inquiry of truth, which is the love-making, or wooing of it, the knowledge of truth, which is the presence of it, and the belief of truth, which is the enjoying of it, is the sovereign good of human nature. The first creature of God, in the works of the days, was the light of the sense: the last was the light of reason: and his sabbath work ever since, is the illumination of his Spirit. First, he breathed light upon the face of the matter, or chaos; then he breathed light into the face of man; and still he breatheth and inspireth light into the face of his chosen. The poet that beautified the sect, that was otherwise inferior to the rest, saith yet excellently well:—'It is a pleasure to stand upon the shore, and to see ships tossed upon the sea: a pleasure to stand in the window of a castle, and to see a battle, and the adventures thereof below: but no pleasure is comparable to the standing upon the vantage ground of truth' (a hill not to be commanded, and where the air is always clear and serene), 'and to see the errors, and wanderings, and mists, and tempests, in the vale below': so always that this prospect be with pity, and not with swelling or pride. Certainly, it is heaven upon earth, to have a man's mind move in charity, rest in providence, and turn upon the poles of truth.

To pass from theological and philosophical truth to the truth of civil business; it will be acknowledged even by those that practise it not, that clear and round dealing is the honour of man's nature, and that mixture of falsehood is like alloy in coin of gold and silver, which may make the metal work the better, but it embaseth it. For these winding and crooked courses are the goings of the serpent; which goeth basely upon the belly, and not upon the feet. There is no vice that doth so cover a man with shame as to be found false and perfidious; and therefore Montaigne saith prettily, when he inquired the reason why the word of the lie should be such a disgrace, and such an odious charge, saith he, 'If it be well weighed, to say that a man lieth, is as much as to say that he is brave towards God and a coward towards men. For a lie faces God, and shrinks from man.' Surely the wickedness of falsehood and breach of faith cannot possibly be so highly expressed, as in that it shall be the last peal to call the judgments of God upon the generations of men: it being foretold, that, when 'Christ cometh,' he shall not 'find faith upon the earth.'

II. OF DEATH

MEN fear death as children fear to go in the dark; and as that natural fear in children is increased with tales, so is the other. Certainly, the contemplation of death, as the wages of sin, and passage to another world, is holy and religious; but the fear of it, as a tribute due unto nature, is weak. Yet in religious meditations there is sometimes mixture of vanity and of superstition. You shall read in some of the friars' books of mortification, that a man should think with himself, what the pain is, if he have but his finger's end pressed or tortured; and thereby imagine what the pains of death are, when the whole body is corrupted and dissolved; when many times death passeth with less pain than the torture of a limb; for the most vital parts are not the quickest of sense. And by him that spake only as a philosopher, and natural man, it was well said, 'Pompa mortis magis terret, quam mors ipsa.' Groans and convulsions, and a discoloured face, and friends weeping, and blacks and obsequies, and the like, show death terrible. It is worthy the observing, that there is no passion in the mind of man so weak, but it mates and masters the fear of death;

and therefore death is no such terrible enemy when a man hath so many attendants about him that can win the combat of him. Revenge triumphs over death; love slights it; honour aspireth to it; grief flieth to it; fear preoccupateth it; nay, we read, after Otho the emperor had slain himself, pity (which is the tenderest of affections) provoked many to die out of mere compassion to their sovereign, and as the truest sort of followers. Nay, Seneca adds, niceness and satiety: 'Cogita quamdiu eadem feceris; mori velle, non tantum fortis, aut miser, sed etiam fastidiosus potest.' A man would die, though he were neither valiant nor miserable, only upon a weariness to do the same thing so oft over and over. It is no less worthy to observe, how little alteration in good spirits the approaches of death make: for they appear to be the same men till the last instant. Augustus Cæsar died in a compliment; 'Livia, conjugii nostri memor, vive et vale.' Tiberius in dissimulation, as Tacitus saith of him, 'Jam Tiberium vires et corpus, non dissimulatio, deserebant': Vespasian in a jest, sitting upon the stool, 'Ut puto Deus fio': Galba with a sentence, 'Feri, si ex re sit populi Romani,' holding forth his neck; Septimius Severus in dispatch, 'Adeste, si quid mihi restat agendum,' and the like. Certainly the Stoics bestowed too much cost upon death, and by their great preparations made it appear more fearful. Better, saith he, 'qui finem vitæ extremum inter munera ponat naturæ.' It is as natural to die as to be born; and to a little infant, perhaps, the one is as painful as the other. He that dies in an earnest pursuit, is like one that is wounded in hot blood; who, for the time, scarce feels the hurt; and therefore a mind fixed and bent upon somewhat that is good, doth avert the dolours of death; but, above all, believe it, the sweetest canticle is 'Nunc dimittis,' when a man hath obtained worthy ends and expectations. Death hath this also, that it openeth the gate to good fame, and extinguisheth envy: 'Extinctus amabitur idem.'

III. OF REVENGE

REVENGE is a kind of wild justice, which the more man's nature runs to, the more ought law to weed it out; for as for the first wrong, it doth but offend the law, but the revenge of that wrong putteth the law out of office. Certainly, in taking revenge, a man is but even with his enemy; but in passing it over, he is superior; for it is a prince's part to pardon: and Solomon, I am sure, saith, 'It is the glory of a man to pass by an offence.' That which is past is gone and irrevocable, and wise men have enough to do with things present and to come; therefore they do but trifle with themselves that labour in past matters. There is no man doth a wrong for the wrong's sake, but thereby to purchase himself profit, or pleasure, or honour, or the like; therefore why should I be angry with a man for loving himself better than me? And if any man should do wrong, merely out of ill-nature, why, yet it is but like the thorn or briar which prick and scratch, because they can do no other. The most tolerable sort of revenge is for those wrongs which there is no law to remedy; but then, let a man take heed the revenge be such as there is no law to punish, else a man's enemy is still beforehand, and it is two for one. Some, when they take revenge, are desirous the party should know whence it cometh: this is the more generous; for the delight seemeth to be not so much in doing the hurt as in making the party repent: but base and crafty cowards are like the arrow that flieth in the dark. Cosmus, Duke of Florence, had a desperate saying against perfidious or neglecting friends, as if those wrongs were unpardonable. 'You shall read,' saith he, 'that we are commanded to forgive our enemies; but you never read that we are commanded to forgive our friends.' But yet the spirit of Job was in a better tune: 'Shall we,' saith he, 'take good at God's hands, and not be content to take evil also?' and so of friends in a proportion. This is certain, that a man that studieth revenge keeps his own wounds green, which otherwise would heal and do well. Public revenges are for the most part fortunate; as that for the death of Cæsar; for the death of Pertinax; for the death of Henry the Third of France; and many more. But in private revenges it is not so; nay, rather vindictive persons live the life of witches: who, as they are mischievous, so end they unfortunate.

IV. OF ADVERSITY

It was a high speech of Seneca (after the manner of the Stoics), that, 'the good things which belong to prosperity are to be wished, but the good things that belong to adversity are to be admired.' ('Bona rerum secundarum optabilia, adversarum mirabilia.') Certainly, if miracles be the command over nature, they appear most in adversity. It is yet a higher speech of his than the other (much too high for a heathen), 'It is true greatness to have in one the frailty of a man, and the security of a God.' ('Vere magnum habere fragilitatem hominis, securitatem Dei.') This would have done better in poesy, where transcendencies are more allowed; and the poets, indeed, have been busy with it; for it is in effect the thing which is figured in that strange fiction of the ancient poets, which seemeth not to be without mystery; nay, and to have some approach to the state of a Christian, 'that Hercules, when he went to unbind Prometheus (by whom human nature is represented), sailed the length of the great ocean in an earthen pot or pitcher,' lively describing Christian resolution, that saileth in the frail bark of the flesh through the waves of the world. But to speak in a mean, the virtue of prosperity is temperance, the virtue of adversity is fortitude, which in morals is the more heroical virtue. Prosperity is the blessing of the Old Testament, adversity is the blessing of the New, which carrieth the greater benediction, and the clearer revelation of God's favour. Yet even in the Old Testament, if you listen to David's harp, you shall hear as many hearse-like airs as carols; and the pencil of the Holy Ghost hath laboured more in describing the afflictions of Job than the felicities of Solomon. Prosperity is not without many fears and distastes; and adversity is not without comforts and hopes. We see in needle-works and embroideries, it is more pleasing to have a lively work upon a sad and solemn ground, than to have a dark and melancholy work upon a lightsome ground: judge, therefore, of the pleasure of the heart by the pleasure of the eye. Certainly virtue is like precious odours, most fragrant when they are incensed, or crushed: for prosperity doth best discover vice, but adversity doth best discover virtue.

V. OF TRAVEL

TRAVEL, in the younger sort, is a part of education; in the elder, a part of experience. He that travelleth into a country, before he hath some entrance into the language, goeth to school, and not to travel. That young men travel under some tutor or grave servant, I allow well; so that he be such a one that hath the language, and hath been in the country before; whereby he may be able to tell them what things are worthy to be seen in the country where they go, what acquaintances they are to seek, what exercises or discipline the place yieldeth; for else young men shall go hooded, and look abroad little. It is a strange thing, that in sea voyages, where there is nothing to be seen but sky and sea, men should make diaries; but in land travel, wherein so much is to be observed, for the most part they omit it; as if chance were fitter to be registered than observation: let diaries, therefore, be brought in use. The things to be seen and observed are, the courts of princes, especially when they give audience to ambassadors; the courts of justice, while they sit and hear causes; and so of consistories ecclesiastic; the churches and monasteries, with the monuments which are therein extant; the walls and fortifications of cities and towns; and so the havens and harbours, antiquities and ruins, libraries, colleges, disputations, and lectures, where any are; shipping and navies; houses and gardens of state and pleasure, near great cities; armories, arsenals, magazines, exchanges, burses, warehouses, exercises of horsemanship, fencing, training of soldiers, and the like: comedies, such whereunto the better sort of persons do resort; treasuries of jewels and robes; cabinets and rarities; and, to conclude, whatsoever is memorable in the places where they go; after all which the tutors or servants ought to make diligent inquiry. As for triumphs, masks, feasts, weddings, funerals, capital executions, and such shows, men need not to be put in mind of them: yet are they not to be neglected. If you will have a young man to put his travel into a little room, and in short time to gather much, this you must do: first, as was said, he must have some entrance into the language before he goeth; then he must have such a servant, or tutor, as knoweth the country, as was likewise said: let him carry with him also some card, or book, describing the country where he travelleth, which will be a good key to his inquiry; let him keep also a diary; let him not stay long in one city or town, more or less as the place deserveth, but not long; nay, when he stayeth in one city or town, let him change his lodging from one end and part of the town to another, which is a great adamant of acquaintance; let him sequester himself from the company of his countrymen, and diet in such places where there is good company of the nation where he travelleth: let him, upon his removes from one place to another, procure recommendation to some person of quality residing in the place whither he removeth, that he may use his favour in those things he desireth to see or know; thus he may abridge his travel with much profit. As for the acquaintance which is to be sought in travel, that which is most of all profitable, is acquaintance with the secretaries and employed men of ambassadors; for so in travelling in one country he shall suck the experience of many: let him also see and visit eminent persons in all kinds, which are of great name abroad, that he may be able to tell how the life agreeth with the fame; for quarrels, they are with care and discretion to be avoided; they are commonly for mistresses, healths, place, and words; and let a man beware how he keepeth company with choleric and quarrelsome persons; for they will engage him into their own quarrels. When a traveller returneth home, let him not leave the countries where he hath travelled altogether behind him, but maintain a correspondence by letters with those of his acquaintance which are of most worth; and let his travel appear rather in his discourse than in his apparel or gesture; and in his discourse let him be rather advised in his answers, than forward to tell stories: and let it appear that he doth not change his country manners for those of foreign parts; but only prick in some flowers of that he hath learned abroad into the customs of his own country.

VI. OF EMPIRE

It is a miserable state of mind to have few things to desire, and many things to fear; and yet that commonly is the case of Kings, who being at the highest, want matter of desire, which makes their minds more languishing; and have many representations of perils and shadows, which makes their minds the less clear: and this is one reason also of that effect which the Scripture speaketh of, 'That the king's heart is inscrutable': for multitude of jealousies, and lack of some predominant desire, that should marshal and put in order all the rest, maketh any man's heart hard to find or sound. Hence it comes likewise, that princes many times make themselves desires, and set their hearts upon toys; sometimes upon a building; sometimes upon erecting of an order; sometimes upon the advancing of a person; sometimes upon obtaining excellency in some art, or feat of the hand: as Nero for playing on the harp; Domitian for certainty of the hand with the arrow; Commodus for playing at fence; Caracalla for driving chariots, and the like. This seemeth incredible unto those that know not the principle, that the mind of man is more cheered and refreshed by profiting in small things than by standing at a stay in great. We see also that Kings that have been fortunate conquerors in their first years, it being not possible for them to go forward infinitely, but that they must have some check or arrest in their fortunes, turn in their latter years to be superstitious and melancholy; as did Alexander the Great, Dioclesian, and in our memory, Charles the Fifth, and others; for he that is used to go forward, and findeth a stop, falleth out of his own favour, and is not the thing he was.

To speak now of the true temper of empire, it is a thing rare and hard to keep; for both temper and distemper consist of contraries; but it is one thing to mingle contraries, another to interchange them. The answer of Apollonius to Vespasian is full of excellent instruction. Vespasian asked him, 'What was Nero's overthrow?' he answered, 'Nero could touch and tune the harp well; but in government sometimes he used to wind the pins too high, sometimes to let them down too low.' And certain it is, that nothing destroyeth authority so much as the unequal and untimely interchange of power pressed too far, and relaxed too much.

This is true, that the wisdom of all these latter times in princes' affairs is rather fine deliveries, and shiftings of dangers and mischiefs, when they are near, than solid and grounded courses to keep them aloof: but this is but to try masteries with fortune; and let men beware how they neglect and suffer matter of trouble to be prepared. For no man can forbid the spark, nor tell whence it may come. The difficulties in princes' business are many and great; but the greatest difficulty is often in their own mind. For it is common with princes (saith Tacitus) to will contradictories: 'Sunt plerumque regum voluntates vehementes, et inter se contrariæ'; for it is the solecism of power to think to command the end, and yet not to endure the mean.

Kings have to deal with their neighbours, their wives, their children, their prelates or clergy, their nobles, their second nobles or gentlemen, their merchants, their commons, and their men of war; and from all these arise dangers, if care and circumspection be not used.

First, for their neighbours, there can no general rule be given (the occasions are so variable), save one which ever holdeth; which is, that princes do keep due sentinel, that none of their neighbours do overgrow so (by increase of territory, by embracing of trade, by approaches, or the like), as they become more able to annoy them than they were; and this is generally the work of standing counsels to foresee and to hinder it. During that triumvirate of kings, King Henry the Eighth of England, Francis the First, King of France, and Charles the Fifth, Emperor, there was such a watch kept that none of the three could win a palm of ground, but the other two would straightways balance it, either by confederation, or, if need were, by a war; and would not in anywise take up peace at interest: and the like was done by that league (which Guicciardini saith was the security of Italy), made between Ferdinando, King of Naples, Lorenzius Medicis, and Ludovicus Sforza, potentates, the one of Florence, the other of Milan. Neither is the opinion of some of the schoolmen to be received, that a war cannot justly be made, but upon a precedent injury or provocation; for there is no question, but a just fear of an imminent danger, though there be no blow given, is a lawful cause of a war.

For their wives, there are cruel examples of them. Livia is infamed for the poisoning of her husband; Roxolana, Solyman's wife, was the destruction of that renowned prince, Sultan Mustapha, and otherwise troubled his house and succession; Edward the Second of England's Queen had the principal hand in the deposing and murder of her husband.

This kind of danger is then to be feared chiefly when the wives have plots for the raising of their own children, or else that they be advoutresses.[1]

For their children, the tragedies likewise of dangers from them have been many; and generally the entering of fathers into suspicion of their children hath been ever unfortunate. The destruction of Mustapha (that we named before) was so fatal to Solyman's line, as the succession of the Turks from Solyman until this day is suspected to be untrue, and of strange blood; for that Selymus the Second was thought to be supposititious. The destruction of Crispus, a young prince of rare towardness, by Constantinus the Great, his father, was in like manner fatal to his house; for both Constantinus and Constance, his sons, died violent deaths; and Constantius, his other son, did little better, who died indeed of sickness, but after that Julianus had taken arms against him. The destruction of Demetrius, son to Philip the Second of Macedon, turned upon the father, who died of repentance. And many like examples there are; but few or none where the fathers had good by such distrust, except it were where the sons were up in open arms against them; as was Selymus the First against Bajazet, and the three sons of Henry the Second, King of England.

For their prelates, when they are proud and great, there is also danger from them; as it was in the times of Anselmus and Thomas Becket, Archbishops of

[1] Adulteresses.

Canterbury, who with their crosiers did almost try it with the King's sword; and yet they had to deal with stout and haughty Kings: William Rufus, Henry the First, and Henry the Second. The danger is not from that state, but where it hath a dependence of foreign authority; or where the churchmen come in and are elected, not by the collation of the King, or particular patrons, but by the people.

For their nobles, to keep them at a distance it is not amiss; but to depress them may make a King more absolute, but less safe, and less able to perform anything that he desires. I have noted it in my history of King Henry the Seventh of England, who depressed his nobility, whereupon it came to pass that his times were full of difficulties and troubles; for the nobility, though they continued loyal unto him, yet did they not co-operate with him in his business; so that in effect he was fain to do all things himself.

For their second nobles, there is not much danger from them, being a body dispersed: they may sometimes discourse high, but that doth little hurt: besides, they are a counterpoise to the higher nobility, that they grow not too potent; and, lastly, being the most immediate in authority with the common people, they do best temper popular commotions.

For their merchants, they are 'vena porta'; and if they flourish not, a kingdom may have good limbs, but will have empty veins, and nourish little. Taxes and imposts upon them do seldom good to the King's revenue, for that which he wins in the hundred, he loseth in the shire; the particular rates being increased, but the total bulk of trading rather decreased.

For their commons, there is little danger from them, except it be where they have great and potent heads; or where you meddle with the point of religion, or their customs, or means of life.

For their men of war, it is a dangerous state where they live and remain in a body, and are used to donatives; whereof we see examples in the Janizaries and

Prætorian bands of Rome; but trainings of men, and arming them in several places, and under several commanders, and without donatives, are things of defence, and no danger.

Princes are like to heavenly bodies, which cause good or evil times; and which have much veneration, but no rest. All precepts concerning Kings are in effect comprehended in those two remembrances, 'Memento quod es homo'; and 'Memento quod es Deus,' or 'vice Dei'; the one bridleth their power, and the other their will.

VII. OF FRIENDSHIP

It had been hard for him that spake it to have put more truth and untruth together in few words than in that speech, 'Whosoever is delighted in solitude, is either a wild beast or a god': for it is most true, that a natural and secret hatred and aversion towards society in any man hath somewhat of the savage beast; but it is most untrue that it should have any character at all of the divine nature, except it proceed, not out of a pleasure in solitude, but out of a love and desire to sequester a man's self for a higher conversation: such as is found to have been falsely and feignedly in some of the heathen; as Epimenides, the Candian; Numa, the Roman; Empedocles, the Sicilian; and Apollonius of Tyana; and truly and really in divers of the ancient hermits and holy fathers of the Church. But little do men perceive what solitude is, and how far it extendeth; for a crowd is not company, and faces are but a gallery of pictures, and talk but a tinkling cymbal where there is no love. The Latin adage meeteth with it a little, 'Magna civitas, magna solitudo'; because in a great town friends are scattered, so that there is not that fellowship, for the most part, which is in less neighbourhoods: but we may go further, and affirm most truly, that it is a mere and miserable solitude to want true friends, without which the world is but a wilderness; and even in this sense also of solitude, whosoever in the frame of his nature and affections is unfit for friendship, he taketh it of the beast, and not from humanity.

A principal fruit of friendship is the ease and discharge of the fulness and swellings of the heart, which passions of all kinds do cause and induce. We know diseases of stoppings and suffocations are the most dangerous in the body; and it is not much otherwise in the mind; you may take sarza to open the liver, steel to open the spleen, flower of sulphur for the lungs, castoreum for the brain; but no receipt openeth the heart but a true friend, to whom you may impart griefs, joys, fears, hopes, suspicions, counsels, and whatsoever lieth upon the heart to oppress it, in a kind of civil shrift or confession.

It is a strange thing to observe how high a rate great kings and monarchs do set upon this fruit of friendship whereof we speak: so great, as they purchase it many times at the hazard of their own safety and greatness: for princes, in regard of the distance of their fortune from that of their subjects and servants, cannot gather this fruit, except (to make themselves capable thereof) they raise some persons to be as it were companions, and almost equals to themselves, which many times sorteth to inconvenience. The modern languages give unto such persons the name of favourites, or privadoes, as if it were matter of grace, or conversation; but the Roman name attaineth the true use and cause thereof, naming them 'participes curarum'; for it is that which tieth the knot: and we see plainly that this hath been done, not by weak and passionate princes only, but by the wisest and most politic that ever reigned, who have oftentimes joined to themselves some of their servants, whom both themselves have called friends, and allowed others likewise to call them in the same manner, using the word which is received between private men.

L. Sylla, when he commanded Rome, raised Pompey

(after surnamed the Great) to that height that Pompey vaunted himself for Sylla's overmatch, for when he had carried the consulship for a friend of his, against the pursuit of Sylla, and that Sylla did a little resent thereat, and began to speak great, Pompey turned upon him again, and in effect bade him be quiet; for that more men adored the sun rising than the sun setting. With Julius Cæsar, Decimus Brutus had obtained that interest, as he set him down in his testament for heir in remainder after his nephew; and this was the man that had power with him to draw him forth to his death: for when Cæsar would have discharged the senate, in regard of some ill presages, and specially a dream of Calpurnia, this man lifted him gently by the arm out of his chair, telling him he hoped he would not dismiss the senate till his wife had dreamt a better dream; and it seemeth his favour was so great, as Antonius, in a letter which is recited verbatim in one of Cicero's Philippics, calleth him 'venefica,'—'witch'; as if he had enchanted Cæsar. Augustus raised Agrippa (though of mean birth) to that height, as, when he consulted with Mæcenas about the marriage of his daughter Julia, Mæcenas took the liberty to tell him, that he must either marry his daughter to Agrippa, or take away his life: there was no third way, he had made him so great. With Tiberius Cæsar, Sejanus had ascended to that height, as they two were termed and reckoned as a pair of friends. Tiberius, in a letter to him, saith, 'Hæc pro amicitiâ nostrâ non occultavi'; and the whole senate dedicated an altar to Friendship, as to a goddess, in respect of the great dearness of friendship between them two. The like, or more, was between Septimius Severus and Plautianus; for he forced his eldest son to marry the daughter of Plautianus, and would often maintain Plautianus in doing affronts to his son; and did write also, in a letter to the senate, by these words: 'I love the man so well, as I wish he may over-live me.' Now, if these princes had been as a Trajan, or a Marcus Aurelius, a man might have thought that this had proceeded of an abundant goodness of nature; but being men so wise, of such strength and severity of mind, and so extreme lovers of themselves, as all these were, it proveth most plainly that they found their own felicity (though as great as ever happened to mortal men) but as an half-piece, except they might have a friend to make it entire; and yet, which is more, they were princes that had wives, sons, nephews; and yet all these could not supply the comfort of friendship.

It is not to be forgotten what Comineus observeth of his first master, Duke Charles the Hardy, namely, that he would communicate his secrets with none; and least of all, those secrets which troubled him most. Whereupon he goeth on, and saith, that towards his latter time that closeness did impair and a little perish his understanding. Surely Comineus might have made the same judgment also, if it had pleased him, of his second master, Louis the Eleventh, whose closeness was indeed his tormentor. The parable of Pythagoras is dark, but true, 'Cor ne edito,'—'eat not the heart.' Certainly, if a man would give it a hard phrase, those that want friends to open themselves unto are cannibals of their own hearts: but one thing is most admirable (wherewith I will conclude this first fruit of friendship), which is, that this communicating of a man's self to his friend works two contrary effects; for it redoubleth joys, and cutteth griefs in halves: for there is no man that imparteth his joys to his friend, but he joyeth the more; and no man that imparteth his griefs to his friend, but he grieveth the less. So that it is, in truth of operation upon a man's mind, of like virtue as the alchymists used to attribute to their stone for a man's body, that it worketh all contrary effects, but still to the good and benefit of nature: but yet, without praying in aid of alchymists, there is a manifest image of this in the ordinary course of nature; for, in bodies, union strengtheneth and cherisheth any natural action, and, on the other side, weakeneth and dulleth any violent impression; and even so is it of minds.

The second fruit of friendship is healthful and sovereign for the understanding, as the first is for the affections; for friendship maketh indeed a fair day in the affections from storm and tempests, but it maketh daylight in the understanding, out of darkness and confusion of thoughts: neither is this to be understood only of faithful counsel, which a man receiveth from his friend; but before you come to that, certain it is, that whosoever hath his mind fraught with many thoughts, his wits and understanding do clarify and break up in the communicating and discoursing with another; he tosseth his thoughts more easily; he marshalleth them more orderly; he seeth how they look when they are turned into words: finally, he waxeth wiser than himself; and that more by an hour's discourse than by a day's meditation. It was well said by Themistocles to the King of Persia, 'That speech was like cloth of Arras, opened and put abroad; whereby the imagery doth appear in figure; whereas in thoughts they lie but as in packs.' Neither is this second fruit of friendship, in opening the understanding, restrained only to such friends as are able to give a man counsel (they indeed are best), but even without that a man learneth of himself, and bringeth his own thoughts to light, and whetteth his wits as against a stone, which itself cuts not. In a word, a man were better relate himself to a statue or picture, than to suffer his thoughts to pass in smother.

Add now, to make this second fruit of friendship complete, that other point which lieth more open, and falleth within vulgar observation: which is faithful counsel from a friend. Heraclitus saith well in one of his enigmas, 'Dry light is ever the best': and certain it is, that the light that a man receiveth by counsel from another, is drier and purer than that which cometh from his own understanding and judgment;

which is ever infused and drenched in his affections and customs. So as there is as much difference between the counsel that a friend giveth, and that a man giveth himself, as there is between the counsel of a friend and of a flatterer; for there is no such flatterer as is a man's self, and there is no such remedy against flattery of a man's self as the liberty of a friend. Counsel is of two sorts; the one concerning manners, the other concerning business: for the first, the best preservative to keep the mind in health, is the faithful admonition of a friend. The calling of a man's self to a strict account is a medicine sometimes too piercing and corrosive; reading good books of morality is a little flat and dead; observing our faults in others is sometimes improper for our case; but the best receipt (best I say to work and best to take) is the admonition of a friend. It is a strange thing to behold what gross errors and extreme absurdities many (especially of the greater sort) do commit for want of a friend to tell them of them, to the great damage both of their fame and fortune: for, as St. James saith, they are as men 'that look sometimes into a glass, and presently forget their own shape and favour.' As for business, a man may think, if he will, that two eyes see no more than one; or, that a gamester seeth always more than a looker-on; or, that a man in anger is as wise as he that hath said over the four-and-twenty letters; or, that a musket may be shot off as well upon the arm as upon a rest; and such other fond and high imaginations, to think himself all in all: but when all is done, the help of good counsel is that which setteth business straight: and if any man think that he will take counsel, but it shall be by pieces; asking counsel in one business of one man, and in another business of another man; it is well (that is to say, better, perhaps, than if he asked none at all); but he runneth two dangers: one, that he shall not be faithfully counselled; for it is a rare thing, except it be from a perfect and entire friend, to have counsel given, but such as shall be bowed and crooked to some ends which he hath that giveth it: the other, that he shall have counsel given, hurtful and unsafe (though with good meaning), and mixed partly of mischief, and partly of remedy; even as if you would call a physician, that is thought good for the cure of the disease you complain of, but is unacquainted with your body; and, therefore, may put you in a way for a present cure, but overthroweth your health in some other kind, and so cure the disease and kill the patient: but a friend, that is wholly acquainted with a man's estate, will beware, by furthering any present business, how he dasheth upon other inconvenience; and therefore, rest not upon scattered counsels; they will rather distract and mislead, than settle and direct.

After these two noble fruits of friendship (peace in the affections, and support of the judgment), followeth the last fruit, which is like the pomegranate, full of many kernels; I mean aid, and bearing a part in all actions and occasions. Here the best way to represent to life the manifold use of friendship, is to cast and see how many things there are which a man cannot do himself: and then it will appear that it was a sparing speech of the ancients to say, 'that a friend is another himself': for that a friend is far more than himself. Men have their time, and die many times in desire of some things which they principally take to heart; the bestowing of a child, the finishing of a work, or the like. If a man have a true friend, he may rest almost secure that the care of those things will continue after him; so that a man hath, as it were, two lives in his desires. A man hath a body, and that body is confined to a place: but where friendship is, all offices of life are, as it were, granted to him and his deputy; for he may exercise them by his friend. How many things are there, which a man cannot, with any face or comeliness, say or do himself? A man can scarce allege his own merits with modesty, much less extol them: a man cannot sometimes brook to supplicate, or beg, and a number of the like: but all these things are graceful in a friend's mouth, which are blushing in a man's own. So again, a man's person hath many proper relations which he cannot put off. A man cannot speak to his son but as a father; to his wife but as a husband; to his enemy but upon terms: whereas a friend may speak as the case requires, and not as it sorteth with the person: but to enumerate these things were endless; I have given the rule, where a man cannot fitly play his own part, if he have not a friend, he may quit the stage.

VIII. OF STUDIES

Studies serve for delight, for ornament, and for ability. Their chief use for delight, is in privateness and retiring; for ornament, is in discourse; and for ability, is in the judgment and disposition of business; for expert men can execute, and perhaps judge of particulars, one by one: but the general counsels, and the plots and marshalling of affairs come best from those that are learned. To spend too much time in studies, is sloth; to use them too much for ornament, is affectation; to make judgment wholly by their rules, is the humour of a scholar: they perfect nature, and are perfected by experience: for natural abilities are like natural plants, that need pruning by study; and studies themselves do give forth directions too much at large, except they be bounded in by experience. Crafty men contemn studies, simple men admire them, and wise men use them; for they teach not their own use; but that is a wisdom without them and above them, won by observation. Read not to contradict and confute, nor to believe and take for granted, nor to find talk and discourse, but to weigh and consider. Some books are to be tasted, others to be swallowed, and some few to be chewed and digested; that is, some books are to be read only in parts; others to be read but not curiously; and some few to be read wholly, and with diligence and attention. Some books also may be read by deputy, and extracts made of them by others; but that would be only in the less important arguments and the meaner sort of books; else distilled books are, like common distilled waters, flashy things. Reading maketh a full man; conference a ready man; and writing an exact man; and, therefore, if a man write little, he had need have a great memory; if he confer little, he had need have a present wit; and if he read little, he had need have much cunning, to seem to know that he doth not. Histories make men wise; poets, witty; the mathematics, subtle; natural philosophy, deep; moral, grave; logic and rhetoric, able to contend: 'Abeunt studia in mores'; nay, there is no stand or impediment in the wit, but may be wrought out by fit studies: like as diseases of the body may have appropriate exercises; bowling is good for the stone and reins, shooting for the lungs and breast, gentle walking for the stomach, riding for the head and the like; so if a man's wit be wandering, let him study the mathematics; for in demonstrations, if his wit be called away never so little, he must begin again; if his wit be not apt to distinguish or find difference, let him study the schoolmen; for they are 'Cymini sectores.' If he be not apt to beat over matters, and to call up one thing to prove and illustrate another, let him study the lawyers' cases: so every defect of the mind may have a special receipt.

IX. OF GARDENS

God Almighty first planted a garden; and, indeed, it is the purest of human pleasures; it is the greatest refreshment to the spirits of man; without which buildings and palaces are but gross handyworks: and a man shall ever see, that, when ages grow to civility and elegancy, men come to build stately, sooner than to garden finely; as if gardening were the greater perfection. I do hold it in the royal ordering of gardens, there ought to be gardens for all the months in the year, in which, severally, things of beauty may be then in season. For December, and January, and the latter part of November, you must take such things as are green all winter: holly, ivy, bays, juniper, cypress-trees, yew, pineapple-trees; fir-trees, rosemary, lavender; periwinkle, the white, the purple, and the blue; germander, flags, orange-trees, lemon-trees, and myrtles, if they be stoved; and sweet marjoram, warm set. There followeth, for the latter part of January and February, the mezereon-tree, which then blossoms: crocus vernus, both the yellow and the grey; primroses, anemones, the early tulip, the hyacinthus orientalis, chamaïris, fritellaria. For March, there come violets, especially the single blue, which are the earliest; the yellow daffodil, the daisy, the almond-tree in blossom, the peach-tree in blossom, the cornelian-tree in blossom, sweet-briar. In April follow the double white violet, the wallflower, the stock-gilliflower, the cowslip, flower-de-luces and lilies of all natures; rosemary-flowers, the tulip, the double peony, the pale daffodil, the French honeysuckle, the cherry-tree in blossom, the damascene and plum-trees in blossom, the white thorn in leaf, the lilac-tree. In May and June come pinks of all sorts, specially the blush-pink; roses of all kinds, except the musk, which comes later; honeysuckles, strawberries, bugloss, columbine, the French marygold, flos Africanus, cherry-tree in fruit, ribes, figs in fruit, rasps, vine-flowers, lavender in flowers, the sweet satyrian, with the white flower; herba muscaria, lilium convallium, the apple-tree in blossom. In July come gilliflowers of all varieties, musk-roses, the lime-tree in blossom, early pears, and plums in fruit, genitings, codlins. In August come plums of all sorts in fruit, pears, apricots, barberries, filberts, musk-melons, monks-hoods, of all colours. In September come grapes, apples, poppies of all colours, peaches, melocotones, nectarines, cornelians, wardens, quinces. In October, and the beginning of November come services, medlars, bullaces, roses cut or removed to come late, hollyoaks, and such like. These particulars are for the climate of London; but my meaning is perceived, that you may have 'ver perpetuum,' as the place affords.

And because the breath of flowers is far sweeter in the air (where it comes and goes, like the warbling of music), than in the hand, therefore nothing is more fit for that delight, than to know what be the flowers and plants that do best perfume the air. Roses, damask and red, are fast flowers of their smells; so that you may walk by a whole row of them, and find nothing of their sweetness; yea, though it be in a morning's dew. Bays, likewise, yield no smell as they grow, rosemary little, nor sweet marjoram; that which, above all others, yields the sweetest smell in the air, is the violet, especially the white double violet, which comes twice a year, about the middle of April, and about Bartholomew-tide. Next to that is the musk-rose; then the strawberry leaves dying, with a most excellent cordial smell; then the flower of the vines, it is a little dust like the dust of a bent, which grows upon the cluster in the first coming forth; then sweet-briar, then wallflowers, which are very delightful to be set under a parlour or lower chamber window; then pinks and gilliflowers, specially the matted pink and clove gilliflower; then the flowers of the lime-trees; then the honeysuckles, so they be somewhat afar off. Of bean-flowers I speak not, because they are field-flowers; but those which perfume the air most delightfully, not passed by as the rest, but being trodden upon and crushed, are three; that is, burnet, wild thyme, and water-mints; therefore you are to set whole alleys of them, to have the pleasure when you walk or tread.

For gardens (speaking of those which are indeed prince-like, as we have done of buildings), the contents ought not well to be under thirty acres of ground, and to be divided into three parts; a green in the entrance, a heath, or desert, in the going forth, and the main garden in the midst, besides alleys on both sides; and I like well, that four acres of ground be assigned to the green, six to the heath, four and four to either side, and twelve to the main garden. The green hath two pleasures: the one, because nothing is more pleasant to the eye than green grass kept finely shorn; the other, because it will give you a fair alley in the midst, by which you may go in front upon a stately hedge, which is to enclose the garden: but because the alley will be long, and in great heat of the year, or day, you ought not to buy the shade in the garden by going in the sun through the green; therefore you are, of either side the green, to plant a covert alley, upon carpenter's work, about twelve foot in height, by which you may go in shade into the garden. As for the making of knots, or figures, with divers coloured earths, that they may lie under the windows of the house on that side which the garden stands, they be but toys; you may see as good sights many times in tarts. The garden is best to be square, encompassed on all the four sides with a stately arched hedge; the arches to be upon pillars of carpenter's work, of some ten foot high, and six foot broad, and the spaces between of the same dimensions with the breadth of the arch. Over the arches let there be an entire hedge of some four foot high, framed also upon carpenter's work; and upon the upper hedge, over every arch, a little turret, with a belly enough to receive a cage of birds: and over every space between the arches some other little figure, with broad plates of round coloured glass gilt, for the sun to play upon: but this hedge I intend to be raised upon a bank, not steep, but gently slope, of some six foot, set all with flowers. Also I understand, that this square of the garden should not be the whole breadth of the ground, but to leave on either side ground enough for diversity of side alleys, unto which the two covert alleys of the green may deliver you; but there must be no alleys with hedges at either end of this great enclosure; not at the hither end, for letting[1] your prospect upon this fair hedge from the green; nor at the further end, for letting your prospect from the hedge through the arches upon the heath.

For the ordering of the ground within the great hedge, I leave it to variety of device; advising, nevertheless, that whatsoever form you cast it into first, it be not too busy,[2] or full of work; wherein I, for my part, do not like images cut out in juniper or other garden stuff; they be for children. Little low hedges, round like welts, with some pretty pyramids, I like well; and in some places fair columns, upon frames of carpenter's work. I would also have the alleys spacious and fair. You may have closer alleys upon the side grounds, but none in the main garden. I wish also, in the very middle, a fair mount, with three ascents and alleys, enough for four to walk abreast; which I would have to be perfect circles, without any bulwarks or embossments; and the whole mount to be thirty foot high, and some fine banqueting-house with some chimneys neatly cast, and without too much glass.

For fountains, they are a great beauty and refreshment; but pools mar all, and make the garden unwholesome, and full of flies and frogs. Fountains I intend to be of two natures; the one that sprinkleth or spouteth water: the other a fair receipt of water, of some thirty or forty foot square, but without fish, or slime, or mud. For the first, the ornaments of images, gilt or of marble, which are in use, do well: but the main matter is so to convey the water, as it never stay, either in the bowls or in the cistern: that the water be never by rest discoloured, green, or red, or the like, or gather any mossiness or putrefaction; besides that, it is to be cleansed every day by the hand: also some steps up to it, and some fine pavement about it doth well. As for the other kind of fountain, which we may call a bathing-pool, it may

[1] Hindering. [2] Elaborate.

admit much curiosity and beauty, wherewith we will not trouble ourselves: as, that the bottom be finely paved, and with images; the sides likewise; and withal embellished with coloured glass, and such things of lustre; encompassed also with fine rails of low statues: but the main point is the same which we mentioned in the former kind of fountain; which is, that the water be in perpetual motion, fed by a water higher than the pool, and delivered into it by fair spouts, and then discharged away under ground, by some equality of bores, that it stay little; and for fine devices, of arching water without spilling, and making it rise in several forms (of feathers, drinking-glasses, canopies, and the like), they be pretty things to look on, but nothing to health and sweetness.

For the heath, which was the third part of our plot, I wish it to be framed as much as may be to a natural wildness. Trees I would have none in it, but some thickets made only of sweet-briar and honeysuckle, and some wild vine amongst; and the ground set with violets, strawberries, and primroses; for these are sweet, and prosper in the shade; and these to be in the heath here and there, not in any order. I like also little heaps, in the nature of mole-hills (such as are in wild heaths), to be set, some with wild thyme, some with pinks, some with germander, that gives a good flower to the eye; some with periwinkle, some with violets, some with strawberries, some with cowslips, some with daisies, some with red roses, some with lilium convallium, some with sweet-williams red, some with bear's foot, and the like low flowers, being withal sweet and sightly; part of which heaps to be with standards of little bushes pricked upon their top, and part without: the standards to be roses, juniper, holly, barberries (but here and there, because of the smell of their blossom), red currants, gooseberries, rosemary, bays, sweet-briar, and such like: but these standards to be kept with cutting, that they grow not out of course.

For the side grounds, you are to fill them with variety of alleys, private, to give a full shade; some of them, wheresoever the sun be. You are to frame some of them likewise for shelter, that when the wind blows sharp, you may walk as in a gallery: and those alleys must be likewise hedged at both ends, to keep out the wind; and these closer alleys must be ever finely gravelled, and no grass, because of going wet. In many of these alleys, likewise, you are to set fruit-trees of all sorts, as well upon the walls as in ranges; and this should be generally observed, that the borders wherein you plant your fruit-trees be fair, and large, and low, and not steep; and set with fine flowers, but thin and sparingly, lest they deceive the trees. At the end of both the side grounds I would have a mount of some pretty height, leaving the wall of the enclosure breast-high, to look abroad into the fields.

For the main garden I do not deny but there should be some fair alleys ranged on both sides, with fruit-trees, and some pretty tufts of fruit-trees and arbours with seats, set in some decent order; but these to be by no means set too thick, but to leave the main garden so as it be not close, but the air open and free. For as for shade, I would have you rest upon the alleys of the side grounds, there to walk, if you be disposed, in the heat of the year or day; but to make account that the main garden is for the more temperate parts of the year, and, in the heat of summer, for the morning and the evening or overcast days.

For aviaries, I like them not, except they be of that largeness as they may be turfed, and have living plants and bushes set in them; that the birds may have more scope and natural nestling, and that no foulness appear in the floor of the aviary. So I have made a platform of a princely garden, partly by precept, partly by drawing; not a model, but some general lines of it; and in this I have spared for no cost: but it is nothing for great princes, that for the most part, taking advice with workmen, with no less cost set their things together, and sometimes add statues and such things, for state and magnificence, but nothing to the true pleasure of a garden.

ABRAHAM COWLEY

1618–1667

OF SOLITUDE

'*NUNQUAM minus solus, quam cum solus*,' is now become a very vulgar saying. Every man, and almost every boy, for these seventeen hundred years has had it in his mouth. But it was at first spoken by the excellent Scipio, who was without question a most eloquent and witty person, as well as the most wise, most worthy, most happy, and the greatest of all mankind. His meaning no doubt was this: that he found more satisfaction to his mind, and more improvement of it by solitude than by company; and to show that he spoke not this loosely or out of vanity, after he had made Rome mistress of almost the whole world, he retired himself from it by a voluntary exile, and at a private house in the middle of a wood near Linternum passed the remainder of his glorious life no less gloriously. This house Seneca went to see so long after with great veneration, and, among other things, describes his bath to have been of so mean a structure that now, says he, the basest of the people would despise them, and cry out, 'Poor Scipio understood not how to live.' What an authority is here for the credit of retreat! and happy had it been for Hannibal if adversity could have taught him as much wisdom as was learnt by Scipio from the highest prosperities. This would be no wonder if it were as truly as it is colourably and wittily said by Monsieur de Montaigne, that ambition itself might teach us to love solitude: there is nothing does so much hate to have companions. It is true, it loves to have its elbows free, it detests to have company on either side, but it delights above all things in a train behind, ay, and ushers, too, before it. But the greater part of men are so far from the opinion of that noble Roman, that if they chance at any time to be without company they are like a becalmed ship; they never move but by the wind of other men's breath, and have no oars of their own to steer withal. It is very fantastical and contradictory in human nature that men should love themselves above all the rest of the world, and yet never endure to be with themselves. When they are in love with a mistress, all other persons are importunate and burdensome to them. '*Tecum vivere amem, tecum obeam lubens,*' They would live and die with her alone.

Sic ego secretis possum benè vivere silvis
Quà nulla humano sit via trita pede,
Tu mihi curarum requies, tu nocte vel atrâ
Lumen, et in solis tu mihi turba locis.

With thee for ever I in woods could rest,
Where never human foot the ground has pressed
Thou from all shades the darkness canst exclude
And from a desert banish solitude.

And yet our dear self is so wearisome to us that we can scarcely support its conversation for an hour together. This is such an odd temper of mind as Catullus expresses towards one of his mistresses, whom we may suppose to have been of a very unsociable humour.

Odi et Amo, qua nam id faciam ratione requiris?
Nescio, sed fieri sentio, et excrucior.

I hate, and yet I love thee too;
How can that be? I know not how;
Only that so it is I know,
And feel with torment that 'tis so.

It is a deplorable condition this, and drives a man sometimes to pitiful shifts in seeking how to avoid himself.

The truth of the matter is, that neither he who is a fop in the world is a fit man to be alone, nor he who has set his heart much upon the world, though he has ever so much understanding; so that solitude can be well fitted and set right but upon a very few persons. They must have enough knowledge of the world to see the vanity of it, and enough virtue to despise all vanity; if the mind be possessed with any lust or passions, a man had better be in a fair than in a wood alone. They may, like petty thieves, cheat us perhaps, and pick our pockets in the midst of company, but like robbers, they use[1] to strip and bind, or murder us when they catch us alone. This is but to retreat from men, and fall into the hands of devils. It is like the punishment of parricides among the Romans, to be sewed into a bag with an ape, a dog and a serpent. The first work, therefore, that a man must do to make himself capable of the good of solitude is the very eradication of all lusts, for how is it possible for a man to enjoy himself while his affections are tied to things without himself? In the second place, he must learn the art and get the habit of thinking; for this too, no less than well speaking, depends upon much practice; and cogitation is the thing which distinguishes the solitude of a god from a wild beast. Now because the soul of man is not by its own nature or observation furnished with sufficient materials to work upon; it is necessary for it to have continual resource to learning and books for fresh supplies, so that the solitary life will grow indigent, and be ready to starve without them; but if once we be thoroughly engaged in the love of letters, instead of being wearied with the length of any day, we shall only complain of the shortness of our whole life.

O vita, stulto longa, sapienti brevis!

O life, long to the fool, short to the wise!

The First Minister of State has not so much business in public as a wise man has in private; if the one have little leisure to be alone, the other has less leisure to be in company; the one has but part of the affairs of

[1] Are wont.

one nation, the other all the works of God and nature under his consideration. There is no saying shocks me so much as that which I hear very often, 'That a man does not know how to pass his time.' It would have been but ill spoken by Methuselah in the nine hundred and sixty-ninth year of his life, so far it is from us, who have not time enough to attain to the utmost perfection of any part of any science, to have cause to complain that we are forced to be idle for want of work. But this you will say is work only for the learned, others are not capable either of the employments or the divertisements that arise from letters. I know they are not, and therefore cannot much recommend solitude to a man totally illiterate. But if any man be so unlearned as to want entertainment of the little intervals of accidental solitude, which frequently occur in almost all conditions (except the very meanest of the people, who have business enough in the necessary provisions for life), it is truly a great shame both to his parents and himself; for a very small portion of any ingenious art will stop up all those gaps of our time, either music, or painting, or designing, or chemistry, or history, or gardening, or twenty other things, will do it usefully and pleasantly; and if he happen to set his affections upon poetry (which I do not advise him too immoderately) that will overdo it; no wood will be thick enough to hide him from the importunities of company or business, which would abstract him from his beloved.

> —— *O quis me gelidis sub montibus Hæmi*
> *Sistat, et ingenti ramorum protegat umbrâ?*

I

Hail, old patrician trees, so great and good!
  Hail, ye plebeian underwood!
  Where the poetic birds rejoice,
And for their quiet nests and plenteous food
  Pay with their grateful voice.

II

Hail, the poor Muses' richest manor seat!
  Ye country houses and retreat
  Which all the happy gods so love,
That for you oft they quit their bright and great
  Metropolis above.

III

Here Nature does a house for me erect,
  Nature the wisest architect,
  Who those fond artists does despise
That can the fair and living trees neglect,
  Yet the dead timber prize.

IV

Here let me, careless and unthoughtful lying,
  Hear the soft winds, above me flying,
  With all their wanton boughs dispute,
And the more tuneful birds to both replying,
  Nor be myself too mute.

V

A silver stream shall roll his waters near,
  Gilt with the sunbeams here and there,
  On whose enamelled bank I'll walk,
And see how prettily they smile, and hear
  How prettily they talk.

VI

Ah wretched, and too solitary he
  Who loves not his own company!
  He'll feel the weight of't many a day,
Unless he call in sin or vanity
  To help to bear't away.

VII

Oh solitude, first state of human-kind!
  Which blest remained till man did find
  Even his own helper's company.
As soon as two, alas, together joined,
  The serpent made up three.

VIII

Though God himself, through countless ages, thee
His sole companion chose to be,
Thee, sacred Solitude alone;
Before the branchy head of number's Tree
Sprang from the trunk of One.

IX

Thou (though men think thine an unactive part)
Dost break and tame th' unruly heart,
Which else would know no settled pace,
Making it move, well managed by thy art,
With swiftness and with grace.

X

Thou the faint beams of Reason's scattered light
Dost like a burning-glass unite;
Dost multiply the feeble heat,
And fortify the strength, till thou dost bright
And noble fires beget.

XI

Whilst this hard truth I teach, methinks, I see
The monster London laugh at me;
I should at thee too, foolish city,
If it were fit to laugh at misery.
But thy estate, I pity.

XII

Let but thy wicked men from out thee go,
And the fools that crowd thee so,—
Even thou, who dost thy millions boast,
A village less than Islington wilt grow,
A solitude almost.

OF GREATNESS

Since we cannot attain to greatness, says the Sieur de Montaigne, let us have our revenge by railing at it: this he spoke but in jest. I believe he desired it no more than I do, and had less reason, for he enjoyed so plentiful and honourable a fortune in a most excellent country, as allowed him all the real conveniences of it, separated and purged from the incommodities. If I were but in his condition, I should think it hard measure, without being convinced of any crime, to be sequestered from it and made one of the principal officers of state. But the reader may think that what I now say is of small authority, because I never was, nor ever shall be, put to the trial; I can therefore only make my protestation.

If ever I more riches did desire
Than cleanliness and quiet do require;
If e'er ambition did my fancy cheat,
With any wish so mean as to be great,
Continue, Heaven, still from me to remove
The humble blessings of that life I love.

I know very many men will despise, and some pity me, for this humour, as a poor-spirited fellow; but I am content, and, like Horace, thank God for being so. *Dii bene fecerunt inopis me, quodque pusilli finxerunt animi.* I confess I love littleness almost in all things. A little convenient estate, a little cheerful house, a little company, and a very little feast; and if I were ever to fall in love again (which is a great passion, and therefore I hope I have done with it) it would be, I think, with prettiness rather than with majestical beauty. I would neither wish that my mistress, nor my fortune, should be a *bona roba*, nor, as Homer used to describe his beauties, like a daughter of great Jupiter, for the stateliness and largeness of her person, but, as Lucretius says, '*Parvula, pumilio, Χαρίτων μία, tota merum sal.*'

Where there is one man of this, I believe there are

a thousand of Senecio's mind, whose ridiculous affectation of grandeur Seneca the elder describes to this effect. Senecio was a man of a turbid and confused wit, who could not endure to speak any but mighty words and sentences, till this humour grew at last into so notorious a habit, or rather disease, as became the sport of the whole town: he would have no servants but huge massy fellows, no plate or household stuff but thrice as big as the fashion; you may believe me, for I speak it without raillery, his extravagancy came at last into such a madness that he would not put on a pair of shoes each of which was not big enough for both his feet; he would eat nothing but what was great, nor touch any fruit but horse-plums and pound-pears. He kept a concubine that was a very giantess, and made her walk, too, always in *chiopins*, till at last he got the surname of '*Senecio Grandio*,' which, Messala said, was not his cognomen, but his cognomentum. When he declaimed for the three hundred Lacedæmonians, who also opposed Xerxes' army of above three hundred thousand, he stretched out his arms and stood on tiptoes, that he might appear the taller, and cried out in a very loud voice, 'I rejoice, I rejoice!' We wondered, I remember, what new great fortune had befallen his eminence. 'Xerxes,' says he, 'is all mine own. He who took away the sight of the sea with the canvas veils of so many ships . . .' and then he goes on so, as I know not what to make of the rest, whether it be the fault of the edition, or the orator's own burly way of nonsense.

This is the character that Seneca gives of this hyperbolical fop, whom we stand amazed at, and yet there are very few men who are not, in some things, and to some degrees, grandios. Is anything more common than to see our ladies of quality wear such high shoes as they cannot walk in without one to lead them? and a gown as long again as their body, so that they cannot stir to the next room without a page or two to hold it up? I may safely say that all the ostentation of our grandees is just like a train, of no use in the world, but horribly cumbersome and incommodious. What is all this but spice of *grandio*! How tedious would this be if we were always bound to it! I do believe there is no king who would not rather be deposed than endure every day of his reign all the ceremonies of his coronation. The mightiest princes are glad to fly often from these majestic pleasures (which is, methinks, no small disparagement to them), as it were for refuge, to the most contemptible divertisements and meanest recreations of the vulgar, nay, even of children. One of the most powerful and fortunate princes of the world of late could find out no delight so satisfactory as the keeping of little singing-birds, and hearing of them and whistling to them. What did the emperors of the whole world? If ever any men had the free and full enjoyment of all human greatness (nay, that would not suffice, for they would be gods too) they certainly possessed it; and yet one of them, who styled himself 'Lord and God of the Earth,' could not tell how to pass his whole day pleasantly, without spending constant two or three hours in catching of flies, and killing them with a bodkin, as if his godship had been Beelzebub. One of his predecessors, Nero (who never put any bounds, nor met with any stop to his appetite), could divert himself with no pastime more agreeable than to run about the streets all night in a disguise, and abuse the women and affront the men whom he met, and sometimes to beat them, and sometimes to be beaten by them. This was one of his imperial nocturnal pleasures; his chiefest in the day was to sing and play upon a fiddle, in the habit of a minstrel, upon the public stage; he was prouder of the garlands that were given to his divine voice (as they called it then) in those kind of prizes, than all his forefathers were of their triumphs over nations. He did not at his death complain that so mighty an emperor, and the last of all the Cæsarian race of deities, should be brought to so shameful and miserable an end, but only cried out, 'Alas! what pity it is that so excellent a musician should perish in this manner!' His uncle Claudius spent half his time at playing at dice; that was the main fruit of his sovereignty. I omit the madnesses of Caligula's delights, and the execrable sordidness of those of Tiberius. Would one think that Augustus himself, the highest and most fortunate of mankind, a person endowed too with many excellent parts of nature, should be so hard put to it sometimes for want of recreations, as to be found playing at nuts and bounding-stones with little Syrian and Moorish boys, whose company he took delight in for their prating and their wantonness?

> Was it for this, that Rome's best blood he spilt,
> With so much falsehood, so much guilt?
> Was it for this that his ambition strove
> To equal Cæsar first, and after Jove?
> Greatness is barren sure of solid joys;
> Her merchandise, I fear, is all in toys;
> She could not else sure so uncivil be,
> To treat his universal majesty,
> His new created Deity,
> With nuts and bounding-stones and boys.

But we must excuse her for this meagre entertainment; she has not really wherewithal to make such feasts as we imagine; her guests must be contented sometimes with but slender cates, and with the same cold meats served over and over again, even till they become nauseous. When you have pared away all the vanity, what solid and natural contentment does there remain which may not be had with five hundred pounds a year? Not so many servants or horses, but a few good ones, which will do all the business as well; not so many choice dishes at every meal, but at several meals all of them, which makes them both the more healthy and the more pleasant; not so rich garments nor so frequent changes, but as warm and as comely, and so frequent change, too, as is every jot as good for the master, though not for the tailor or valet-de-chambre; not such a stately palace, nor gilt rooms, nor the costlier sorts of tapestry, but a convenient brick house, with decent wainscot and pretty forest-work hangings. Lastly (for I omit all other particulars, and will end with that which I love most in both conditions), not whole woods cut in walks, nor vast parks, nor fountain or cascade gardens, but herb and flower and fruit gardens, which are more useful, and the water every whit as clear and wholesome as if it darted from the breasts of a marble nymph or the urn of a river-god. If for all this you like better the substance of that former estate of life, do but consider the inseparable accidents of both: servitude, disquiet, danger, and most commonly guilt, inherent in the one; in the other, liberty, tranquillity, security, and innocence: and when you have thought upon this, you will confess that to be a truth which appeared to you before but a ridiculous paradox, that a low fortune is better guarded and attended than a high one. If, indeed, we look only upon the flourishing head of the tree, it appears a most beautiful object.

> —— *Sed quantum vertice ad auras*
> *Ætherias, tantum radice ad Tartara tendit.*

> As far up towards heaven the branches grow,
> So far the roots sinks down to hell below.

Another horrible disgrace to greatness is, that it is for the most part in pitiful want and distress. What a wonderful thing is this, unless it degenerate into avarice, and so cease to be greatness. It falls perpetually into such necessities as drive it into all the meanest and most sordid ways of borrowing, cozenage, and robbery, *Mancipiis locuples, eget aeris Cappadocum Rex.* This is the case of almost all great men, as well as of the poor king of Cappadocia. They abound with slaves, but are indigent of money. The ancient Roman emperors, who had the riches of the whole world for their revenue, had wherewithal to live, one would have thought, pretty well at ease, and to have been exempt from the pressures of extreme poverty. But yet with most of them it was much otherwise, and they fell perpetually into such miserable penury, that they were forced to devour or squeeze most of their friends and servants, to cheat with infamous projects, to ransack and pillage all their provinces. This fashion of imperial grandeur is imitated by all inferior and subordinate sorts of it, as if it were a point of honour. They must be cheated of a third part of their estates, two other thirds they must expend in vanity, so that they remain debtors for all the necessary provisions of life, and have no way to satisfy those debts but out of the succours and supplies of rapine; 'as riches increase,' says Solomon, 'so do the mouths that devour it.' The master mouth has no more than before; the owner, methinks, is like Ocnus in the fable, who is perpetually winding a rope of hay and an ass at the end perpetually eating it. Out of these inconveniences arises naturally one more, which is, that no greatness can be satisfied or contented with itself: still, if it could mount up a little higher, it would be happy; if it could but gain that point, it would obtain all its desires; but yet at last, when it is got up to the very top of the peak of Teneriffe, it is in very great danger of breaking its neck downwards, but in no possibility of ascending upwards into the seat of tranquillity above the moon. The first ambitious men in the world, the old giants, are said to have made an heroical attempt of scaling Heaven in despite of the gods, and they cast Ossa upon Olympus and Pelion upon Ossa, two or three mountains more they thought would have done their business, but the thunder spoiled all the work when they were come up to the third storey;

> And what a noble plot was crossed,
> And what a brave design was lost.

A famous person of their offspring, the late giant of

our nation, when, from the condition of a very inconsiderable captain, he had made himself lieutenant-general of an army of little Titans, which was his first mountain; and afterwards general, which was his second; and after that absolute tyrant of three kingdoms, which was the third, and almost touched the heaven which he affected; is believed to have died with grief and discontent because he could not attain to the honest name of a king, and the old formality of a crown, though he had before exceeded the power by a wicked usurpation. If he could have compassed that, he would perhaps have wanted something else that is necessary to felicity, and pined away for the want of the title of an emperor or a god. The reason of this is, that greatness has no reality in nature, but is a creature of the fancy—a notion that consists only in relation and comparison. It is indeed an idol; but St. Paul teaches us that an idol is nothing in the world. There is in truth no rising or meridian of the sun, but only in respect to several places: there is no right or left, no upper hand in nature; everything is little and everything is great according as it is diversely compared. There may be perhaps some villages in Scotland or Ireland where I might be a great man; and in that case I should be like Cæsar—you would wonder how Cæsar and I should be like one another in anything—and choose rather to be the first man of the village than second at Rome. Our country is called Great Britain, in regard only of a lesser of the same name; it would be but a ridiculous epithet for it when we consider it together with the kingdom of China. That, too, is but a pitiful rood of ground in comparison of the whole earth besides; and this whole globe of earth, which we account so immense a body, is but one point or atom in relation to those numberless worlds that are scattered up and down in the infinite space of the sky which we behold. The other many inconveniences of grandeur I have spoken of dispersedly in several chapters, and shall end this with an ode of Horace, not exactly copied but rudely imitated.

HORACE. LIB. 3. ODE I

Odi profanum vulgus, etc.

I

Hence, ye profane; I hate ye all;
Both the great vulgar, and the small.
To virgin minds, which yet their native whiteness
hold,
Not yet discoloured with the love of gold
(That jaundice of the soul,
Which makes it look so gilded and so foul),
To you, ye very few, these truths I tell;
The muse inspires my song, hark, and observe it well.

II

We look on men, and wonder at such odds
'Twixt things that were the same by birth;
We look on kings as giants of the earth,
These giants are but pigmies to the gods.
The humblest bush and proudest oak
Are but of equal proof against the thunder-stroke.
Beauty and strength, and wit, and wealth, and power
Have their short flourishing hour,
And love to see themselves, and smile,
And joy in their pre-eminence a while;
Even so in the same land,
Poor weeds, rich corn, gay flowers together stand;
Alas, death mows down all with an impartial hand.

III

And all you men, whom greatness does so please,
Ye feast, I fear, like Damocles.
If you your eyes could upwards move,
(But you, I fear, think nothing is above)
You would perceive by what a little thread
The sword still hangs over your head.

No tide of wine would drown your cares,
No mirth or music over-noise your fears;
The fear of death would you so watchful keep,
As not to admit the image of it, sleep.

IV

Sleep is a god too proud to wait in palaces;
And yet so humble, too, as not to scorn
The meanest country cottages,
His poppy grows among the corn.
The halcyon sleep will never build his nest
In any stormy breast.
'Tis not enough that he does find
Clouds and darkness in their mind;
Darkness but half his work will do,
'Tis not enough; he must find quiet too.

V

The man who, in all wishes he does make,
Does only Nature's counsel take,
That wise and happy man will never fear
The evil aspects of the year,
Nor tremble, though two comets should appear.
He does not look in almanacks to see
Whether he fortunate shall be ;
Let Mars and Saturn in the heavens conjoin,
And what they please against the world design,
So Jupiter within him shine.

VI

If of their pleasures and desires no end be found;
God to their cares and fears will set no bound.
What would content you? Who can tell?
Ye fear so much to lose what you have got
As if ye liked it well.
Ye strive for more, as if ye liked it not.
Go, level hills, and fill up seas,
Spare nought that may your wanton fancy please;
But trust me, when you have done all this,
Much will be missing still, and much will be amiss.

45

OF MYSELF

It is a hard and nice subject for a man to write of himself; it grates his own heart to say anything of disparagement and the reader's ears to hear anything of praise for him. There is no danger from me of offending him in this kind; neither my mind, nor my body, nor my fortune allow me any materials for that vanity. It is sufficient for my own contentment that they have preserved me from being scandalous, or remarkable on the defective side. But besides that, I shall here speak of myself only in relation to the subject of these precedent discourses, and shall be likelier thereby to fall into the contempt than rise up to the estimation of most people. As far as my memory can return back into my past life, before I knew or was capable of guessing what the world, or glories, or business of it were, the natural affections of my soul gave me a secret bent of aversion from them, as some plants are said to turn away from others, by an antipathy imperceptible to themselves and inscrutable to man's understanding. Even when I was a very young boy at school, instead of running about on holidays and playing with my fellows, I was wont to steal from them and walk into the fields, either alone with a book, or with some one companion, if I could find any of the same temper. I was then, too, so much an enemy to all constraint, that my masters could never prevail on me, by any persuasions or encouragements, to learn without book the common rules of grammar, in which they dispensed with me alone, because they found I made a shift to do the usual exercises out of my own reading and observation. That I was then of the same mind as I am now (which I confess I wonder at myself) may appear by the latter end of an ode which I made when I was but thirteen years old, and which was then printed with many other verses. The beginning of it is boyish, but of this part which I here set down, if a very little were corrected, I should hardly now be much ashamed.

IX

This only grant me, that my means may lie
Too low for envy, for contempt too high.
  Some honour I would have,
Not from great deeds, but good alone.
The unknown are better than ill known.
  Rumour can ope the grave;
Acquaintance I would have, but when it depends
Not on the number, but the choice of friends.

X

Books should, not business, entertain the light,
And sleep, as undisturbed as death, the night.
  My house a cottage, more
Than palace, and should fitting be
For all my use, no luxury.
  My garden painted o'er
With Nature's hand, not Art's; and pleasures yield,
Horace might envy in his Sabine field.

XI

Thus would I double my life's fading space,
For he that runs it well twice runs his race.
  And in this true delight,
These unbought sports, this happy state,
I would not fear, nor wish my fate,
  But boldly say each night,
To-morrow let my sun his beams display
Or in clouds hide them—I have lived to-day.

You may see by it I was even then acquainted with the poets (for the conclusion is taken out of Horace), and perhaps it was the immature and immoderate love of them which stamped first, or rather engraved, these characters in me. They were like letters cut into the bark of a young tree, which with the tree still grow proportionably. But how this love came to be produced in me so early is a hard question. I believe I can tell the particular little chance that filled my head first with such chimes of verse as have never since left ringing there. For I remember when I began to read, and to take some pleasure in it, there was wont to lie in my mother's parlour (I know not by what accident, for she herself never in her life read any book but of devotion), but there was wont to lie Spenser's works; this I happened to fall upon, and was infinitely delighted with the stories of the knights, and giants, and monsters, and brave houses, which I found everywhere there (though my understanding had little to do with all this); and by degrees with the tinkling of the rhyme and dance of the numbers, so that I think I had read him all over before I was twelve years old, and was thus made a poet as immediately as a child is made an eunuch. With these affections of mind, and my heart wholly set upon letters, I went to the university, but was soon torn from thence by that violent public storm which would suffer nothing to stand where it did, but rooted up every plant, even from the princely cedars to me, the hyssop. Yet I had as good fortune as could have befallen me in such a tempest; for I was cast by it into the family of one of the best persons, and into the court of one of the best princesses of the world. Now though I was here engaged in ways most contrary to the original design of my life, that is, into much company, and no small business, and into a daily sight of greatness, both militant and triumphant, for that was the state then of the English and French Courts; yet all this was so far from altering my opinion, that it only added the confirmation of reason to that which was before but natural inclination. I saw plainly all the paint of that kind of life, the nearer I came to it; and that beauty which I did not fall in love with when, for aught I knew, it was real, was not like to bewitch or entice me when I saw that it was adulterate. I met with several great persons, whom I liked very well, but could not perceive that any part of their greatness was to be liked or desired, no more than I would be glad or content to be in a storm, though I saw many ships which rode safely and bravely in it. A storm would not agree with my stomach, if it did with my courage. Though I was in a crowd of as good company as could be found anywhere, though I was in business of great and honourable trust, though I ate at the best table, and enjoyed the best conveniences for present subsistence that ought to be desired by a man of my condition in banishment and public distresses, yet I could not abstain from renewing my old schoolboy's wish in a copy of verses to the same effect.

> Well then; I now do plainly see,
> This busy world and I shall ne'er agree, &c.

And I never then proposed to myself any other advantage from his Majesty's happy restoration, but the getting into some moderately convenient retreat in the country, which I thought in that case I might easily have compassed, as well as some others, with no greater probabilities or pretences, have arrived to extraordinary fortunes. But I had before written a shrewd prophecy against myself, and I think Apollo inspired me in the truth, though not in the elegance of it.

> Thou, neither great at court nor in the war,
> Nor at th' exchange shalt be, nor at the wrangling bar;
> Content thyself with the small barren praise,
> Which neglected verse does raise, etc.

However, by the failing of the forces which I had expected, I did not quit the design which I had resolved on; I cast myself into it *A corps perdu*, without making capitulations or taking counsel of fortune. But God laughs at a man who says to his soul, 'Take thy ease': I met presently not only with many little encumbrances and impediments, but with so much sickness (a new misfortune to me) as would have spoiled the happiness of an emperor as well as mine. Yet I do neither repent nor alter my course. *Non ego perfidum dixi sacramentum.* Nothing shall separate me from a mistress which I have loved so long, and have now at last married, though she neither has brought me a rich portion, nor lived yet so quietly with me as I hoped from her.

> —— *Nec vos, dulcissima mundi*
> *Nomina, vos Musæ, libertas, otia, libri,*
> *Hortique sylvæque anima remanente relinquam.*

> Nor by me e'er shall you,
> You of all names the sweetest, and the best,
> You Muses, books, and liberty, and rest;
> You gardens, fields, and woods forsaken be,
> As long as life itself forsakes not me.

But this is a very petty ejaculation. Because I have concluded all the other chapters with a copy of verses, I will maintain the humour to the last.

MARTIAL, LIB. 10, EP. 47

Vitam quæ faciunt beatiorem, etc.

Since, dearest friend, 'tis your desire to see
A true receipt of happiness from me;
These are the chief ingredients, if not all:
Take an estate neither too great nor small,
Which *quantum sufficit* the doctors call;
Let this estate from parents' care descend:
The getting it too much of life does spend.
Take such a ground, whose gratitude may be
A fair encouragement for industry.
Let constant fires the winter's fury tame,
And let thy kitchens be a vestal flame.
Thee to the town let never suit at law,
And rarely, very rarely, business draw.
Thy active mind in equal temper keep,
In undisturbèd peace, yet not in sleep.
Let exercise a vigorous health maintain,
Without which all the composition 's vain.
In the same weight prudence and innocence take.
Ana of each does the just mixture make.
But a few friendships wear, and let them be
By Nature and by Fortune fit for thee.

Instead of art and luxury in food,
Let mirth and freedom make thy table good.
If any cares into thy daytime creep,
At night, without wines, opium, let them sleep.
Let rest, which Nature does to darkness wed,
And not lust, recommend to thee thy bed,
Be satisfied, and pleased with what thou art;
Act cheerfully and well the allotted part.
Enjoy the present hour, be thankful for the past,
And neither fear, nor wish the approaches of the last.

MARTIAL, LIB. 10, EP. 96

Me, who have lived so long among the great,
You wonder to hear talk of a retreat:
And a retreat so distant, as may show
No thoughts of a return when once I go.
Give me a country, how remote so e'er,
Where happiness a moderate rate does bear,
Where poverty itself in plenty flows
And all the solid use of riches knows.
The ground about the house maintains it there,
The house maintains the ground about it here.
Here even hunger's dear, and a full board
Devours the vital substance of the lord.
The land itself does there the feast bestow,
The land itself must here to market go.
Three or four suits one winter here does waste,
One suit does there three or four winters last.
Here every frugal man must oft be cold,
And little lukewarm fires are to you sold.
There fire 's an element as cheap and free
Almost as any of the other three.
Stay you then here, and live among the great,
Attend their sports, and at their tables eat.
When all the bounties here of men you score:
The Place's bounty there, shall give me more.

DANIEL DEFOE

1661–1731

THE INSTABILITY OF HUMAN GLORY

SIR, I have employed myself of late pretty much in the study of history, and have been reading the stories of the great men of past ages, Alexander the Great, Julius Cæsar, the great Augustus, and many more down, down, down, to the still greater Louis XIV, and even to the still greatest John, Duke of Marlborough. In my way I met with Tamerlane, the Scythian, Tomornbejus, the Egyptian, Solyman, the Magnificent, and others of the Mahometan or Ottoman race; and after all the great things they have done I find it said of them all, one after another, AND THEN HE DIED, all dead, dead, dead! *hic jacet* is the finishing part of their history. Some lie in the bed of honour, and some in honour's truckle bed; some were bravely slain in battle on the field of honour, some in the storm of a counterscarp and died in the ditch of honour: some here, some there;—the bones of the bold and the brave, the cowardly and the base, the hero and the scoundrel, are heaped up together;—there they lie in oblivion, and under the ruins of the earth, undistinguished from one another, nay, even from the common earth.

> Huddled in dirt the blust'ring engine lies,
> That was so great, and thought himself so wise.

How many hundreds of thousands of the bravest fellows then in the world lie on heaps in the ground, whose bones are to this day ploughed up by the rustics, or dug up by the labourer, and the earth their more noble vital parts are converted to has been perhaps applied to the meanest uses!

How have we screened the ashes of heroes to make

our mortar, and mingled the remains of a Roman general to make a hog sty! Where are the ashes of a Cæsar, and the remains of a Pompey, a Scipio, or a Hannibal? All are vanished, they and their very monuments are mouldered into earth, their dust is lost, and their place knows them no more. They live only in the immortal writings of their historians and poets, the renowned flatterers of the age they lived in, and who have made us think of the persons, not as they really were, but as they were pleased to represent them.

As the greatest men, so even the longest lived. The Methuselahs of the antediluvian world—the accounts of them all end with the same. Methuselah lived nine hundred sixty and nine years and begat sons and daughters—and what then? AND THEN HE DIED.

> Death like an overflowing stream
> Sweeps us away; our life's a dream.

We are now solemnising the obsequies of the great Marlborough; all his victories, all his glories, his great projected schemes of war, his uninterrupted series of conquests, which are called his, as if he alone had fought and conquered by his arm, what so many men obtained for him with their blood—all is ended, where other men, and, indeed, where all men ended: HE IS DEAD.

Not all his immense wealth, the spoils and trophies of his enemies, the bounty of his grateful Mistress, and the treasure amassed in war and peace, not all that mighty bulk of gold—which some suggest is such, and so great, as I care not to mention—could either give him life, or continue it one moment, but he is dead; and some say the great treasure he was possessed of here had one strange particular quality attending it, which might have been very dissatisfying to him if he had considered much on it, namely, that he could not carry much of it with him.

We have now nothing left us of this great man

that we can converse with but his monument and his history. He is now numbered among things past. The funeral as well as the battles of the Duke of Marlborough are like to adorn our houses in sculpture as things equally gay and to be looked on with pleasure. Such is the end of human glory, and so little is the world able to do for the greatest men that come into it, and for the greatest merit those men can arrive to.

What then is the work of life? What the business of great men, that pass the stage of the world in seeming triumph as these men, we call heroes, have done? Is it to grow great in the mouth of fame and take up many pages in history? Alas! that is no more than making a tale for the reading of posterity till it turns into fable and romance. Is it to furnish subject to the poets, and live in their immortal rhymes, as they call them? That is, in short, no more than to be hereafter turned into ballad and song and be sung by old women to quiet children, or at the corner of a street to gather crowds in aid of the pickpocket and the poor. Or is their business rather to add virtue and piety to their glory, which alone will pass them into eternity and make them truly immortal? What is glory without virtue? A great man without religion is no more than a great beast without a soul. What is honour without merit? And what can be called true merit but that which makes a person be a good man as well as a great man?

If we believe in a future state of life, a place for the rewards of good men and for the punishment of the haters of virtue, how few crowned heads wear the crowns of immortal felicity!

Let no man envy the great and glorious men, as we call them! Could we see them now, how many of them would move our pity rather than call for our congratulations! These few thoughts, sir, I send to prepare your readers' minds when they go to see the magnificent funeral of the late Duke of Marlborough.

JONATHAN SWIFT

1667–1745

ON STYLE

THE following letter has laid before me many great and manifest evils in the world of letters, which I had overlooked; but they open to me a very busy scene, and it will require no small care and application to amend errors which are become so universal. The affectation of politeness is exposed in this epistle with a great deal of wit and discernment; so that whatever discourses I may fall into hereafter upon the subjects the writer treats of, I shall at present lay the matter before the world, without the least alteration from the words of my correspondent.

'*To Isaac Bickerstaff*, *Esquire*.

'Sir,

'There are some abuses among us of great consequence, the reformation of which is properly your province; though, as far as I have been conversant in your papers, you have not yet considered them. These are the deplorable ignorance that for some years hath reigned among our English writers, the great depravity of our taste, and the continual corruption of our style. I say nothing here of those who handle particular sciences, divinity, law, physic, and the like; I mean the traders in history, politics, and the *belles lettres*, together with those by whom books are not translated, but as the common expressions are, *done* out of French, Latin, or other language, and made English. I cannot but observe to you that until of late years a Grub Street book was always bound in sheep-skin, with suitable print and paper, the price never above a shilling, and taken off wholly by common tradesmen or country pedlars; but now they appear in all sizes and shapes, and in all places. They are handed about from lapfuls in every coffee-house to persons of quality; are shown in Westminster Hall and the Court of Requests. You may see them gilt, and in royal paper of five or six hundred pages, and rated accordingly. I would engage to furnish you with a catalogue of English books, published within the compass of seven years past, which at the first hand would cost you a hundred pounds, wherein you shall not be able to find ten lines together of common grammar or common sense.

'These two evils, ignorance and want of taste, have produced a third; I mean the continual corruption of our English tongue, which, without some timely remedy, will suffer more by the false refinements of twenty years past than it hath been improved in the foregoing hundred. And this is what I design chiefly to enlarge upon, leaving the former evils to your animadversion.

'But instead of giving you a list of the late refinements crept into our language, I here send you the copy of a letter I received, some time ago, from a most accomplished person in this way of writing; upon which I shall make some remarks. It is in these terms:

' "Sir,

' "I *cou'd n't* get the things you sent for all *about town*—I *thot* to *ha* come down myself, and then *I'd h' brot'um*; but I *ha'nt don 't*, and I believe I *can't do 't*, that 's *pozz*—Tom begins to *gi 'mself* airs, because *he 's* going with the *plenipo's*—'T is said the *French* king will *bamboozl us agen*, which causes many speculations. The *Jacks* and others of that *kidney* are very *uppish* and *alert upon 't*, as you may see by their *phizz's*—Will Hazard has got the *hipps*, having lost *to the tune of* five *hundr'd* pound, *tho'* he understands play very well, *no body better*. He has *promis't* me upon *rep*, to leave off play; but you know 't is a weakness *he 's* too apt to *give in to*, *tho'* he has as much wit as any man, *no body more*. He has lain *incog* ever since—The *mob 's* very quiet with us now—I believe you *thot I banter'd* you in my last, like a *country put*—I *shan't* leave town this month," etc.

'This letter is in every point an admirable pattern of the present polite way of writing; nor is it of less authority for being an epistle. You may gather every flower in it, with a thousand more of equal sweetness, from the books, pamphlets, and single papers offered us every day in the coffee-houses: and these are the beauties introduced to supply the want of wit, sense, humour, and learning, which formerly were looked upon as qualifications for a writer. If a man of wit, who died forty years ago, were to rise from the grave on purpose, how would he be able to read this letter? and after he had got through that difficulty, how would he be able to understand it? The first thing that strikes your eye is the breaks at the end of almost every sentence; of which I know not the use, only that it is a refinement, and very frequently practised. Then you will observe the abbreviations and elisions, by which consonants of most obdurate sound are joined together, without one softening vowel to intervene; and all this only to make one syllable of two, directly contrary to the example of the Greek and Romans, altogether of the Gothic strain, and a natural tendency towards relapsing into barbarity, which delights in monosyllables, and uniting of mute consonants, as it is observable in all the northern languages. And this is still more visible in the next refinement, which consists in pronouncing the first syllable in a word that has many, and dismissing the rest, such as *phizz*, *hipps*, *mob*, *pozz*, *rep*, and many more, when we are already overloaded with monosyllables, which are the disgrace of our language. Thus we cram one syllable, and cut off the rest, as the owl fattened her mice after she had bitten off their legs to prevent them from running away; and if ours be the same reason for maiming our words, it will certainly answer the end; for I am sure no other nation will desire to borrow them. Some words are hitherto but fairly split, and therefore only in their way to perfection, as *incog* and *plenipo*: but in a short time it is to be hoped they will be further docked to *inc* and *plen*. This reflection has made me of late years very impatient for a peace, which I believe would save the lives of many brave words, as well as men. The war has introduced abundance of polysyllables, which will never be able to live many more campaigns: *speculations*, *operations*, *preliminaries*, *ambassadors*, *pallisadoes*, *communication*, *circumvallation*, *battalions*: as numerous as they are, if they attack us too frequently in our coffee-houses, we shall certainly put them to flight, and cut off the rear.

'The third refinement observable in the letter I send you consists in the choice of certain words, invented by some pretty fellows, such as *banter*, *bamboozle*, *country put*, and *kidney*, as it is there applied; some of which are now struggling for the vogue, and others are in possession of it. I have done my utmost for some years past to stop the progress of *mob* and *banter*, but have been plainly borne down by numbers, and betrayed by those who promised to assist me.

'In the last place, you are to take notice of certain choice phrases scattered through the letter, some of them tolerable enough, until they were worn to rags by servile imitators. You might easily find them though they were not in a different print, and therefore I need not disturb them.

'These are the false refinements in our style which you ought to correct: first, by argument and fair means; but if these fail, I think you are to make use of your authority as Censor, and by an annual *Index Expurgatorius* expunge all words and phrases that are offensive to good sense, and condemn those barbarous mutilations of vowels and syllables. In this last point the usual pretence is, that they spell as they speak. A noble standard for language! to depend upon the caprice of every coxcomb who, because words are the clothing of our thoughts, cuts them out and shapes them as he pleases, and changes them oftener than his dress. I believe all reasonable people would be content that such refiners were more sparing in their words, and liberal in their syllables: and upon this head I should be glad you would bestow some advice upon several young readers in our churches, who, coming up from the university full fraught with admiration of our town politeness, will needs correct the style of their prayer-books. In reading the Absolution, they are very careful to say *pardons* and *absolves*: and in the prayer for the royal family, it must be *endue 'um*, *enrich 'um*, *prosper 'um*, and *bring 'um*. Then in their sermons they use all the modern terms of art, *sham*, *banter*, *mob*, *bubble*, *bully*, *cutting*, *shuffling*, and *palming*; all which, and many more of the like stamp, as I have heard them often in the pulpit from such young sophisters, so I have read them in some of *those sermons that have made most noise of late*. The design, it seems, is to avoid the dreadful imputation of pedantry; to show us that they know the town, understand men and manners, and have not been poring upon old unfashionable books in the university.

'I should be glad to see you the instrument of introducing into our style that simplicity which is the best and truest ornament of most things in life, which the politer age always aimed at in their building and dress, *simplex munditiis*, as well as in their productions of wit. It is manifest that all new affected modes of speech, whether borrowed from the court, the town, or the theatre, are the first perishing parts in any language; and, as I could prove by many hundred instances, have been so in ours. The writings of Hooker, who was a country clergyman, and of Parsons the Jesuit, both in the reign of Queen Elizabeth, are in a style that, with very few allowances, would not offend any present reader, and are much more clear and intelligible than those of Sir Harry Wotton, Sir Robert Naunton, Osborn, Daniel the historian, and several others who wrote later; but being men of the court, and affecting the phrases then in fashion, they are often either not to be understood, or appear perfectly ridiculous.

'What remedies are to be applied to these evils I have not room to consider, having, I fear, already taken up most of your paper. Besides, I think it is our office only to represent abuses, and yours to redress them. I am, with great respect, Sir, yours,' etc.

RICHARD STEELE

1672–1729

MR. BICKERSTAFF VISITS A FRIEND

Interea dulces pendent circum oscula nati,
Casta pudicitiam servat domus.——

VIRG. *Georg*. ii. 523.

THERE are several persons who have many pleasures and entertainments in their possession, which they do not enjoy. It is, therefore, a kind and good office to acquaint them with their own happiness, and turn their attention to such instances of their good fortune as they are apt to overlook. Persons in the married state often want such a monitor; and pine away their days, by looking upon the same condition in anguish and murmur, which carries with it in the opinion of others a complication of all the pleasures of life, and a retreat from its inquietudes.

I am led into this thought by a visit I made an old friend, who was formerly my school-fellow. He came to town last week with his family for the winter, and yesterday morning sent me word his wife expected me to dinner. I am, as it were, at home at that house, and every member of it knows me for their well-wisher. I cannot indeed express the pleasure it is, to be met by the children with so much joy as I am when I go thither. The boys and girls strive who shall come first, when they think it is I that am knocking at the door; and that child which loses the race to me runs back again to tell the father it is Mr. Bickerstaff. This day I was led in by a pretty girl, that we all thought must have forgotten me; for the family has been out of town these two years. Her knowing me again was a mighty subject with us, and took up our discourse at the first entrance. After which, they began to rally me upon a thousand little stories they heard in the country, about my marriage to one of my neighbour's daughters. Upon which the gentleman, my friend, said, 'Nay, if Mr. Bickerstaff marries a child of any of his old companions, I hope mine shall have the preference; there is Mrs. Mary is now sixteen, and would make him as fine a widow as the best of them. But I know him too well; he is so enamoured with the very memory of those who flourished in our youth, that he will not so much as look upon the modern beauties. I remember, old gentleman, how often you went home in a day to refresh your countenance and dress when Teraminta reigned in your heart. As we came up in the coach, I repeated to my wife some of your verses on her.' With such reflections on little passages which happened long ago, we passed our time, during a cheerful and elegant meal. After dinner, his lady left the room, as did also the children. As soon as we were alone, he took me by the hand; 'Well, my good friend,' says he, 'I am heartily glad to see thee; I was afraid you would never have seen all the company that dined with you to-day again. Do not you think the good woman of the house a little altered since you followed her from the play-house, to find out who she was, for me?' I perceived a tear fall down his cheek as he spoke, which moved me not a little. But, to turn the discourse, I said, 'She is not indeed quite that creature she was, when she returned me the letter I carried from you; and told me, "she hoped, as I was a gentleman, I would be employed no more to trouble her, who had never offended me; but would be so much the gentleman's friend, as to dissuade him from a pursuit, which he could never succeed in." You may remember, I thought her in earnest; and you were forced to employ your cousin Will, who made his sister get acquainted with her, for you. You cannot expect her to be for ever fifteen.' 'Fifteen!' replied my good friend: 'Ah! you little understand, you that have lived a bachelor, how great, how exquisite a pleasure there is, in being really beloved! It is impossible, that the most beauteous face in nature should raise in me such pleasing ideas, as when I look upon that excellent woman. That fading in her countenance is chiefly caused by her watching with me in my fever. This was followed by a fit of sickness, which had like to have carried her off last winter. I tell you sincerely, I have so many obligations to her, that I cannot, with any sort of moderation, think of her present state of health. But as to what you say of fifteen, she gives me every day pleasures beyond what I ever knew in the possession of her beauty, when I was in the vigour of youth. Every moment of her life brings me fresh instances of her complacency to my inclinations, and her prudence in regard to my fortune. Her face is to me much more beautiful than when I first saw it; there is no decay in any feature, which I cannot trace, from the very instant it was occasioned by some anxious concern for my welfare and interests. Thus, at the same time, methinks, the love I conceived towards her for what she was, is heightened by my gratitude for what she is. The love of a wife is as much above the idle passion commonly called by that name, as the loud laughter of buffoons is inferior to the elegant mirth of gentlemen. Oh! she is an inestimable jewel. In her examination of her household affairs, she shows a certain fearfulness to find a fault, which makes her servants obey her like children; and the meanest we have has an ingenuous shame for an offence, not always to be seen in children in other families. I speak freely to you, my old friend; ever since her sickness, things that gave me the quickest joy before, turn now to a certain anxiety. As the children play in the next room, I know the poor things by their steps, and am considering what they must do, should they lose their mother in their tender years. The pleasure I used to take in telling my boy stories of battles, and asking my girl questions about the disposal of her baby, and the gossiping of it, is turned into inward reflection and melancholy.'

He would have gone on in this tender way, when the good lady entered, and with an inexpressible sweetness in her countenance told us, 'she had been searching her closet for something very good, to treat such an old friend as I was.' Her husband's eyes sparkled with pleasure at the cheerfulness of her countenance; and I saw all his fears vanish in an instant. The lady observing something in our looks which showed we had been more serious than ordinary, and seeing her husband receive her with great concern under a forced cheerfulness, immediately guessed at what we had been talking of; and applying herself to me, said, with a smile, 'Mr. Bickerstaff, do not believe a word of what he tells you; I shall still live to have you for my second, as I have often promised you, unless he takes more care of himself than he has done since his coming to town. You must know, he tells me that he finds London is a much more healthy place than the country; for he sees several of his old acquaintance and school-fellows are here, young fellows with fair full-bottomed periwigs. I could scarce keep him in this morning from going out open-breasted.' My friend, who is always extremely delighted with her agreeable humour, made her sit down with us. She did it with that easiness which is peculiar to women of sense; and to keep up the good humour she had brought in with her, turned her raillery upon me. 'Mr. Bickerstaff, you remember you followed me one night from the play-house; suppose you should carry me thither to-morrow night, and lead me into the front box.' This put us into a long field of discourse about the beauties, who were mothers to the present, and shined in the boxes twenty years ago. I told her, 'I was glad she had transferred so many of her charms, and I did not question but her eldest daughter was within half-a-year of being a toast.'

We were pleasing ourselves with this fantastical preferment of the young lady, when on a sudden we were alarmed with the noise of a drum, and immediately entered my little godson to give me a point of war. His mother, between laughing and chiding, would have put him out of the room; but I would not part with him so. I found, upon conversation with him, though he was a little noisy in his mirth, that the child had excellent parts, and was a great master of all the learning on the other side eight years old. I perceived him a very great historian in Æsop's Fables: but he frankly declared to me his mind, 'that he did not delight in that learning, because he did not believe they were true'; for which reason I found he had very much turned his studies, for about a twelvemonth past, into the lives and adventures of Don Belianis of Greece, Guy of Warwick, the Seven Champions, and other historians of that age. I could not but observe the satisfaction the father took in the forwardness of his son; and that these diversions might turn to some profit, I found the boy had made remarks, which might be of service to him during the course of his whole life. He would tell you the mismanagements of John Hickerthrift, find fault with the passionate temper in Bevis of Southampton, and loved Saint George for being the champion of England; and by this means had his thoughts insensibly moulded into the notions of discretion, virtue, and honour. I was extolling his accomplishments, when the mother told me, 'that the little girl who led me in this morning was in her way a better scholar than he. Betty,' said she, 'deals chiefly in fairies and sprights; and sometimes in a winter-night will terrify the maids with her accounts, until they are afraid to go up to bed.'

I sat with them until it was very late, sometimes in merry, sometimes in serious discourse, with this particular pleasure, which gives the only true relish to all conversation, a sense that every one of us liked each other. I went home, considering the different conditions of a married life and that of a bachelor; and I must confess it struck me with a secret concern, to reflect, that whenever I go off I shall leave no traces behind me. In this pensive mood I returned to my family; that is to say, to my maid, my dog, and my cat, who only can be the better or worse for what happens to me.

MR. BICKERSTAFF VISITS A FRIEND

(continued)

Ut in vita, sic in studiis, pulcherrimum et humanissimum existimo, severitatem comitatemque miscere, ne illa in tristitiam, haec in petulantiam procedat.—PLIN. *Epist.*

I WAS walking about my chamber this morning in a very gay humour, when I saw a coach stop at my door, and a youth about fifteen alighting out of it, whom I perceived to be the eldest son of my bosom friend that I gave some account of in my paper of the seventeenth of the last month. I felt a sensible pleasure rising in me at the sight of him, my acquaintance having begun with his father when he was just such a stripling, and about that very age. When he came up to me, he took me by the hand, and burst out in tears. I was extremely moved, and immediately said, 'Child, how does your father do?' He began to reply, 'My mother ——' but could not go on for weeping. I went down with him into the coach, and gathered out of him, that his mother was then dying, and that, while the holy man was doing the last offices to her, he had taken that time to come and call me to his father, who, he said, would certainly break his heart, if I did not go and comfort him. The child's discretion in coming to me of his own head, and the tenderness he showed for his parents, would have quite overpowered me, had I not resolved to fortify myself for the seasonable performance of those duties which I owed to my friend. As we were going, I could not but reflect upon the character of that excellent woman, and the greatness of his grief for the loss of one who has ever been the support to him under all other afflictions. How, thought I, will he be able to bear the hour of her death, that could not, when I was lately with him, speak of a sickness, which was then past, without sorrow! We were now got pretty far into Westminster, and arrived at my friend's house. At the door of it I met Favonius, not without a secret satisfaction to find he had been there. I had formerly conversed with him at this house; and as he abounds with that sort of virtue and knowledge which makes religion beautiful, and never leads the conversation into the violence and rage of party-disputes, I listened to him with great pleasure. Our discourse chanced to be upon the subject of death, which he treated with such a strength of reason, and greatness of soul, that, instead of being terrible, it appeared to a mind rightly cultivated, altogether to be contemned, or rather to be desired. As I met him at the door, I saw in his face a certain glowing of grief and humanity, heightened with an air of fortitude and resolution, which, as I afterwards found, had such an irresistible force, as to suspend the pains of the dying, and the lamentation of the nearest friends who attended her. I went up directly to the room where she lay, and was met at the entrance by my friend, who, notwithstanding his thoughts had been composed a little before, at the sight of me turned away his face and wept. The little family of children renewed the expressions of their sorrow according to their several ages and degrees of understanding. The eldest daughter was in tears, busied in attendance upon her mother; others were kneeling about the bedside; and what troubled me most was, to see a little boy, who was too young to know the reason, weeping only because his sisters did. The only one in the room who seemed resigned and comforted was the dying person. At my approach to the bedside, she told me, with a low broken voice, 'This is kindly done—take care of your friend—do not go from him!' She had before taken leave of her husband and children, in a manner proper for so solemn a parting, and with a gracefulness peculiar to a woman of her character. My heart was torn in pieces, to see the husband on one side suppressing and keeping down the swellings of his grief, for fear of disturbing her in her last moments; and the wife, even at that time, concealing the pains she endured, for fear of increasing his affliction. She kept her eyes upon him for some moments after she grew speechless, and soon after closed them for ever. In the moment of her departure, my friend, who had thus far commanded himself, gave a deep groan, and fell into a swoon by her bedside. The distraction of the children, who thought they saw both their parents expiring together, and now lying dead before them, would have melted the hardest heart; but they soon perceived their father recover, whom I helped to remove into another room, with a resolution to accompany him until the first pangs of his affliction were abated. I knew consolation would now be impertinent; and therefore contented myself to sit by him, and condole with him in silence. For I shall here use the method of an ancient author, who, in one of his epistles, relating the virtues and death of Macrinus's wife, expresses himself thus: 'I shall suspend my advice to this best of friends, until he is made capable of receiving it by those three great remedies—*Necessitas ipsa, dies longa, et satietas doloris* —the necessity of submission, length of time, and satiety of grief.'

In the mean time, I cannot but consider, with much commiseration, the melancholy state of one who has had such a part of himself torn from him, and which he misses in every circumstance of life. His condition is like that of one who has lately lost his right arm, and is every moment offering to help himself with it. He does not appear to himself the same person in his house, at his table, in company, or in retirement; and loses the relish of all the pleasures and diversions that were before entertaining to him by her participation of them. The most agreeable objects recall the sorrow for her with whom he used to enjoy them. This additional satisfaction, from the taste of pleasures in the society of one we love, is admirably described in Milton, who represents Eve, though in Paradise itself, no further pleased with the beautiful objects around her, than as she sees them in company with Adam, in that passage so inexpressibly charming:

> With thee conversing, I forget all time;
> All seasons, and their change; all please alike.
> Sweet is the breath of morn, her rising sweet
> With charm of earliest birds; pleasant the sun,
> When first on this delightful land he spreads
> His orient beams, on herb, tree, fruit, and flower
> Glist'ring with dew; fragrant the fertile earth
> After soft showers; and sweet the coming on
> Of grateful evening mild; the silent night,
> With this her solemn bird, and this fair moon,
> And these the gems of heaven, her starry train.
> But neither breath of morn when she ascends
> With charm of earliest birds; nor rising sun
> On this delightful land; nor herb, fruit, flower,
> Glist'ring with dew; nor fragrance after showers;
> Nor grateful evening mild; nor silent night,
> With this her solemn bird, nor walk by moon,
> Or glittering starlight, without thee is sweet.

The variety of images in this passage is infinitely pleasing, and the recapitulation of each particular image, with a little varying of the expression, makes one of the finest turns of words that I have ever seen; which I rather mention, because Mr. Dryden has said, in his preface to Juvenal, that he could meet with no turn of words in Milton.

It may be further observed, that though the sweetness of these verses has something in it of a pastoral, yet it excels the ordinary kind, as much as the scene of it is above an ordinary field or meadow. I might here, since I am accidentally led into this subject, show several passages in Milton that have as excellent turns of this nature as any of our English poets whatsoever; but shall only mention that which follows, in which he describes the fallen angels engaged in the intricate disputes of predestination, free-will, and fore-knowledge; and, to humour the perplexity, makes a kind of labyrinth in the very words that describe it.

> Others apart sat on a hill retir'd,
> In thoughts more elevate, and reason'd high
> Of Providence, fore-knowledge, will, and fate,
> Fix'd fate, free-will, fore-knowledge absolute,
> And found no end, in wand'ring mazes lost.

THE TRUMPET CLUB

Habeo senectuti magnam gratiam, quæ mihi sermonis aviditatem auxit, potionis et cibi sustulit.—TULL. *de Senect.*

AFTER having applied my mind with more than ordinary attention to my studies, it is my usual custom to relax and unbend it in the conversation of such as are rather easy than shining companions. This I find particularly necessary for me before I retire to rest, in order to draw my slumbers upon me by degrees, and fall asleep insensibly. This is the particular use I make of a set of heavy honest men, with whom I have passed many hours with much indolence, though not with great pleasure. Their conversation is a kind of preparative for sleep: it takes the mind down from its abstractions, leads it into the familiar traces of thought, and lulls it into that state of tranquillity, which is the condition of a thinking man when he is but half awake. After this, my reader will not be surprised to hear the account which I am about to give of a club of my own contemporaries, among whom I pass two or three hours every evening. This I look upon as taking my first nap before I go to bed. The truth of it is, I should think myself unjust to posterity, as well as to the society at the *Trumpet*, of which I am a member, did not I in some part of my writings give an account of the persons among whom I have passed almost a sixth part of my time for these last forty years. Our club consisted originally of fifteen; but, partly by the severity of the law in arbitrary times, and partly by the natural effects of old age, we are at present reduced to a third part of that number; in which, however, we have this consolation, that the best company is said to consist of five persons. I must confess, besides the aforementioned benefit which I meet with in the conversation of this select society, I am not the less pleased with the company, in that I find myself the greatest wit among them, and am heard as their oracle in all points of learning and difficulty.

Sir Jeoffery Notch, who is the oldest of the club, has been in possession of the right-hand chair time out of mind, and is the only man among us that has the liberty of stirring the fire. This, our foreman, is a gentleman of an ancient family, that came to a great estate some years before he had discretion, and run it out in hounds, horses, and cock-fighting: for which reason he looks upon himself as an honest, worthy gentleman, who has had misfortunes in the world, and calls every thriving man a pitiful upstart.

Major Matchlock is the next senior, who served in the last civil wars, and has all the battles by heart. He does not think any action in Europe worth talking of since the fight of Marston Moor; and every night tells us of his having been knocked off his horse at the rising of the London apprentices; for which he is in great esteem among us.

Honest old Dick Reptile is the third of our society. He is a good-natured indolent man, who speaks little himself, but laughs at our jokes; and brings his young nephew along with him, a youth of eighteen years old, to show him good company and give him a taste of the world. This young fellow sits generally silent; but whenever he opens his mouth, or laughs at any thing that passes, he is constantly told by his uncle, after a jocular manner, 'Ay, ay, Jack, you young men think us fools; but we old men know you are.'

The greatest wit of our company, next to myself, is a bencher of the neighbouring inn, who in his youth frequented the ordinaries about Charing-cross, and pretends to have been intimate with Jack Ogle. He has about ten distichs of Hudibras without book, and never leaves the club until he has applied them all. If any modern wit be mentioned, or any town-frolic spoken of, he shakes his head at the dulness of the present age, and tells us a story of Jack Ogle.

For my own part, I am esteemed among them, because they see I am something respected by others; though at the same time I understand by their behaviour, that I am considered by them as a man of a great deal of learning, but no knowledge of the world; insomuch that the major sometimes, in the height of his military pride, calls me the Philosopher: and Sir Jeoffery, no longer ago than last night, upon a dispute what day of the month it was then in Holland, pulled his pipe out of his mouth, and cried, 'What does the scholar say to it?'

Our club meets precisely at six o'clock in the evening; but I did not come last evening until half an hour after seven, by which means I escaped the battle of Naseby, which the major usually begins at about three quarters after six: I found also, that my good friend the bencher had already spent three of his distichs; and only waited an opportunity to hear a sermon spoken of, that he might introduce the couplet where 'a stick' rhymes to 'ecclesiastic.' At my entrance into the room, they were naming a red petticoat and a cloak, by which I found that the bencher had been diverting them with a story of Jack Ogle.

I had no sooner taken my seat, but Sir Jeoffery, to show his good-will towards me, gave me a pipe of his own tobacco, and stirred up the fire. I look upon it as a point of morality, to be obliged by those who endeavour to oblige me; and therefore, in requital for his kindness, and to set the conversation a-going, I took the best occasion I could to put him upon telling us the story of old Gauntlett, which he always does with very particular concern. He traced up his descent on both sides for several generations, describing his diet and manner of life, with his several battles, and particularly that in which he fell. This Gauntlett was a game cock, upon whose head the knight, in his youth, had won five hundred pounds, and lost two thousand. This naturally set the major upon the account of Edge-hill fight, and ended in a duel of Jack Ogle's.

Old Reptile was extremely attentive to all that was said, though it was the same he had heard every night for these twenty years, and, upon all occasions, winked upon his nephew to mind what passed.

This may suffice to give the world a taste of our innocent conversation, which we spun out until about ten of the clock, when my maid came with a lantern to light me home. I could not but reflect with myself, as I was going out, upon the talkative humour of old men, and the little figure which that part of life makes in one who cannot employ his natural propensity in discourses which would make him venerable. I must own, it makes me very melancholy in company, when I hear a young man begin a story; and have often observed, that one of a quarter of an hour long in a man of five-and-twenty, gathers circumstances every time he tells it, until it grows into a long Canterbury tale of two hours by that time he is threescore.

The only way of avoiding such a trifling and frivolous old age is, to lay up in our way to it such stores of knowledge and observation, as may make us useful and agreeable in our declining years. The mind of man in a long life will become a magazine of wisdom or folly, and will consequently discharge itself in something impertinent or improving. For which reason, as there is nothing more ridiculous than an old trifling story-teller, so there is nothing more venerable, than one who has turned his experience to the entertainment and advantage of mankind.

In short, we, who are in the last stage of life, and are apt to indulge ourselves in talk, ought to consider, if what we speak be worth being heard, and endeavour to make our discourse like that of Nestor, which Homer compares to the flowing of honey for its sweetness.

I am afraid I shall be thought guilty of this excess I am speaking of, when I cannot conclude without observing, that Milton certainly thought of this passage in Homer, when, in his description of an eloquent spirit, he says,

His tongue dropped manna.

RECOLLECTIONS OF CHILDHOOD

Dies, ni fallor, adest, quem semper acerbum,
Semper honoratum, sic dii voluistis, habebo.

VIRG. *Æn.* v. 49.

THERE are those among mankind, who can enjoy no relish of their being, except the world is made acquainted with all that relates to them, and think every thing lost that passes unobserved; but others find a solid delight in stealing by the crowd, and modelling their life after such a manner, as is as much above the approbation as the practice of the vulgar. Life being too short to give instances great enough of true friendship or good will, some sages have thought it pious to preserve a certain reverence for the names of their deceased friends; and have withdrawn themselves from the rest of the world at certain seasons, to commemorate in their own thoughts such of their acquaintance who have gone before them out of this life. And indeed, when we are advanced in years, there is not a more pleasing entertainment, than to recollect in a gloomy moment the many we have parted with, that have been dear and agreeable to us, and to cast a melancholy thought or two after those, with whom, perhaps, we have indulged ourselves in whole nights of mirth and jollity. With such inclinations in my heart I went to my closet yesterday in the evening, and resolved to be sorrowful; upon which occasion I could not but look with disdain upon myself, that though all the reasons which I had to lament the loss of many of my friends are now as forcible as at the moment of their departure, yet did not my heart swell with the same sorrow which I felt at the time; but I could, without tears, reflect upon many pleasing adventures I have had with some, who have long been blended with common earth. Though it is by the benefit of nature, that length of time thus blots out the violence of afflictions; yet, with tempers too much given to pleasure, it is almost necessary to revive the old places of grief in our memory; and ponder step by step on past life, to lead the mind into that sobriety of thought which poises the heart, and makes it beat with due time, without being quickened with desire, or retarded with despair, from its proper and equal motion. When we wind up a clock that is out of order, to make it go well for the future, we do not immediately set the hand to the present instant, but we make it strike the round of all its hours, before it can recover the regularity of its time. Such, thought I, shall be my method this evening; and since it is that day of the year which I dedicate to the memory of such in another life as I much delighted in when living, an hour or two shall be sacred to sorrow and their memory, while I run over all the melancholy circumstances of this kind which have occurred to me in my whole life.

The first sense of sorrow I ever knew was upon the death of my father, at which time I was not quite five years of age; but was rather amazed at what all the house meant, than possessed with a real understanding why nobody was willing to play with me. I remember I went into the room where his body lay, and my mother sat weeping alone by it. I had my battledore in my hand, and fell a-beating the coffin, and calling Papa; for, I know not how, I had some slight idea that he was locked up there. My mother caught me in her arms, and, transported beyond all patience of the silent grief she was before in, she almost smothered me in her embraces; and told me in a flood of tears, Papa could not hear me, and would play with me no more, for they were going to put him under ground, whence he could never come to us again. She was a very beautiful woman, of a noble spirit, and there was a dignity in her grief amidst all the wildness of her transport, which, methought, struck me with an instinct of sorrow, that, before I was sensible of what it was to grieve, seized my very soul, and has made pity the weakness of my heart ever since. The mind in infancy is, methinks, like the body in embryo; and receives impressions so forcible, that they are as hard to be removed by reason, as any mark with which a child is born is to be taken away by any future application. Hence it is, that good nature in me is no merit; but having been so frequently overwhelmed with her tears before I knew the cause of any affliction, or could draw defences from my own judgment, I imbibed commiseration, remorse, and an unmanly gentleness of mind, which has since insnared me into ten thousand calamities; and from whence I can reap no advantage, except it be, that, in such a humour as I am now in, I can the better indulge myself in the softnesses of humanity, and enjoy that sweet anxiety which arises from the memory of past afflictions.

We, that are very old, are better able to remember things which befell us in our distant youth, than the passages of later days. For this reason it is, that the companions of my strong and vigorous years present themselves more immediately to me in this office of sorrow. Untimely and unhappy deaths are what we are most apt to lament; so little are we able to make it indifferent when a thing happens, though we know it must happen. Thus we groan under life, and bewail those who are relieved from it. Every object that returns to our imagination raises different passions, according to the circumstances of their departure. Who can have lived in an army, and in a serious hour reflect upon the many gay and agreeable men that might long have flourished in the arts of peace, and not join with the imprecations of the fatherless and widows on the tyrant to whose ambition they fell sacrifices? But gallant men, who are cut off by the sword, move rather our veneration than our pity; and we gather relief enough from their own contempt of death, to make that no evil, which was approached with so much cheerfulness, and attended with so much honour. But when we turn our thoughts from the great parts of life on such occasions, and instead of lamenting those who stood ready to give death to those from whom they had the fortune to receive it; I say, when we let our thoughts wander from such noble objects, and consider the havoc which is made among the tender and the innocent, pity enters with an unmixed softness, and possesses all our souls at once.

Here (were there words to express such sentiments with proper tenderness) I should record the beauty, innocence, and untimely death, of the first object my eyes ever beheld with love. The beauteous virgin! how ignorantly did she charm, how carelessly excel? Oh death! thou hast right to the bold, to the ambitious, to the high, and to the haughty; but why this cruelty to the humble, to the meek, to the undiscerning, to the thoughtless? Nor age, nor business, nor distress, can erase the dear image from my imagination. In the same week I saw her dressed for a ball, and in a shroud. How ill did the habit of death become the pretty trifler? I still behold the smiling earth——A large train of disasters were coming on to my memory, when my servant knocked at my closet-door, and interrupted me with a letter, attended with a hamper of wine, of the same sort with that which is to be put to sale on Thursday next, at Garraway's coffee-house. Upon the receipt of it, I sent for three of my friends. We are so intimate, that we can be company in whatever state of mind we meet, and can entertain each other without expecting always to rejoice. The wine we found to be generous and warming, but with such a heat as moved us rather to be cheerful than frolicsome. It revived the spirits, without firing the blood. We commended it until two of the clock this morning; and having to-day met a little before dinner, we found, that though we drank two bottles a man, we had much more reason to recollect than forget what had passed the night before.

A RAMBLE FROM RICHMOND TO LONDON

> Sine me, vacivum tempus ne quod dem mihi
> Laboris.—TER. *Heaut.* Act. i. Sc. 1.

IT is an inexpressible pleasure to know a little of the world, and be of no character or significancy in it.

To be ever unconcerned, and ever looking on new objects with an endless curiosity, is a delight known only to those who are turned for speculation: nay, they who enjoy it must value things only as they are the objects of speculation, without drawing any worldly advantage to themselves from them, but just as they are what contribute to their amusement, or the improvement of the mind. I lay one night last week at Richmond; and being restless, not out of dissatisfaction, but a certain busy inclination one sometimes has, I rose at four in the morning, and took boat for London, with a resolution to rove by boat and coach for the next four-and-twenty hours, till the many different objects I must needs meet with should tire my imagination, and give me an inclination to repose more profound than I was at that time capable of. I beg people's pardon for an odd humour I am guilty of, and was often that day, which is saluting any person whom I like, whether I know him or not. This is a particularity would be tolerated in me, if they considered that the greatest pleasure I know I receive at my eyes, and that I am obliged to an agreeable person for coming abroad into my view, as another is for a visit of conversation at their own houses.

The hours of the day and night are taken up in the cities of London and Westminster, by people as different from each other as those who are born in different centuries. Men of six o'clock give way to those of nine, they of nine to the generation of twelve; and they of twelve disappear, and make room for the fashionable world, who have made two o'clock the noon of the day.

When we first put off from shore, we soon fell in with a fleet of gardeners, bound for the several market ports of London; and it was the most pleasing scene imaginable to see the cheerfulness with which those industrious people plied their way to a certain sale of their goods. The banks on each side are as well peopled, and beautified with as agreeable plantations, as any spot on the earth; but the Thames itself, loaded with the product of each shore, added very much to the landscape. It was very easy to observe by their sailing, and the countenances of the ruddy virgins, who were supercargoes, the parts of the town to which they were bound. There was an air in the purveyors for Covent-garden, who frequently converse with morning rakes, very unlike the seeming sobriety of those bound for Stocks-market.

Nothing remarkable happened in our voyage; but I landed with ten sail of apricot-boats, at Strand-bridge, after having put in at Nine-Elms, and taken in melons, consigned by Mr. Cuffe, of that place, to Sarah Sewell and Company, at their stall in Covent-garden. We arrived at Strand-bridge at six of the clock, and were unloading; when the hackney-coachmen of the foregoing night took their leave of each other at the Dark-house, to go to bed before the day was too far spent.

Chimney-sweepers passed by us as we made up to the market, and some raillery happened between one of the fruit-wenches and those black men about the Devil and Eve, with allusion to their several professions. I could not believe any place more entertaining than Covent-garden; where I strolled from one fruit-shop to another, with crowds of agreeable young women around me, who were purchasing fruit for their respective families. It was almost eight of the clock before I could leave that variety of objects. I took coach and followed a young lady, who tripped into another just before me, attended by her maid. I saw immediately she was of the family of the Vainloves. There are a set of these, who, of all things, affect the play of Blind-man's-buff, and leading men into love for they know not whom, who are fled they know not where. This sort of woman is usually a jaunty slattern; she hangs on her clothes, plays her head, varies her posture, and changes place incessantly, and all with an appearance of striving at the same time to hide herself, and yet give you to understand she is in humour to laugh at you. You must have often seen the coachmen make signs with their fingers, as they drive by each other, to intimate how much they have got that day. They can carry on that language to give intelligence where they are driving. In an instant my coachman took the wink to pursue; and the lady's driver gave the hint that he was going through Long-acre towards St. James's; while he whipped up James-street, we drove for King-street, to save the pass at St. Martin's-lane. The coachmen took care to meet, jostle, and threaten each other for way, and be entangled at the end of Newport-street and Long-acre. The fright, you must believe, brought down the lady's coach-door, and obliged her, with her mask off, to inquire into the bustle,—when she sees the man she would avoid. The tackle of the coach-window is so bad she cannot draw it up again, and she drives on sometimes wholly discovered, and sometimes half-escaped, according to the accident of carriages in her way. One of these ladies keeps her seat in a hackney-coach, as well as the best rider does on a managed horse. The laced shoe on her left foot, with a careless gesture, just appearing on the opposite cushion, held her both firm, and in a proper attitude to receive the next jolt.

As she was an excellent coach-woman, many were the glances at each other which we had for an hour and a half, in all parts of the town, by the skill of our drivers; till at last my lady was conveniently lost, with notice from her coachman to ours to make off, and he should hear where she went. This chase was now at an end: and the fellow who drove her came to us, and discovered that he was ordered to come again in an hour, for that she was a silk-worm. I was surprised with this phrase, but found it was a cant among the hackney fraternity for their best customers, women who ramble twice or thrice a week from shop to shop, to turn over all the goods in town without buying anything. The silk-worms are, it seems, indulged by the tradesmen; for, though they never buy, they are ever talking of new silks, laces, and ribbons, and serve the owners in getting them customers, as their common dunners do in making them pay.

The day of people of fashion began now to break, and carts and hacks were mingled with equipages of show and vanity; when I resolved to walk it out of cheapness; but my unhappy curiosity is such, that I find it always my interest to take coach; for some odd adventure among beggars, ballad-singers, or the like, detains and throws me into expense. It happened so immediately: for at the corner of Warwick-street, as I was listening to a new ballad, a ragged rascal, a beggar who knew me, came up to me, and began to turn the eyes of the good company upon me, by telling me he was extremely poor, and should die in the street for want of drink, except I immediately would have the charity to give him sixpence to go into the next alehouse and save his life. He urged, with a melancholy face, that all his family had died of thirst. All the mob have humour, and two or three began to take the jest; by which Mr. Sturdy carried his point, and let me sneak off to a coach. As I drove along, it was a pleasing reflection to see the world so prettily checkered since I left Richmond, and the scene still filling with children of a new hour. This satisfaction increased as I moved towards the city; and gay signs, well-disposed streets, magnificent public structures, and wealthy shops adorned with contented faces, made the joy still rising till we came into the centre of the city, and centre of the world of trade, the Exchange of London. As other men in the crowds about me were pleased with their hopes and bargains, I found my account in observing them, in attention to their several interests. I, indeed, looked upon myself as the richest man that walked the Exchange that day; for my benevolence made me share the gains of every bargain that was made. It was not the least of my satisfaction in my survey, to go upstairs, and pass the shops of agreeable females; to observe so many pretty hands busy in the folding of ribbons, and the utmost eagerness of agreeable faces in the sale of patches, pins, and wires, on each side of the counters, was an amusement in which I could longer have indulged myself, had not the dear creatures called to me, to ask what I wanted, when I could not answer, only 'To look at you.' I went to one of the windows which opened to the area below, where all the several voices lost their distinction, and rose up in a confused humming; which created in me a reflection that could not come into the mind of any but of one a little too studious; for I said to myself with a kind of pun in thought, 'What nonsense is all the hurry of this world to those who are above it?' In these, or not much wiser thoughts, I had like to have lost my place at the chop-house, where every man, according to the natural bashfulness or sullenness of our nation, eats in a public room a mess of broth, or chop of meat, in dumb silence, as if they had no pretence to speak to each other on the foot of being men, except they were of each other's acquaintance.

I went afterward to Robin's, and saw people, who had dined with me at the five-penny ordinary just before, give bills for the value of large estates; and could not but behold with great pleasure, property lodged in, and transferred in a moment from, such as would never be masters of half as much as is seemingly in them, and given from them, every day they live. But before five in the afternoon I left the city, came to my common scene of Covent-garden, and passed the evening at Will's in attending the discourses of several sets of people, who relieved each other within my hearing on the subjects of cards, dice, love, learning, and politics. The last subject kept me till I heard the streets in the possession of the bellman, who had now the world to himself, and cried, 'Past two o'clock.' This roused me from my seat; and I went to my lodgings, led by a light, whom I put into the discourse of his private economy, and made him give me an account of the charge, hazard, profit, and loss of a family that depended upon a link, with a design to end my trivial day with the generosity of sixpence, instead of a third part of that sum. When I came to my chambers, I writ down these minutes; but was at a loss what instruction I should propose to my reader from the enumeration of so many insignificant matters and occurrences; and I thought it of great use, if they could learn with me to keep their minds open to gratification, and ready to receive it from any thing it meets with. This one circumstance will make every face you see give you the satisfaction you now take in beholding that of a friend; will make every object a pleasing one; will make all the good which arrives to any man, an increase of happiness to yourself.

83

THE SPECTATOR CLUB

Ast alii sex
Et plures, uno conclamant ore.—JUV. *Sat.* vii. 167.

THE first of our society is a gentleman of Worcestershire, of ancient descent, a baronet, his name Sir Roger de Coverley. His great-grandfather was inventor of that famous country-dance which is called after him. All who know that shire are very well acquainted with the parts and merits of Sir Roger. He is a gentleman that is very singular in his behaviour, but his singularities proceed from his good sense, and are contradictions to the manners of the world only as he thinks the world is in the wrong. However, this humour creates him no enemies, for he does nothing with sourness or obstinacy; and his being unconfined to modes and forms makes him but the readier and more capable to please and oblige all who know him. When he is in town, he lives in Soho-square. It is said, he keeps himself a bachelor by reason he was crossed in love by a perverse beautiful widow of the next county to him. Before this disappointment, Sir Roger was what you call a fine gentleman, had often supped with my Lord Rochester and Sir George Etherege, fought a duel upon his first coming to town, and kicked bully Dawson in a public coffee-house for calling him youngster. But being ill-used by the above-mentioned widow, he was very serious for a year and a half; and though, his temper being naturally jovial, he at last got over it, he grew careless of himself, and never dressed afterward. He continues to wear a coat and doublet of the same cut that were in fashion at the time of his repulse, which, in his merry humours, he tells us, has been in and out twelve times since he first wore it. . . . He is now in his fifty-sixth year, cheerful, gay, and hearty; keeps a good house both in town and country; a great lover of mankind; but there is such a mirthful cast in his behaviour, that he is rather beloved than esteemed.

His tenants grow rich, his servants look satisfied, all the young women profess love to him, and the young men are glad of his company. When he comes into a house he calls the servants by their names, and talks all the way upstairs to a visit. I must not omit, that Sir Roger is a justice of the quorum; that he fills the chair at a quarter-session with great abilities, and three months ago gained universal applause, by explaining a passage in the game act.

The gentleman next in esteem and authority among us is another bachelor, who is a member of the Inner Temple, a man of great probity, wit, and understanding; but he has chosen his place of residence rather to obey the direction of an old humorsome father, than in pursuit of his own inclinations. He was placed there to study the laws of the land, and is the most learned of any of the house in those of the stage. Aristotle and Longinus are much better understood by him than Littleton or Coke. The father sends up every post questions relating to marriage-articles, leases, and tenures in the neighbourhood; all which questions he agrees with an attorney to answer and take care of in the lump. He is studying the passions themselves when he should be inquiring into the debates among men which arise from them. He knows the argument of each of the orations of Demosthenes and Tully, but not one case in the reports of our own courts. No one ever took him for a fool; but none, except his intimate friends, know he has a great deal of wit. This turn makes him at once both disinterested and agreeable: as few of his thoughts are drawn from business, they are most of them fit for conversation. His taste of books is a little too just for the age he lives in; he has read all, but approves of very few. His familiarity with the customs, manners, actions, and writings of the ancients, makes him a very delicate observer of what occurs to him in the present world. He is an excellent critic, and the time of the play is his hour of business; exactly at five he passes through

New-Inn, crosses through Russell-court, and takes a turn at Will's till the play begins; he has his shoes rubbed and his periwig powdered at the barber's as you go into the Rose. It is for the good of the audience when he is at a play, for the actors have an ambition to please him.

The person of next consideration is Sir Andrew Freeport, a merchant of great eminence in the city of London; a person of indefatigable industry, strong reason, and great experience. His notions of trade are noble and generous, and (as every rich man has usually some sly way of jesting, which would make no great figure were he not a rich man) he calls the sea the British Common. He is acquainted with commerce in all its parts, and will tell you that it is a stupid and barbarous way to extend dominion by arms: for true power is to be got by arts and industry. He will often argue, that if this part of our trade were well cultivated, we should gain from one nation; and if another, from another. I have heard him prove, that diligence makes more lasting acquisitions than valour, and that sloth has ruined more nations than the sword. He abounds in several frugal maxims, amongst which the greatest favourite is 'A penny saved is a penny got.' A general trader of good sense is pleasanter company than a general scholar; and Sir Andrew having a natural unaffected eloquence, the perspicuity of his discourse gives the same pleasure that wit would in another man. He has made his fortunes himself; and says that England may be richer than other kingdoms, by as plain methods as he himself is richer than other men; though at the same time I can say this of him, that there is not a point in the compass, but blows home a ship in which he is an owner.

Next to Sir Andrew in the club-room sits Captain Sentry, a gentleman of great courage, good understanding, but invincible modesty. He is one of those that deserve very well, but are very awkward at putting their talents within the observation of such as should take notice of them. He was some years a captain, and behaved himself with great gallantry in several engagements and at several sieges; but having a small estate of his own, and being next heir to Sir Roger, he has quitted a way of life in which no man can rise suitably to his merit, who is not something of a courtier as well as a soldier. I have heard him often lament, that in a profession where merit is placed in so conspicuous a view, impudence should get the better of modesty. When he had talked to this purpose, I never heard him make a sour expression, but frankly confess that he left the world, because he was not fit for it. A strict honesty, and an even regular behaviour, are in themselves obstacles to him that must press through crowds, who endeavour at the same end with himself, the favour of a commander. He will, however, in his way of talk excuse generals, for not disposing according to men's desert, or inquiring into it; for, says he, that great man who has a mind to help me, has as many to break through to come at me, as I have to come at him: therefore he will conclude, that the man who would make a figure, especially in a military way, must get over all false modesty, and assist his patron against the importunity of other pretenders, by a proper assurance in his own vindication. He says it is a civil cowardice to be backward in asserting what you ought to expect, as it is a military fear to be slow in attacking when it is your duty. With this candour does the gentleman speak of himself and others. The same frankness runs through all his conversation. The military part of his life has furnished him with many adventures, in the relation of which he is very agreeable to the company; for he is never overbearing, though accustomed to command men in the utmost degree below him; nor ever too obsequious, from a habit of obeying men highly above him.

But that our society may not appear a set of humorists, unacquainted with the gallantries and pleasures of the age, we have amongst us the gallant Will Honeycomb, a gentleman who, according to his years, should be in the decline of his life, but having been very careful of his person, and always had a very easy fortune, time has made but very little impression, either by wrinkles on his forehead, or traces on his brain. His person is well turned, and of a good height. He is very ready at that sort of discourse with which men usually entertain women. He has all his life dressed very well, and remembers habits as others do men. He can smile when one speaks to him, and laughs easily. He knows the history of every mode, and can inform you from which of the French king's wenches our wives and daughters had this manner of curling their hair, that way of placing their hoods; . . . and whose vanity to show her foot made that part of the dress so short in such a year. In a word, all his conversation and knowledge has been in the female world. As other men of his age will take notice to you what such a minister said upon such an occasion, he will tell you, when the Duke of Monmouth danced at court, such a woman was then smitten—another was taken with him at the head of his troop in the Park. In all these important relations, he has ever about the same time received a kind glance, or a blow of a fan from some celebrated beauty, mother of the present Lord Such-a-one. . . . This way of talking of his very much enlivens the conversation among us of a more sedate turn; and I find there is not one of the company, but myself, who rarely speak at all, but speaks of him as of that sort of man who is usually called a well-bred fine gentleman. To conclude his character, where women are not concerned, he is an honest worthy man.

I cannot tell whether I am to account him whom I am next to speak of, as one of our company; for he visits us but seldom; but when he does, it adds to every man else a new enjoyment of himself. He is a clergyman, a very philosophic man, of general learning, great sanctity of life, and the most exact good breeding. He has the misfortune to be of a very weak constitution, and consequently, cannot accept of such cares and business as preferments in his function would oblige him to; he is therefore among divines what a chamber-counsellor is among lawyers. The probity of his mind, and the integrity of his life, create him followers, as being eloquent or loud advances others. He seldom introduces the subject he speaks upon; but we are so far gone in years, that he observes, when he is among us, an earnestness to have him fall on some divine topic, which he always treats with much authority, as one who has no interest in this world, as one who is hastening to the object of all his wishes, and conceives hope from his decays and infirmities. These are my ordinary companions.

SIR ROGER DE COVERLEY'S PORTRAIT GALLERY

Abnormis sapiens.—HOR. *Sat.* ii. 2, 3.

I WAS this morning walking in the gallery, when Sir Roger entered at the end opposite to me, and advancing towards me, said he was glad to meet me among his relations the De Coverleys, and hoped I liked the conversation of so much good company, who were as silent as myself. I knew he alluded to the pictures, and as he is a gentleman who does not a little value himself upon his ancient descent, I expected he would give me some account of them. We were now arrived at the upper end of the gallery, when the knight faced towards one of the pictures, and, as we stood before it, he entered into the matter after his blunt way of saying things as they occur to his imagination, without regular introduction, or care to preserve the appearance of chain of thought.

'It is,' said he, 'worth while to consider the force of dress; and how the persons of one age differ from those of another, merely by that only. One may observe also, that the general fashion of one age has been followed by one particular set of people in another, and by them preserved from one generation to another. Thus the vast jetting coat and small bonnet, which was the habit in Henry the Seventh's time, is kept on in the yeomen of the guard; not without a good and politic view, because they look a foot taller, and a foot and a half broader—besides that the cap leaves the face expanded, and consequently more terrible and fitter to stand at the entrance of palaces.

'This predecessor of ours, you see, is dressed after this manner, and his cheeks would be no larger than mine were he in a hat as I am. He was the last man that won a prize in the Tilt-yard (which is now a common street before Whitehall). You see the broken lance that lies there by his right foot. He shivered that lance of his adversary all to pieces; and bearing himself, look you, Sir, in this manner, at the same time he came within the target of the gentleman who rode against him, and taking him with incredible force before him on the pommel of his saddle, he in that manner rode the tournament over, with an air that showed he did it rather to perform the rules of the lists. than expose his enemy: however, it appeared he knew how to make use of a victory, and with a gentle trot he marched up to a gallery where their mistress sat (for they were rivals), and let him down with laudable courtesy and pardonable insolence. I do not know but it might be exactly where the coffee-house is now.

'You are to know this my ancestor was not only of a military genius, but fit also for the arts of peace, for he played on the bass-viol as well as any gentleman at court; you see where his viol hangs by his basket-hilt sword. The action at the Tilt-yard, you may be sure, won the fair lady, who was a maid of honour and the greatest beauty of her time; here she stands, the next picture. You see, Sir, my great great great grandmother has on a new-fashioned petticoat, except that the modern is gathered at the waist; my grandmother appears as if she stood in a large drum, whereas the ladies now walk as if they were in a go-cart. For all this lady was bred at court, she became an excellent country-wife; she brought ten children, and when I show you the library, you shall see in her own hand (allowing for the difference of the language) the best receipt now in England both for a hasty-pudding and a white-pot.

'If you please to fall back a little, because it is necessary to look at the three next pictures at one view; these are three sisters. She on the right hand who is so very beautiful, died a maid; the next to her, still handsomer, had the same fate, against her will; this homely thing in the middle had both their portions added to her own, and was stolen by a neighbouring gentleman, a man of stratagem and resolution; for he poisoned three mastiffs to come at her, and knocked down two deer-stealers in carrying her off. Misfortunes happen in all families. The theft of this romp, and so much money, was no great matter to our estate. But the next heir that possessed it was this soft gentleman whom you see there. Observe the small buttons, the little boots, the laces, the slashes about his clothes, and above all the posture he is drawn in (which to be sure was his own choosing): you see he sits with one hand on a desk, writing, and looking as it were another way, like an easy writer, or a sonnetteer. He was one of those that had too much wit to know how to live in the world; he was a man of no justice, but great good manners; he ruined every body that had any thing to do with him, but never said a rude thing in his life; the most indolent person in the world, he would sign a deed that passed away half his estate with his gloves on, but would not put on his hat before a lady if it were to save his country. He is said to be the first that made love by squeezing the hand. He left the estate with ten thousand pounds debt upon it; but, however, by all hands I have been informed, that he was every way the finest gentleman in the world. That debt lay heavy on our house for one generation, but it was retrieved by a gift from that honest man you see there, a citizen of our name, but nothing at all akin to us. I know Sir Andrew Freeport has said behind my back, that this man was descended from one of the ten children of the maid of honour I showed you above: but it was never made out. We winked at the thing indeed, because money was wanting at that time.'

Here I saw my friend a little embarrassed, and turned my face to the next portraiture.

Sir Roger went on with his account of the gallery in the following manner: 'This man (pointing to him I looked at) I take to be the honour of our house, Sir Humphry de Coverley; he was in his dealings as punctual as a tradesman, and as generous as a gentleman. He would have thought himself as much undone by breaking his word, as if it were to be followed by bankruptcy. He served his country as knight of this shire to his dying day. He found it no easy matter to maintain an integrity in his words and actions, even in things that regarded the offices which were incumbent upon him, in the care of his own affairs and relations of life, and therefore dreaded (though he had great talents) to go into employments of state, where he must be exposed to the snares of ambition. Innocence of life, and great ability, were the distinguishing parts of his character; the latter, he had often observed, had led to the destruction of the former, and he used frequently to lament that great and good had not the same signification. He was an excellent husbandman, but had resolved not to exceed such a degree of wealth; all above it he bestowed in secret bounties many years after the sum he aimed at for his own use was attained. Yet he did not slacken his industry, but to a decent old age spent the life and fortune which were superfluous to himself, in the service of his friends and neighbours.'

Here we were called to dinner, and Sir Roger ended the discourse of this gentleman, by telling me, as we followed the servant, that this his ancestor was a brave man, and narrowly escaped being killed in the civil wars; 'for,' said he, 'he was sent out of the field upon a private message, the day before the battle of Worcester.' The whim of narrowly escaping by having been within a day of danger, with other matters abovementioned, mixed with good sense, left me at a loss whether I was more delighted with my friend's wisdom or simplicity.

JOSEPH ADDISON

1672–1719

SIR ROGER DE COVERLEY AT HOME

Hic tibi copia
Manabit ad plenum, benigno
Ruris honorum opulenta cornu.

HOR. *Od.* i. 17.

HAVING often received an invitation from my friend Sir Roger de Coverley to pass away a month with him in the country, I last week accompanied him thither, and am settled with him for some time at his country-house, where I intend to form several of my ensuing speculations. Sir Roger, who is very well acquainted with my humour, lets me rise and go to bed when I please; dine at his own table or in my chamber as I think fit, sit still and say nothing without bidding me be merry. When the gentlemen of the country come to see him, he only shows me at a distance: as I have been walking in his fields I have observed them stealing a sight of me over a hedge, and have heard the knight desiring them not to let me see them, for that I hated to be stared at.

I am the more at ease in Sir Roger's family, because it consists of sober and staid persons: for as the knight is the best master in the world, he seldom changes his servants; and as he is beloved by all about him, his servants never care for leaving him; by this means his domestics are all in years, and grown old with their master. You would take his valet-de-chambre for his brother, his butler is grey-headed, his groom is one of the gravest men that I have ever seen, and his coachman has the looks of a privy-counsellor. You see the goodness of the master even in the old house-dog, and in a grey pad that is kept in the stable with great care and tenderness out of regard to his past services, though he has been useless for several years.

I could not but observe with a great deal of pleasure the joy that appeared in the countenance of these ancient domestics upon my friend's arrival at his country-seat. Some of them could not refrain from tears at the sight of their old master; every one of them pressed forward to do something for him, and seemed discouraged if they were not employed. At the same time the good old knight, with a mixture of the father and the master of the family, tempered the inquiries after his own affairs with several kind questions relating to themselves. This humanity and good nature engages everybody to him, so that when he is pleasant upon any of them, all his family are in good humour, and none so much as the person whom he diverts himself with: on the contrary, if he coughs, or betrays any infirmity of old age, it is easy for a stander by to observe a secret concern in the looks of all his servants.

My worthy friend has put me under the particular care of his butler, who is a very prudent man, and, as well as the rest of his fellow-servants, wonderfully desirous of pleasing me, because they have often heard their master talk of me as of his particular friend.

My chief companion, when Sir Roger is diverting himself in the woods or the fields, is a very venerable man who is ever with Sir Roger, and has lived at his house in the nature of a chaplain above thirty years. This gentleman is a person of good sense and some learning, of a very regular life and obliging conversation: he heartily loves Sir Roger, and knows that he is very much in the old knight's esteem, so that he lives in the family rather as a relation than a dependant.

I have observed in several of my papers, that my friend Sir Roger, amidst all his good qualities, is something of an humorist; and that his virtues, as well as imperfections, are, as it were, tinged by a certain extravagance, which makes them particularly his, and distinguishes them from those of other men.

This cast of mind, as it is generally very innocent in itself, so it renders his conversation highly agreeable, and more delightful than the same degree of sense and virtue would appear in their common or ordinary colours. As I was walking with him last night, he asked me how I liked the good man whom I have just now mentioned; and, without staying for my answer, told me that he was afraid of being insulted with Latin and Greek at his own table; for which reason he desired a particular friend of his at the university to find him out a clergyman rather of plain sense than much learning, of a good aspect, a clear voice, a sociable temper: and, if possible, a man that understood a little of back-gammon. 'My friend,' says Sir Roger, 'found me out this gentleman, who, besides the endowments required of him, is, they tell me, a good scholar, though he does not show it: I have given him the parsonage of the parish; and because I know his value, have settled upon him a good annuity for life. If he outlives me, he shall find that he was higher in my esteem than perhaps he thinks he is. He has now been with me thirty years; and though he does not know I have taken notice of it, has never in all that time asked anything of me for himself, though he is every day soliciting me for something in behalf of one or other of my tenants, his parishioners. There has not been a law-suit in the parish since he has lived among them; if any dispute arises they apply themselves to him for the decision; if they do not acquiesce in his judgment, which I think never happened above once or twice at most, they appeal to me. At his first settling with me, I made him a present of all the good sermons which have been printed in English, and only begged of him that every Sunday he would pronounce one of them in the pulpit. Accordingly, he has digested them into such a series, that they follow one another naturally, and make a continued system of practical divinity.'

As Sir Roger was going on in his story, the gentleman we were talking of came up to us; and upon the knight's asking him who preached to-morrow (for it was Saturday night) told us, the Bishop of St. Asaph in the morning, and Dr. South in the afternoon. He then showed us his list of preachers for the whole year, where I saw with a great deal of pleasure Archbishop Tillotson, Bishop Saunderson, Dr. Barrow, Dr. Calamy, with several living authors who have published discourses of practical divinity. I no sooner saw this venerable man in the pulpit, but I very much approved of my friend's insisting upon the qualifications of a good aspect and a clear voice; for I was so charmed with the gracefulness of his figure and delivery, as well as with the discourses he pronounced, that I think I never passed any time more to my satisfaction. A sermon repeated after this manner, is like the composition of a poet in the mouth of a graceful actor.

I could heartily wish that more of our country clergy would follow this example; and instead of wasting their spirits in laborious compositions of their own, would endeavour after a handsome elocution, and all those other talents that are proper to enforce what has been penned by greater masters. This would not only be more easy to themselves, but more edifying to the people.

SIR ROGER AND WILL WIMBLE

Gratis anhelans, multa agendo nihil agens.

PHÆDR. *Fab.* v. 2.

As I was yesterday morning walking with Sir Roger before his house, a country fellow brought him a huge fish, which, he told him, Mr. Will Wimble had caught that morning; and that he presented it with his service to him, and intended to come and dine with him. At the same time he delivered a letter, which my friend read to me as soon as the messenger left him.

'SIR ROGER,

'I desire you to accept of a jack, which is the best I have caught this season. I intend to come and stay with you a week, and see how the perch bite in the Black River. I observed with some concern, the last time I saw you upon the bowling-green, that your whip wanted a lash to it; I will bring half-a-dozen with me that I twisted last week, which I hope will serve you all the time you are in the country. I have not been out of the saddle for six days past, having been at Eton with Sir John's eldest son. He takes to his learning hugely.—I am, Sir, your humble servant, WILL WIMBLE.'

This extraordinary letter, and message that accompanied it, made me very curious to know the character and quality of the gentleman who sent them; which I found to be as follows. Will Wimble is younger brother to a baronet, and descended of the ancient family of the Wimbles. He is now between forty and fifty: but being bred to no business, and born to no estate, he generally lives with his elder brother as superintendent of his game. He hunts a pack of dogs better than any man in the country, and is very famous for finding out a hare. He is extremely well versed in all the little handicrafts of an idle man: he makes a May-fly to a miracle; and furnishes the whole country with angle rods. As he is a good-natured officious fellow, and very much esteemed upon account of his family, he is a welcome guest at every house, and keeps up a good correspondence among all the gentlemen about him. He carries a tulip-root in his pocket from one to another, or exchanges a puppy between a couple of friends that live perhaps in the opposite sides of the county. Will is a particular favourite of all the young heirs, whom he frequently obliges with a net that he has weaved, or a setting dog that he has made himself. He now and then presents a pair of garters of his own knitting to their mothers or sisters; and raises a great deal of mirth among them, by inquiring as often as he meets them, how they wear? These gentleman-like manufactures and obliging little humours make Will the darling of the country.

Sir Roger was proceeding in the character of him, when we saw him make up to us with two or three hazel twigs in his hand that he had cut in Sir Roger's woods, as he came through them in his way to the house. I was very much pleased to observe, on one side the hearty and sincere welcome with which Sir Roger received him, and on the other the secret joy which his guest discovered at sight of the good old knight. After the first salutes were over, Will desired Sir Roger to lend him one of his servants to carry a set of shuttle-cocks he had with him in a little box to a lady that lived about a mile off, to whom it seems he had promised such a present for above this half year. Sir Roger's back was no sooner turned but honest Will began to tell me of a large cock-pheasant that he had sprung in one of the neighbouring woods, with two or three other adventures of the same nature. Odd and uncommon characters are the game that I look for, and most delight in; for which reason I was so much pleased with the novelty of the person that talked with me, as he could be for his life with the springing of a pheasant, and therefore listened to him with more than ordinary attention.

In the midst of his discourse the bell rung to dinner, where the gentleman I have been speaking of had the pleasure of seeing the huge jack he had caught, served up for the first dish in a most sumptuous manner. Upon our sitting down to it, he gave us a long account how he had hooked it, played with it, foiled it, and at length drew it out upon the bank, with several other particulars that lasted all the first course. A dish of wild fowl that came afterwards furnished conversation for the rest of the dinner, which concluded with a late invention of Will's for improving the quail-pipe.

Upon withdrawing into my room after dinner, I was secretly touched with compassion towards the honest gentleman that had dined with us; and could not but consider with a great deal of concern, how so good an heart and such busy hands were wholly employed in trifles; that so much humanity should be so little beneficial to others, and so much industry so little advantageous to himself. The same temper of mind and application to affairs might have recommended him to the public esteem, and might have raised his fortune in another station of life. What good to his country or himself might not a trader or a merchant have done with such useful though ordinary qualifications!

Will Wimble's is the case of many a younger brother of a great family, who had rather see their children starve like gentlemen, than thrive in a trade or profession that is beneath their quality. This humour fills several parts of Europe with pride and beggary. It is the happiness of a trading nation like ours, that the younger sons, though incapable of any liberal art or profession, may be placed in such a way of life as may perhaps enable them to vie with the best of their family: accordingly we find several citizens that were launched into the world with narrow fortunes, rising by honest industry to greater estates than those of their elder brothers. It is not improbable but Will was formerly tried at divinity, law, or physic; and that, finding his genius did not lie that way, his parents at length gave him up to his own inventions. But certainly, however improper he might have been for studies of a higher nature, he was perfectly well turned for the occupations of trade and commerce. As I think this is a point which cannot be too much inculcated, I shall desire my reader to compare what I have here written with what I have said in my twenty-first speculation.

SIR ROGER AT CHURCH

Ἀθανάτους μὲν πρῶτα θεούς, νόμῳ ὡς διάκειται,
Τίμα—— PYTH.

I AM always very well pleased with a country Sunday, and think, if keeping holy the seventh day were only a human institution, it would be the best method that could have been thought of for the polishing and civilising of mankind. It is certain the country people would soon degenerate into a kind of savages and barbarians, were there not such frequent returns of a stated time in which the whole village meet together with their best faces, and in their cleanliest habits, to converse with one another upon indifferent subjects, hear their duties explained to them, and join together in adoration of the Supreme Being. Sunday clears away the rust of the whole week, not only as it refreshes in their minds the notions of religion, but as it puts both the sexes upon appearing in their most agreeable forms, and exerting all such qualities as are apt to give them a figure in the eye of the village. A country fellow distinguishes himself as much in the churchyard, as a citizen does upon the Change, the whole parish politics being generally discussed in that place either after sermon or before the bell rings.

My friend Sir Roger, being a good churchman, has beautified the inside of his church with several texts of his own choosing; he has likewise given a handsome pulpit-cloth, and railed in the communion table at his own expense. He has often told me, that at his coming to his estate he found his parishioners very irregular; and that in order to make them kneel and join in the responses, he gave every one of them a hassock and a common-prayer book: and at the same time employed an itinerant singing master, who goes about the country for that purpose, to instruct them rightly in the tunes of the psalms; upon which they now very much value themselves, and indeed outdo most of the country churches that I have ever heard.

As Sir Roger is landlord to the whole congregation, he keeps them in very good order, and will suffer nobody to sleep in it besides himself; for if by chance he has been surprised into a short nap at sermon, upon recovering out of it he stands up and looks about him, and if he sees anybody else nodding, either wakes them himself, or sends his servants to them. Several other of the old knight's particularities break out upon these occasions: sometimes he will be lengthening out a verse in the singing-psalms, half a minute after the rest of the congregation have done with it; sometimes, when he is pleased with the matter of his devotion, he pronounces *Amen* three or four times to the same prayer; and sometimes stands up when everybody else is upon their knees, to count the congregation, or see if any of his tenants are missing.

I was yesterday very much surprised to hear my old friend, in the midst of the service, calling out to one John Matthews to mind what he was about, and not disturb the congregation. This John Matthews it seems is remarkable for being an idle fellow, and at that time was kicking his heels for his diversion. This authority of the knight, though exerted in that odd manner which accompanies him in all circumstances of life, has a very good effect upon the parish, who are not polite enough to see anything ridiculous in his behaviour; besides that the general good sense and worthiness of his character makes his friends observe these little singularities as foils that rather set off than blemish his good qualities.

As soon as the sermon is finished, nobody presumes to stir till Sir Roger is gone out of the church. The knight walks down from his seat in the chancel between a double row of his tenants, that stand bowing to him on each side; and every now and then inquires how such an one's wife, or mother, or son, or father do, whom he does not see at church; which is understood as a secret reprimand to the person that is absent.

The chaplain has often told me, that upon a catechising day, when Sir Roger has been pleased with a boy that answers well, he has ordered a bible to be given him next day for his encouragement; and sometimes accompanies it with a flitch of bacon to his mother. Sir Roger has likewise added five pounds a year to the clerk's place; and that he may encourage the young fellows to make themselves perfect in the church service, has promised, upon the death of the present incumbent, who is very old, to bestow it according to merit.

The fair understanding between Sir Roger and his chaplain, and their mutual concurrence in doing good, is the more remarkable, because the very next village is famous for the differences and contentions that rise between the parson and the 'squire, who live in a perpetual state of war. The parson is always preaching at the 'squire, and the 'squire to be revenged on the parson never comes to church. The 'squire has made all his tenants atheists, and tithe-stealers; while the parson instructs them every Sunday in the dignity of his order, and insinuates to them in almost every sermon that he is a better man than his patron. In short, matters are come to such an extremity, that the 'squire has not said his prayers either in public or private this half year; and that the parson threatens him, if he does not mend his manners, to pray for him in the face of the whole congregation.

Feuds of this nature, though too frequent in the country, are very fatal to the ordinary people; who are so used to be dazzled with riches, that they pay as much deference to the understanding of a man of an estate, as of a man of learning: and are very hardly brought to regard any truth, how important soever it may be, that is preached to them, when they know there are several men of five hundred a year who do not believe it.

SIR ROGER AT THE ASSIZES

Comes jucundus in via pro vehiculo est.

PUB. SYR. *Frag.*

A MAN'S first care should be to avoid the reproaches of his own heart; his next, to escape the censures of the world; if the last interferes with the former, it ought to be entirely neglected; but otherwise there cannot be a greater satisfaction to an honest mind, than to see those approbations which it gives itself seconded by the applauses of the public: a man is more sure of his conduct, when the verdict which he passes upon his own behaviour is thus warranted and confirmed by the opinion of all that know him.

My worthy friend Sir Roger is one of those who is not only at peace within himself, but beloved and esteemed by all about him. He receives a suitable tribute for his universal benevolence to mankind, in the returns of affection and good-will, which are paid him by every one that lives within his neighbourhood. I lately met with two or three odd instances of that general respect which is shown to the good old knight. He would needs carry Will Wimble and myself with him to the county assizes: as we were upon the road Will Wimble joined a couple of plain men who rode before us, and conversed with them for some time; during which my friend Sir Roger acquainted me with their characters.

'The first of them,' says he, 'that has a spaniel by his side, is a yeoman of about an hundred pounds a year, an honest man: he is just within the game act, and qualified to kill an hare or a pheasant: he knocks down a dinner with his gun twice or thrice a week: and by that means lives much cheaper than those who have not so good an estate as himself. He would be a good neighbour if he did not destroy so many partridges: in short he is a very sensible man; shoots flying; and has been several times foreman of the petty jury.

'The other that rides along with him is Tom Touchy, a fellow famous for taking the law of every body. There is not one in the town where he lives that he has not sued at a quarter-sessions. The rogue had once the impudence to go to law with the widow. His head is full of costs, damages, and ejectments; he plagued a couple of honest gentlemen so long for a trespass in breaking one of his hedges, till he was forced to sell the ground it enclosed to defray the charges of the prosecution: his father left him four-score pounds a year; but he has cast and been cast so often, that he is not now worth thirty. I suppose he is going upon the old business of the willow tree.'

As Sir Roger was giving me this account of Tom Touchy, Will Wimble and his two companions stopped short until we came up to them. After having paid their respects to Sir Roger, Will told him that Mr. Touchy and he must appeal to him upon a dispute that arose between them. Will it seems had been giving his fellow-traveller an account of his angling one day in such a hole; when Tom Touchy, instead of hearing out his story, told him, that Mr. such an one, if he pleased, might *take the law of him* for fishing in that part of the river. My friend Sir Roger heard them both upon a round trot; and after having paused some time, told them, with the air of a man who would not give his judgment rashly, that *much might be said on both sides*. They were neither of them dissatisfied with the knight's determination, because neither of them found himself in the wrong by it; upon which we made the best of our way to the assizes.

The court was sat before Sir Roger came; but notwithstanding all the justices had taken their places upon the bench, they made room for the old knight at the head of them; who, for his reputation in the country, took occasion to whisper in the judge's ear, *that he was glad his lordship had met with so much good weather in his circuit*. I was listening to the proceedings of the court with much attention, and infinitely pleased with that great appearance and solemnity which so properly accompanies such a public administration of our laws; when, after about an hour's sitting, I observed to my great surprise, in the midst of a trial, that my friend Sir Roger was getting up to speak. I was in some pain for him till I found he had acquitted himself of two or three sentences, with a look of much business and great intrepidity.

Upon his first rising the court was hushed, and a general whisper ran among the country people that Sir Roger *was up*. The speech he made was so little to the purpose, that I shall not trouble my readers with an account of it; and I believe was not so much designed by the knight himself to inform the court, as to give him a figure in my eye, and keep up his credit in the country.

I was highly delighted, when the court rose, to see the gentlemen of the country gathering about my old friend, and striving who should compliment him most; at the same time that the ordinary people gazed upon him at a distance, not a little admiring his courage, that was not afraid to speak to the judge.

In our return home we met with a very odd accident; which I cannot forbear relating, because it shows how desirous all who know Sir Roger are of giving him marks of their esteem. When we were arrived upon the verge of his estate, we stopped at a little inn to rest ourselves and our horses. The man of the house had, it seems, been formerly a servant in the knight's family; and to do honour to his old master, had some time since, unknown to Sir Roger, put him up in a sign-post before the door; so that 'the Knight's Head' had hung out upon the road about a week before he himself knew anything of the matter. As soon as Sir Roger was acquainted with it, finding that his servant's indiscretion proceeded wholly from affection and good-will, he only told him that he had made him too high a compliment; and when the fellow seemed to think that could hardly be, added with a more decisive look, that it was too great an honour for any man under a duke; but told him at the same time, that it might be altered with a very few touches, and that he himself would be at the charge of it. Accordingly, they got a painter by the knight's directions to add a pair of whiskers to the face, and by a little aggravation of the features to change it into the *Saracen's Head*. I should not have known this story, had not the innkeeper, upon Sir Roger's alighting, told him in my hearing, that his honour's head was brought back last night with the alterations that he had ordered to be made in it. Upon this my friend with his usual cheerfulness related the particulars above mentioned, and ordered the head to be brought into the room. I could not forbear discovering greater expressions of mirth than ordinary upon the appearance of this monstrous face, under which, notwithstanding it was made to frown and stare in a most extraordinary manner, I could still discover a distant resemblance of my old friend. Sir Roger, upon seeing me laugh, desired me to tell him truly if I thought it possible for people to know him in that disguise. I at first kept my usual silence: but upon the knight conjuring me to tell him whether it was not still more like himself than a Saracen, I composed my countenance in the best manner I could, and replied, *That much might be said on both sides.*

These several adventures, with the knight's behaviour in them, gave me as pleasant a day as ever I met with in any of my travels.

SIR ROGER IN LONDON

Ævo rarissima nostro
Simplicitas. OVID, *Ars Am.* i. 241.

I WAS this morning surprised with a great knocking at the door, when my landlady's daughter came up to me, and told me, that there was a man below desired to speak with me. Upon my asking her who it was, she told me it was a very grave elderly person, but that she did not know his name. I immediately went down to him, and found him to be the coachman of my worthy friend Sir Roger de Coverley. He told me that his master came to town last night, and would be glad to take a turn with me in Gray's Inn walks. As I was wondering in myself what had brought Sir Roger to town, not having lately received any letter from him, he told me that his master was come up to get a sight of Prince Eugene, and that he desired I would immediately meet him.

I was not a little pleased with the curiosity of the old knight, though I did not much wonder at it, having heard him say more than once in private discourse, that he looked upon Prince Eugenio (for so the knight always calls him) to be a greater man than Scanderbeg.

I was no sooner come into Gray's Inn walks, but I heard my friend upon the terrace hemming twice or thrice to himself with great vigour, for he loves to clear his pipes in good air (to make use of his own phrase), and is not a little pleased with any one who takes notice of the strength which he still exerts in his morning hems.

I was touched with a secret joy at the sight of the good old man, who before he saw me was engaged in conversation with a beggar man that had asked an alms of him. I could hear my friend chide him for not finding out some work; but at the same time saw him put his hand into his pocket and give him sixpence.

Our salutations were very hearty on both sides, consisting of many kind shakes of the hand, and several affectionate looks which we cast upon one another. After which the knight told me, my good friend his chaplain was very well, and much at my service, and that the Sunday before he had made a most incomparable sermon out of Dr. Barrow. 'I have left,' says he, 'all my affairs in his hands, and being willing to lay an obligation upon him, have deposited with him thirty marks, to be distributed among his poor parishioners.'

He then proceeded to acquaint me with the welfare of Will Wimble. Upon which he put his hand into his fob, and presented me in his name with a tobacco-stopper, telling me, that Will had been busy all the beginning of the winter in turning great quantities of them; and that he made a present of one to every gentleman in the country who has good principles, and smokes. He added, that poor Will was at present under great tribulation, for that Tom Touchy had taken the law of him for cutting some hazel sticks out of one of his hedges.

Among other pieces of news which the knight brought from his country-seat, he informed me that Moll White was dead; and that about a month after her death the wind was so very high, that it blew down the end of one of his barns. 'But for my own part,' says Sir Roger, 'I do not think that the old woman had any hand in it.'

He afterwards fell into an account of the diversions which had passed in his house during the holidays; for Sir Roger, after the laudable custom of his ancestors, always keeps open house at Christmas. I learned from him, that he had killed eight fat hogs for this season; that he had dealt about his chines very liberally amongst his neighbours; and that in particular he had sent a string of hog's puddings with a pack of cards to every poor family in the parish. 'I have often thought,' says Sir Roger, 'it happens very well that Christmas should fall out in the middle of winter. It is the most dead and uncomfortable time of the year, when the poor people would suffer very much from their poverty and cold, if they had not good cheer, warm fires, and Christmas gambols to support them. I love to rejoice their poor hearts at this season, and to see the whole village merry in my great hall. I allow a double quantity of malt to my small beer, and set it a-running for twelve days to every one that calls for it. I have always a piece of cold beef and a mince-pie upon the table, and am wonderfully pleased to see my tenants pass away a whole evening in playing their innocent tricks, and smutting one another. Our friend Will Wimble is as merry as any of them, and shows a thousand roguish tricks upon these occasions.'

I was very much delighted with the reflection of my old friend, which carried so much goodness in it. He then launched out into the praise of the late act of parliament for securing the Church of England, and told me, with great satisfaction, that he believed it already began to take effect, for that a rigid dissenter who chanced to dine at his house on Christmas day had been observed to eat very plentifully of his plumb-porridge.

After having dispatched all our country matters, Sir Roger made several inquiries concerning the club, and particularly of his old antagonist Sir Andrew Freeport. He asked me with a kind of smile, whether Sir Andrew had not taken the advantage of his absence to vent among them some of his republican doctrines; but soon after, gathering up his countenance into a more than ordinary seriousness, 'Tell me truly,' said he, 'don't you think Sir Andrew had a hand in the pope's procession'—but without giving me time to answer him, 'Well, well,' says he, 'I know you are a wary man, and do not care for talking of public matters.'

The knight then asked me if I had seen Prince Eugenio, and made me promise to get him a stand in some convenient place where he might have a full sight of that extraordinary man, whose presence does so much honour to the British nation. He dwelt very long on the praises of this great general, and I found that, since I was with him in the country, he had drawn many observations together out of his reading in Baker's Chronicle, and other authors, who always lie in his hall window, which very much redound to the honour of this prince.

Having passed away the greatest part of the morning in hearing the knight's reflections, which were partly private and partly political, he asked me if I would smoke a pipe with him over a dish of coffee at Squire's. As I love the old man, I take delight in complying with every thing that is agreeable to him, and accordingly waited on him to the coffee-house, where his venerable aspect drew upon us the eyes of the whole room. He had no sooner seated himself at the upper end of the high table, but he called for a clean pipe, a paper of tobacco, a dish of coffee, a wax-candle, and the Supplement, with such an air of cheerfulness and good humour, that all the boys in the coffee-room (who seemed to take pleasure in serving him) were at once employed on his several errands, insomuch that nobody else could come at a dish of tea, till the knight had got all his conveniences about him.

SIR ROGER AT THE THEATRE

Respicere exemplar vitæ morumque jubebo
Doctum imitatorem, et veras hinc ducere voces.
HOR. *Ars Poet.* 317.

MY friend Sir Roger de Coverley, when we last met together at the club, told me that he had a great mind to see the new tragedy with me, assuring me at the same time, that he had not been at a play these twenty years. 'The last I saw,' said Sir Roger, 'was *The Committee*, which I should not have gone to neither, had not I been told beforehand that it was a good Church of England comedy.' He then proceeded to inquire of me who this *Distressed Mother* was; and upon hearing that she was Hector's widow, he told me that her husband was a brave man, and that when he was a school-boy he had read his life at the end of the dictionary. My friend asked me, in the next place, if there would not be some danger in coming home late, in case the Mohocks should be abroad. 'I assure you,' says he, 'I thought I had fallen into their hands last night; for I observed two or three lusty black men that followed me half way up Fleet Street, and mended their pace behind me in proportion as I put on to get away from them. You must know,' continued the knight, with a smile, 'I fancied they had a mind to *hunt* me; for I remember an honest gentleman in my neighbourhood, who was served such a trick in King Charles II.'s time, for which reason he has not ventured himself in town ever since. I might have shown them very good sport, had this been their design; for as I am an old fox-hunter, I should have turned and dodged, and have played them a thousand tricks they had never seen in their lives before.' Sir Roger added that if these gentlemen had any such intention, they did not succeed very well in it; 'for I threw them out,' says he, 'at the end of Norfolk Street, where I doubled the corner, and got shelter in my lodgings before they could imagine what was become of me. However,' says the knight, 'if Captain Sentry will make one with us to-morrow night, and if you will both of you call upon me about four o'clock, that we may be at the house before it is full, I will have my own coach in readiness to attend you, for John tells me he has got the fore-wheels mended.'

The Captain, who did not fail to meet me there at the appointed hour, bade Sir Roger fear nothing, for that he had put on the same sword which he made use of at the battle of Steenkirk. Sir Roger's servants, and among the rest my old friend the butler, had, I found, provided themselves with good oaken plants, to attend their master upon this occasion. When we had placed him in his coach, with myself at his left hand, the Captain before him, and his butler at the head of his footmen in the rear, we convoyed him in safety to the play-house, where, after having marched up the entry in good order, the Captain and I went in with him, and seated him betwixt us in the pit. As soon as the house was full, and the candles lighted, my old friend stood up and looked about him with that pleasure, which a mind seasoned with humanity naturally feels in itself, at the sight of a multitude of people who seem pleased with one another, and partake of the same common entertainment. I could not but fancy myself, as the old man stood up in the middle of the pit, that he made a very proper centre to a tragic audience. Upon the entering of Pyrrhus, the knight told me that he did not believe the King of France himself had a better strut. I was indeed very attentive to my old friend's remarks, because I looked upon them as a piece of natural criticism; and was well pleased to hear him, at the conclusion of almost every scene, telling me that he could not imagine how the play would end. One while he appeared much concerned for Andromache, and a little while after as much for Hermione; and was extremely puzzled to think what would become of Pyrrhus.

When Sir Roger saw Andromache's obstinate refusal to her lover's importunities, he whispered me in the ear, that he was sure she would never have him; to which he added, with a more than ordinary vehemence, 'You can't imagine, Sir, what it is to have to do with a widow.' Upon Pyrrhus his threatening afterwards to leave her, the knight shook his head and muttered to himself, 'Ay, do if you can.' This part dwelt so much upon my friend's imagination, that at the close of the third act, as I was thinking of something else, he whispered in my ear, 'These widows, Sir, are the most perverse creatures in the world. But pray,' says he, 'you that are a critic, is this play according to your dramatic rules, as you call them? Should your people in tragedy always talk to be understood? Why, there is not a single sentence in this play that I do not know the meaning of.'

The fourth act very unluckily began before I had

time to give the old gentleman an answer: 'Well,' says the knight, sitting down with great satisfaction, 'I suppose we are now to see Hector's ghost.' He then renewed his attention, and, from time to time, fell a-praising the widow. He made, indeed, a little mistake as to one of her pages, whom at his first entering he took for Astyanax: but he quickly set himself right in that particular, though, at the same time, he owned he should have been very glad to have seen the little boy, 'Who,' said he, 'must needs be a very fine child by the account that is given of him.' Upon Hermione's going off with a menace to Pyrrhus, the audience gave a loud clap; to which Sir Roger added, 'On my word, a notable young baggage!'

As there was a very remarkable silence and stillness in the audience during the whole action, it was natural for them to take the opportunity of these intervals between the acts, to express their opinion of the players and of their respective parts. Sir Roger hearing a cluster of them praise Orestes, struck in with them, and told them that he thought his friend Pylades was a very sensible man; as they were afterwards applauding Pyrrhus, Sir Roger put in a second time, 'And let me tell you,' says he, 'though he speaks but little, I like the old fellow in whiskers as well as any of them.' Captain Sentry seeing two or three wags who sat near us, lean with an attentive ear towards Sir Roger, and fearing lest they should smoke the knight, plucked him by the elbow, and whispered something in his ear, that lasted till the opening of the fifth act. The knight was wonderfully attentive to the account which Orestes gives of Pyrrhus his death, and at the conclusion of it told me, it was such a bloody piece of work, that he was glad it was not done upon the stage. Seeing afterwards Orestes in his raving fit, he grew more than ordinary serious, and took occasion to moralise (in his way) upon an evil conscience, adding, that Orestes, in his madness, looked as if he saw something.

As we were the first that came into the house, so we were the last that went out of it; being resolved to have a clear passage for our old friend, whom we did not care to venture among the justling of the crowd. Sir Roger went out fully satisfied with his entertainment, and we guarded him to his lodgings in the same manner that we brought him to the play-house; being highly pleased, for my own part, not only with the performance of the excellent piece which had been presented, but with the satisfaction which it had given to the good old man.

DEATH OF SIR ROGER

Heu pietas! heu prisca fides!
VIRG. *Æn.* vi. 878.

WE last night received a piece of ill news at our club, which very sensibly afflicted every one of us. I question not but my readers themselves will be troubled at the hearing of it. To keep them no longer in suspense, Sir Roger de Coverley *is dead*. He departed this life at his house in the country, after a few weeks' sickness. Sir Andrew Freeport has a letter from one of his correspondents in those parts, that informs him the old man caught a cold at the county-sessions, as he was very warmly promoting an address of his own penning, in which he succeeded according to his wishes. But this particular comes from a Whig justice of peace, who was always Sir Roger's enemy and antagonist. I have letters both from the chaplain and Captain Sentry which mention nothing of it, but are filled with many particulars to the honour of the good old man. I have likewise a letter from the butler, who took so much care of me last summer when I was at the knight's house. As my friend the butler mentions, in the simplicity of his heart, several circumstances the others have passed over in silence, I shall give my reader a copy of his letter, without any alteration or diminution.

'HONOURED SIR,

'Knowing that you was my old master's good friend, I could not forbear sending you the melancholy news of his death, which has afflicted the whole country, as well as his poor servants, who loved him, I may say, better than we did our lives. I am afraid he caught his death the last county-sessions, where he would go to see justice done to a poor widow woman, and her fatherless children, that had been wronged by a neighbouring gentleman; for you know, sir, my good master was always the poor man's friend. Upon his coming home, the first complaint he made was, that he had lost his roast-beef stomach, not being able to touch a sirloin, which was served up according to custom; and you know he used to take great delight in it. From that time forward he grew worse and worse, but still kept a good heart to the last. Indeed we were once in great hope of his recovery, upon a kind message that was sent him from the widow lady whom he had made love to the forty last years of his life, but this only proved a lightning before death. He has bequeathed to this lady, as a token of his love, a great pearl necklace, and a couple of silver bracelets set with jewels, which belonged to my good old lady his mother: he has bequeathed the fine white gelding, that he used to ride a-hunting upon, to his chaplain, because he thought he would be kind to him, and has left you all his books. He has, moreover, bequeathed to the chaplain a very pretty tenement with good lands about it. It being a very cold day when he made his will, he left for mourning, to every man in the parish, a great frieze-coat, and to every woman a black riding-hood. It was a most moving sight to see him take leave of his poor servants, commending us all for our fidelity, whilst we were not able to speak a word for weeping. As we most of us are grown grey-headed in our dear master's service, he has left us pensions and legacies, which we may live very comfortably upon the remaining part of our days. He has bequeathed a great deal more in charity, which is not yet come to my knowledge, and it is peremptorily said in the parish, that he has left money to build a steeple to the church; for he was heard to say some time ago that if he lived two years longer, Coverley church should have a steeple to it. The chaplain tells everybody that he made a very good end, and never speaks of him without tears. He was buried, according to his own directions, among the family of the Coverleys, on the left hand of his father Sir Arthur. The coffin was carried by six of his tenants, and the pall held up by six of the *quorum*: the whole parish followed the corpse with heavy hearts, and in their mourning suits, the men in frieze, and the women in riding-hoods. Captain Sentry, my master's nephew, has taken possession of the hall-house, and the whole estate. When my old master saw him a little before his death, he shook him by the hand, and wished him joy of the estate which was falling to him, desiring him only to make a good use of it, and to pay the several legacies, and the gifts of charity which he told him he had left as quit-rents upon the estate. The Captain truly seems a courteous man, though he says but little. He makes much of those whom my master loved, and shows great kindnesses to the old house-dog, that you know my poor master was so fond of. It would have gone to your heart to have heard the moans the dumb creature made on the day of my master's death. He has never joyed himself since; no more has any of us. 'Twas the melancholiest day for the poor people that ever happened in Worcestershire. This is all from,—Honoured sir, your most sorrowful servant,

EDWARD BISCUIT.

'*P.S.*—My master desired, some weeks before he died, that a book which comes up to you by the carrier, should be given to Sir Andrew Freeport, in his name.'

This letter, notwithstanding the poor butler's man

ner of writing it, gave us such an idea of our good old friend, that upon the reading of it there was not a dry eye in the club. Sir Andrew, opening the book, found it to be a collection of acts of parliament. There was in particular the Act of Uniformity, with some passages in it marked by Sir Roger's own hand. Sir Andrew found that they related to two or three points, which he had disputed with Sir Roger the last time he appeared at the club. Sir Andrew, who would have been merry at such an incident on another occasion, at the sight of the old man's handwriting burst into tears, and put the book into his pocket. Captain Sentry informs me, that the knight has left rings and mourning for every one in the club.

THE ADVENTURES OF A SHILLING

Per varios casus, per tot discrimina rerum,
Tendimus. VIRG.

I WAS last night visited by a friend of mine, who has an inexhaustible fund of discourse, and never fails to entertain his company with a variety of thoughts and hints that are altogether new and uncommon. Whether it were in complaisance to my way of living or his real opinion, he advanced the following paradox, 'That it required much greater talents to fill up and become a retired life, than a life of business.' Upon this occasion he rallied very agreeably the busy men of the age, who only valued themselves for being in motion and passing through a series of trifling and insignificant actions. In the heat of his discourse, seeing a piece of money lying on my table, 'I defy,' says he, 'any of these active persons to produce half the adventures that this twelvepenny piece has been engaged in, were it possible for him to give us an account of his life.'

My friend's talk made so odd an impression upon my mind, that soon after I was a-bed I fell insensibly into a most unaccountable reverie, that had neither moral nor design in it, and cannot be so properly called a dream as a delirium.

Methought that the shilling that lay upon the table reared itself upon its edge, and turning the face towards me, opened its mouth, and in a soft silver sound, gave me the following account of his life and adventures:

'I was born (says he) on the side of a mountain, near a little village of Peru, and made a voyage to England in an ingot, under the convoy of Sir Francis Drake. I was, soon after my arrival, taken out of my Indian habit, refined, naturalised, and put into the British mode, with the face of Queen Elizabeth on one side, and the arms of the country on the other. Being thus equipped, I found in me a wonderful inclination to ramble, and visit all parts of the new world into which I was brought. The people very much favoured my natural disposition, and shifted me so fast from hand to hand, that before I was five years old, I had travelled into almost every corner of the nation. But in the beginning of my sixth year, to my unspeakable grief, I fell into the hands of a miserable old fellow, who clapped me into an iron chest, where I found five hundred more of my own quality who lay under the same confinement. The only relief we had, was to be taken out and counted over in the fresh air every morning and evening. After an imprisonment of several years, we heard somebody knocking at our chest, and breaking it open with a hammer. This we found was the old man's heir, who, as his father lay a-dying, was so good as to come to our release: he separated us that very day. What was the fate of my companions I know not: as for myself, I was sent to the apothecary's shop for a pint of sack. The apothecary gave me to an herb-woman, the herb-woman to a butcher, the butcher to a brewer, and the brewer to his wife, who made a present of me to a nonconformist preacher. After this manner I made my way merrily through the world; for, as I told you before, we shillings love nothing so much as travelling. I sometimes fetched in a shoulder of mutton, sometimes a play-book, and often had the satisfaction to treat a Templar at a twelvepenny ordinary, or carry him, with three friends, to Westminster Hall.

'In the midst of this pleasant progress which I made from place to place, I was arrested by a superstitious old woman, who shut me up in a greasy purse, in pursuance of a foolish saying, "That while she kept a Queen Elizabeth's shilling about her, she should never be without money." I continued here a close prisoner for many months, till at last I was exchanged for eight and forty farthings.

'I thus rambled from pocket to pocket till the beginning of the civil wars, when, to my shame be it spoken, I was employed in raising soldiers against the king: for being of a very tempting breadth, a sergeant made use of me to inveigle country fellows, and list them in the service of the parliament.

'As soon as he had made one man sure, his way was to oblige him to take a shilling of a more homely figure, and then practise the same trick upon another. Thus I continued doing great mischief to the crown, till my officer, chancing one morning to walk abroad earlier than ordinary, sacrificed me to his pleasures, and made use of me to seduce a milk-maid. This wench bent me, and gave me to her sweetheart, applying more properly than she intended the usual form of, "To my love and from my love." This ungenerous gallant marrying her within a few days after, pawned me for a dram of brandy, and drinking me out next day, I was beaten flat with a hammer, and again set a-running.

'After many adventures, which it would be tedious to relate, I was sent to a young spendthrift, in company with the will of his deceased father. The young fellow, who I found was very extravagant, gave great demonstrations of joy at the receiving of the will: but opening it, he found himself disinherited and cut off from the possession of a fair estate, by virtue of my being made a present to him. This put him into such a passion, that after having taken me in his hand, and cursed me, he squirred me away from him as far as he could fling me. I chanced to light in an unfrequented place under a dead wall, where I lay undiscovered and useless, during the usurpation of Oliver Cromwell.

'About a year after the king's return, a poor cavalier that was walking there about dinner-time, fortunately cast his eye upon me, and, to the great joy of us both, carried me to a cook's shop, where he dined upon me, and drank the king's health. When I came again into the world, I found that I had been happier in my retirement than I thought, having probably, by that means, escaped wearing a monstrous pair of breeches.

'Being now of great credit and antiquity, I was rather looked upon as a medal than an ordinary coin; for which reason a gamester laid hold of me, and converted me to a counter, having got together some dozens of us for that use. We led a melancholy life in his possession, being busy at those hours wherein current coin is at rest, and partaking the fate of our master, being in a few moments valued at a crown, a pound, or a sixpence, according to the situation in which the fortune of the cards placed us. I had at length the good luck to see my master break, by which means I was again sent abroad under my primitive denomination of a shilling.

'I shall pass over many other accidents of less moment, and hasten to that fatal catastrophe, when I fell into the hands of an artist, who conveyed me under ground, and with an unmerciful pair of shears, cut off my titles, clipped my brims, retrenched my shape, rubbed me to my inmost ring, and, in short, so spoiled and pillaged me, that he did not leave me worth a groat. You may think what a confusion I was in, to see myself thus curtailed and disfigured. I should have been ashamed to have shown my head, had not all my old acquaintance been reduced to the same shameful figure, excepting some few that were punched through the belly. In the midst of this general calamity, when everybody thought our misfortune irretrievable, and our case desperate, we were thrown into the furnace together, and (as it often happens with cities rising out of a fire) appeared with greater beauty and lustre than we could ever boast of before. What has happened to me since this change of sex which you now see, I shall take some other opportunity to relate. In the meantime, I shall only repeat two adventures, as being very extraordinary, and neither of them having ever happened to me above once in my life. The first was, my being in a poet's pocket, who was so taken with the brightness and novelty of my appearance, that it gave occasion to the finest burlesque poem in the British language, entitled from me, "The Splendid Shilling." The second adventure, which I must not omit, happened to me in the year 1703, when I was given away in charity to a blind man; but indeed this was by a mistake, the person who gave me having heedlessly thrown me into the hat among a pennyworth of farthings.'

MEDITATIONS IN WESTMINSTER ABBEY

Pallida mors æquo pulsat pede pauperum tabernas
Regumque turres. O beate Sesti,
Vitæ summa brevis spem nos vetat inchoare longam.
Iam te premet nox, fabulæque manes,
Et domus exilis Plutonia. HOR.

WHEN I am in a serious humour, I very often walk by myself in Westminster Abbey, where the gloominess of the place, and the use to which it is applied, with the solemnity of the building, and the condition of the people who lie in it, are apt to fill the mind with a kind of melancholy, or rather thoughtfulness, that is not disagreeable. I yesterday passed a whole afternoon in the churchyard, the cloisters, and the church, amusing myself with the tombstones and inscriptions that I met with in those several regions of the dead. Most of them recorded nothing else of the buried person, but that he was born upon one day, and died upon another; the whole history of his life being comprehended in those two circumstances that are common to all mankind. I could not but look upon these registers of existence, whether of brass or marble, as a kind of satire upon the departed persons; who had left no other memorial of them, but that they were born and that they died. They put me in mind of several persons mentioned in the battles of heroic poems, who have sounding names given them, for no other reason but that they may be killed, and are celebrated for nothing but being knocked on the head.

> *Γλαῦκόν τε Μέδοντά τε Θερσίλοχόν τε.* HOM.
> Glaucumque, Medontaque, Thersilochumque. VIRG.

The life of these men is finely described in holy writ by 'the path of an arrow,' which is immediately closed up and lost.

Upon my going into the church, I entertained myself with the digging of a grave; and saw in every shovelful of it that was thrown up, the fragment of a bone or skull intermixed with a kind of fresh mouldering earth, that some time or other had a place in the composition of a human body. Upon this I began to consider with myself what innumerable multitudes of people lay confused together under the pavement of that ancient cathedral; how men and women, friends and enemies, priests and soldiers, monks and prebendaries, were crumbled amongst one another, and blended together in the same common mass; how beauty, strength, and youth, with old age, weakness, and deformity, lay undistinguished in the same promiscuous heap of matter.

After having thus surveyed this great magazine of mortality, as it were, in the lump; I examined it more particularly by the accounts which I found on several of the monuments which are raised in every quarter of that ancient fabric. Some of them were covered with such extravagant epitaphs, that, if it were possible for the dead person to be acquainted with them, he would blush at the praises which his friends have bestowed upon him. There are others so excessively modest, that they deliver the character of the person departed in Greek or Hebrew, and by that means are not understood once in a twelvemonth. In the poetical quarter, I found there were poets who had no monuments, and monuments which had no poets. I observed, indeed, that the present war had filled the church with many of these uninhabited monuments, which had been erected to the memory of persons whose bodies were perhaps buried in the plains of Blenheim, or in the bosom of the ocean.

I could not but be very much delighted with several modern epitaphs which are written with great elegance of expression and justness of thought, and therefore do honour to the living as well as to the dead. As a foreigner is very apt to conceive an idea of the ignorance or politeness of a nation from the turn of their public monuments and inscriptions, they should be submitted to the perusal of men of learning and genius, before they are put in execution. Sir Cloudesley Shovel's monument has very often given me great offence: instead of the brave rough English Admiral, which was the distinguishing character of that plain gallant man, he is represented on his tomb by the figure of a beau, dressed in a long periwig, and reposing himself upon velvet cushions under a canopy of state. The inscription is answerable to the monument; for instead of celebrating the many remarkable actions he had performed in the service of his country, it acquaints us only with the manner of his death, in which it was impossible for him to reap any honour. The Dutch, whom we are apt to despise for want of genius, show an infinitely greater taste of antiquity and politeness in their buildings and works of this nature, than what we meet with in those of our own country. The monuments of their admirals, which have been erected at the public expense, represent them like themselves; and are adorned with rostral crowns and naval ornaments, with beautiful festoons of seaweed, shells, and coral.

But to return to our subject. I have left the repository of our English kings for the contemplation of another day, when I shall find my mind disposed for so serious an amusement. I know that entertainments of this nature are apt to raise dark and dismal thoughts in timorous minds and gloomy imaginations; but for my own part, though I am always serious, I do not know what it is to be melancholy; and can therefore take a view of nature in her deep and solemn scenes, with the same pleasure as in her most gay and delightful ones. By this means I can improve myself with those objects which others consider with terror. When I look upon the tombs of the great, every emotion of envy dies in me; when I read the epitaphs of the beautiful, every inordinate desire goes out; when I meet with the grief of parents upon a tombstone, my heart melts with compassion; when I see the tomb of the parents themselves, I consider the vanity of grieving for those whom we must quickly follow; when I see kings lying by those who deposed them, when I consider rival wits placed side by side, or the holy men that divided the world with their contests and disputes, I reflect with sorrow and astonishment on the little competitions, factions, and debates of mankind. When I read the several dates of the tombs, of some that died yesterday, and some six hundred years ago, I consider that great day when we shall all of us be contemporaries, and make our appearance together.

THE TORY FOX-HUNTER

Studiis rudis, sermone barbarus, impetu strenuus, manu promptus, cogitatione celer. VELL. PATERC.

FOR the honour of his Majesty, and the safety of his government, we cannot but observe that those who have appeared the greatest enemies to both are of that rank of men, who are commonly distinguished by the title of Fox-hunters. As several of these have had no part of their education in cities, camps, or courts, it is doubtful whether they are of greater ornament or use to the nation in which they live. It would be an everlasting reproach to politics, should such men be able to overturn an establishment which has been formed by the wisest laws, and is supported by the ablest heads. The wrong notions and prejudices which cleave to many of these country gentlemen, who have always lived out of the way of being better informed, are not easy to be conceived by a person who has never conversed with them.

That I may give my readers an image of these rural statesmen, I shall, without further preface, set down an account of a discourse I chanced to have with one of them some time ago. I was travelling towards one of the remote parts of England, when about three o'clock in the afternoon, seeing a country gentleman trotting before me with a spaniel by his horse's side, I made up to him. Our conversation opened, as usual, upon the weather; in which we were very unanimous; having both agreed that it was too dry for the season of the year. My fellow-traveller, upon this, observed to me that there had been no good weather since the Revolution. I was a little startled at so extraordinary a remark, but would not interrupt him till he proceeded to tell me of the fine weather they used to have in King Charles the Second's reign. I only answered that I did not see how the badness of the weather could be the king's fault; and, without waiting for his reply, asked him whose house it was we saw upon the rising ground at a little distance from us. He told me it belonged to an old fanatical cur, Mr. Such-a-one. 'You must have heard of him,' says he, 'he 's one of the Rump.' I knew the gentleman's character upon hearing his name, but assured him, that to my knowledge he was a good churchman: 'Ay!' says he, with a kind of surprise, 'We were told in the country, that he spoke twice, in the queen's time, against taking off the duties upon French claret.' This naturally led us into the proceedings of late parliaments, upon which occasion he affirmed roundly, that there had not been one good law passed since King William's accession to the throne, except the act for preserving the game. I had a mind to see him out, and therefore did not care for contradicting him. 'Is it not hard,' says he, 'that honest gentlemen should be taken into custody of messengers to prevent them from acting according to their consciences? But,' says he, 'what can we expect when a parcel of factious sons of whores——' He was going on in great passion, but chanced to miss his dog, who was amusing himself about a bush, that grew at some distance behind us. We stood still till he had whistled him up; when he fell into a long panegyric upon his spaniel, who seemed, indeed, excellent in his kind: but I found the most remarkable adventure of his life was, that he had once like to have worried a dissenting teacher. The master could hardly sit on his horse for laughing all the while he was giving me the particulars of his story, which I found had mightily endeared his dog to him, and as he himself told me, had made him a great favourite among all the honest gentlemen of the country. We were at length diverted from this piece of mirth by a post-boy, who winding his horn at us, my companion gave him two or three curses, and left the way clear for him. 'I fancy,' said I, 'that post brings news from Scotland. I shall long to see the next Gazette.' 'Sir,' says he, 'I make it a rule never to believe any of your printed news. We never see, sir, how things go, except now and then in Dyer's Letter, and I read that more for the style than the news. The man has a clever pen, it must be owned. But is it not strange that we should be making war upon Church of England men with Dutch and Swiss soldiers, men of anti-monarchical principles? these foreigners will never be loved in England, sir; they have not that wit and good-breeding that we have.' I must confess I did not expect to hear my new acquaintance value himself upon these qualifications, but finding him such a critic upon foreigners, I asked him if he had ever travelled; he told me, he did not know what travelling was good for, but to teach a man to ride the great horse, to jabber French, and to talk against passive obedience; to which he added, that he scarce ever knew a traveller in his life who had not forsaken his principles, and lost his hunting-seat. 'For my part,' says he, 'I and my father before me have always been for passive obedience, and shall be always for opposing a prince who makes use of ministers that are of another opinion. But where do you intend to inn to-night? (for we were now come in sight of the next town;) I can help you to a very good landlord if you will go along with me. He is a lusty, jolly fellow, that lives well, at least three yards in the girth, and the best Church of England man upon the road.' I had a curiosity to see this high-church inn-keeper, as well as to enjoy more of the conversation of my fellow traveller, and therefore readily consented to set our horses together for that night. As we rode side by side through the town, I was let into the characters of all the principal inhabitants whom we met in our way. One was a dog, another a whelp, another a cur, and another the son of a bitch, under which several denominations were comprehended all that voted on the Whig side, in the last election of burgesses. As for those of his own party, he distinguished them by a nod of his head, and asking them how they did by their Christian names. Upon our arrival at the inn, my companion fetched out the jolly landlord, who knew him by his whistle. Many endearments and private whispers passed between them; though it was easy to see by the landlord's scratching his head that things did not go to their wishes. The landlord had swelled his body to a prodigious size, and worked up his complexion to a standing crimson by his zeal for the prosperity of the church, which he expressed every hour of the day, as his customers dropped in, by repeated bumpers. He had not time to go to church himself, but, as my friend told me in my ear, had headed a mob at the pulling down of two or three meeting-houses. While supper was preparing, he enlarged upon the happiness of the neighbouring shire; 'For,' says he, 'there is scarce a Presbyterian in the whole county, except the bishop.' In short, I found by his discourse that he had learned a great deal of politics, but not one word of religion, from the parson of his parish; and, indeed, that he had scarce any other notion of religion, but that it consisted in hating Presbyterians. I had a remarkable instance of his notions in this particular. Upon seeing a poor decrepit old woman pass under the window where we sat, he desired me to take notice of her; and afterwards informed me, that she was generally reputed a witch by the country people, but that, for his part, he was apt to believe that she was a Presbyterian.

Supper was no sooner served in, than he took occasion from a shoulder of mutton that lay before us, to cry up the plenty of England, which would be the happiest country in the world, provided we would live within ourselves. Upon which, he expatiated on the inconveniences of trade, that carried from us the commodities of our country, and made a parcel of upstarts as rich as men of the most ancient families of England. He then declared frankly, that he had always been against all treaties and alliances with foreigners: 'Our wooden walls,' says he, 'are our security, and we may bid defiance to the whole world, especially if they should attack us when the militia is out.' I ventured to reply, that I had as great an opinion of the English fleet as he had; but I could not see how they could be paid, and manned, and fitted out, unless we encouraged trade and navigation. He replied, with some vehemence, that he would undertake to prove trade would be the ruin of the English nation. I would fain have put him upon it; but he contented himself with affirming it more eagerly, to which he added two or three curses upon the London merchants, not forgetting the directors of the bank. After supper he asked me if I was an admirer of punch; and immediately called for a sneaker. I took this occasion to insinuate the advantages of trade, by observing to him, that water was the only native of England that could be made use of on this occasion: but that the lemons, the brandy, the sugar, and the nutmeg were all foreigners. This put him into some confusion; but the landlord, who overheard me, brought him off, by affirming, that for constant use, there was no liquor like a cup of English water, provided it had malt enough in it. My squire laughed heartily at the conceit, and made the landlord sit down with us. We sat pretty late over our punch; and, amidst a great deal of improving discourse, drank the healths of several persons in the country, whom I had never heard of, that, they both assured me, were the ablest statesmen in the nation; and of some Londoners, whom they extolled to the skies for their wit, and who, I knew, passed in town for silly fellows. It being now midnight, and my friend perceiving by his almanac that the moon was up, he called for his horse, and took a sudden resolution to go to his house, which was at three miles' distance from the town, after having bethought himself that he never slept well out of his own bed. He shook me very heartily by the hand at parting, and discovered a great air of satisfaction in his looks, that he had met with an opportunity of showing his parts, and left me a much wiser man than he found me.

ON ASKING ADVICE ON AFFAIRS OF LOVE

Quæ res in se neque consilium neque modum
Habet ullum, eam consilio regere non potes.

TER.

It is an old observation, which has been made of politicians who would rather ingratiate themselves with their sovereign, than promote his real service, that they accommodate their counsels to his inclinations and advise him to such actions only as his heart is naturally set upon. The privy-counsellor of one in love must observe the same conduct, unless he would forfeit the friendship of the person who desires his advice. I have known several odd cases of this nature. Hipparchus was going to marry a common woman, but being resolved to do nothing without the advice of his friend Philander, he consulted him upon the occasion. Philander told him his mind freely, and represented his mistress to him in such strong colours, that the next morning he received a challenge for his pains, and before twelve o'clock was run through the body by the man who had asked his advice. Celia was more prudent on the like occasion: she desired Leonilla to give her opinion freely upon a young fellow who made his addresses to her. Leonilla, to oblige her, told her with great frankness that she looked upon him as one of the most worthless—— Celia, foreseeing what a character she was to expect, begged her not to go on, for that she had been privately married to him above a fortnight. The truth of it is, a woman seldom asks advice before she has bought her wedding-clothes. When she has made her own choice, for form's sake she sends a *congé d'élire* to her friends.

If we look into the secret springs and motives that set people at work on these occasions, and put them upon asking advice, which they never intend to take; I look upon it to be none of the least, that they are incapable of keeping a secret which is so very pleasing to them. A girl longs to tell her confidant, that she hopes to be married in a little time, and, in order to talk of the pretty fellow that dwells so much in her thoughts, asks her very gravely, what she would advise her to in a case of so much difficulty. Why else should Melissa, who had not a thousand pounds in the world, go into every quarter of the town to ask her acquaintance whether they would advise her to take Tom Townly, that made his addresses to her with an estate of five thousand a year? 'Tis very pleasant on this occasion to hear the lady propose her doubts, and to see the pains she is at to get over them.

I must not here omit a practice that is in use among the vainer part of our own sex, who will often ask a friend's advice, in relation to a fortune whom they are never likely to come at. Will Honeycomb, who is now on the verge of threescore, took me aside not long since, and asked me in his most serious look, whether I would advise him to marry my Lady Betty Single, who, by the way, is one of the greatest fortunes about town. I stared him full in the face upon so strange a question; upon which he immediately gave me an inventory of her jewels and estate, adding, that he was resolved to do nothing in a matter of such consequence without my approbation. Finding he would have an answer, I told him, if he could get the lady's consent, he had mine. This is about the tenth match which, to my knowledge, Will has consulted his friends upon, without ever opening his mind to the party herself.

I have been engaged in this subject by the following letter, which comes to me from some notable young female scribe, who, by the contents of it, seems to have carried matters so far, that she is ripe for asking advice; but as I would not lose her good-will, nor forfeit the reputation which I have with her for wisdom, I shall only communicate the letter to the public, without returning any answer to it.

'Mr. Spectator,—Now, sir, the thing is this: Mr.

Shapely is the prettiest gentleman about town. He is very tall, but not too tall neither. He dances like an angel. His mouth is made I do not know how, but it is the prettiest that I ever saw in my life. He is always laughing, for he has an infinite deal of wit. If you did but see how he rolls his stockings! He has a thousand pretty fancies, and I am sure, if you saw him, you would like him. He is a very good scholar, and can talk Latin as fast as English. I wish you could but see him dance. Now you must understand poor Mr. Shapely has no estate; but how can he help that, you know? and yet my friends are so unreasonable as to be always teasing me about him, because he has no estate: but I am sure he has that that is better than an estate; for he is a good-natured, ingenious, modest, civil, tall, well-bred, handsome man, and I am obliged to him for his civilities ever since I saw him. I forgot to tell you that he has black eyes, and looks upon me now and then as if he had tears in them. And yet my friends are so unreasonable, that they would have me be uncivil to him. I have a good portion which they cannot hinder me of, and I shall be fourteen on the 29th day of August next, and am therefore willing to settle in the world as soon as I can, and so is Mr. Shapely. But everybody I advise with here is poor Mr. Shapely's enemy. I desire, therefore, you will give me your advice, for I know you are a wise man; and if you advise me well, I am resolved to follow it. I heartily wish you could see him dance, and am, Sir, your most humble servant,

B. D.

'He loves your *Spectators* mightily.'

ALEXANDER POPE

1688–1744

ON EPIC POETRY

Docebo
Unde parentur opes; quid alat formetque poetam.
HOR. *Ars Poet.* 306.

IT is no small pleasure to me, who am zealous in the interests of learning, to think I may have the honour of leading the town into a very new and uncommon road of criticism. As that kind of literature is at present carried on, it consists only in a knowledge of mechanic rules which contribute to the structure of different sorts of poetry; as the receipts of good housewives do to the making puddings of flour, oranges, plums, or any other ingredients. It would, methinks, make these my instructions more easily intelligible to ordinary readers, if I discoursed of these matters in the style in which ladies learned in economies dictate to their pupils for the improvement of the kitchen and larder.

I shall begin with epic poetry, because the critics agree it is the greatest work human nature is capable of. I know the French have already laid down many mechanical rules for compositions of this sort, but at the same time they cut off almost all undertakers from the possibility of ever performing them; for the first qualification they unanimously require in a poet, is a genius. I shall here endeavour (for the benefit of my countrymen) to make it manifest, that epic poems may be made 'without a genius,' nay, without learning or much reading. This must necessarily be of great use to all those poets who confess they never read, and of whom the world is convinced they never learn. What Molière observes of making a dinner, that any man can do it with money, and if a professed cook cannot without, he has his art for nothing; the same may be said of making a poem, it is easily brought about by him that has a genius, but the skill lies in doing it without one. In pursuance of this end, I shall present the reader with a plain and certain receipt, by which even sonneteers and ladies may be qualified for this grand performance.

I know it will be objected that one of the chief qualifications of an epic poet is to be knowing in all arts and sciences. But this ought not to discourage those that have no learning, as long as indexes and dictionaries may be had, which are the compendium of all knowledge. Besides, since it is an established rule that none of the terms of those arts and sciences are to be made use of, one may venture to affirm, our poet cannot impertinently offend in this point. The learning which will be more particularly necessary to him, is the ancient geography of towns, mountains, and rivers: for this let him take Cluverius, value fourpence.

Another quality required is a complete skill in languages. To this I answer, that it is notorious persons of no genius have been oftentimes great linguists. To instance in the Greek, of which there are two sorts; the original Greek, and that from which our modern authors translate. I should be unwilling to promise impossibilities, but modestly speaking, this may be learned in about an hour's time with ease. I have known one, who became a sudden professor of Greek immediately upon application of the left-hand page of the Cambridge Homer to his eye. It is in these days with authors as with other men, the well-bred are familiarly acquainted with them at first sight; and as it is sufficient for a good general to have surveyed the ground he is to conquer, so it is enough for a good poet to have seen the author he is to be master of. But to proceed to the purpose of this paper.

A RECEIPT TO MAKE AN EPIC POEM

FOR THE FABLE

Take out of any old poem, history book, romance, or legend (for instance, Geoffrey of Monmouth, or Don Belianis of Greece), those parts of story which afford most scope for long descriptions. Put these pieces together, and throw all the adventures you fancy into one tale. Then take a hero whom you may choose for the sound of his name, and put him into the midst of these adventures. There let him work for twelve books; at the end of which you may take him out ready prepared to conquer, or to marry; it being necessary that the conclusion of an epic poem be fortunate.

To make an Episode.—Take any remaining adventure of your former collection, in which you could no way involve your hero; or any unfortunate accident that was too good to be thrown away; and it will be of use applied to any other person, who may be lost and evaporate in the course of the work, without the least damage to the composition.

For the Moral and Allegory.—These you may extract out of the fable afterwards, at your leisure. Be sure you strain them sufficiently.

FOR THE MANNERS

For those of the hero, take all the best qualities you can find in all the celebrated heroes of antiquity; if they will not be reduced to a consistency, lay them all on a heap upon him. But be sure they are qualities which your patron would be thought to have; and, to prevent any mistake which the world may be subject to, select from the alphabet those capital letters that compose his name, and set them at the head of a dedication before your poem. However, do not absolutely observe the exact quantity of these virtues, it not being determined whether or no it be necessary for the hero of the poem to be an honest man. For the under characters, gather them from Homer and Virgil, and change the names as occasion serves.

FOR THE MACHINES

Take of deities, male and female, as many as you can use. Separate them into two equal parts, and keep Jupiter in the middle. Let Juno put him in a ferment, and Venus mollify him. Remember on all occasions to make use of volatile Mercury. If you have need of devils, draw them out of Milton's Paradise, and extract your spirits from Tasso. The use of these machines is evident; and since no epic poem can possibly subsist without them, the wisest way is to reserve them for your greatest necessities. When you cannot extricate your hero by any human means, or yourself by your own wits, seek relief from heaven, and the gods will do your business very readily. This is according to the direct prescription of Horace in his *Art of Poetry*:

> *Nec deus intersit, nisi dignus vindice nodus*
> *Inciderit.*
>
> Never presume to make a God appear,
> But for a business worthy of a God.—ROSCOMMON.

That is to say, a poet should never call upon the gods for their assistance but when he is in great perplexity.

FOR THE DESCRIPTIONS

For a Tempest.—Take Eurus, Zephyr, Auster, and Boreas, and cast them together in one verse. Add to these of rain, lightning, and of thunder (the loudest you can) *quantum sufficit.* Mix your clouds and billows well together until they foam, and thicken your description here and there with a quicksand. Brew your tempest well in your head, before you set a-blowing.

For a Battle.—Pick a large quantity of images and descriptions from Homer's *Iliad*, with a spice or two of Virgil, and if there remain any overplus you may lay them by for a skirmish. Season it well with similes, and it will make an excellent battle.

For Burning a Town.—If such a description be necessary, because it is certain there is one in Virgil, Old Troy is ready burnt to your hands. But if you fear that would be thought borrowed, a chapter or two of the *Theory of the Conflagration*, well circumstanced, and done into verse, will be a good succedaneum.

As for *Similes and Metaphors*, they may be found all over the creation; the most ignorant may gather them, but the danger is in applying them. For this, advise with your bookseller.

FOR THE LANGUAGE

(I mean the diction.) Here it will do well to be an imitator of Milton, for you will find it easier to imitate him in this than anything else. Hebraisms and Grecisms are to be found in him, without the trouble of learning the languages. I knew a painter, who (like our poet) had no genius, made his daubings to be thought originals by setting them in the smoke. You may in the same manner give the venerable air of antiquity to your piece, by darkening it up and down with Old English. With this you may be easily furnished upon any occasion by the dictionary commonly printed at the end of Chaucer.

I must not conclude, without cautioning all writers without genius in one material point, which is, never to be afraid of having too much fire in their works. I should advise rather to take their warmest thoughts, and spread them abroad upon paper; for they are observed to cool before they are read.

HENRY FIELDING

1707–1754

ON TASTE IN THE CHOICE OF BOOKS

At nostri proavi Plautinos et numeros, et
Laudavere sales; nimium patienter utrumque
Ne dicam stultè, mirati.

MODERNISED

In former times this tasteless, silly town
Too fondly prais'd Tom D'Urfey and Tom Brown.

THE present age seems pretty well agreed in an opinion, that the utmost scope and end of reading is amusement only; and such, indeed, are now the fashionable books, that a reader can propose no more than mere entertainment, and it is sometimes very well for him if he finds even this, in his studies.

Letters, however, were surely intended for a much more noble and profitable purpose than this. Writers are not, I presume, to be considered as mere jack-puddings, whose business it is only to excite laughter; this, indeed, may sometimes be intermixed and served up with graver matters, in order to titillate the palate, and to recommend wholesome food to the mind; and for this purpose it hath been used by many excellent authors: 'For why,' as Horace says, 'should not any one promulgate truth with a smile on his countenance?' Ridicule indeed, as he again intimates, is commonly a stronger and better method of attacking vice than the severer kind of satire.

When wit and humour are introduced for such good purposes, when the agreeable is blended with the useful, then is the writer said to have succeeded in every point. Pleasantry (as the ingenious author of *Clarissa* says of a story) should be made only the vehicle of instruction; and thus romances themselves, as well as epic poems, may become worthy the perusal of the greatest of men: but when no moral, no lesson, no instruction, is conveyed to the reader, where the whole design of the composition is no more than to make us laugh, the writer comes very near to the character of a buffoon; and his admirers, if an old Latin proverb be true, deserve no great compliments to be paid to their wisdom.

After what I have here advanced I cannot fairly, I think, be represented as an enemy to laughter, or to all those kinds of writing that are apt to promote it. On the contrary, few men, I believe, do more admire the works of those great masters who have sent their satire (if I may use the expression) laughing into the world. Such are the great triumvirate, Lucian, Cervantes, and Swift. These authors I shall ever hold in the highest degree of esteem; not indeed for that wit and humour alone which they all so eminently possessed, but because they all endeavoured, with the utmost force of their wit and humour, to expose and extirpate those follies and vices which chiefly prevailed in their several countries. I would not be thought to confine wit and humour to these writers, Shakespeare, Molière, and some other authors, have been blessed with the same talents, and have employed them to the same purposes. There are some, however, who, though not void of these talents, have made so wretched a use of them, that, had the consecration of their labours been committed to the hands of the hangman, no good man would have regretted their loss; nor am I afraid to mention Rabelais, and Aristophanes himself, in this number. For, if I may speak my opinion freely of these two last writers, and of their works, their design appears to me very plainly to have been to ridicule all sobriety, modesty, decency, virtue, and religion, out of the world. Now, whoever reads over the five great writers first mentioned in this paragraph, must either have a very bad head or a very bad heart if he doth not become both a wiser and a better man.

In the exercise of the mind, as well as in the exercise of the body, diversion is a secondary consideration, and designed only to make that agreeable which is at the same time useful, to such noble purposes as health and wisdom. But what should we say to a man who mounted his chamber-hobby, or fought with his own shadow, for his amusement only? how much more absurd and weak would he appear who swallowed poison because it was sweet?

How differently did Horace think of study from our modern readers!

Quid verum atque decens curo et rogo, et omnis in hoc sum:
Condo et compono, quae mox depromere possim.

'Truth and decency are my whole care and inquiry. In this study I am entirely occupied; these I am always laying up, and so disposing that I can at any time draw forth my stores for my immediate use.' The whole epistle, indeed, from which I have paraphrased this passage, is a comment upon it, and affords many useful lessons of philosophy.

When we are employed in reading a great and good author, we ought to consider ourselves as searching after treasures, which, if well and regularly laid up in the mind, will be of use to us on sundry occasions in our lives. If a man, for instance, should be overloaded with prosperity or adversity (both of which cases are liable to happen to us), who is there so very wise, or so very foolish, that, if he was a master of Seneca and Plutarch, could not find great matter of comfort and utility from their doctrines? I mention these rather than Plato and Aristotle, as the works of the latter are not, I think, yet completely made English, and, consequently, are less within the reach of most of my countrymen.

But perhaps it may be asked, will Seneca or Plutarch make us laugh? Perhaps not; but if you are not a fool, my worthy friend, which I can hardly with civility suspect, they will both (the latter especially) please you more than if they did. For my own part, I declare, I have not read even Lucian himself with more delight than I have Plutarch; but surely it is astonishing that such scribblers as Tom Brown, Tom D'Urfey, and the wits of our age, should find readers, while the writings of so excellent, so entertaining, and so voluminous an author as Plutarch remain in the world, and, as I apprehend, are very little known.

The truth I am afraid is, that real taste is a quality with which human nature is very slenderly gifted. It is indeed so very rare, and so little known, that scarce two authors have agreed in their notions of it; and those who have endeavoured to explain it to others seem to have succeeded only in showing us that they know it not themselves. If I might be allowed to give my own sentiments, I should derive it from a nice harmony between the imagination and the judgment; and hence perhaps it is that so few have ever possessed this talent in any eminent degree. Neither of these will alone bestow it; nothing is indeed more common than to see men of very bright imaginations, and of very accurate learning (which can hardly be acquired without judgment), who are entirely devoid of taste; and Longinus, who of all men seems most exquisitely to have possessed it, will puzzle his reader very much if he should attempt to decide whether imagination or judgment shine the brighter in that inimitable critic.

But as for the bulk of mankind, they are clearly void of any degree of taste. It is a quality in which they advance very little beyond a state of infancy. The first thing a child is fond of in a book is a picture, the second is a story, and the third a jest. Here then is the true Pons Asinorum, which very few readers ever get over.

From what I have said it may perhaps be thought to appear that true taste is the real gift of nature only; and if so, some may ask to what purpose have I endeavoured to show men that they are without a blessing which it is impossible for them to attain?

Now, though it is certain that to the highest consummation of taste, as well as of every other excellence, nature must lend much assistance, yet great is the power of art, almost of itself, or at best with only slender aids from nature; and, to say the truth, there are very few who have not in their minds some small seeds of taste. 'All men,' says Cicero, 'have a sort of tacit sense of what is right or wrong in arts and sciences, even without the help of arts.' This surely it is in the power of art very greatly to improve. That most men, therefore, proceed no farther than as I have above declared, is owing either to the want of any, or (which is perhaps yet worse) to an improper education.

I shall probably, therefore, in a future paper endeavour to lay down some rules by which all men may acquire at least some degree of taste. In the meanwhile, I shall (according to the method observed in inoculation) recommend to my readers, as a preparative for their receiving my instructions, a total abstinence from all bad books. I do therefore most earnestly entreat all my young readers that they would cautiously avoid the perusal of any modern book till it hath first had the sanction of some wise and learned man; and the same caution I propose to all fathers, mothers, and guardians.

'Evil communications corrupt good manners,' is a quotation of St. Paul from Menander. *Evil books corrupt at once both our manners and our taste.*

SAMUEL JOHNSON

1709–1784

DICK MINIM THE CRITIC

CRITICISM is a study by which men grow important and formidable at a very small expense. The power of invention has been conferred by nature upon few, and the labour of learning those sciences which may by mere labour be obtained is too great to be willingly endured; but every man can exert such judgment as he has upon the works of others; and he whom nature has made weak, and idleness keeps ignorant, may yet support his vanity by the name of a Critic.

I hope it will give comfort to great numbers who are passing through the world in obscurity, when I inform them how easily distinction may be obtained. All the other powers of literature are coy and haughty, they must be long courted, and at last are not always gained; but Criticism is a goddess easy of access and forward of advance, who will meet the slow, and encourage the timorous; the want of meaning she supplies with words, and the want of spirit she recompenses with malignity.

This profession has one recommendation peculiar to itself, that it gives vent to malignity without real mischief. No genius was ever blasted by the breath of critics. The poison which, if confined, would have burst the heart, fumes away in empty hisses, and malice is set at ease with very little danger to merit. The Critic is the only man whose triumph is without another's pain, and whose greatness does not rise upon another's ruin.

To a study at once so easy and so reputable, so malicious and so harmless, it cannot be necessary to invite my readers by a long or laboured exhortation;

it is sufficient, since all would be Critics if they could, to show by one eminent example that all can be Critics if they will.

Dick Minim, after the common course of puerile studies, in which he was no great proficient, was put apprentice to a brewer, with whom he had lived two years, when his uncle died in the city, and left him a large fortune in the stocks. Dick had for six months before used the company of the lower players, of whom he had learned to scorn a trade, and, being now at liberty to follow his genius, he resolved to be a man of wit and humour. That he might be properly initiated in his new character, he frequented the coffee-houses near the theatres, where he listened very diligently, day after day, to those who talked of language and sentiments, and unities and catastrophes, till, by slow degrees, he began to think that he understood something of the stage, and hoped in time to talk himself.

But he did not trust so much to natural sagacity as wholly to neglect the help of books. When the theatres were shut, he retired to Richmond with a few select writers, whose opinions he impressed upon his memory by unwearied diligence; and, when he returned with other wits to the town, was able to tell, in very proper phrases, that the chief business of art is to copy nature; that a perfect writer is not to be expected, because genius decays as judgment increases; that the great art is the art of blotting; and that, according to the rule of Horace, every piece should be kept nine years.

Of the great authors he now began to display the characters, laying down as an universal position, that all had beauties and defects. His opinion was, that Shakespeare, committing himself wholly to the impulse of nature, wanted the correctness which learning would have given him; and that Jonson, trusting to learning, did not sufficiently cast his eyes on nature. He blamed the stanzas of Spenser, and could not bear the hexameters of Sidney. Denham and Waller he held the first reformers of English numbers; and thought that if Waller could have obtained the strength of Denham, or Denham the sweetness of Waller, there had been nothing wanting to complete a poet. He often expressed his commiseration of Dryden's poverty, and his indignation at the age which suffered him to write for bread; he repeated with rapture the first lines of All for Love, but wondered at the corruption of taste which could bear anything so unnatural as rhyming tragedies. In Otway he found uncommon powers of moving the passions, but was disgusted by his general negligence, and blamed him for making a conspirator his hero; and never concluded his disquisition, without remarking how happily the sound of the clock is made to alarm the audience. Southern would have been his favourite, but that he mixes comic with tragic scenes, intercepts the natural course of the passions, and fills the mind with a wild confusion of mirth and melancholy. The versification of Rowe he thought too melodious for the stage, and too little varied in different passions. He made it the great fault of Congreve, that all his persons were wits, and that he always wrote with more art than nature. He considered Cato rather as a poem than play, and allowed Addison to be the complete master of allegory and grave humour, but paid no great deference to him as a critic. He thought the chief merit of Prior was in his easy tales and lighter poems, though he allowed that his *Solomon* had many noble sentiments elegantly expressed. In Swift he discovered an inimitable vein of irony, and an easiness which all would hope and few would attain. Pope he was inclined to degrade from a poet to a versifier, and thought his numbers rather luscious than sweet. He often lamented the neglect of Phædra and Hippolitus, and wished to see the stage under better regulations.

These assertions passed commonly uncontradicted; and if now and then an opponent started up, he was quickly repressed by the suffrages of the company, and Minim went away from every dispute with elation of heart and increase of confidence.

He now grew conscious of his abilities, and began to talk of the present state of dramatic poetry; wondered what had become of the comic genius which supplied our ancestors with wit and pleasantry, and why no writer could be found that durst now venture beyond a farce. He saw no reason for thinking that the vein of humour was exhausted, since we live in a country where liberty suffers every character to spread itself to its utmost bulk, and which therefore produces more originals than all the rest of the world together. Of tragedy he concluded business to be the soul, and yet often hinted that love predominates too much upon the modern stage.

He was now an acknowledged critic, and had his own seat in a coffee-house, and headed a party in the pit. Minim has more vanity than ill-nature, and seldom desires to do much mischief; he will perhaps murmur a little in the ear of him that sits next him, but endeavours to influence the audience to favour, by clapping when an actor exclaims, 'Ye gods!' or laments the misery of his country.

By degrees he was admitted to rehearsals; and many of his friends are of opinion, that our present poets are indebted to him for their happiest thoughts: by his contrivance the bell was rung twice in *Barbarossa*, and by his persuasion the author of *Cleone* concluded his play without a couplet; for what can be more absurd, said Minim, than that part of a play should be rhymed, and part written in blank verse? and by what acquisition of faculties is the speaker, who never could find rhymes before, enabled to rhyme at the conclusion of an act?

He is the great investigator of hidden beauties, and is particularly delighted when he finds 'the sound an echo to the sense.' He has read all our poets with particular attention to this delicacy of versification, and wonders at the supineness with which their works have been hitherto perused, so that no man has found the sound of a drum in this distich:

> When pulpit, drum ecclesiastic,
> Was beat with fist instead of a stick;

and that the wonderful lines upon honour and a bubble have hitherto passed without notice:

> Honour is like the glassy bubble,
> Which cost philosophers such trouble;
> Where, one part crack'd, the whole does fly,
> And wits are crack'd to find out why.

In these verses, says Minim, we have two striking accommodations of the sound to the sense. It is impossible to utter the first two lines emphatically without an act like that which they describe; *bubble* and *trouble* causing a momentary inflation of the cheeks by the retention of the breath, which is afterwards forcibly emitted, as in the practice of *blowing bubbles*. But the greatest excellence is in the third line, which is *crack'd* in the middle to express a crack, and then shivers into monosyllables. Yet has this diamond lain neglected with common stones, and among the innumerable admirers of Hudibras, the observation of this superlative passage has been reserved for the sagacity of Minim.

DICK MINIM THE CRITIC—(*continued*)

Mr. Minim had now advanced himself to the zenith of critical reputation; when he was in the pit, every eye in the boxes was fixed upon him: when he entered his coffee-house, he was surrounded by circles of candidates, who passed their noviciate of literature under his tuition: his opinion was asked by all who had no opinion of their own, and yet loved to debate and decide; and no composition was supposed to pass in safety to posterity, till it had been secured by Minim's approbation.

Minim professes great admiration of the wisdom and munificence by which the academies of the continent were raised; and often wishes for some standard of taste, for some tribunal, to which merit may appeal from caprice, prejudice, and malignity. He has formed a plan for an academy of criticism, where every work of imagination may be read before it is printed, and which shall authoritatively direct the theatres what pieces to receive or reject, to exclude or to revive.

Such an institution would, in Dick's opinion, spread the fame of English literature over Europe, and make London the metropolis of elegance and politeness, the place to which the learned and ingenious of all countries would repair for instruction and improvement, and where nothing would any longer be applauded or endured that was not conformed to the nicest rules, and finished with the highest elegance.

Till some happy conjunction of the planets shall dispose our princes or ministers to make themselves immortal by such an academy, Minim contents himself to preside four nights in a week in a critical society selected by himself, where he is heard without contradiction, and whence his judgment is disseminated through the great vulgar and the small.

When he is placed in the chair of criticism, he declares loudly for the noble simplicity of our ancestors, in opposition to the petty refinements and ornamental luxuriance. Sometimes he is sunk in despair, and perceives false delicacy daily gaining ground, and sometimes brightens his countenance with a gleam of hope, and predicts the revival of the true sublime. He then fulminates his loudest censures against the monkish barbarity of rhyme; wonders how beings that pretend to reason can be pleased with one line always ending like another; tells how unjustly and unnaturally sense is sacrificed to sound; how often the best thoughts are mangled by the necessity of confining or extending them to the dimensions of a couplet; and rejoices that genius has, in our days, shaken off the shackles which had encumbered it so long. Yet he allows that rhyme may sometimes be borne, if the lines be often broken, and the pauses judiciously diversified.

From blank verse he makes an easy transition to Milton, whom he produces as an example of the slow advance of lasting reputation. Milton is the only writer in whose books Minim can read for ever without weariness. What cause it is that exempts this pleasure from satiety he has long and diligently inquired, and believes it to consist in the perpetual variation of the numbers, by which the ear is gratified and the attention awakened. The lines that are commonly thought rugged and unmusical, he conceives to have been written to temper the melodious luxury of the rest, or to express things by a proper cadence: for he scarcely finds a verse that has not this favourite beauty; he declares that he could shiver in a hot-house when he reads that

> the ground
> Burns frore, and cold performs th' effect of fire;

and that, when Milton bewails his blindness, the verse,

> So thick a drop serene has quenched these orbs,

has, he knows not how, something that strikes him with an obscure sensation like that which he fancies would be felt from the sound of darkness.

Minim is not so confident of his rules of judgment as not very eagerly to catch new light from the name of the author. He is commonly so prudent as to spare those whom he cannot resist, unless, as will sometimes happen, he finds the public combined against them. But a fresh pretender to fame he is strongly inclined to censure, till his own honour requires that he commend him. Till he knows the success of a composition, he entrenches himself in general terms; there are some new thoughts and beautiful passages, but there is likewise much which he would have advised the author to expunge. He has several favourite epithets, of which he never settled the meaning, but which are very commodiously applied to books which he has not read, or cannot understand. One is *manly*, another is *dry*, another *stiff*, and another *flimsy*; sometimes he discovers delicacy of style, and sometimes meets with *strange expressions*.

He is never so great, nor so happy, as when a youth of promising parts is brought to receive his directions for the prosecution of his studies. He then puts on a very serious air; he advises the pupil to read none but the best authors, and, when he finds one congenial to his own mind, to study his beauties, but avoid his faults; and, when he sits down to write, to consider how his favourite author would think at the present time on the present occasion. He exhorts him to catch those moments when he finds his thoughts expanded and his genius exalted, but to take care lest imagination hurry him beyond the bounds of nature. He holds diligence the mother of success; yet enjoins him, with great earnestness, not to read more than he can digest, and not to confuse his mind by pursuing studies of contrary tendencies. He tells him, that every man has his genius, and that Cicero could never be a poet. The boy retires illuminated, resolves to follow his genius, and to think how Milton would have thought: and Minim feasts upon his own beneficence till another day brings another pupil.

DAVID HUME

1711–1776

OF SIMPLICITY AND REFINEMENT IN WRITING

FINE writing, according to Addison, consists of sentiments, which are natural, without being obvious. There cannot be a juster and more concise definition of fine writing.

Sentiments which are merely natural, affect not the mind with any pleasure, and seem not worthy of our attention. The pleasantries of a waterman, the observations of a peasant, the ribaldry of a porter or hackney coachmen, all of these are natural and disagreeable. What an insipid comedy should we make of the chit-chat of the tea-table, copied faithfully and at full length? Nothing can please persons of taste, but nature drawn with all her graces and ornaments, *la belle nature*; or if we copy low life, the strokes must be strong and remarkable, and must convey a lively image to the mind. The absurd naïveté of Sancho Panza is represented in such inimitable colours by Cervantes, that it entertains as much as the picture of the most magnanimous hero or the softest lover.

The case is the same with orators, philosophers, critics, or any author who speaks in his own person, without introducing other speakers or actors. If his language be not elegant, his observations uncommon, his sense strong and masculine, he will in vain boast his nature and simplicity. He may be correct; but he never will be agreeable. It is the unhappiness of such authors, that they are never blamed or censured. The good fortune of a book and that of a man, are not the same. The secret deceiving path of life, which Horace talks of, *fallentis semita vitæ*, may be the happiest lot of the one; but it is the greatest misfortune which the other can possibly fall into.

On the other hand, productions which are merely surprising, without being natural, can never give any lasting entertainment to the mind. To draw chimeras is not, properly speaking, to copy or imitate. The justness of representation is lost, and the mind is displeased to find a picture which bears no resemblance to any original. Nor are such excessive refinements more agreeable in the epistolary or philosophic style, than in the epic or tragic. Too much ornament is a fault in every kind of production. Uncommon expressions, strong flashes of wit, pointed similes, and epigrammatic turns, especially when they recur too frequently, are a disfigurement rather than any embellishment of discourse. As the eye, in surveying a Gothic building, is distracted by the multiplicity of ornaments, and loses the whole by a minute attention to the parts; so the mind, in perusing a work overstocked with wit, is fatigued and disgusted with the constant endeavour to shine and surprise. This is the case where the writer over-abounds in wit, even though that wit in itself should be just and agreeable. But it commonly happens to such writers, that they seek for their favourite ornaments, even where the subject does not afford them; and by that means have twenty insipid conceits for one thought which is really beautiful.

There is no object in critical learning more copious than this of the just mixture of simplicity and refinement in writing; and therefore, not to wander in too large a field, I shall confine myself to a few general observations on that head.

1. I observe, *That though excesses of both kinds are to be avoided, and though a proper medium ought to be studied in all productions; yet this medium lies not in a point, but admits of a considerable latitude.* Consider the wide distance, in this respect, between Pope and Lucretius. These seem to lie in the two greatest extremes of refinement and simplicity in which a poet can indulge himself, without being guilty of any blameable excess.

All this interval may be filled with poets, who may differ from each other, but may be equally admirable, each in his peculiar style and manner. Corneille and Congreve, who carry their wit and refinement somewhat further than Pope (if poets of so different a kind can be compared together), and Sophocles and Terence, who are more simple than Lucretius, seem to have gone out of that medium, in which the most perfect productions are found, and to be guilty of some excess in these opposite characters. Of all the great poets, Virgil and Racine, in my opinion, lie nearest the centre, and are the furthest removed from both the extremities.

2. My observation on this head is, *That it is very difficult, if not impossible, to explain by words, where the just medium lies between the excesses of simplicity and refinement, or to give any rule by which we can know precisely the bounds between the fault and the beauty.* A critic may not only discourse very judiciously on this head without instructing his readers, but even without understanding the matter perfectly himself. There is not a finer piece of criticism than the 'Dissertation on Pastorals' by Fontenelle; in which, by a number of reflections and philosophical reasonings, he endeavours to fix the just medium which is suitable to that species of writing. But let any one read the pastorals of that author, and he will be convinced that this judicious critic, notwithstanding his fine reasonings, had a false taste, and fixed the point of perfection much nearer the extreme of refinement than pastoral poetry will admit of. The sentiments of his shepherds are better suited to the toilettes of Paris than to the forests of Arcadia. But this it is impossible to discover from his critical reasonings. He blames all excessive painting and ornament as much as Virgil could have done, had that great poet written a dissertation on this species of poetry. However different the tastes of men, their general discourse on these subjects is commonly the same. No criticism can be instructive which descends not to

particulars, and is not full of examples and illustrations. It is allowed on all hands, that beauty, as well as virtue, always lies in a medium; but where this medium is placed is a great question, and can never be sufficiently explained by general reasonings.

3. I shall deliver on this subject, *That we ought to be more on our guard against the excess of refinement than that of simplicity; and that because the former excess is both less* beautiful, *and more* dangerous *than the latter.*

It is a certain rule, that wit and passion are entirely incompatible. When the affections are moved, there is no place for the imagination. The mind of man being naturally limited, it is impossible that all its faculties can operate at once: and the more any one predominates the less room is there for the others to exert their vigour. For this reason, a greater simplicity is required in all compositions, where men, and actions, and passions, are painted, than in such as consist of reflections and observations. And, as the former species of writing is the more engaging and beautiful, one may safely upon this account give the preference to the extreme of simplicity above that of refinement.

We may also observe, that those compositions which we read the oftenest, and which every man of taste has got by heart, have the recommendation of simplicity, and have nothing surprising in the thought, when divested of that elegance of expression, and harmony of numbers, with which it is clothed. If the merit of the composition lie in a point of wit, it may strike at first; but the mind anticipates the thought in the second perusal, and is no longer affected by it. When I read an epigram of Martial, the first line recalls the whole; and I have no pleasure in repeating to myself what I know already. But each line, each word in Catullus, has its merit; and I am never tired with the perusal of him. It is sufficient to run over Cowley once; but Parnell, after the fiftieth reading, is as fresh as at the first. Besides, it is with books as with women, where a certain plainness of manner and of dress is more engaging than the glare of paint, and airs, and apparel, which may dazzle the eye, but reaches not the affections. Terence is a modest and bashful beauty, to whom we grant everything, because he assumes nothing, and whose purity and nature make a durable though not a violent impression on us.

But refinement, as it is the less *beautiful*, so is it the more *dangerous* extreme, and what we are the aptest to fall into. Simplicity passes for dulness, when it is not accompanied with great elegance and propriety. On the contrary, there is something surprising in a blaze of wit and conceit. Ordinary readers are mightily struck with it, and falsely imagine it to be the most difficult, as well as most excellent way of writing. Seneca abounds with agreeable faults, says Quintilian, *abundat dulcibus vitiis*; and for that reason is the more dangerous, and the more apt to pervert the taste of the young and the inconsiderate.

I shall add, that the excess of refinement is now more to be guarded against than ever; because it is the extreme, which men are the most apt to fall into, after learning has made some progress, and after eminent writers have appeared in every species of composition. The endeavour to please by novelty leads men wide of simplicity and nature, and fills their writings with affectation and conceit. It was thus the Asiatic eloquence degenerated so much from the Attic: it was thus the age of Claudius and Nero became so much inferior to that of Augustus in taste and genius. And perhaps there are at present some symptoms of a like degeneracy of taste in France as well as in England.

OLIVER GOLDSMITH

1728–1774

THE MAN IN BLACK

THOUGH fond of many acquaintances, I desire an intimacy only with a few. The Man in Black, whom I have often mentioned, is one whose friendship I could wish to acquire, because he possesses my esteem. His manners, it is true, are tinctured with some strange inconsistencies; and he may be justly termed an humorist in a nation of humorists. Though he is generous even to profusion, he affects to be thought a prodigy of parsimony and prudence; though his conversation be replete with the most sordid and selfish maxims, his heart is dilated with the most unbounded love. I have known him profess himself a man-hater, while his cheek was glowing with compassion; and, while his looks were softened into pity, I have heard him use the language of the most unbounded ill-nature. Some affect humanity and tenderness, others boast of having such dispositions from Nature; but he is the only man I ever knew who seemed ashamed of his natural benevolence. He takes as much pains to hide his feelings, as any hypocrite would to conceal his indifference; but on every unguarded moment the mask drops off, and reveals him to the most superficial observer.

In one of our late excursions into the country, happening to discourse upon the provision that was made for the poor in England, he seemed amazed how any of his countrymen could be so foolishly weak as to relieve occasional objects of charity, when the laws had made such ample provision for their support. 'In every parish-house,' says he, 'the poor are supplied with food, clothes, fire, and a bed to lie on; they want no more, I desire no more myself; yet still they seem discontented. I'm surprised at the inactivity of our magistrates in not taking up such vagrants, who are only a weight upon the industrious; I'm surprised that the people are found to relieve them, when they must be at the same time sensible that it, in some measure, encourages idleness, extravagance, and imposture. Were I to advise any man for whom I had the least regard, I would caution him by all means not to be imposed upon by their false pretences: let me assure you, sir, they are impostors, every one of them; and rather merit a prison than relief.'

He was proceeding in this strain earnestly, to dissuade me from an imprudence of which I am seldom guilty, when an old man, who still had about him the remnants of tattered finery, implored our compassion. He assured us that he was no common beggar, but forced into the shameful profession to support a dying wife and five hungry children. Being prepossessed against such falsehoods, his story had not the least influence upon me; but it was quite otherwise with the Man in Black; I could see it visibly operate upon his countenance, and effectually interrupt his harangue. I could easily perceive that his heart burned to relieve the five starving children, but he seemed ashamed to discover his weakness to me. While he thus hesitated between compassion and pride, I pretended to look another way, and he seized this opportunity of giving the poor petitioner a piece of silver, bidding him at the same time, in order that I should hear, go work for his bread, and not tease passengers with such impertinent falsehoods for the future.

As he had fancied himself quite unperceived, he continued, as we proceeded, to rail against beggars with as much animosity as before; he threw in some episodes on his own amazing prudence and economy, with his profound skill in discovering impostors; he explained the manner in which he would deal with beggars, were he a magistrate, hinted at enlarging some of the prisons for their reception, and told two stories of ladies that were robbed by beggarmen. He was beginning a third to the same purpose, when a sailor with a wooden leg once more crossed our walks, desiring our pity, and blessing our limbs. I was for going on without taking any notice, but my friend, looking wistfully upon the poor petitioner, bade me stop, and he would show me with how much ease he could at any time detect an impostor.

He now, therefore, assumed a look of importance, and in an angry tone began to examine the sailor, demanding in what engagement he was thus disabled and rendered unfit for service. The sailor replied in a tone as angrily as he, that he had been an officer on board a private ship of war, and that he had lost his leg abroad, in defence of those who did nothing at home. At this reply, all my friend's importance vanished in a moment; he had not a single question more to ask; he now only studied what method he should take to relieve him unobserved. He had, however, no easy part to act, as he was obliged to preserve the appearance of ill-nature before me, and yet relieve himself by relieving the sailor. Casting, therefore, a furious look upon some bundles of chips which the fellow carried in a string at his back, my friend demanded how he sold his matches; but not waiting for a reply, desired in a surly tone to have a shilling's worth. The sailor seemed at first surprised at his demand, but soon recollecting himself, and presenting his whole bundle—'Here, master,' says he, 'take all my cargo, and a blessing into the bargain.'

It is impossible to describe with what an air of triumph my friend marched off with his new purchase; he assured me that he was firmly of opinion that those fellows must have stolen their goods who could thus afford to sell them for half value. He informed me of several different uses to which those chips might be applied; he expatiated largely upon the savings that would result from lighting candles with a match instead of thrusting them into the fire. He averred that he would as soon have parted with a tooth as his money to those vagabonds, unless for some valuable consideration. I cannot tell how long this panegyric upon frugality and matches might have continued, had not his attention been called off by another object more distressful than either of the former. A woman in rags, with one child in her arms, and another on her back, was attempting to sing ballads, but with such a mournful voice that it was difficult to determine whether she was singing or crying. A wretch who in the deepest distress still aimed at good-humour, was an object my friend was by no means capable of withstanding; his vivacity and his discourse were instantly interrupted; upon this occasion his very dissimulation had forsaken him. Even in my presence, he immediately applied his hands to his pockets, in order to relieve her; but guess his confusion, when he found he had already given away all the money he carried about him to former objects. The misery painted in the woman's visage was not half so strongly expressed as the agony in his. He continued to search for some time, but to no purpose, till, at length, recollecting himself, with a face of ineffable good-nature, as he had no money, he put into her hands his shilling's worth of matches.

BEAU TIBBS

THOUGH naturally pensive, yet I am fond of gay company, and take every opportunity of thus dismissing the mind from duty. From this motive I am often found in the centre of a crowd; and wherever pleasure is to be sold, am always a purchaser. In those places, without being remarked by any, I join in whatever goes forward; work my passions into a similitude of frivolous earnestness, shout as they shout, and condemn as they happen to disapprove. A mind thus sunk for awhile below its natural standard, is qualified for stronger flights, as those first retire who would spring forward with greater vigour.

Attracted by the serenity of the evening, a friend and I lately went to gaze upon the company in one of the public walks near the city. Here we sauntered together for some time, either praising the beauty of such as were handsome, or the dresses of such as had nothing else to recommend them. We had gone thus deliberately forward for some time, when my friend, stopping on a sudden, caught me by the elbow, and led me out of the public walk, I could perceive by the quickness of his pace, and by his frequently looking behind, that he was attempting to avoid somebody who followed; we now turned to the right, then to the left; as we went forward, he still went faster, but in vain; the person whom he attempted to escape, hunted us through every doubling, and gained upon us each moment; so that at last we fairly stood still, resolving to face what we could not avoid.

Our pursuer soon came up, and joined us with all the familiarity of an old acquaintance. 'My dear Charles,' cries he, shaking my friend's hand, 'where have you been hiding this half a century? Positively I had fancied you were gone down to cultivate matrimony and your estate in the country.' During the reply I had an opportunity of surveying the appearance of our new companion. His hat was pinched up with peculiar smartness; his looks were pale, thin, and sharp; round his neck he wore a broad black ribbon, and in his bosom a buckle studded with glass; his coat was trimmed with tarnished twist; he wore by his side a sword with a black hilt, and his stockings of silk, though newly washed, were grown yellow by long service. I was so much engaged with the peculiarity of his dress, that I attended only to the latter part of my friend's reply, in which he complimented Mr. Tibbs on the taste of his clothes, and the bloom in his countenance. 'Psha, psha, Charles,' cried the figure, 'no more of that if you love me; you know I hate flattery, on my soul I do; and yet, to be sure, an intimacy with the great will improve one's appearance, and a course of venison will fatten; and yet, faith, I despise the great as much as you do; but there are a great many honest fellows among them; and we must not quarrel with one half because the other wants breeding. If they were all such as my Lord Mudler, one of the most good-natured creatures that ever squeezed a lemon, I should myself be among the number of their admirers. I was yesterday to dine at the Duchess of Piccadilly's. My lord was there. "Ned," says he to me, "Ned," says he, "I'll hold gold to silver I can tell where you were poaching last night." "Poaching, my lord?" says I; "faith, you have missed already; for I stayed at home, and let the girls poach for me. That 's my way; I take a fine woman as some animals do their prey; stand still, and swoop, they fall into my mouth." '

'Ah, Tibbs, thou art an happy fellow,' cried my companion, with looks of infinite pity; 'I hope your fortune is as much improved as your understanding in such company?' 'Improved,' replied the other; 'you shall know—but let it go no further—a great secret—five hundred a year to begin with. My lord's word of honour for it. His lordship took me down in his own chariot yesterday, and we had a *tête-à-tête* dinner in the country; where we talked of nothing else.' 'I fancy you forgot, sir,' cried I; 'you told us but this moment of your dining yesterday in town.' 'Did I say so?' replied he coolly. 'To be sure, if I said so it was so. Dined in town: egad, now I do remember, I did dine in town; but I dined in the country too; for you must know, my boys, I eat two dinners. By the bye, I am grown as nice as the devil in my eating. I'll tell you a pleasant affair about that: We were a select party of us to dine at Lady Grogram's, an affected piece, but let it go no further; a secret. "Well," says I, "I'll hold a thousand guineas, and say done first, that——" But, dear Charles, you are an honest creature, lend me half-a-crown for a minute or two, or so, just till—— But, harkee, ask me for it the next time we meet, or it may be twenty to one but I forget to pay you.'

When he left us, our conversation naturally turned upon so extraordinary a character. 'His very dress,' cries my friend, 'is not less extraordinary than his conduct. If you meet him this day you find him in rags; if the next, in embroidery. With those persons of distinction, of whom he talks so familiarly, he has scarce a coffee-house acquaintance. However, both for the interests of society, and perhaps for his own, Heaven has made him poor; and while all the world perceives his wants, he fancies them concealed from every eye. An agreeable companion, because he understands flattery; and all must be pleased with the first part of his conversation, though all are sure of its ending with a demand on their purse. While his youth countenances the levity of his conduct, he may thus earn a precarious subsistence; but when age comes on, the gravity of which is incompatible with buffoonery, then will he find himself forsaken by all; condemned, in the decline of life, to hang upon some rich family whom he once despised, there to undergo all the ingenuity of studied contempt, to be employed only as a spy upon the servants, or a bugbear to fright children into duty.'

BEAU TIBBS AT HOME

There are some acquaintances whom it is no easy matter to shake off. My little beau yesterday overtook me again in one of the public walks, and, slapping me on the shoulder, saluted me with an air of the most perfect familiarity. His dress was the same as usual, except that he had more powder in his hair; wore a dirtier shirt, and had on a pair of temple spectacles, and his hat under his arm.

As I knew him to be an harmless amusing little thing, I could not return his smiles with any degree of severity; so we walked forward on the terms of the utmost intimacy, and in a few minutes discussed all the usual topics preliminary to particular conversation.

The oddities that marked his character, however, soon began to appear; he bowed to several well-dressed persons, who, by their manner of returning the compliment, appeared perfect strangers. At intervals he drew out a pocket-book, seeming to take memorandums before all the company, with much importance and assiduity. In this manner he led me through the length of the whole Mall, fretting at his absurdities, and fancying myself laughed at as well as he by every spectator.

When we were got to the end of our procession, 'Hang me,' cries he, with an air of vivacity, 'I never saw the park so thin in my life before; there 's no company at all to-day. Not a single face to be seen.' 'No company,' interrupted I, peevishly; 'no company where there is such a crowd? Why, man, there is too much. What are the thousands that have been laughing at us but company?' 'Lord, my dear,' returned he, with the utmost good humour, 'you seem immensely chagrined; but hang me, when the world laughs at me, I laugh at all the world, and so we are even. My Lord Trip, Bill Squash, the Creolian, and I, sometimes make a party at being ridiculous; and so we say and do a thousand things for the joke's sake. But I see you are grave; and if you are for a fine grave sentimental companion, you shall dine with my wife to-day; I must insist on't; I'll introduce you to Mrs. Tibbs, a lady of as elegant qualifications as any in nature; she was bred, but that 's between ourselves, under the inspection of the Countess of Shoreditch. A charming body of voice! But no more of that, she shall give us a song. You shall see my little girl too. Carolina Wilhelma Amelia Tibbs, a sweet pretty creature; I design her for my Lord Drumstick's eldest son; but that 's in friendship, let it go no further; she' s but six years old, and yet she walks a minuet, and plays on the guitar immensely already. I intend she shall be as perfect as possible in every accomplishment. In the first place I'll make her a scholar; I'll teach her Greek myself, and I intend to learn that language purposely to instruct her; but let that be a secret.'

Thus saying, without waiting for a reply, he took me by the arm and hauled me along. We passed through many dark alleys and winding ways; for, from some motives to me unknown, he seemed to have a particular aversion to every frequented street; at last, however, we got to the door of a dismal-looking house in the outlets of the town, where he informed me he chose to reside for the benefit of the air.

We entered the lower door, which seemed ever to lie most hospitably open: and I began to ascend an old and creaking staircase, when, as he mounted to show me the way, he demanded whether I delighted in prospects; to which answering in the affirmative, 'Then,' says he, 'I shall show you one of the most charming out of my windows; we shall see the ships sailing, and the whole country for twenty miles round, tip top, quite high. My Lord Swamp would give ten thousand guineas for such a one; but, as I sometimes pleasantly tell him, I always love to keep my prospects at home, that my friends may come to see me the oftener.'

By this time we were arrived as high as the stairs would permit us to ascend, till we came to what he was facetiously pleased to call the first floor down the chimney; and knocking at the door, a voice with a Scotch accent, from within, demanded, 'Wha 's there?' My conductor answered that it was him. But this not satisfying the querist, the voice again repeated the demand: to which he answered louder than before, and now the door was opened by an old maid-servant with cautious reluctance.

When we were got in, he welcomed me to his house with great ceremony, and turning to the old woman, asked where her lady was? 'Good troth,' replied she, in the northern dialect, 'she 's washing your twa shirts at the next door, because they have taken an oath against lending out the tub any longer.' 'My two shirts!' cries he in a tone that faltered with confusion, 'what does the idiot mean?' 'I ken what I mean well enough,' replied the other; 'she' s washing your twa shirts at the next door, because——' 'Fire and fury! no more of thy stupid explanations,' cried he. 'Go and inform her we have got company. Were that Scotch hag,' continued he, turning to me, 'to be for ever in the family, she would never learn politeness, nor forget that absurd poisonous accent of hers, or testify the smallest specimen of breeding or high life; and yet it is very surprising too, as I had her from a parliament man, a friend of mine, from the Highlands, one of the politest men in the world; but that 's a secret.'

We waited some time for Mrs. Tibbs' arrival, during which interval I had a full opportunity of surveying the chamber and all its furniture; which consisted of four chairs with old wrought bottoms, that he assured me were his wife's embroidery; a square table that had been once japanned, a cradle in one corner, a lumbering cabinet in the other; a broken shepherdess, and a mandarin without a head, were stuck over the chimney; and round the walls several paltry, unframed pictures, which, he observed, were all of his own drawing. 'What do you think, sir, of that head in the corner, done in the manner of Grisoni? There 's the true keeping in it; it 's my own face: and though there happens to be no likeness, a countess offered me an hundred for its fellow: I refused her; for, hang it, that would be mechanical, you know.'

The wife, at last, made her appearance, at once a slattern and a coquette; much emaciated, but still carrying the remains of beauty. She made twenty apologies for being seen in such odious dishabille, but hoped to be excused, as she had stayed out all night at Vauxhall Gardens with the countess, who was excessively fond of the horns. 'And indeed, my dear,' added she, turning to her husband, 'his lordship drank your health in a bumper.' 'Poor Jack,' cries he, 'a dear good-natured creature, I know he loves me; but I hope, my dear, you have given orders for dinner? You need make no great preparations neither, there are but three of us; something elegant, and little will do; a turbot, an ortolan, or a——' 'Or what do you think, my dear,' interrupts the wife, 'of a nice pretty bit of ox-cheek, piping hot, and dressed with a little of my own sauce?' 'The very thing,' replies he; 'it will eat best with some smart bottled beer; but be sure to let's have the sauce his grace was so fond of. I hate your immense loads of meat; that is country all over; extreme disgusting to those who are in the least acquainted with high life.'

By this time my curiosity began to abate, and my appetite to increase; the company of fools may at first make us smile, but at last never fails of rendering us melancholy. I therefore pretended to recollect a prior engagement, and after having shown my respect to the house, by giving the old servant a piece of money at the door, I took my leave: Mr. Tibbs assuring me that dinner, if I stayed, would be ready at least in less than two hours.

WILLIAM COWPER

1731–1800

COUNTRY CONGREGATIONS

Delicta majorum immeritus lues,
Romane, donec templa refeceris
Ædesque labentes deorum, et
Fœda nigro simulacra fumo.—HOR.

'DEAR COUSIN,—The country at present, no less than the metropolis, abounding with politicians of every kind, I began to despair of picking up any intelligence that might possibly be entertaining to your readers. However, I have lately visited some of the most distant parts of the kingdom with a clergyman of my acquaintance: I shall not trouble you with an account of the improvements that have been made in the seats we saw according to the modern taste, but proceed to give you some reflections, which occurred to us on observing several country churches, and the behaviour of the congregations.

'The ruinous condition of some of these edifices gave me great offence; and I could not help wishing that the honest vicar, instead of indulging his genius for improvements, by enclosing his gooseberry bushes within a Chinese rail, and converting half an acre of his glebe-land into a bowling green, would have applied part of his income to the more laudable purpose of sheltering his parishioners from the weather, during their attendance on divine service. It is no uncommon thing to see the parsonage house well thatched, and in exceeding good repair, while the church perhaps has scarce any other roof than the ivy that grows over it. The noise of owls, bats, and magpies makes the principal part of the church music in many of these ancient edifices; and the walls, like a large map, seem to be portioned out into capes, seas, and promontories, by the various colours by which the damps have stained them. Sometimes, the foundation being too weak to support the steeple any longer, it has been expedient to pull down that part of the building, and to hang the bells under a wooden shed on the ground beside it. This is the case in a parish in Norfolk, through which I lately passed, and where the clerk and the sexton, like the two figures at St. Dunstan's, serve the bells in capacity of clappers, by striking them alternately with a hammer.

'In other churches I have observed, that nothing unseemly or ruinous is to be found, except in the clergyman, and the appendages of his person. The squire of the parish, or his ancestors, perhaps to testify their devotion, and leave a lasting monument of their magnificence, have adorned the altar-piece with the richest crimson velvet, embroidered with vine leaves and ears of wheat; and have dressed up the pulpit with the same splendour and expense; while the gentleman, who fills it, is exalted in the midst of all this finery, with a surplice as dirty as a farmer's frock, and a periwig that seems to have transferred its faculty of curling to the band which appears in full buckle beneath it.

'But if I was concerned to see several distressed pastors, as well as many of our country churches, in a tottering condition, I was more offended with the indecency of worship in others. I could wish that the clergy would inform their congregations, that there is no occasion to scream themselves hoarse in making the responses; that the town-crier is not the only person qualified to pray with due devotion; and that he who bawls the loudest may nevertheless be the wickedest fellow in the parish. The old women too in the aisle might be told, that their time would be better employed in attending to the sermon, than in fumbling over their tattered testaments till they have found the text; by which time the discourse is near drawing to a conclusion: while a word or two of instruction might not be thrown away upon the younger part of the congregation, to teach them that making posies in summer time, and cracking nuts in autumn, is no part of the religious ceremony.

'The good old practice of psalm-singing is, indeed, wonderfully improved in many country churches since the days of Sternhold and Hopkins; and there is scarce a parish clerk who has so little taste as not to pick his staves out of the New Version. This has occasioned great complaints in some places, where the clerk has been forced to bawl by himself, because the rest of the congregation cannot find the psalm at the end of their prayer-books; while others are highly disgusted at the innovation, and stick as obstinately to the Old Version as to the Old Style. The tunes themselves have also been new set to jiggish measures; and the sober drawl, which used to accompany the two first staves of the hundredth psalm, with the *gloria patri*, is now split into as many quavers as an Italian air. For this purpose there is in every county an itinerant band of vocal musicians, who make it their business to go round to all the churches in their turns, and, after a prelude with the pitch-pipe, astonish the audience with hymns set to the new Winchester measure, and anthems of their own composing. As these new-fashioned psalmodists are necessarily made up of young men and maids, we may naturally suppose, that there is a perfect concord and symphony between them: and, indeed, I have known it happen that these sweet singers have more than once been brought into disgrace, by too close an unison between the thorough-bass and the treble.

'It is a difficult matter to decide, which is looked upon as the greatest man in a country church, the parson or his clerk. The latter is most certainly held in higher veneration, where the former happens to be only a poor curate, who rides post every Sabbath from village to village, and mounts and dismounts at the church door. The clerk's office is not only to tag the prayers with an Amen, or usher in the sermon with a stave; but he is also the universal father to give away the brides, and the standing godfather to all the new-born bantlings. But in many places there is a still greater man belonging to the church, than either the parson or the clerk himself. The person I mean is the Squire; who, like the King, may be styled Head of the Church in his own parish. If the benefice be in his own gift, the vicar is his creature, and of consequence entirely at his devotion; or, if the care of the church be left to a curate, the Sunday fees of roast beef and plum pudding, and a liberty to shoot in the manor, will bring him as much under the Squire's command as his dogs and horses. For this reason the bell is often kept tolling and the people waiting in the churchyard an hour longer than the usual time; nor must the service begin until the Squire has strutted up the aisle, and seated himself in the great pew in the chancel. The length of the sermon is also measured by the will of the Squire, as formerly by the hour-glass: and I know one parish where the preacher has always the complaisance to conclude his discourse, however abruptly, the minute that the Squire gives the signal, by rising up after his nap.

'In a village church, the Squire's lady or the vicar's wife are perhaps the only females that are stared at for their finery: but in the larger cities and towns, where the newest fashions are brought down weekly by the stage-coach or wagon, all the wives and daughters of the most topping tradesmen vie with each other every Sunday in the elegance of their apparel. I could even trace their gradations in their dress, according to the opulence, the extent, and the distance of the place from London. I was at church in a populous city in the North, where the mace-bearer cleared the way for Mrs. Mayoress, who came sidling after him in an enormous fan-hoop, of a pattern which had never been seen before in those parts. At another church, in a corporation town, I saw several negligées with furbelowed aprons, which had long disputed the prize of superiority: but these were most woefully eclipsed by a burgess's daughter, just come from London, who appeared in a Trollops or Slammerkin, with treble ruffles to the cuffs, pinked and gimped, and the sides of the petticoat drawn up in festoons. In some lesser borough towns, the contest, I found, lay between three or four black and green bibs and aprons; at one, a grocer's wife attracted our eyes, by a new-fashioned cap, called a Joan; and at another, they were wholly taken up by a mercer's daughter in a nun's hood.

'I need not say anything of the behaviour of the congregations in these more polite places of religious resort; as the same genteel ceremonies are practised there, as at the most fashionable churches in town. The ladies, immediately on their entrance, breathe a pious ejaculation through their fan-sticks, and the beaux very gravely address themselves to the haberdashers' bills, glued upon the linings of their hats. This pious duty is no sooner performed, than the exercise of bowing and curtsying succeeds; the locking and unlocking of the pews drowns the reader's voice at the beginning of the service; and the rustling of silks, added to the whispering and tittering of so much good company, renders him totally unintelligible to the very end of it.—I am, dear Cousin, yours,' etc.

CHARLES LAMB

1775–1834

MRS. BATTLE'S OPINIONS ON WHIST

'A CLEAR fire, a clean hearth,[1] and the rigour of the game.' This was the celebrated *wish* of old Sarah Battle (now with God), who, next to her devotions, loved a good game of whist. She was none of your lukewarm gamesters, your half-and-half players, who have no objection to take a hand, if you want one to make up a rubber; who affirm that they have no pleasure in winning; that they like to win one game and lose another; that they can while away an hour very agreeably at a card-table, but are indifferent whether they play or no; and will desire an adversary, who has slipped a wrong card, to take it up and play another.[2] These insufferable triflers are the curse of a table. One of these flies will spoil a whole pot. Of such it may be said that they do not play at cards, but only play at playing at them.

Sarah Battle was none of that breed. She detested them, as I do, from her heart and soul, and would not, save upon a striking emergency, willingly seat herself at the same table with them. She loved a thorough-paced partner, a determined enemy. She took, and gave, no concessions. She hated favours. She never made a revoke, nor ever passed it over in her adversary without exacting the utmost forfeiture. She fought a good fight: cut and thrust. She held not her good sword (her cards) 'like a dancer.' She sate bolt upright; and neither showed you her cards,

[1 This was before the introduction of rugs, Reader. You must remember the intolerable crash of the unswept cinders betwixt your foot and the marble.]

[2 As if a sportsman should tell you he liked to kill a fox one day and lose him the next.]

nor desired to see yours. All people have their blind side—their superstitions; and I have heard her declare, under the rose, that Hearts was her favourite suit.

I never in my life—and I knew Sarah Battle many of the best years of it—saw her take out her snuff-box when it was her turn to play; or snuff a candle in the middle of a game; or ring for a servant, till it was fairly over. She never introduced, or connived at, miscellaneous conversation during its process. As she emphatically observed, cards were cards; and if I ever saw unmingled distaste in her fine last-century countenance, it was at the airs of a young gentleman of a literary turn, who had been with difficulty persuaded to take a hand; and who, in his excess of candour, declared, that he thought there was no harm in unbending the mind now and then, after serious studies, in recreations of that kind! She could not bear to have her noble occupation, to which she wound up her faculties, considered in that light. It was her business, her duty, the thing she came into the world to do,—and she did it. She unbent her mind afterwards—over a book.

Pope was her favourite author: his *Rape of the Lock* her favourite work. She once did me the favour to play over with me (with the cards) his celebrated game of Ombre in that poem; and to explain to me how far it agreed with, and in what points it would be found to differ from, tradrille. Her illustrations were apposite and poignant; and I had the pleasure of sending the substance of them to Mr. Bowles; but I suppose they came too late to be inserted among his ingenious notes upon that author.

Quadrille, she has often told me, was her first love; but whist had engaged her maturer esteem. The former, she said, was showy and specious, and likely to allure young persons. The uncertainty and quick shifting of partners—a thing which the constancy of whist abhors; the dazzling supremacy and regal investiture of Spadille—absurd, as she justly observed, in the pure aristocracy of whist, where his crown and garter give him no proper power above his brother-nobility of the Aces;—the giddy vanity, so taking to the inexperienced, of playing alone; above all, the overpowering attractions of a *Sans Prendre Vole*,—to the triumph of which there is certainly nothing parallel or approaching, in the contingencies of whist; —all these, she would say, make quadrille a game of captivation to the young and enthusiastic. But whist was the *solider* game: that was her word. It was a long meal; not like quadrille, a feast of snatches. One or two rubbers might co-extend in duration with an evening. They gave time to form rooted friendships, to cultivate steady enmities. She despised the chance-started, capricious, and ever-fluctuating alliances of the other. The skirmishes of quadrille, she would say, reminded her of the petty ephemeral embroilments of the little Italian states, depicted by Machiavel: perpetually changing postures and connexions; bitter foes to-day, sugared darlings to-morrow; kissing and scratching in a breath;—but the wars of whist were comparable to the long, steady, deep-rooted, rational antipathies of the great French and English nations.

A grave simplicity was what she chiefly admired in her favourite game. There was nothing silly in it, like the nob in cribbage—nothing superfluous. No *flushes*—that most irrational of all pleas that a reasonable being can set up:—that any one should claim four by virtue of holding cards of the same mark and colour, without reference to the playing of the game, or the individual worth or pretensions of the cards themselves! She held this to be a solecism; as pitiful an ambition at cards as alliteration is in authorship. She despised superficiality, and looked deeper than the colour of things.—Suits were soldiers, she would say, and must have a uniformity of array to distinguish them: but what should we say to a foolish squire, who should claim a merit from dressing up his tenantry in red jackets, that never were to be marshalled—never to take the field?—She even wished that whist were more simple than it is; and, in my mind, would have stripped it of some appendages, which, in the state of human frailty, may be venially, and even commendably, allowed of. She saw no reason for the deciding of the trump by the turn of the card. Why not one suit always trumps?—Why two colours, when the mark of the suit would have sufficiently distinguished them without it?

'But the eye, my dear madam, is agreeably refreshed with the variety. Man is not a creature of pure reason—he must have his senses delightfully appealed to. We see it in Roman Catholic countries, where the music and the paintings draw in many to worship, whom your quaker spirit of unsensualising would have kept out.—You yourself have a pretty collection of paintings—but confess to me, whether, walking in your gallery at Sandham, among those clear Vandykes, or among the Paul Potters in the ante-room, you ever felt your bosom glow with an elegant delight, at all comparable to *that* you have it in your power to experience most evenings over a well-arranged assortment of the court-cards?—the pretty antic habits, like heralds in a procession—the gay triumph-assuring scarlets—the contrasting deadly-killing sables—the "hoary majesty of spades"—Pam in all his glory!—

'All these might be dispensed with; and with their naked names upon the drab pasteboard, the game might go on very well, pictureless; but the *beauty* of cards would be extinguished for ever. Stripped of all that is imaginative in them, they must degenerate into mere gambling. Imagine a dull deal board, or drum head, to spread them on, instead of that nice verdant carpet (next to nature's), fittest arena for those courtly combatants to play their gallant jousts and turneys in!—Exchange those delicately-turned ivory markers—(work of Chinese artist, unconscious of their symbol,—or as profanely slighting their true application as the arrantest Ephesian journeyman that turned out those little shrines for the goddess) —exchange them for little bits of leather (our ancestors' money), or chalk and a slate!'—

The old lady, with a smile, confessed the soundness of my logic; and to her approbation of my arguments on her favourite topic that evening I have always fancied myself indebted for the legacy of a curious cribbage-board, made of the finest Sienna marble, which her maternal uncle (old Walter Plumer, whom I have elsewhere celebrated) brought with him from Florence:—this, and a trifle of five hundred pounds, came to me at her death.

The former bequest (which I do not least value) I have kept with religious care; though she herself, to confess a truth, was never greatly taken with cribbage. It was an essentially vulgar game, I have heard her say,—disputing with her uncle, who was very partial to it. She could never heartily bring her mouth to pronounce '*Go*,' or '*That 's a go*.' She called it an ungrammatical game. The pegging teased her. I once knew her to forfeit a rubber (a five-dollar stake) because she would not take advantage of the turn-up knave, which would have given it her, but which she must have claimed by the disgraceful tenure of declaring '*two for his heels*.' There is something extremely genteel in this sort of self-denial. Sarah Battle was a gentlewoman born.

Piquet she held the best game at the cards for two persons, though she would ridicule the pedantry of the terms—such as pique—repique—the capot—they savoured (she thought) of affectation. But games for two, or even three, she never greatly cared for. She loved the quadrate, or square. She would argue thus: —Cards are warfare: the ends are gain, with glory. But cards are war, in disguise of a sport: when single adversaries encounter, the ends proposed are too palpable. By themselves, it is too close a fight; with spectators, it is not much bettered. No looker-on can be interested, except for a bet, and then it is a mere affair of money; he cares not for your luck *sympathetically*, or for your play.—Three are still worse; a mere naked war of every man against every man, as in cribbage, without league or alliance; or a rotation of petty and contradictory interests, a succession of heartless leagues, and not much more hearty infractions of them, as in tradrille.—But in square games (*she meant whist*), all that is possible to be attained in card-playing is accomplished. There are the incentives of profit with honour, common to every species—though the *latter* can be but very imperfectly enjoyed in those other games, where the spectator is only feebly a participator. But the parties in whist are spectators and principals too. They are a theatre to themselves, and a looker-on is not wanted. He is rather worse than nothing, and an impertinence. Whist abhors neutrality, or interests beyond its sphere. You glory in some surprising stroke of skill or fortune, not because a cold—or even an interested—bystander witnesses it, but because your *partner* sympathises in the contingency. You win for two. You triumph for two. Two are exalted. Two again are mortified; which divides their disgrace, as the conjunction doubles (by taking off the invidiousness) your glories. Two losing to two are better reconciled, than one to one in that close butchery. The hostile feeling is weakened by multiplying the channels. War becomes a civil game. By such reasonings as these the old lady was accustomed to defend her favourite pastime.

No inducement could ever prevail upon her to play at any game, where chance entered into the composition, *for nothing*. Chance, she would argue—and here again, admire the subtlety of her conclusion;—chance is nothing, but where something else depends upon it. It is obvious that cannot be *glory*. What rational cause of exultation could it give to a man to turn up size ace a hundred times together by himself? or before spectators, where no stake was depending?—Make a lottery of a hundred thousand tickets with but one fortunate number—and what possible principle of our nature, except stupid wonderment, could it gratify to gain that number as many times successively without a prize? Therefore she disliked the mixture of chance in backgammon, where it was not played for money. She called it foolish, and those people idiots, who were taken with a lucky hit under such circumstances. Games of pure skill were as little to her fancy. Played for a stake, they were a mere system of over-reaching. Played for glory, they were a mere setting of one man's wit,—his memory, or combination-faculty rather—against another's; like a mock-engagement at a review, bloodless and profitless. She could not conceive a *game* wanting the spritely infusion of chance, the handsome excuses of good fortune. Two people playing at chess in a corner of a room, whilst whist was stirring in the centre, would inspire her with insufferable horror and ennui. Those well-cut similitudes of Castles and Knights, the *imagery* of the board, she would argue (and I think in this case justly), were entirely misplaced and senseless. Those hard-head contests can in no instance ally with the fancy. They reject form and colour. A pencil and dry slate (she used to say) were the proper arena for such combatants.

To those puny objectors against cards, as nurturing the bad passions, she would retort, that man is a gaming animal. He must be always trying to get the better in something or other:—that this passion can scarcely be more safely expended than upon a game at cards: that cards are a temporary illusion; in truth, a mere drama; for we do but *play* at being mightily concerned, where a few idle shillings are at stake, yet, during the illusion, we *are* as mightily concerned as those whose stake is crowns and kingdoms. They are a sort of dream-fighting; much ado; great battling, and little bloodshed; mighty means for disproportioned ends: quite as diverting, and a great deal more innoxious, than many of those more serious *games* of life, which men play without esteeming them to be such.

With great deference to the old lady's judgment in these matters, I think I have experienced some moments in my life when playing at cards *for nothing* has even been very agreeable. When I am in sickness, or not in the best spirits, I sometimes call for the cards, and play a game at piquet *for love* with my cousin Bridget—Bridget Elia.

I grant there is something sneaking in it; but with a toothache, or a sprained ankle,—when you are subdued and humble,—you are glad to put up with an inferior spring of action.

There is such a thing in nature, I am convinced, as *sick whist.*

I grant it is not the highest style of man—I deprecate the manes of Sarah Battle—she lives not, alas! to whom I should apologise.

At such times, those *terms* which my old friend objected to, come in as something admissible—I love to get a tierce or a quatorze, though they mean nothing. I am subdued to an inferior interest. Those shadows of winning amuse me.

That last game I had with my sweet cousin (I capotted her)—(dare I tell thee, how foolish I am?)—I wished it might have lasted for ever, though we gained nothing, and lost nothing, though it was a mere shade of play: I would be content to go on in that idle folly for ever. The pipkin should be ever boiling, that was to prepare the gentle lenitive to my foot, which Bridget was doomed to apply after the game was over: and, as I do not much relish appliances, there it should ever bubble. Bridget and I should be ever playing.

ALL FOOLS' DAY

THE compliments of the season to my worthy masters, and a merry first of April to us all!

Many happy returns of this day to you—and you—and *you*, Sir—nay, never frown, man, nor put a long face upon the matter. Do not we know one another? what need of ceremony among friends? we have all a touch of *that same*—you understand me—a speck of the motley. Beshrew the man who on such a day as this, the *general festival*, should affect to stand aloof. I am none of those sneakers. I am free of the corporation, and care not who knows it. He that meets me in the forest to-day, shall meet me with no wise-acre, I can tell him. *Stultus sum.* Translate me that, and take the meaning of it to yourself for your pains. What! man, we have four quarters of the globe on our side, at the least computation.

Fill us a cup of that sparkling gooseberry—we will drink no wise, melancholy, politic port on this day—and let us troll the catch of Amiens—*duc ad me—duc ad me*—how goes it?

> Here shall he see
> Gross fools as he.

Now would I give a trifle to know, historically and authentically, who was the greatest fool that ever lived. I would certainly give him in a bumper. Marry, of the present breed, I think I could without much difficulty name you the party.

Remove your cap a little further, if you please: it hides my bauble. And now each man bestride his hobby, and dust away his bells to what tune he pleases. I will give you, for my part,

> ———The crazy old church clock,
> And the bewildered chimes.

Good master Empedocles, you are welcome. It is long since you went a salamander-gathering down Ætna. Worse than samphire-picking by some odds.

'Tis a mercy your worship did not singe your mustachios.

Ha! Cleombrotus! and what salads in faith did you light upon at the bottom of the Mediterranean? You were founder, I take it, of the disinterested sect of the Calenturists.

Gebir, my old freemason, and prince of plasterers at Babel, bring in your trowel, most Ancient Grand! You have claim to a seat here at my right hand, as patron of the stammerers. You left your work, if I remember Herodotus correctly, at eight hundred million toises, or thereabout, above the level of the sea. Bless us, what a long bell you must have pulled, to call your top workmen to their nuncheon on the low grounds of Shinar. Or did you send up your garlic and onions by a rocket? I am a rogue if I am not ashamed to show you our Monument on Fish-street Hill, after your altitudes. Yet we think it somewhat.

What, the magnanimous Alexander in tears?—cry, baby, put its finger in its eye, it shall have another globe, round as an orange, pretty moppet!

Mister Adams—— 'odso, I honour your coat—pray do us the favour to read to us that sermon, which you lent to Mistress Slipslop—the twenty and second in your portmanteau there—on Female Incontinence—the same—it will come in most irrelevantly and impertinently seasonable to the time of the day.

Good Master Raymund Lully, you look wise. Pray correct that error.——

Duns, spare your definitions. I must fine you a bumper, or a paradox. We will have nothing said or done syllogistically this day. Remove those logical forms, waiter, that no gentleman break the tender shins of his apprehension stumbling across them.

Master Stephen, you are late.—Ha! Cokes, is it you?—Aguecheek, my dear knight, let me pay my devoir to you.—Master Shallow, your worship's poor servant to command.—Master Silence, I will use few words with you.—Slender, it shall go hard if I edge not you in somewhere.—You six will engross all the poor wit of the company to-day.—I know it, I know it.

Ha! honest R——, my fine old Librarian of Ludgate, time out of mind, art thou here again? Bless thy doublet, it is not over-new, threadbare as thy stories:—what dost thou flitting about the world at this rate?—Thy customers are extinct, defunct, bedrid, have ceased to read long ago.—Thou goest still among them, seeing if, peradventure, thou canst hawk a volume or two.—Good Granville S——, thy last patron, is flown.

> King Pandion, he is dead,
> All thy friends are lapt in lead.—

Nevertheless, noble R——, come in, and take your seat here, between Armado and Quisada; for in true courtesy, in gravity, in fantastic smiling to thyself, in courteous smiling upon others, in the goodly ornature of well-apparelled speech, and the commendation of wise sentences, thou art nothing inferior to those accomplished Dons of Spain. The spirit of chivalry forsake me for ever, when I forget thy singing the song of Macheath, which declares that he might be *happy with either*, situated between those two ancient spinsters—when I forget the inimitable formal love which thou didst make, turning now to the one, and now to the other, with that Malvolian smile—as if Cervantes, not Gay, had written it for his hero; and as if thousands of periods must revolve, before the mirror of courtesy could have given his invidious preference between a pair of so goodly-propertied and meritorious-equal damsels. * * * * *

To descend from these altitudes, and not to protract our Fools' Banquet beyond its appropriate day, —for I fear the second of April is not many hours distant—in sober verity I will confess a truth to thee, reader. I love a *Fool*—as naturally as if I were of kith and kin to him. When a child, with child-like apprehensions, that dived not below the surface of the matter, I read those *Parables*—not guessing at the involved wisdom—I had more yearnings towards that simple architect, that built his house upon the sand, than I entertained for his more cautious neighbour: I grudged at the hard censure pronounced upon the quiet soul that kept his talent; and—prizing their simplicity beyond the more provident, and, to my apprehension, somewhat *unfeminine* wariness of their competitors—I felt a kindliness, that almost amounted to a *tendre*, for those five thoughtless virgins.—I have never made an acquaintance since, that lasted: or a friendship, that answered; with any that had not some tincture of the absurd in their characters. I venerate an honest obliquity of understanding. The more laughable blunders a man shall commit in your company, the more tests he giveth you, that he will not betray or overreach you. I love the safety which a palpable hallucination warrants; the security, which a word out of season ratifies. And take my word for this, reader, and say a fool told it you, if you please, that he who hath not a dram of folly in his mixture, hath pounds of much worse matter in his composition. It is observed, that 'the foolisher the fowl or fish,—woodcocks,—dotterels—cods'-heads, etc., the finer the flesh thereof,' and what are commonly the world's received fools but such whereof the world is not worthy? and what have been some of the kindliest patterns of our species, but so many darlings of absurdity, minions of the goddess, and her white boys?—Reader, if you wrest my words beyond their fair construction, it is you, and not I, that are the *April Fool.*

GRACE BEFORE MEAT

The custom of saying grace at meals had, probably, its origin in the early times of the world, and the hunter-state of man, when dinners were precarious things, and a full meal was something more than a common blessing! when a belly-full was a windfall, and looked like a special providence. In the shouts and triumphal songs with which, after a season of sharp abstinence, a lucky booty of deer's or goat's flesh would naturally be ushered home, existed, perhaps, the germ of the modern grace. It is not otherwise easy to be understood, why the blessing of food —the act of eating—should have had a particular expression of thanksgiving annexed to it, distinct from that implied and silent gratitude with which we are expected to enter upon the enjoyment of the many other various gifts and good things of existence.

I own that I am disposed to say grace upon twenty other occasions in the course of the day besides my dinner. I want a form for setting out upon a pleasant walk, for a moonlight ramble, for a friendly meeting, or a solved problem. Why have we none for books, those spiritual repasts—a grace before Milton—a grace before Shakespeare—a devotional exercise proper to be said before reading the *Fairy Queen*?—but the received ritual having prescribed these forms to the solitary ceremony of manducation, I shall confine my observations to the experience which I have had of the grace, properly so called; commending my new scheme for extension to a niche in the grand philosophical, poetical, and perchance in part heretical, liturgy, now compiling by my friend Homo Humanus, for the use of a certain snug congregation of Utopian Rabelæsian Christians, no matter where assembled.

The form, then, of the benediction before eating has its beauty at a poor man's table, or at the simple and unprovocative repast of children. It is here that the grace becomes exceedingly graceful. The indigent man, who hardly knows whether he shall have a meal the next day or not, sits down to his fare with a present sense of the blessing, which can be but feebly acted by the rich, into whose minds the conception of wanting a dinner could never, but by some extreme theory, have entered. The proper end of food—the animal sustenance—is barely contemplated by them. The poor man's bread is his daily bread, literally his bread for the day. Their courses are perennial.

Again, the plainest diet seems the fittest to be preceded by the grace. That which is least stimulative to appetite, leaves the mind most free for foreign considerations. A man may feel thankful, heartily thankful, over a dish of plain mutton with turnips, and have leisure to reflect upon the ordinance and institution of eating; when he shall confess a perturbation of mind, inconsistent with the purposes of the grace, at the presence of venison or turtle. When I have sate (a *rarus hospes*) at rich men's tables, with the savoury soup and messes steaming up the nostrils, and moistening the lips of the guests with desire and a distracted choice, I have felt the introduction of that ceremony to be unseasonable. With the ravenous orgasm upon you, it seems impertinent to interpose a religious sentiment. It is a confusion of purpose to mutter out praises from a mouth that waters. The heats of epicurism put out the gentle flame of devotion. The incense which rises round is pagan, and the belly-god intercepts it for its own. The very excess of the provision beyond the needs, takes away all sense of proportion between the end and means. The giver is veiled by his gifts. You are startled at the injustice of returning thanks—for what?—for having too much while so many starve. It is to praise the Gods amiss.

I have observed this awkwardness felt, scarce consciously perhaps, by the good man who says the grace. I have seen it in clergymen and others—a sort of shame—a sense of the co-presence of circumstances which unhallow the blessing. After a devotional tone put on for a few seconds, how rapidly the speaker will fall into his common voice! helping himself or his neighbour, as if to get rid of some uneasy sensation of hypocrisy. Not that the good man was a hypocrite, or was not most conscientious in the discharge of the duty; but he felt in his inmost mind the incompatibility of the scene and the viands before him with the exercise of a calm and rational gratitude.

I hear somebody exclaim,—Would you have Christians sit down at table like hogs to their troughs, without remembering the Giver?—no—I would have them sit down as Christians, remembering the Giver, and less like hogs. Or, if their appetites must run riot, and they must pamper themselves with delicacies for which east and west are ransacked, I would have them postpone their benediction to a fitter season, when appetite is laid; when the still small voice can be heard, and the reason of the grace returns—with temperate diet and restricted dishes. Gluttony and surfeiting are no proper occasions for thanksgiving. When Jeshurun waxed fat, we read that he kicked. Virgil knew the harpy-nature better, when he put into the mouth of Celæno anything but a blessing. We may be gratefully sensible of the deliciousness of some kinds of food beyond others, though that is a meaner and inferior gratitude: but the proper object of the grace is sustenance, not relishes; daily bread, not delicacies; the means of life, and not the means of pampering the carcass. With what frame or composure, I wonder, can a city chaplain pronounce his benediction at some great Hall-feast, when he knows that his last concluding pious word—and that in all probability, the sacred name which he preaches—is but the signal for so many impatient harpies to commence their foul orgies, with as little sense of true thankfulness (which is temperance) as those Virgilian fowl! It is well if the good man himself does not feel his devotions a little clouded, those foggy sensuous steams mingling with and polluting the pure altar sacrifice.

The severest satire upon full tables and surfeits is the banquet which Satan, in the *Paradise Regained*, provides for a temptation in the wilderness:

> A table richly spread in regal mode
> With dishes piled, and meats of noblest sort

And savour; beasts of chase, or fowl of game,
In pastry built, or from the spit, or boiled,
Gris-amber-steamed; all fish from sea or shore,
Freshet or purling brook, for which was drained
Pontus, and Lucrine bay, and Afric coast.

The Tempter, I warrant you, thought these cates would go down without the recommendatory preface of a benediction. They are like to be short graces where the devil plays the host. I am afraid the poet wants his usual decorum in this place. Was he thinking of the old Roman luxury, or of a gaudy day at Cambridge? This was a temptation fitter for a Heliogabalus. The whole banquet is too civic and culinary, and the accompaniments altogether a profanation of that deep, abstracted, holy scene. The mighty artillery of sauces, which the cook-fiend conjures up, is out of proportion to the simple wants and plain hunger of the guest. He that disturbed him in his dreams, from his dreams might have been taught better. To the temperate fantasies of the famished Son of God, what sort of feasts presented themselves? —He dreamed indeed,

——As appetite is wont to dream,
Of meats and drinks, nature's refreshment sweet.

But what meats?—

Him thought he by the brook of Cherith stood,
And saw the ravens with their horny beaks
Food to Elijah bringing even and morn;
Though ravenous, taught to abstain from what they brought.
He saw the prophet also how he fled
Into the desert, and how there he slept
Under a juniper; then how awaked
He found his supper on the coals prepared,
And by the angel was bid rise and eat,
And ate the second time after repose,
The strength whereof sufficed him forty days:
Sometimes, that with Elijah he partook,
Or as a guest with Daniel at his pulse.

Nothing in Milton is finelier fancied than these temperate dreams of the divine Hungerer. To which of these two visionary banquets, think you, would the introduction of what is called the grace have been the most fitting and pertinent?

Theoretically I am no enemy to graces; but practically I own that (before meat especially) they seem to involve something awkward and unseasonable. Our appetites, of one or another kind, are excellent spurs to our reason, which might otherwise but feebly set about the great ends of preserving and continuing the species. They are fit blessings to be contemplated at a distance with a becoming gratitude; but the moment of appetite (the judicious reader will apprehend me) is, perhaps, the least fit season for that exercise. The Quakers, who go about their business of every description with more calmness than we, have more title to the use of these benedictory prefaces. I have always admired their silent grace, and the more because I have observed their applications to the meat and drink following to be less passionate and sensual than ours. They are neither gluttons nor wine-bibbers as a people. They eat, as a horse bolts his chopped hay, with indifference, calmness, and cleanly circumstances. They neither grease not slop themselves. When I see a citizen in his bib and tucker, I cannot imagine it a surplice.

I am no Quaker at my food. I confess I am not indifferent to the kinds of it. Those unctuous morsels of deer's flesh were not made to be received with dispassionate services. I hate a man who swallows it, affecting not to know what he is eating. I suspect his taste in higher matters. I shrink instinctively from one who professes to like minced veal. There is a physiognomical character in the tastes for food. C—— holds that a man cannot have a pure mind who refuses apple-dumplings. I am not certain but he is right. With the decay of my first innocence, I confess a less and less relish daily for those innocuous cates.

The whole vegetable tribe have lost their gust with me. Only I stick to asparagus, which still seems to inspire gentle thoughts. I am impatient and querulous under culinary disappointments, as to come home at the dinner hour, for instance, expecting some savoury mess, and to find one quite tasteless and sapidless. Butter ill melted—that commonest of kitchen failures—puts me beside my tenor.—The author of the *Rambler* used to make inarticulate animal noises over a favourite food. Was this the music quite proper to be preceded by the grace? or would the pious man have done better to postpone his devotions to a season when the blessing might be contemplated with less perturbation? I quarrel with no man's tastes, nor would set my thin face against those excellent things, in their way, jollity and feasting. But as these exercises, however laudable, have little in them of grace or gracefulness, a man should be sure, before he ventures so to grace them, that while he is pretending his devotions otherwhere, he is not secretly kissing his hand to some great fish—his Dagon—with a special consecration of no art but the fat tureen before him. Graces are the sweet preluding strains to the banquets of angels and children; to the roots and severer repasts of the Chartreuse; to the slender, but not slenderly acknowledged, refection of the poor and humble man: but at the heaped-up boards of the pampered and the luxurious they become of dissonant mood, less timed and tuned to the occasion, methinks, than the noise of those better befitting organs would be which children hear tales of, at Hog's Norton. We sit too long at our meals, or are too curious in the study of them, or too disordered in our application to them, or engross too great a portion of those good things (which should be common) to our share, to be able with any grace to say grace. To be thankful for what we grasp exceeding our proportion, is to add hypocrisy to injustice. A lurking sense of this truth is what makes the performance of this duty so cold and spiritless a service at most tables. In houses where the grace is as indispensable as the napkin, who has not seen that never-settled question arise, as to *who shall say it?* while the good man of the house and the visitor clergyman, or some other guest belike of next authority, from years or gravity, shall be bandying about the office between them as a matter of compliment, each of them not unwilling to shift the awkward burthen of an equivocal duty from his own shoulders?

I once drank tea in company with two Methodist divines of different persuasions, whom it was my fortune to introduce to each other for the first time that evening. Before the first cup was handed round, one of these reverend gentlemen put it to the other, with all due solemnity, whether he chose to *say anything.* It seems it is the custom with some sectaries to put up a short prayer before this meal also. His reverend brother did not at first quite apprehend him, but upon an explanation, with little less importance he made answer that it was not a custom known in his church: in which courteous evasion the other acquiescing for good manners' sake, or in compliance with a weak brother, the supplementary or tea grace was waived altogether. With what spirit might not Lucian have painted two priests, of *his* religion, playing into each other's hands the compliment of performing or omitting a sacrifice,—the hungry God meantime, doubtful of his incense, with expectant nostrils hovering over the two flamens, and (as between two stools) going away in the end without his supper.

A short form upon these occasions is felt to want reverence; a long one, I am afraid, cannot escape the charge of impertinence. I do not quite approve of the epigrammatic conciseness with which that equivocal wag (but my pleasant school-fellow) C. V. L., when importuned for a grace, used to inquire, first slyly leering down the table, 'Is there no clergyman here?'—significantly adding, 'thank G—.' Nor do

I think our old form at school quite pertinent, where we were used to preface our bald bread-and-cheese-suppers with a preamble, connecting with that humble blessing a recognition of benefits the most awful and overwhelming to the imagination which religion has to offer. *Non tunc illis erat locus.* I remember we were put to it to reconcile the phrase 'good creatures,' upon which the blessing rested, with the fare set before us, wilfully understanding that expression in a low and animal sense,—till some one recalled a legend, which told how, in the golden days of Christ's, the young Hospitallers were wont to have smoking joints of roast meat upon their nightly boards, till some pious benefactor, commiserating the decencies, rather than the palates, of the children, commuted our flesh for garments, and gave us—*horresco referens*—trousers instead of mutton.

A DISSERTATION UPON ROAST PIG

MANKIND, says a Chinese manuscript, which my friend M. was obliging enough to read and explain to me, for the first seventy thousand ages ate their meat raw, clawing or biting it from the living animal, just as they do in Abyssinia to this day. This period is not obscurely hinted at by their great Confucius in the second chapter of his Mundane Mutations, where he designates a kind of golden age by the term Cho-fang, literally the Cooks' Holiday. The manuscript goes on to say, that the art of roasting, or rather broiling (which I take to be the elder brother) was accidentally discovered in the manner following. The swine-herd, Ho-ti, having gone out into the woods one morning, as his manner was, to collect mast for his hogs, left his cottage in the care of his eldest son Bo-bo, a great lubberly boy, who being fond of playing with fire, as younkers of his age commonly are, let some sparks escape into a bundle of straw, which kindling quickly, spread the conflagration over every part of their poor mansion, till it was reduced to ashes. Together with the cottage (a sorry antediluvian make-shift of a building, you may think it), what was of much more importance, a fine litter of new-farrowed pigs, no less than nine in number, perished. China pigs have been esteemed a luxury all over the East, from the remotest periods that we read of. Bo-bo was in the utmost consternation, as you may think, not so much for the sake of the tenement, which his father and he could easily build up again with a few dry branches, and the labour of an hour or two, at any time, as for the loss of the pigs. While he was thinking what he should say to his father, and wringing his hands over the smoking remnants of one of those untimely sufferers, an odour assailed his nostrils, unlike any scent which he had before experienced. What could it proceed from?—not from the burnt cottage—he had smelt that smell before—indeed, this was by no means the first accident of the kind which had occurred through the negligence of this unlucky young firebrand. Much less did it resemble that of any known herb, weed, or flower. A premonitory moistening at the same time overflowed his nether lip. He knew not what to think. He next stooped down to feel the pig, if there were any signs of life in it. He burnt his fingers, and to cool them he applied them in his booby fashion to his mouth. Some of the crumbs of the scorched skin had come away with his fingers, and for the first time in his life (in the world's life indeed, for before him no man had known it) he tasted—*crackling!* Again he felt and fumbled at the pig. It did not burn him so much now, still he licked his fingers from a sort of habit. The truth at length broke into his slow understanding, that it was the pig that smelt so, and the pig that tasted so delicious; and surrendering himself up to the new-born pleasure, he fell to tearing up whole handfuls of the scorched skin with the flesh next it, and was cramming it down his throat in his beastly fashion, when his sire entered amid the smoking rafters, armed with retributory cudgel, and finding how affairs stood, began to rain blows upon the young rogue's shoulders, as thick as hailstones, which Bo-bo heeded not any more than if they had been flies. The tickling pleasure, which he experienced in his lower regions, had rendered him quite callous to any inconveniences he might feel in those remote quarters. His father might lay on, but he could not beat him from his pig, till he had fairly made an end of it, when, becoming a little more sensible of his situation, something like the following dialogue ensued.

'You graceless whelp, what have you got there devouring? Is it not enough that you have burnt me down three houses with your dog's tricks, and be hanged to you! but you must be eating fire, and I know not what—what have you got there, I say?'

'O father, the pig, the pig! do come and taste how nice the burnt pig eats.'

The ears of Ho-ti tingled with horror. He cursed his son, and he cursed himself that ever he should beget a son that should eat burnt pig.

Bo-bo, whose scent was wonderfully sharpened since morning, soon raked out another pig, and fairly rending it asunder, thrust the lesser half by main force into the fists of Ho-ti, still shouting out, 'Eat, eat, eat the burnt pig, father, only taste—O Lord!'—with such-like barbarous ejaculations, cramming all the while as if he would choke.

Ho-ti trembled in every joint while he grasped the abominable thing, wavering whether he should not put his son to death for an unnatural young monster, when the crackling scorching his fingers, as it had done his son's, and applying the same remedy to them, he in his turn tasted some of its flavour, which, make what sour mouths he would for a pretence, proved not altogether displeasing to him. In conclusion (for the manuscript here is a little tedious), both father and son fairly set down to the mess, and never left off till they had despatched all that remained of the litter.

Bo-bo was strictly enjoined not to let the secret escape, for the neighbours would certainly have stoned them for a couple of abominable wretches, who could think of improving upon the good meat which God had sent them. Nevertheless, strange stories got about. It was observed that Ho-ti's cottage was burnt down now more frequently than ever. Nothing but fires from this time forward. Some would break out in broad day, others in the night-time. As often as the sow farrowed, so sure was the house of Ho-ti to be in a blaze; and Ho-ti himself, which was the more remarkable, instead of chastising his son, seemed to grow more indulgent to him than ever. At length they were watched, the terrible mystery discovered, and father and son summoned to take their trial at Pekin, then an inconsiderable assize town. Evidence was given, the obnoxious food itself produced in court, and verdict about to be pronounced, when the foreman of the jury begged that some of the burnt pig, of which the culprits stood accused, might be handed into the box. He handled it, and they all handled it; and burning their fingers, as Bo-bo and his father had done before them, and nature prompting to each of them the same remedy, against the face of all the facts, and the clearest charge which judge had ever given,—to the surprise of the whole court, townsfolk, strangers, reporters, and all present—without leaving the box, or any manner of consultation whatever, they brought in a simultaneous verdict of Not Guilty.

The judge, who was a shrewd fellow, winked at the manifest iniquity of the decision: and when the court was dismissed, went privily and bought up all the pigs that could be had for love or money. In a few days his lordship's town-house was observed to be on fire. The thing took wing, and now there was nothing to be seen but fires in every direction. Fuel and pigs grew enormously dear all over the district. The insurance-offices one and all shut up shop. People built slighter and slighter every day, until it was feared that the very science of architecture would in no long time be lost to the world. Thus this custom of firing houses continued, till in process of time, says my manuscript, a sage arose, like our Locke, who made a discovery that the flesh of swine, or indeed of any other animal, might be cooked (*burnt*, as they called it) without the necessity of consuming a whole house to dress it. Then first began the rude form of a gridiron. Roasting by the string or spit came in a century or two later, I forget in whose dynasty. By such slow degrees, concludes the manuscript, do the most useful, and seemingly the most obvious, arts make their way among mankind——

Without placing too implicit faith in the account above given, it must be agreed that if a worthy pretext for so dangerous an experiment as setting houses on fire (especially in these days) could be assigned in favour of any culinary object, that pretext and excuse might be found in ROAST PIG.

Of all the delicacies in the whole *mundus edibilis*, I will maintain it to be the most delicate—*princeps obsoniorum*.

I speak not of your grown porkers—things between pig and pork—these hobbledehoys—but a young and tender suckling—under a moon old—guiltless as yet of the sty—with no original speck of the *amor immunditiæ*, the hereditary failing of the first parent, yet manifest—his voice as yet not broken, but something between a childish treble and a grumble—the mild forerunner or *prœludium* of a grunt.

He must be roasted. I am not ignorant that our ancestors ate them seethed, or boiled—but what a sacrifice of the exterior tegument!

There is no flavour comparable, I will contend, to that of the crisp, tawny, well-watched, not over-roasted, *crackling*, as it is well called—the very teeth are invited to their share of the pleasure at this banquet, in overcoming the coy, brittle resistance—with the adhesive oleaginous—O call it not fat! but an indefinable sweetness growing up to it—the tender blossoming of fat—fat cropped in the bud—taken in the shoot—in the first innocence—the cream and quintessence of the child-pig's yet pure food—the lean, no lean, but a kind of animal manna—or, rather, fat and lean (if it must be so) so blended and running into each other, that both together make but one ambrosian result or common substance.

Behold him while he is 'doing'—it seemeth rather a refreshing warmth, than a scorching heat, that he is so passive to. How equably he twirleth round the string! Now he is just done. To see the extreme sensibility of that tender age! he hath wept out his pretty eyes—radiant jellies—shooting stars.—

See him in the dish, his second cradle, how meek he lieth!—wouldst thou have had this innocent grow up to the grossness and indocility which too often accompany maturer swinehood? Ten to one he would have proved a glutton, a sloven, an obstinate, disagreeable animal—wallowing in all manner of filthy conversation—from these sins he is happily snatched away—

> Ere sin could blight or sorrow fade,
> Death came with timely care—

his memory is odoriferous—no clown curseth, while his stomach half rejecteth, the rank bacon—no coal-heaver bolteth him in reeking sausages—he hath a fair sepulchre in the grateful stomach of the judicious epicure—and for such a tomb might be content to die.

He is the best of sapors. Pine-apple is great. She is indeed almost too transcendent—a delight, if not sinful, yet so like to sinning, that really a tender-conscienced person would do well to pause—too ravishing for mortal taste, she woundeth and excoriateth the lips that approach her—like lovers' kisses, she biteth—she is a pleasure bordering on pain from the fierceness and insanity of her relish—but she stoppeth at the palate—she meddleth not with the appetite—and the coarsest hunger might barter her consistently for a mutton-chop.

Pig—let me speak his praise—is no less provocative of the appetite than he is satisfactory to the criticalness of the censorious palate. The strong man may batten on him, and the weakling refuseth not his mild juices.

Unlike to mankind's mixed characters, a bundle of virtues and vices, inexplicably intertwisted, and not to be unravelled without hazard, he is—good throughout. No part of him is better or worse than another. He helpeth, as far as his little means extend, all around. He is the least envious of banquets. He is all neighbours' fare.

I am one of those who freely and ungrudgingly impart a share of the good things of this life which fall to their lot (few as mine are in this kind) to a friend. I protest I take as great an interest in my friend's pleasures, his relishes, and proper satisfactions, as in mine own. 'Presents,' I often say, 'endear Absents.' Hares, pheasants, partridges, snipes, barn-door chickens (those 'tame villatic fowl'), capons, plovers, brawn, barrels of oysters, I dispense as freely as I receive them. I love to taste them, as it were, upon the tongue of my friend. But a stop must be put somewhere. One would not, like Lear, 'give everything.' I make my stand upon pig. Methinks it is an ingratitude to the Giver of all good flavours to extra-domiciliate, or send out of the house slightingly (under pretext of friendship, or I know not what) a blessing so particularly adapted, predestined, I may say, to my individual palate.—It argues an insensibility.

I remember a touch of conscience in this kind at school. My good old aunt, who never parted from me at the end of a holiday without stuffing a sweet-meat, or some nice thing, into my pocket, had dismissed me one evening with a smoking plum-cake, fresh from the oven. In my way to school (it was over London Bridge) a grey-headed old beggar saluted me (I have no doubt at this time of day, that he was a counterfeit). I had no pence to console him with, and in the vanity of self-denial, and the very coxcombry of charity, schoolboy like, I made him a present of—the whole cake! I walked on a little, buoyed up, as one is on such occasions, with a sweet soothing of self-satisfaction; but, before I had got to the end of the bridge, my better feelings returned, and I burst into tears, thinking how ungrateful I had been to my good aunt, to go and give her good gift away to a stranger that I had never seen before, and who might be a bad man for aught I knew; and then I thought of the pleasure my aunt would be taking in thinking that I—I myself, and not another—would eat her nice cake—and what should I say to her the next time I saw her—how naughty I was to part with her pretty present!—and the odour of that spicy cake came back upon my recollection, and the pleasure and the curiosity I had taken in seeing her make it, and her joy when she sent it to the oven, and how disappointed she would feel that I had never had a bit of it in my mouth at last—and I blamed my impertinent spirit of alms-giving, and out-of-place hypocrisy of goodness; and above all I wished never to see the face again of that insidious, good-for-nothing, old grey impostor.

Our ancestors were nice in their method of sacrificing these tender victims. We read of pigs whipt to death with something of a shock, as we hear of any other obsolete custom. The age of discipline is gone by, or it would be curious to inquire (in a philosophical light merely) what effect this process might have towards intenerating and dulcifying a substance, naturally so mild and dulcet as the flesh of young pigs. It looks like refining a violet. Yet we should be cautious, while we condemn the inhumanity, how we censure the wisdom of the practice. It might impart a gusto.—

I remember an hypothesis, argued upon by the young students, when I was at St. Omer's, and maintained with much learning and pleasantry on both sides, 'Whether, supposing that the flavour of a pig who obtained his death by whipping (*per flagellationem extremam*) superadded a pleasure upon the palate of a man more intense than any possible suffering we can conceive in the animal, is man justified in using that method of putting the animal to death?' I forget the decision.

His sauce should be considered. Decidedly, a few bread crumbs, done up with his liver and brains, and a dash of mild sage. But banish, dear Mrs. Cook, I beseech you, the whole onion tribe. Barbecue your whole hogs to your palate, steep them in shalots, stuff them out with plantations of the rank and guilty garlic; you cannot poison them, or make them stronger than they are—but consider, he is a weakling—a flower.

A BACHELOR'S COMPLAINT OF THE BEHAVIOUR OF MARRIED PEOPLE

As a single man, I have spent a good deal of my time in noting down the infirmities of Married People, to console myself for those superior pleasures, which they tell me I have lost by remaining as I am.

I cannot say that the quarrels of men and their wives ever made any great impression upon me, or had much tendency to strengthen me in those anti-social resolutions which I took up long ago upon more substantial considerations. What oftenest offends me at the houses of married persons where I visit, is an error of quite a different description;—it is that they are too loving.

Not too loving neither: that does not explain my meaning. Besides, why should that offend me? The very act of separating themselves from the rest of the world, to have the fuller enjoyment of each other's society, implies that they prefer one another to all the world.

But what I complain of is, that they carry this preference so undisguisedly, they perk it up in the faces of us single people so shamelessly, you cannot be in their company a moment without being made to feel, by some indirect hint or open avowal, that *you* are not the object of this preference. Now there are some things which give no offence, while implied or taken for granted merely; but expressed, there is much offence in them. If a man were to accost the first homely-featured or plain-dressed young woman of his acquaintance, and tell her bluntly, that she was not handsome or rich enough for him, and he could not marry her, he would deserve to be kicked for his ill-manners; yet no less is implied in the fact, that having access and opportunity of putting the question to her, he has never yet thought fit to do it. The young woman understands this as clearly as if it were put into words; but no reasonable young woman would think of making this the ground of a quarrel. Just as little right have a married couple to tell me by speeches, and looks that are scarce less plain than speeches, that I am not the happy man,—the lady's choice. It is enough that I know I am not: I do not want this perpetual reminding.

The display of superior knowledge or riches may be made sufficiently mortifying, but these admit of a palliative. The knowledge which is brought out to insult me, may accidentally improve me; and in the rich man's houses and pictures,—his parks and gardens, I have a temporary usufruct at least. But the display of married happiness has none of these palliatives: it is throughout pure, unrecompensed, unqualified insult.

Marriage by its best title is a monopoly, and not of the least invidious sort. It is the cunning of most possessors of any exclusive privilege to keep their advantage as much out of sight as possible, that their less favoured neighbours, seeing little of the benefit, may the less be disposed to question the right. But these married monopolists thrust the most obnoxious part of their patent into our faces.

Nothing is to me more distasteful than that entire complacency and satisfaction which beam in the countenances of a new-married couple,—in that of the lady particularly: it tells you, that her lot is disposed of in this world: that *you* can have no hopes of her. It is true, I have none: nor wishes either, perhaps: but this is one of those truths which ought, as I said before, to be taken for granted, not expressed.

The excessive airs which those people give themselves, founded on the ignorance of us unmarried people, would be more offensive if they were less irrational. We will allow them to understand the mysteries belonging to their own craft better than we, who have not had the happiness to be made free of the company: but their arrogance is not content within these limits. If a single person presume to offer his opinion in their presence, though upon the most indifferent subject, he is immediately silenced as an incompetent person. Nay, a young married lady of my acquaintance, who, the best of the jest was, had not changed her condition above a fortnight before, in a question on which I had the misfortune to differ from her, respecting the properest mode of breeding oysters for the London market, had the assurance to ask with a sneer, how such an old Bachelor as I could pretend to know anything about such matters!

But what I have spoken of hitherto is nothing to the airs which these creatures give themselves when they come, as they generally do, to have children. When I consider how little of a rarity children are,—that every street and blind alley swarms with them,—that the poorest people commonly have them in most abundance,—that there are few marriages that are not blest with at least one of these bargains,—how often they turn out ill, and defeat the fond hopes of their parents, taking to vicious courses, which end in poverty, disgrace, the gallows, etc.—I cannot for my life tell what cause for pride there can possibly be in having them. If they were young phœnixes, indeed, that were born but one in a year, there might be a pretext. But when they are so common——

I do not advert to the insolent merit which they assume with their husbands on these occasions. Let *them* look to that. But why *we*, who are not their natural-born subjects, should be expected to bring our spices, myrrh, and incense,—our tribute and homage of admiration,—I do not see.

'Like as the arrows in the hand of the giant, even so are the young children'; so says the excellent office in our Prayer-book appointed for the churching of women. 'Happy is the man that hath his quiver full of them.' So say I; but then don't let him discharge his quiver upon us that are weaponless;—let them be arrows, but not to gall and stick us. I have generally observed that these arrows are double-headed: they have two forks, to be sure to hit with one or the other. As for instance, where you come into a house which is full of children, if you happen to take no notice of them (you are thinking of something else, perhaps, and turn a deaf ear to their innocent caresses), you are set down as untractable, morose, a hater of children. On the other hand, if you find them more than usually engaging,—if you are taken with their pretty manners, and set about in earnest to romp and play with them,—some pretext or other is sure to be found for sending them out of the room; they are too noisy or boisterous, or Mr. —— does not like children. With one or other of these forks the arrow is sure to hit you.

I could forgive their jealousy, and dispense with toying with their brats, if it gives them any pain; but I think it unreasonable to be called upon to *love* them, where I see no occasion,—to love a whole family, perhaps eight, nine, or ten indiscriminately,—to love all the pretty dears, because children are so engaging!

I know there is a proverb, 'Love me, love my dog': that is not always so very practicable, particularly if the dog be set upon you to tease you or snap at you in sport. But a dog, or a lesser thing—any inanimate substance, as a keepsake, a watch or a ring, a tree, or the place where we last parted when my friend went away upon a long absence, I can make shift to love, because I love him, and anything that reminds me of him; provided it be in its nature indifferent, and apt to receive whatever hue fancy can give it. But children have a real character, and an essential being of themselves: they are amiable or unamiable *per se*; I must love or hate them as I see cause for either in their qualities. A child's nature is too serious a thing to admit of its being regarded as a mere appendage to another being, and to be loved or hated accordingly; they stand with me upon their own stock, as much as men and women do. Oh! but you will say, sure it is an attractive age,—there is something in the tender years of infancy that of itself charms us. That is the very reason why I am more nice about them. I know that a sweet child is the sweetest thing in nature, not even excepting the delicate creatures which bear them; but the prettier the kind of a thing is, the more desirable it is that it should be pretty of its kind. One daisy differs not much from another in glory; but a violet should look and smell the daintiest.—I was always rather squeamish in my women and children.

But this is not the worst: one must be admitted into their familiarity at least, before they can complain of inattention. It implies visits, and some kind of intercourse. But if the husband be a man with whom you have lived on a friendly footing before marriage—if you did not come in on the wife's side—if you did not sneak into the house in her train, but were an old friend in fast habits of intimacy before their courtship was so much as thought on,—look about you—your tenure is precarious—before a twelvemonth shall roll over your head, you shall find your old friend gradually grow cool and altered towards you, and at last seek opportunities of breaking with you. I have scarce a married friend of my acquaintance, upon whose firm faith I can rely, whose friendship did not commence *after the period of his marriage.* With some limitations they can endure that? but that the good man should have dared to enter into a solemn league of friendship in which they were not consulted, though it happened before they knew him,—before they that are now man and wife ever met,—this is intolerable to them. Every long friendship, every old authentic intimacy, must be brought into their office to be new stamped with their currency, as a sovereign prince calls in the good old money that was coined in some reign before he was born or thought of, to be new marked and minted with the stamp of his authority, before he will let it pass current in the world. You may guess what luck generally befalls such a rusty piece of metal as I am in these *new mintings.*

Innumerable are the ways which they take to insult and worm you out of their husband's confidence. Laughing at all you say with a kind of wonder, as if you were a queer kind of fellow that said good things, *but an oddity*, is one of the ways;—they have a particular kind of stare for the purpose;—till at last the husband, who used to defer to your judgment, and would pass over some excrescences of understanding and manner for the sake of a general vein of observation (not quite vulgar) which he perceived in you, begins to suspect whether you are not altogether a humorist,—a fellow well enough to have consorted with in his bachelor days, but not quite so proper to be introduced to ladies. This may be called the staring way; and is that which has oftenest been put in practice against me.

Then there is the exaggerating way, or the way of irony; that is, where they find you an object of especial regard with their husband, who is not so easily to be shaken from the lasting attachment founded on esteem which he has conceived towards you, by never qualified exaggerations to cry up all that you say or do, till the good man, who understands well enough that it is all done in compliment to him, grows weary of the debt of gratitude which is due to so much candour, and by relaxing a little on his part, and taking down a peg or two in his enthusiasm, sinks at length to the kindly level of moderate esteem—that 'decent affection and complacent kindness' towards you, where she herself can join in sympathy with him without much stretch and violence to her sincerity.

Another way (for the ways they have to accomplish so desirable a purpose are infinite) is, with a kind of innocent simplicity, continually to mistake what it was which first made their husband fond of you. If an esteem for something excellent in your moral character was that which riveted the chain which she is to break, upon any imaginary discovery of a want of poignancy in your conversation, she will cry, 'I thought, my dear, you described your friend Mr. ——, as a great wit?' If, on the other hand, it was for some supposed charm in your conversation that he first grew to like you, and was content for this to overlook some trifling irregularities in your moral deportment, upon the first notice of any of these she as readily exclaims, 'This, my dear, is your good Mr. ——!' One good lady whom I took the liberty of expostulating with for not showing me quite so much respect as I thought due to her husband's old friend, had the candour to confess to me that she had often heard Mr. —— speak of me before marriage, and that she had conceived a great desire to be acquainted with me, but that the sight of me had very much disappointed her expectations; for, from her husband's representations of me, she had formed a notion that she was to see a fine, tall, officer-like looking man (I use her very words), the very reverse of which proved to be the truth. This was candid; and I had the civility not to ask her in return how she came to pitch upon a standard of personal accomplishments for her husband's friends which differed so much from his own; for my friend's dimensions as near as possible approximate to mine; he standing five feet five in his shoes, in which I have the advantage of him by about half an inch; and he no more than myself exhibiting any indications of a martial character in his air or countenance.

These are some of the mortifications which I have encountered in the absurd attempt to visit at their houses. To enumerate them all would be a vain endeavour; I shall therefore just glance at the very common impropriety of which married ladies are guilty,—of treating us as if we were their husbands, and *vice versâ*. I mean, when they use us with familiarity, and their husbands with ceremony. *Testacea*, for instance, kept me the other night two or three hours beyond my usual time of supping, while she was fretting because Mr. —— did not come home, till the oysters were all spoiled, rather than she would be guilty of the impoliteness of touching one in his absence. This was reversing the point of good manners: for ceremony is an invention to take off the uneasy feeling which we derive from knowing ourselves to be less the object of love and esteem with a fellow-creature than some other person is. It endeavours to make up, by superior attentions in little points, for that invidious preference which it is forced to deny in the greater. Had *Testacea* kept the oysters back for me, and withstood her husband's importunities to go to supper, she would have acted according to the strict rules of propriety. I know no ceremony that ladies are bound to observe to their husbands, beyond the point of a modest behaviour and decorum: therefore I must protest against the vicarious gluttony of

Cerasia, who at her own table sent away a dish of Morellas, which I was applying to with great good-will, to her husband at the other end of the table, and recommended a plate of less extraordinary gooseberries to my unwedded palate in their stead. Neither can I excuse the wanton affront of——

But I am weary of stringing up all my married acquaintance by Roman denominations. Let them amend and change their manners, or I promise to record the full-length English of their names, to the terror of all such desperate offenders in future.

THE CONVALESCENT

A PRETTY severe fit of indisposition which, under the name of a nervous fever, has made a prisoner of me for some weeks past, and is but slowly leaving me, has reduced me to an incapacity of reflecting upon any topic foreign to itself. Expect no healthy conclusions from me this month, reader; I can offer you only sick men's dreams.

And truly the whole state of sickness is such; for what else is it but a magnificent dream for a man to lie a-bed, and draw daylight curtains about him; and, shutting out the sun, to induce a total oblivion of all the works which are going on under it? To become insensible to all the operations of life, except the beatings of one feeble pulse?

If there be a regal solitude, it is a sick-bed. How the patient lords it there; what caprices he acts without control! how king-like he sways his pillow—tumbling, and tossing, and shifting, and lowering, and thumping, and flatting, and moulding it, to the ever-varying requisitions of his throbbing temples.

He changes *sides* oftener than a politician. Now he lies full length, then half length, obliquely, transversely, head and feet quite across the bed; and none accuses him of tergiversation. Within the four curtains he is absolute. They are his Mare Clausum.

How sickness enlarges the dimensions of a man's self to himself! he is his own exclusive object. Supreme selfishness is inculcated upon him as his only duty. 'Tis the Two Tables of the Law to him. He has nothing to think of but how to get well. What passes out of doors, or within them, so he hear not the jarring of them, affects him not.

A little while ago he was greatly concerned in the event of a lawsuit, which was to be the making or the marring of his dearest friend. He was to be seen trudging about upon this man's errand to fifty quarters of the town at once, jogging this witness, refreshing that solicitor. The cause was to come on yesterday. He is absolutely as indifferent to the decision as if it were a question to be tried at Pekin. Peradventure from some whispering, going on about the house, not intended for his hearing, he picks up enough to make him understand that things went cross-grained in the court yesterday, and his friend is ruined. But the word 'friend,' and the word 'ruin,' disturb him no more than so much jargon. He is not to think of anything but how to get better.

What a world of foreign cares are merged in that absorbing consideration!

He has put on his strong armour of sickness, he is wrapped in the callous hide of suffering; he keeps his sympathy, like some curious vintage, under trusty lock and key, for his own use only.

He lies pitying himself, honing and moaning to himself; he yearneth over himself; his bowels are even melted within him, to think what he suffers; he is not ashamed to weep over himself.

He is for ever plotting how to do some good to himself; studying little stratagems and artificial alleviations.

He makes the most of himself; dividing himself, by an allowable fiction, into as many distinct individuals as he hath sore and sorrowing members. Sometimes he meditates—as of a thing apart from him—upon his poor aching head, and that dull pain which, dozing or waking, lay in it all the past night like a log, or palpable substance of pain, not to be removed without opening the very skull, as it seemed, to take it thence. Or he pities his long, clammy, attenuated fingers. He compassionates himself all over; and his bed is a very discipline of humanity, and tender heart.

He is his own sympathiser; and instinctively feels that none can so well perform that office for him. He cares for few spectators to his tragedy. Only that punctual face of the old nurse pleases him, that announces his broths and his cordials. He likes it because it is so unmoved, and because he can pour forth his feverish ejaculations before it as unreservedly as to his bed-post.

To the world's business he is dead. He understands not what the callings and occupations of mortals are; only he has a glimmering conceit of some such thing, when the doctor makes his daily call; and even in the lines on that busy face he reads no multiplicity of patients, but solely conceives of himself as *the sick man*. To what other uneasy couch the good man is hastening, when he slips out of his chamber, folding up his thin douceur so carefully, for fear of rustling —is no speculation which he can at present entertain. He thinks only of the regular return of the same phenomenon at the same hour to-morrow.

Household rumours touch him not. Some faint murmur, indicative of life going on within the house, soothes him, while he knows not distinctly what it is. He is not to know anything, not to think of anything. Servants gliding up or down the distant staircase, treading as upon velvet, gently keep his ear awake, so long as he troubles not himself further than with some feeble guess at their errands. Exacter knowledge would be a burthen to him: he can just endure the pressure of conjecture. He opens his eye faintly at the dull stroke of the muffled knocker, and closes it again without asking 'Who was it?' He is flattered by a general notion that inquiries are making after him, but he cares not to know the name of the inquirer. In the general stillness, and awful hush of the house, he lies in state, and feels his sovereignty.

To be sick is to enjoy monarchal prerogatives. Compare the silent tread and quiet ministry, almost by the eye only, with which he is served—with the careless demeanour, the unceremonious goings in and out (slapping of doors, or leaving them open) of the very same attendants, when he is getting a little better—and you will confess, that from the bed of sickness (throne let me rather call it) to the elbow-chair of convalescence, is a fall from dignity, amounting to a deposition.

How convalescence shrinks a man back to his pristine stature! Where is now the space, which he occupied so lately, in his own, in the family's eye?

The scene of his regalities, his sick-room, which was his presence-chamber, where he lay and acted his despotic fancies—how is it reduced to a common bedroom! The trimness of the very bed has something petty and unmeaning about it. It is *made* every day. How unlike to that wavy, many-furrowed, oceanic surface, which it presented so short a time since, when to *make* it was a service not to be thought of at oftener than three or four day revolutions, when the patient was with pain and grief to be lifted for a little while out of it, to submit to the encroachments of unwelcome neatness, and decencies which his shaken frame deprecated; then to be lifted into it again, for another three or four days' respite, to flounder it out of shape again, while every fresh furrow was an historical record of some shifting posture, some uneasy turning, some seeking for a little ease; and the shrunken skin scarce told a truer story than the crumpled coverlid.

Hushed are those mysterious sighs—those groans—so much more awful, while we knew not from what caverns of vast hidden suffering they proceeded. The

Lernean pangs are quenched. The riddle of sickness is solved; and Philoctetes is become an ordinary personage.

Perhaps some relic of the sick man's dream of greatness survives in the still lingering visitations of the medical attendant. But how is he, too, changed with everything else? Can this be he—this man of news—of chat—of anecdote—of everything but physic—can this be he, who so lately came between the patient and his cruel enemy, as on some solemn embassy from Nature, erecting herself into a high mediating party?—Pshaw! 'tis some old woman.

Farewell with him all that made sickness pompous—the spell that hushed the household—the desert-like stillness, felt throughout its inmost chambers—the mute attendance—the inquiry by looks—the still softer delicacies of self-attention—the sole and single eye of distemper alonely fixed upon itself—world-thoughts excluded—the man a world unto himself—his own theatre—

What a speck is he dwindled into!

In this flat swamp of convalescence, left by the ebb of sickness, yet far enough from the terra-firma of established health, your note, dear Editor, reached me, requesting—an article. In Articulo Mortis, thought I; but it is something hard—and the quibble, wretched as it was, relieved me. The summons, unseasonable as it appeared, seemed to link me on again to the petty businesses of life, which I had lost sight of; a gentle call to activity, however trivial; a wholesome weaning from that preposterous dream of self-absorption—the puffy state of sickness—in which I confess to have lain so long, insensible to the magazines and monarchies of the world alike; to its laws, and to its literature. The hypochondriac flatus is subsiding; the acres, which in imagination I had spread over—for the sick man swells in the sole contemplation of his single sufferings, till he becomes a Tityus to himself—are wasting to a span; and for the giant of self-importance, which I was so lately, you have me once again in my natural pretensions—the lean and meagre figure of your insignificant Essayist.

THE SUPERANNUATED MAN

Sera tamen respexit
Libertas. VIRGIL.

A Clerk I was in London gay.—O'KEEFE.

IF peradventure, Reader, it has been thy lot to waste the golden years of thy life—thy shining youth—in the irksome confinement of an office; to have thy prison days prolonged through middle age down to decrepitude and silver hairs, without hope of release or respite; to have lived to forget that there are such things as holidays, or to remember them but as the prerogatives of childhood; then, and then only, will you be able to appreciate my deliverance.

It is now six-and-thirty years since I took my seat at the desk in Mincing Lane. Melancholy was the transition at fourteen from the abundant playtime, and the frequently intervening vacations of school days, to the eight, nine, and sometimes ten hours a day attendance at the counting-house. But time partially reconciles us to anything. I gradually became content—doggedly contented, as wild animals in cages.

It is true I had my Sundays to myself; but Sundays, admirable as the institution of them is for purposes of worship, are for that very reason the very worst adapted for days of unbending and recreation. In particular, there is a gloom for me attendant upon a city Sunday, a weight in the air. I miss the cheerful cries of London, the music, and the ballad-singers—the buzz and stirring murmur of the streets. Those eternal bells depress me. The closed shops repel me. Prints, pictures, all the glittering and endless succession of knacks and gewgaws, and ostentatiously displayed wares of tradesmen, which make a week-day saunter through the less busy parts of the metropolis so delightful—are shut out. No bookstalls deliciously to idle over—no busy faces to recreate the idle man who contemplates them ever passing by—the very face of business a charm by contrast to his temporary relaxation from it. Nothing to be seen but unhappy countenances—or half-happy at best—of emancipated 'prentices and little tradesfolks, with here and there a servant-maid that has got leave to go out, who, slaving all the week, with the habit has lost almost the capacity of enjoying a free hour; and livelily expressing the hollowness of a day's pleasuring. The very strollers in the fields on that day look anything but comfortable.

But besides Sundays, I had a day at Easter, and a day at Christmas, with a full week in the summer to go and air myself in my native fields of Hertfordshire. This last was a great indulgence; and the prospect of its recurrence, I believe, alone kept me up through the year, and made my durance tolerable. But when the week came round, did the glittering phantom of the distance keep touch with me, or rather was it not a series of seven uneasy days, spent in restless pursuit of pleasure, and a wearisome anxiety to find out how to make the most of them? Where was the quiet, where the promised rest? Before I had a taste of it, it was vanished. I was at the desk again, counting upon the fifty-one tedious weeks that must intervene before such another snatch would come. Still the prospect of its coming threw something of an illumination upon the darker side of my captivity. Without it, as I have said, I could scarcely have sustained my thraldom.

Independently of the rigours of attendance, I have ever been haunted with a sense (perhaps a mere caprice) of incapacity for business. This, during my latter years, had increased to such a degree, that it was visible in all the lines of my countenance. My health and my good spirits flagged. I had perpetually a dread of some crisis, to which I should be found unequal. Besides my daylight servitude, I served over again all night in my sleep, and would awake with terrors of imaginary false entries, errors in my accounts, and the like. I was fifty years of age, and no prospect of emancipation presented itself. I had grown to my desk, as it were, and the wood had entered into my soul.

My fellows in the office would sometimes rally me upon the trouble legible in my countenance; but I did not know that it had raised the suspicions of any of my employers, when, on the fifth of last month, a day ever to be remembered by me, L——, the junior partner in the firm, calling me on one side, directly taxed me with my bad looks, and frankly inquired the cause of them. So taxed, I honestly made confession of my infirmity, and added that I was afraid I should eventually be obliged to resign his service. He spoke some words of course to hearten me, and there the matter rested. A whole week I remained labouring under the impression that I had acted imprudently in my disclosure; that I had foolishly given a handle against myself, and had been anticipating my own dismissal. A week passed in this manner—the most anxious one, I verily believe, in my whole life—when on the evening of the 12th of April, just as I was about quitting my desk to go home (it might be about eight o'clock), I received an awful summons to attend the presence of the whole assembled firm in the formidable back parlour. I thought now my time is surely come, I have done for myself, I am going to be told that they have no longer occasion for me. L——, I could see, smiled at the terror I was in, which was a little relief to me,—when to my utter astonishment B——, the eldest partner, began a formal harangue to me on the length of my services, my very meritorious conduct during the whole of the time (the deuce, thought I, how did he find out that? I protest I never had the confidence to think as much). He went on to descant on the expediency of retiring at a certain time of life (how my heart panted!), and asking me a few questions as to the amount of my own property, of which I have a little, ended with a proposal, to which his three partners nodded a grave assent, that I should accept from the house, which I had served so well, a pension for life to the amount of two-thirds of my accustomed salary—a magnificent offer! I do not know what I answered between surprise and gratitude, but it was understood that I accepted their proposal, and I was told that I was free from that hour to leave their service. I stammered out a bow, and at just ten minutes after eight I went home—for ever. This noble benefit—gratitude forbids me to conceal their names—I owe to the kindness of the most munificent firm in the world—the house of Boldero, Merryweather, Bosanquet, and Lacy.

Esto perpetua!

For the first day or two I felt stunned—overwhelmed. I could only apprehend my felicity; I was too confused to taste it sincerely. I wandered about, thinking I was happy, and knowing that I was not. I was in the condition of a prisoner in the old Bastile, suddenly let loose after a forty years' confinement. I could scarce trust myself with myself. It was like passing out of Time into Eternity—for it is a sort of Eternity for a man to have all his Time to himself. It seemed to me that I had more time on my hands than I could ever manage. From a poor man, poor in Time, I was suddenly lifted up into a vast revenue; I could see no end of my possessions; I wanted some steward, or judicious bailiff, to manage my estates in Time for me. And here let me caution persons grown old in active business, not lightly, nor without weighing their own resources, to forego their customary employment all at once, for there may be danger in it. I feel it by myself, but I know that my resources are sufficient; and now that those first giddy raptures have subsided, I have a quiet home-feeling of the blessedness of my condition. I am in no hurry. Having all holidays, I am as though I had none. If Time hung heavy upon me, I could walk it away; but I do *not* walk all day long, as I used to do in those old transient holidays, thirty miles a day, to make the most of them. If Time were troublesome, I could read it away; but I do *not* read in that violent measure, with which, having no Time my own but candlelight Time, I used to weary out my head and eyesight in bygone winters. I walk, read, or scribble (as now) just when the fit seizes me. I no longer hunt after pleasure; I let it come to me. I am like the man

> ————that's born, and has his years come to him,
> In some green desert.

'Years!' you will say; 'what is this superannuated simpleton calculating upon? He has already told us he is past fifty.'

I have indeed lived nominally fifty years, but deduct out of them the hours which I have lived to other people, and not to myself, and you will find me still a young fellow. For *that* is the only true Time, which a man can properly call his own—that which he has all to himself; the rest, though in some sense he may be said to live it, is other people's Time, not his. The remnant of my poor days, long or short, is at least multiplied for me threefold. My ten next years, if I stretch so far, will be as long as any preceding thirty. 'Tis a fair rule-of-three sum.

Among the strange fantasies which beset me at the commencement of my freedom, and of which all traces are not yet gone, one was, that a vast tract of time had intervened since I quitted the Counting House. I could not conceive of it as an affair of yesterday. The partners, and the clerks with whom I had for so many years, and for so many hours in each day of the year, been closely associated—being suddenly removed from them—they seemed as dead to me. There is a fine passage, which may serve to illustrate this fancy, in a Tragedy by Sir Robert Howard, speaking of a friend's death:—

> ———'Twas but just now he went away;
> I have not since had time to shed a tear;
> And yet the distance does the same appear
> As if he had been a thousand years from me.
> Time takes no measure in Eternity.

To dissipate this awkward feeling, I have been fain to go among them once or twice since; to visit my old desk-fellows—my co-brethren of the quill—that I had left below in the state militant. Not all the kindness with which they received me could quite restore to me that pleasant familiarity, which I had heretofore enjoyed among them. We cracked some of our old jokes, but methought they went off but faintly. My old desk; the peg where I hung my hat, were appropriated to another. I knew it must be, but I could not take it kindly. D——l take me, if I did not feel some remorse—beast, if I had not—at quitting my old compeers, the faithful partners of my toils for six-and-thirty years, that smoothed for me with their jokes and conundrums the ruggedness of my professional road. Had it been so rugged then, after all; or was I a coward simply? Well, it is too late to repent; and I also know that these suggestions are a common fallacy of the mind on such occasions. But my heart smote me. I had violently broken the bands betwixt us. It was at least not courteous. I shall be some time before I get quite reconciled to the separation. Farewell, old cronies, yet not for long, for again and again I will come among ye, if I shall have your leave. Farewell, Ch——, dry, sarcastic, and friendly! Do——, mild, slow to move, and gentlemanly! Pl——, officious to do, and to volunteer, good services!—and thou, thou dreary pile, fit mansion for a Gresham or a Whittington of old, stately house of Merchants; with thy labyrinthine passages, and light-excluding, pent-up offices, where candles for one-half the year supplied the place of the sun's light; unhealthy contributor to my weal, stern fosterer of my living, farewell! In thee remain, and not in the obscure collection of some wandering bookseller, my 'works!' There let them rest, as I do from my labours, piled on thy massy shelves, more MSS. in folio than ever Aquinas left, and full as useful! My mantle I bequeath among ye.

A fortnight has passed since the date of my first communication. At that period I was approaching to tranquillity, but had not reached it. I boasted of a calm indeed, but it was comparative only. Something of the first flutter was left; an unsettling sense of novelty; the dazzle to weak eyes of unaccustomed light. I missed my old chains, forsooth, as if they had been some necessary part of my apparel. I was a poor Carthusian, from strict cellular discipline suddenly by some revolution returned upon the world. I am now as if I had never been other than my own master. It is natural to me to go where I please, to do what I please. I find myself at 11 o'clock in the day in Bond Street, and it seems to me that I have been sauntering there at that very hour for years past. I digress into Soho, to explore a bookstall. Methinks I have been thirty years a collector. There is nothing strange nor new in it. I find myself before a fine picture in the morning. Was it ever otherwise? What is become of Fish Street Hill? Where is Fenchurch Street? Stones of old Mincing Lane, which I have worn with my daily pilgrimage for six-and-thirty years, to the footsteps of what toil-worn clerk are your everlasting flints now vocal? I indent the gayer flags of Pall Mall. It is 'Change time, and I am strangely among the Elgin marbles. It was no hyperbole when I ventured to compare the change in my condition to a passing into another world. Time stands still in a manner to me. I have lost all distinction of season. I do not know the day of the week or of the month. Each day used to be individually felt by me in its reference to the foreign post days; in its distance from, or propinquity to, the next Sunday. I had my Wednesday feelings, my Saturday nights' sensations. The genius of each day was upon me distinctly during the whole of it, affecting my appetite, spirits, etc. The phantom of the next day, with the dreary five to follow, sate as a load upon my poor Sabbath recreations. What charm has washed the Ethiop white? What is gone of Black Monday? All days are the same. Sunday itself—that unfortunate failure of a holiday, as it too often proved, what with my sense of its fugitiveness, and over-care to get the greatest quantity of pleasure out of it—is melted down into a week-day. I can spare to go to church now, without grudging the huge cantle which it used to seem to cut out of the holiday. I have time for everything. I can visit a sick friend. I can interrupt the man of much occupation when he is busiest. I can insult over him with an invitation to take a day's pleasure with me to Windsor this fine May morning. It is Lucretian pleasure to behold the poor drudges, whom I have left behind in the world, carking and caring; like horses in a mill, drudging on in the same eternal round—and what is it all for? A man can never have too much Time to himself, nor too little to do. Had I a little son, I would christen him NOTHING-TO-DO; he should do nothing. Man, I verily believe, is out of his element as long as he is operative. I am altogether for the life contemplative. Will no kindly earthquake come and swallow up those accursed cotton-mills? Take me that lumber of a desk there, and bowl it down

As low as to the fiends.

I am no longer * * * * * *, clerk to the Firm of, etc. I am Retired Leisure. I am to be met with in trim gardens. I am already come to be known by my vacant face and careless gesture, perambulating at no fixed pace, nor with any settled purpose. I walk about; not to and from. They tell me, a certain *cum dignitate* air, that has been buried so long with my other good parts, has begun to shoot forth in my person. I grow into gentility perceptibly. When I take up a newspaper, it is to read the state of the opera. *Opus operatum est.* I have done all that I came into this world to do. I have worked task-work, and have the rest of the day to myself.

OLD CHINA

I HAVE an almost feminine partiality for old china. When I go to see any great house, I inquire for the china-closet, and next for the picture-gallery. I cannot defend the order of preference, but by saying that we have all some taste or other, of too ancient a date to admit of our remembering distinctly that it was an acquired one. I can call to mind the first play, and the first exhibition, that I was taken to; but I am not conscious of a time when china jars and saucers were introduced into my imagination.

I had no repugnance then—why should I now have?—to those little, lawless, azure-tinctured grotesques, that, under the notion of men and women, float about, uncircumscribed by any element, in that world before perspective—a china tea-cup.

I like to see my old friends—whom distance cannot diminish—figuring up in the air (so they appear to our optics), yet on *terra firma* still—for so we must in courtesy interpret that speck of deeper blue, which the decorous artist, to prevent absurdity, had made to spring up beneath their sandals.

I love the men with women's faces, and the women, if possible, with still more womanish expressions.

Here is a young and courtly Mandarin, handing tea to a lady from a salver—two miles off. See how distance seems to set off respect! And here the same lady, or another—for likeness is identity on tea-cups—is stepping into a little fairy boat, moored on the hither side of this calm garden river, with a dainty mincing foot, which in a right angle of incidence (as angles go in our world) must infallibly land her in the midst of a flowery mead—a furlong off on the other side of the same strange stream!

Farther on—if far or near can be predicated of their world—see horses, trees, pagodas, dancing the hays.

Here—a cow and rabbit couchant, and co-extensive—so objects show, seen through the lucid atmosphere of fine Cathay.

I was pointing out to my cousin last evening, over our Hyson (which we are old-fashioned enough to drink unmixed still of an afternoon), some of these *speciosa miracula* upon a set of extraordinary old blue china (a recent purchase) which we were now for the first time using; and could not help remarking, how favourable circumstances had been to us of late years, that we could afford to please the eye sometimes with trifles of this sort—when a passing sentiment seemed to overshade the brows of my companion. I am quick at detecting these summer clouds in Bridget.

'I wish the good old times would come again,' she said, 'when we were not quite so rich. I do not mean that I want to be poor; but there was a middle state'—so she was pleased to ramble on,—'in which I am sure we were a great deal happier. A purchase is but a purchase, now that you have money enough and to spare. Formerly it used to be a triumph. When we coveted a cheap luxury (and, O! how much ado I had to get you to consent in those times!)—we were used to have a debate two or three days before, and to weigh the *for* and *against*, and think what we might spare it out of, and what saving we could hit upon, that should be an equivalent. A thing was worth buying then, when we felt the money that we paid for it.

'Do you remember the brown suit, which you made

to hang upon you, till all your friends cried shame upon you, it grew so threadbare—and all because of that folio Beaumont and Fletcher, which you dragged home late at night from Barker's in Covent Garden? Do you remember how we eyed it for weeks before we could make up our minds to the purchase, and had not come to a determination till it was near ten o'clock of the Saturday night, when you set off from Islington, fearing you should be too late—and when the old bookseller with some grumbling opened his shop, and by the twinkling taper (for he was setting bedwards) lighted out the relic from his dusty treasures—and when you lugged it home, wishing it were twice as cumbersome—and when you presented it to me—and when we were exploring the perfectness of it (*collating*, you called it)—and while I was repairing some of the loose leaves with paste, which your impatience would not suffer to be left till daybreak—was there no pleasure in being a poor man? or can those neat black clothes which you wear now, and are so careful to keep brushed, since we have become rich and finical—give you half the honest vanity with which you flaunted it about in that over-worn suit—your old corbeau—for four or five weeks longer than you should have done, to pacify your conscience for the mighty sum of fifteen—or sixteen shillings was it?—a great affair we thought it then—which you had lavished on the old folio. Now you can afford to buy any book that pleases you, but I do not see that you ever bring me home any nice old purchases now.

'When you came home with twenty apologies for laying out a less number of shillings upon that print after Lionardo, which we christened the "Lady Blanch"; when you looked at the purchase, and thought of the money—and thought of the money, and looked again at the picture—was there no pleasure in being a poor man? Now, you have nothing to do but to walk into Colnaghi's, and buy a wilderness of Lionardos. Yet do you?

'Then, do you remember our pleasant walks to Enfield, and Potter's Bar, and Waltham, when we had a holyday—holydays and all other fun are gone now we are rich—and the little hand-basket in which I used to deposit our day's fare of savoury cold lamb and salad—and how you would pry about at noontide for some decent house, where we might go in and produce our store—only paying for the ale that you must call for—and speculate upon the looks of the landlady, and whether she was likely to allow us a tablecloth—and wish for such another honest hostess as Izaak Walton has described many a one on the pleasant banks of the Lea, when he went a-fishing—and sometimes they would prove obliging enough, and sometimes they would look grudgingly upon us—but we had cheerful looks still for one another, and would eat our plain food savourily, scarcely grudging Piscator his Trout Hall? Now—when we go out a day's pleasuring, which is seldom, moreover, we *ride* part of the way, and go into a fine inn, and order the best of dinners, never debating the expense—which, after all, never has half the relish of those chance country snaps, when we were at the mercy of uncertain usage, and a precarious welcome.

'You are too proud to see a play anywhere now but in the pit. Do you remember where it was we used to sit, when we saw the *Battle of Hexham*, and the *Surrender of Calais*, and Bannister and Mrs. Bland in the *Children in the Wood*—when we squeezed out our shillings apiece to sit three or four times in a season in the one-shilling gallery—where you felt all the time that you ought not to have brought me—and more strongly I felt obligation to you for having brought me—and the pleasure was the better for a little shame—and when the curtain drew up, what cared we for our place in the house, or what mattered it where we were sitting, when our thoughts were with Rosalind in Arden, or with Viola at the Court of Illyria? You used to say that the Gallery was the best place of all for enjoying a play socially—that the relish of such exhibitions must be in proportion to the infrequency of going—that the company we met there, not being in general readers of plays, were obliged to attend the more, and did attend, to what was going on, on the stage—because a word lost would have been a chasm, which it was impossible for them to fill up. With such reflections we consoled our pride then—and I appeal to you whether, as a woman, I met generally with less attention and accommodation than I have done since in more expensive situations in the house? The getting in, indeed, and the crowding up those inconvenient staircases, was bad enough—but there was still a law of civility to woman recognised to quite as great an extent as we ever found in the other passages—and how a little difficulty overcome heightened the snug seat and the play, afterwards! Now we can only pay our money and walk in. You cannot see, you say, in the galleries now. I am sure we saw, and heard too, well enough then—but sight, and all, I think, is gone with our poverty.

'There was pleasure in eating strawberries, before they became quite common—in the first dish of peas, while they were yet dear—to have them for a nice supper, a treat. What treat can we have now? If we were to treat ourselves now—that is, to have dainties a little above our means, it would be selfish and wicked. It is the very little more that we allow ourselves beyond what the actual poor can get at, that makes what I call a treat—when two people, living together as we have done, now and then indulge themselves in a cheap luxury, which both like; while each apologises, and is willing to take both halves of the blame to his single share. I see no harm in people making much of themselves, in that sense of the word. It may give them a hint how to make much of others. But now—what I mean by the word—we never *do* make much of ourselves. None but the poor can do it. I do not mean the veriest poor of all, but persons as we were, just above poverty.

'I know what you were going to say, that it is mighty pleasant at the end of the year to make all meet,—and much ado we used to have every Thirty-first Night of December to account for our exceedings—many a long face did you make over your puzzled accounts, and in contriving to make it out how we had spent so much—or that we had not spent so much—or that it was impossible we should spend so much next year—and still we found our slender capital decreasing—but then,—betwixt ways, and projects, and compromises of one sort or another, and talk of curtailing this charge, and doing without that for the future—and the hope that youth brings, and laughing spirits (in which you were never poor till now), we pocketed up our loss, and in conclusion, with "lusty brimmers" (as you used to quote it out of *hearty cheerful Mr. Cotton*, as you called him), we used to welcome in the "coming guest." Now we have no reckoning at all at the end of the old year—no flattering promises about the new year doing better for us.'

Bridget is so sparing of her speech on most occasions, that when she gets into a rhetorical vein, I am careful how I interrupt it. I could not help, however, smiling at the phantom of wealth which her dear imagination had conjured up out of a clear income of poor —— hundred pounds a year. 'It is true we were happier when we were poorer, but we were also younger, my cousin. I am afraid we must put up with the excess, for if we were to shake the superflux into the sea, we should not much mend ourselves. That we had much to struggle with, as we grew up together, we have reason to be most thankful. It strengthened and knit our compact closer. We could never have been what we have been to each other, if we had always had the sufficiency which you now complain of. The resisting power—those natural dilations of the youthful spirit, which circumstances cannot straiten—with us are long since passed away. Competence to age is supplementary youth, a sorry supplement indeed, but I fear the best that is to be had. We must ride where we formerly walked: live better and lie softer—and shall be wise to do so—than we had means to do in those good old days you speak of. Yet could those days return—could you and I once more walk our thirty miles a day—could Bannister and Mrs. Bland again be young, and you and I be young to see them—could the good old one-shilling gallery days return—they are dreams, my cousin, now—but could you and I at this moment, instead of this quiet argument, by our well-carpeted fireside, sitting on this luxurious sofa—be once more struggling up those inconvenient staircases, pushed about and squeezed, and elbowed by the poorest rabble of poor gallery scramblers—could I once more hear those anxious shrieks of yours—and the delicious *Thank God, we are safe*, which always followed when the topmost stair, conquered, let in the first light of the whole cheerful theatre down beneath us—I know not the fathom line that ever touched a descent so deep as I would be willing to bury more wealth in than Crœsus had, or the great Jew R—— is supposed to have, to purchase it. And now do just look at that merry little Chinese waiter holding an umbrella, big enough for a bed-tester, over the head of that pretty insipid half Madonna-ish chit of a lady in that very blue summer-house.'

WILLIAM HAZLITT

1778–1830

ON THE IGNORANCE OF THE LEARNED

For the more languages a man can speak,
His talent has but sprung the greater leak:
And, for the industry he has spent upon 't,
Must full as much some other way discount.
The Hebrew, Chaldee, and the Syriac
Do, like their letters, set men's reason back,
And turn their wits that strive to understand it
(Like those that write the characters) left-handed.
Yet he that is but able to express
No sense at all in several languages,
Will pass for learneder than he that 's known
To speak the strongest reason in his own.

BUTLER.

THE description of persons who have the fewest ideas of all others are mere authors and readers. It is better to be able neither to read nor write than to be able to do nothing else. A lounger who is ordinarily seen with a book in his hand is (we may be almost sure) equally without the power or inclination to attend either to what passes around him or in his own mind. Such a one may be said to carry his understanding about with him in his pocket, or to leave it at home on his library shelves. He is afraid of venturing on any train of reasoning, or of striking out any observation that is not mechanically suggested to him by passing his eyes over certain legible characters; shrinks from the fatigue of thought, which, for want of practice, becomes insupportable to him; and sits down contented with an endless, wearisome succession of words and half-formed images, which fill the void of the mind, and continually efface one another. Learning is, in too many cases, but a foil to common sense; a substitute for true knowledge. Books are less often made use of as 'spectacles' to look at nature with, than as blinds to keep out its strong light and shifting scenery from weak eyes and indolent dispositions. The book-worm wraps himself up in his web of verbal generalities, and sees only the glimmering shadows of things reflected from the minds of others. Nature *puts him out*. The impressions of real objects, stripped of the disguises of words and voluminous roundabout descriptions, are blows that stagger him; their variety distracts, their rapidity exhausts him; and he turns from the bustle, the noise, and glare, and whirling motion of the world about him (which he has not an eye to follow in its fantastic changes, nor an understanding to reduce to fixed principles), to the quiet monotony of the dead languages, and the less startling and more intelligible combinations of the letters of the alphabet. It is well, it is perfectly well. 'Leave me to my repose,' is the motto of the sleeping and the dead. You might as well ask the paralytic to leap from his chair and throw away his crutch, or, without a miracle, to 'take up his bed and walk,' as expect the learned reader to throw down his book and think for himself. He clings to it for his intellectual support; and his dread of being left to himself is like the horror of a vacuum. He can only breathe a learned atmosphere, as other men breathe common air. He is a borrower of sense. He has no ideas of his own, and must live on those of other people. The habit of supplying our ideas from foreign sources 'enfeebles all internal strength of thought,' as a course of dram-drinking destroys the tone of the stomach. The faculties of the mind, when not exerted, or when cramped by custom and authority, become listless, torpid, and unfit for the purposes of thought or action. Can we wonder at the languor and lassitude which is thus produced by a life of learned sloth and ignorance; by poring over lines and syllables that excite little more idea or interest than if they were the characters of an unknown tongue, till the eye closes on vacancy, and the book drops from the feeble hand! I would rather be a woodcutter, or the meanest hind, that all day 'sweats in the eye of Phœbus, and at night sleeps in Elysium,' than wear out my life so, 'twixt dreaming and awake. The learned author differs from the learned student in this, that the one transcribes what the other reads. The learned are mere literary drudges. If you set them upon original composition, their heads turn, they don't know where they are. The indefatigable readers of books are like the everlasting copiers of pictures, who, when they attempt to do anything of their own, find they want an eye quick enough, a hand steady enough, and colours bright enough, to trace the living forms of nature.

Any one who has passed through the regular gradations of a classical education, and is not made a fool by it, may consider himself as having had a very narrow escape. It is an old remark, that boys who shine at school do not make the greatest figure when they grow up and come out into the world. The things, in fact, which a boy is set to learn at school, and on which his success depends, are things which do not require the exercise either of the highest or the most useful faculties of the mind. Memory (and that of the lowest kind) is the chief faculty called into play in conning over and repeating lessons by rote in grammar, in languages, in geography, arithmetic, etc., so that he who has the most of this technical memory, with the least turn for other things, which have a stronger and more natural claim upon his childish attention, will make the most forward schoolboy. The jargon containing the definitions of the parts of speech, the rules for casting up an account, or the inflections of a Greek verb, can have no attraction to the tyro of ten years old, except as they are imposed as a task upon him by others, or from his feeling the want of sufficient relish or amusement in other things. A lad with a sickly constitution and no very active mind, who can just retain what is pointed out to him, and has neither sagacity to distinguish nor spirit to enjoy for himself, will generally be at the head of his form. An idler at school, on the other hand, is one who has high health and spirits, who has the free use of his limbs, with all his wits about him, who feels the circulation of his blood and the motion of his heart, who is ready to laugh and cry in a breath, and who had rather chase a ball or a butterfly, feel the open air in his face, look at the fields or the sky, follow a winding path, or enter with eagerness into all the little conflicts and interests of his acquaintances and friends, than doze over a musty spelling-book, repeat barbarous distichs after his master, sit so many hours pinioned to a writing-desk, and receive his reward for the loss of time and pleasure in paltry prize-medals at Christmas and Midsummer. There is indeed a degree of stupidity which prevents children from learning the usual lessons, or ever arriving at these puny academic honours. But what passes for stupidity is much oftener a want of interest, of a sufficient motive to fix the attention and force a reluctant application to the dry and unmeaning pursuits of school-learning. The best capacities are as much above this drudgery as the dullest are beneath it. Our men of the greatest genius have not been most distinguished for their acquirements at school or at the university.

Th' enthusiast Fancy was a truant ever.

Gray and Collins were among the instances of this wayward disposition. Such persons do not think so highly of the advantages, nor can they submit their imaginations so servilely to the trammels of strict scholastic discipline. There is a certain kind and degree of intellect in which words take root, but into which things have not power to penetrate. A mediocrity of talent, with a certain slenderness of moral constitution, is the soil that produces the most brilliant specimens of successful prize-essayists and Greek epigrammatists. It should not be forgotten that the least respectable character among modern politicians was the cleverest boy at Eton.

Learning is the knowledge of that which is not generally known to others, and which we can only derive at second-hand from books or other artificial sources. The knowledge of that which is before us, or about us, which appeals to our experience, passions, and pursuits, to the bosoms and business of men, is not learning. Learning is the knowledge of that which none but the learned know. He is the most learned man who knows the most of what is farthest removed from common life and actual observation, that is of the least practical utility, and least liable to be brought to the test of experience, and that, having been handed down through the greatest number of intermediate stages, is the most full of uncertainty, difficulties, and contradictions. It is seeing with the eyes of others, hearing with their ears, and pinning our faith on their understandings. The learned man prides himself in the knowledge of names and dates, not of men or things. He thinks and cares nothing about his next-door neighbours, but he is deeply read in the tribes and castes of the Hindoos and Calmuc Tartars. He can hardly find his way into the next street, though he is acquainted with the exact dimensions of Constantinople and Pekin. He does not know whether his oldest acquaintance is a knave or a fool, but he can pronounce a pompous lecture on all the principal characters in history. He cannot tell whether an object is black or white, round or square, and yet he is a professed master of the laws of optics and the rules of perspective. He knows as much of what he talks about as a blind man does of colours. He cannot give a satisfactory answer to the plainest question, nor is he ever in the right in any one of his opinions upon any one matter of fact that really comes before him, and yet he gives himself out for an infallible judge on all these points, of which it is impossible that he or any other person living should know anything but by conjecture. He is expert in all the dead and in most of the living languages; but he can neither speak his own fluently, nor write it correctly. A person of this class, the second Greek scholar of his day, undertook to point out several solecisms in Milton's Latin style; and in his own performance there is hardly a sentence of common English. Such was Dr. ——. Such is Dr. ——. Such was not Porson. He was an exception that confirmed the general rule,—a man that, by uniting talents and knowledge with learning, made the distinction between them more striking and palpable.

A mere scholar, who knows nothing but books, must be ignorant even of them. 'Books do not teach the use of books.' How should he know anything of a work who knows nothing of the subject of it? The learned pedant is conversant with books only as they are made of other books, and those again of others, without end. He parrots those who have parroted others. He can translate the same word into ten different languages, but he knows nothing of the *thing* which it means in any one of them. He stuffs his head with authorities built on authorities, with quotations quoted from quotations, while he locks up his senses, his understanding, and his heart. He is unacquainted with the maxims and manners of the world; he is to seek in the characters of individuals. He sees no beauty in the face of nature or of art. To him 'the mighty world of eye and ear' is hid; and 'knowledge,' except at one entrance, 'quite shut out.' His pride takes part with his ignorance; and his self-importance rises with the number of things of which he does not know the value, and which he therefore despises as unworthy of his notice. He knows nothing of pictures,—'of the colouring of Titian, the grace of Raphael, the purity of Domenichino, the *corregiosity* of Correggio, the learning of Poussin, the airs of Guido, the taste of the Caracci, or the grand contour of Michael Angelo,'—of all those glories of the Italian and miracles of the

Flemish school, which have filled the eyes of mankind with delight, and to the study and imitation of which thousands have in vain devoted their lives. These are to him as if they had never been, a mere dead letter, a by-word; and no wonder, for he neither sees nor understands their prototypes in nature. A print of Rubens' Watering-place or Claude's Enchanted Castle may be hanging on the walls of his room for months without his once perceiving them; and if you point them out to him he will turn away from them. The language of nature, or of art (which is another nature), is one that he does not understand. He repeats indeed the names of Apelles and Phidias, because they are to be found in classic authors, and boasts of their works as prodigies, because they no longer exist; or when he sees the finest remains of Grecian art actually before him in the Elgin Marbles, takes no other interest in them than as they lead to a learned dispute, and (which is the same thing) a quarrel about the meaning of a Greek particle. He is equally ignorant of music; he 'knows no touch of it,' from the strains of the all-accomplished Mozart to the shepherd's pipe upon the mountain. His ears are nailed to his books; and deadened with the sound of the Greek and Latin tongues, and the din and smithery of school-learning. Does he know anything more of poetry? He knows the number of feet in a verse, and of acts in a play; but of the soul or spirit he knows nothing. He can turn a Greek ode into English, or a Latin epigram into Greek verse; but whether either is worth the trouble he leaves to the critics. Does he understand 'the act and practique part of life' better than 'the theorique'? No. He knows no liberal or mechanic art, no trade or occupation, no game of skill or chance. Learning 'has no skill in surgery,' in agriculture, in building, in working in wood or in iron; it cannot make any instrument of labour, or use it when made; it cannot handle the plough or the spade, or the chisel or the hammer; it knows nothing of hunting or hawking, fishing or shooting, of horses or dogs, of fencing or dancing, or cudgel-playing, or bowls, or cards, or tennis, or anything else. The learned professor of all arts and sciences cannot reduce any one of them to practice, though he may contribute an account of them to an Encyclopedia. He has not the use of his hands nor of his feet; he can neither run, nor walk, nor swim; and he considers all those who actually understand and can exercise any of these arts of body or mind as vulgar and mechanical men,—though to know almost any one of them in perfection requires long time and practice, with powers originally fitted, and a turn of mind particularly devoted to them. It does not require more than this to enable the learned candidate to arrive, by painful study, at a doctor's degree and a fellowship, and to eat, drink, and sleep the rest of his life!

The thing is plain. All that men really understand is confined to a very small compass; to their daily affairs and experience; to what they have an opportunity to know, and motives to study or practise. The rest is affectation and imposture. The common people have the use of their limbs; for they live by their labour or skill. They understand their own business and the characters of those they have to deal with; for it is necessary that they should. They have eloquence to express their passions, and wit at will to express their contempt and provoke laughter. Their natural use of speech is not hung up in monumental mockery, in an obsolete language; nor is their sense of what is ludicrous, or readiness at finding out allusions to express it, buried in collections of *Anas*. You will hear more good things on the outside of a stage-coach from London to Oxford than if you were to pass a twelvemonth with the undergraduates, or heads of colleges, of that famous university; and more *home* truths are to be learnt from listening to a noisy debate in an alehouse than from attending to a formal one in the House of Commons. An elderly country gentlewoman will often know more of character, and be able to illustrate it by more amusing anecdotes taken from the history of what has been said, done, and gossiped in a country town for the last fifty years, than the best blue-stocking of the age will be able to glean from that sort of learning which consists in an acquaintance with all the novels and satirical poems published in the same period. People in towns, indeed, are woefully deficient in a knowledge of character, which they see only *in the bust*, not as a whole-length. People in the country not only know all that has happened to a man, but trace his virtues or vices, as they do his features, in their descent through several generations, and solve some contradiction in his behaviour by a cross in the breed half a century ago. The learned know nothing of the matter, either in town or country. Above all, the mass of society have common sense, which the learned in all ages want. The vulgar are in the right when they judge for themselves; they are wrong when they trust to their blind guides. The celebrated non-conformist divine, Baxter, was almost stoned to death by the good women of Kidderminster, for asserting from the pulpit that 'hell was paved with infants' skulls'; but, by the force of argument, and of learned quotations from the Fathers, the reverend preacher at length prevailed over the scruples of his congregation, and over reason and humanity.

Such is the use which has been made of human learning. The labourers in this vineyard seem as if it was their object to confound all common sense, and the distinctions of good and evil, by means of traditional maxims and preconceived notions taken upon trust, and increasing in absurdity with increase of age. They pile hypothesis on hypothesis, mountain high, till it is impossible to come at the plain truth on any question. They see things, not as they are, but as they find them in books, and 'wink and shut their apprehensions up,' in order that they may discover nothing to interfere with their prejudices or convince them of their absurdity. It might be supposed that the height of human wisdom consisted in maintaining contradictions and rendering nonsense sacred. There is no dogma, however fierce or foolish, to which these persons have not set their seals, and tried to impose on the understandings of their followers as the will of Heaven, clothed with all the terrors and sanctions of religion. How little has the human understanding been directed to find out the true and useful! How much ingenuity has been thrown away in the defence of creeds and systems! How much time and talents have been wasted in theological controversy, in law, in politics, in verbal criticism, in judicial astrology, and in finding out the art of making gold! What actual benefit do we reap from the writings of a Laud or a Whitgift, or of Bishop Bull or Bishop Waterland, or Prideaux' Connections, or Beausobre, or Calmet, or St. Augustine, or Puffendorf, or Vattel, or from the more literal but equally learned and unprofitable labours of Scaliger, Cardan, and Scioppius? How many grains of sense are there in their thousand folio or quarto volumes? What would the world lose if they were committed to the flames to-morrow? Or are they not already 'gone to the vault of all the Capulets'? Yet all these were oracles in their time, and would have scoffed at you or me, at common sense and human nature, for differing with them. It is our turn to laugh now.

To conclude this subject. The most sensible people to be met with in society are men of business and of the world, who argue from what they see and know, instead of spinning cobweb distinctions of what things ought to be. Women have often more of what is called *good sense* than men. They have fewer pretensions; are less implicated in theories; and judge of objects more from their immediate and involuntary impression on the mind, and, therefore, more truly and naturally. They cannot reason wrong; for they do not reason at all. They do not think or speak by rule; and they have in general more eloquence and wit, as well as sense, on that account. By their wit, sense, and eloquence together, they generally contrive to govern their husbands. Their style, when they write to their friends (not for the booksellers), is better than that of most authors.—Uneducated people have most exuberance of invention and the greatest freedom from prejudice. Shakespeare's was evidently an uneducated mind, both in the freshness of his imagination and in the variety of his views; as Milton's was scholastic, in the texture both of his thoughts and feelings. Shakespeare had not been accustomed to write themes at school in favour of virtue or against vice. To this we owe the unaffected but healthy tone of his dramatic morality. If we wish to know the force of human genius we should read Shakespeare. If we wish to see the insignificance of human learning we may study his commentators.

THE INDIAN JUGGLERS

COMING forward and seating himself on the ground in his white dress and tightened turban, the chief of the Indian Jugglers begins with tossing up two brass balls, which is what any of us could do, and concludes with keeping up four at the same time, which is what none of us could do to save our lives, nor if we were to take our whole lives to do it in. Is it then a trifling power we see at work, or is it not something next to miraculous? It is the utmost stretch of human ingenuity, which nothing but the bending the faculties of body and mind to it from the tenderest infancy with incessant, ever anxious application up to manhood can accomplish or make even a slight approach to. Man, thou art a wonderful animal, and thy ways past finding out! Thou canst do strange things, but thou turnest them to little account!—To conceive of this effort of extraordinary dexterity distracts the imagination and makes admiration breathless. Yet it costs nothing to the performer, any more than if it were a mere mechanical deception with which he had nothing to do but to watch and laugh at the astonishment of the spectators. A single error of a hair's-breadth, of the smallest conceivable portion of time, would be fatal: the precision of the movements must be like a mathematical truth, their rapidity is like lightning. To catch four balls in succession in less than a second of time, and deliver them back so as to return with seeming consciousness to the hand again; to make them revolve round him at certain intervals, like the planets in their spheres; to make them chase one another like sparkles of fire, or shoot up like flowers or meteors; to throw them behind his back and twine them round his neck like ribbons or like serpents; to do what appears an impossibility, and to do it with all the ease, the grace, the carelessness imaginable; to laugh at, to play with the glittering mockeries; to follow them with his eye as if he could fascinate them with its lambent fire, or as if he had only to see that they kept time with the music on the stage,—there is something in all this which he who does not admire may be quite sure he never really admired anything in the whole course of his life. It is skill surmounting difficulty, and beauty triumphing over skill. It seems as if the difficulty once mastered naturally resolved itself into ease and grace, and as if to be overcome at all, it must be overcome without an effort. The smallest awkwardness or want of pliancy or self-possession would stop the whole process. It is the work of witchcraft, and yet sport for children. Some of the other feats are quite as curious and wonderful, such as the balancing the artificial tree and shooting a bird from each branch through a quill; though none of them have the elegance or facility of the keeping up of the brass balls. You are in pain for the result, and glad when the experiment is over; they are not accompanied with the same unmixed, unchecked delight as the former; and I would not give much to be merely astonished without being pleased at the same time. As to the swallowing of the sword, the police ought to interfere to prevent it. When I saw the Indian Juggler do the same things before, his feet were bare, and he had large rings on the toes, which kept turning round all the time of the performance, as if they moved of themselves.—The hearing a speech in Parliament drawled or stammered out by the Honourable Member or the Noble Lord; the ringing the changes on their common-places, which any one could repeat after them as well as they, stirs me not a jot, shakes not my good opinion of myself; but the seeing the Indian Jugglers does. It makes me ashamed of myself. I ask what there is that I can do as well as this? Nothing. What have I been doing all my life? Have I been idle, or have I nothing to show for all my labour and pains? Or have I passed my time in pouring words like water into empty sieves, rolling a stone up a hill and then down again, trying to prove an argument in the teeth of facts, and looking for causes in the dark and not finding them? Is there no one thing in which I can challenge competition, that I can bring as an instance of exact perfection in which others cannot find a flaw? The utmost I can pretend to is to write a description of what this fellow can do. I can write a book: so can many others who have not even learned to spell. What abortions are these Essays! What errors, what ill-pieced transitions, what crooked reasons, what lame conclusions! How little is made out, and that little how ill! Yet they are the best I can do. I endeavour to recollect all I have ever observed or thought upon a subject, and to express it as nearly as I can. Instead of writing on four subjects at a time, it is as much as I can manage to keep the thread of one discourse clear and unentangled. I have also time on my hands to correct my opinions, and polish my periods; but the one I cannot, and the other I will not do. I am fond of arguing: yet with a good deal of pains and practice it is often as much as I can do to beat my man; though he may be an indifferent hand. A common fencer would disarm his adversary in the twinkling of an eye, unless he were a professor like himself. A stroke of wit will sometimes produce this effect, but there is no such power or superiority in sense or reasoning. There is no complete mastery of execution to be shown there; and you hardly know the professor from the impudent pretender or the mere clown.[1]

I have always had this feeling of the inefficacy and slow progress of intellectual compared to mechanical excellence, and it has always made me somewhat dissatisfied. It is a great many years since I saw Richer, the famous rope-dancer, perform at Sadler's Wells. He was matchless in his art, and added to his extraordinary skill exquisite ease, and unaffected, natural grace. I was at that time employed in copying a half-length picture of Sir Joshua Reynolds's; and it put me out of conceit with it. How ill this part was made out in the drawing! How heavy, how slovenly this other was painted! I could not help saying to myself, 'If the rope-dancer had performed his task in this manner, leaving so many gaps and botches in his work, he would have broken his neck long ago; I should never have seen that vigorous elasticity of nerve and

[1] The celebrated Peter Pindar (Dr. Wolcot) first discovered and brought out the talents of the late Mr. Opie the painter. He was a poor Cornish boy, and was out at work in the fields when the poet went in search of him. 'Well, my lad, can you go and bring me your very best picture?' The other flew like lightning, and soon came back with what he considered as his masterpiece. The stranger looked at it, and the young artist, after waiting for some time without his giving any opinion, at length exclaimed eagerly, 'Well, what do you think of it?' 'Think of it?' said Wolcot; 'why, I think you ought to be ashamed of it—that you, who might do so well, do no better!' The same answer would have applied to this artist's latest performances, that had been suggested by one of his earliest efforts.

precision of movement!'—Is it, then, so easy an undertaking (comparatively) to dance on a tight-rope? Let any one who thinks so get up and try. There is the thing. It is that which at first we cannot do at all which in the end is done to such perfection. To account for this in some degree, I might observe that mechanical dexterity is confined to doing some one particular thing, which you can repeat as often as you please, in which you know whether you succeed or fail, and where the point of perfection consists in succeeding in a given undertaking.—In mechanical efforts you improve by perpetual practice, and you do so infallibly, because the object to be attained is not a matter of taste or fancy or opinion, but of actual experiment, in which you must either do the thing or not do it. If a man is put to aim at a mark with a bow and arrow, he must hit it or miss it, that 's certain. He cannot deceive himself, and go on shooting wide or falling short, and still fancy that he is making progress. The distinction between right and wrong, between true and false, is here palpable; and he must either correct his aim or persevere in his error with his eyes open, for which there is neither excuse nor temptation. If a man is learning to dance on a rope, if he does not mind what he is about he will break his neck. After that it will be in vain for him to argue that he did not make a false step. His situation is not like that of Goldsmith's pedagogue:—

> In argument they own'd his wondrous skill,
> And e'en though vanquish'd, he could argue still.

Danger is a good teacher, and makes apt scholars. So are disgrace, defeat, exposure to immediate scorn and laughter. There is no opportunity in such cases for self-delusion, no idling time away, no being off your guard (or you must take the consequences)—neither is there any room for humour or caprice or prejudice. If the Indian Juggler were to play tricks in throwing up the three case-knives, which keep their positions like the leaves of a crocus in the air, he would cut his fingers. I can make a very bad antithesis without cutting my fingers. The tact of style is more ambiguous than that of double-edged instruments. If the Juggler were told that by flinging himself under the wheels of the Juggernaut, when the idol issues forth on a gaudy day, he would immediately be transported into Paradise, he might believe it, and nobody could disprove it. So the Brahmins may say what they please on that subject, may build up dogmas and mysteries without end, and not be detected; but their ingenious countryman cannot persuade the frequenters of the Olympic Theatre that he performs a number of astonishing feats without actually giving proofs of what he says.—There is, then, in this sort of manual dexterity, first a gradual aptitude acquired to a given exertion of muscular power, from constant repetition, and in the next place, an exact knowledge how much is still wanting and necessary to be supplied. The obvious test is to increase the effort or nicety of the operation, and still to find it come true. The muscles ply instinctively to the dictates of habit. Certain movements and impressions of the hand and eye, having been repeated together an infinite number of times, are unconsciously but unavoidably cemented into closer and closer union; the limbs require little more than to be put in motion for them to follow a regular track with ease and certainty; so that the mere intention of the will acts mathematically like touching the spring of a machine, and you come with Locksley in *Ivanhoe*, in shooting at a mark, 'to allow for the wind.'

Further, what is meant by perfection in mechanical exercises is the performing certain feats to a uniform nicety, that is, in fact, undertaking no more than you can perform. You task yourself, the limit you fix is optional, and no more than human industry and skill can attain to; but you have no abstract, independent standard of difficulty or excellence (other than the extent of your own powers). Thus he who can keep up four brass balls does this *to perfection*; but he cannot keep up five at the same instant, and would fail every time he attempted it. That is, the mechanical performer undertakes to emulate himself, not to equal another.[1] But the artist undertakes to imitate another, or to do what Nature has done, and this it appears is more difficult, viz. to copy what she has set before us in the face of nature or 'human face divine,' entire and without a blemish, than to keep up four brass balls at the same instant, for the one is done by the power of human skill and industry, and the other never was nor will be. Upon the whole, therefore, I have more respect for Reynolds than I have for Richer; for, happen how it will, there have been more people in the world who could dance on a rope like the one than who could paint like Sir Joshua. The latter was but a bungler in his profession to the other, it is true; but then he had a harder taskmaster to obey, whose will was more wayward and obscure, and whose instructions it was more difficult to practise. You can put a child apprentice to a tumbler or rope-dancer with a comfortable prospect of success, if they are but sound of wind and limb; but you cannot do the same thing in painting. The odds are a million to one. You may make indeed as many Haydons and H——s as you put into that sort of machine, but not one Reynolds amongst them all, with his grace, his grandeur, his blandness of gusto, 'in tones and gestures hit,' unless you could make the man over again. To snatch this grace beyond the reach of art is then the height of art—where fine art begins, and where mechanical skill ends. The soft suffusion of the soul, the speechless breathing eloquence, the looks 'commercing with the skies,' the ever-shifting forms of an eternal principle, that which is seen but for a moment, but dwells in the heart always, and is only seized as it

[1] If two persons play against each other at any game, one of them necessarily fails.

passes by strong and secret sympathy, must be taught by nature and genius, not by rules or study. It is suggested by feeling, not by laborious microscopic inspection; in seeking for it without, we lose the harmonious clue to it within; and in aiming to grasp the substance, we let the very spirit of art evaporate. In a word, the objects of fine art are not the objects of sight but as these last are the objects of taste and imagination, that is, as they appeal to the sense of beauty, of pleasure, and of power in the human breast, and are explained by that finer sense, and revealed in their inner structure to the eye in return. Nature is also a language. Objects, like words, have a meaning; and the true artist is the interpreter of this language, which he can only do by knowing its application to a thousand other objects in a thousand other situations. Thus the eye is too blind a guide of itself to distinguish between the warm or cold tone of a deep-blue sky; but another sense acts as a monitor to it and does not err. The colour of the leaves in autumn would be nothing without the feeling that accompanies it; but it is that feeling that stamps them on the canvas, faded, seared, blighted, shrinking from the winter's flaw, and makes the sight as true as touch.—

> And visions, as poetic eyes avow,
> Cling to each leaf and hang on every bough.

The more ethereal, evanescent, more refined and sublime part of art is the seeing nature through the medium of sentiment and passion, as each object is a symbol of the affections and a link in the chain of our endless being. But the unravelling this mysterious web of thought and feeling is alone in the Muse's gift, namely, in the power of that trembling sensibility which is awake to every change and every modification of its ever-varying impressions, that

> Thrills in each nerve, and lives along the line.

This power is indifferently called genius, imagination, feeling, taste; but the manner in which it acts upon the mind can neither be defined by abstract rules, as is the case in science, nor verified by continual, unvarying experiments, as is the case in mechanical performances. The mechanical excellence of the Dutch painters in colouring and handling is that which comes the nearest in fine art to the perfection of certain manual exhibitions of skill. The truth of the effect and the facility with which it is produced are equally admirable. Up to a certain point everything is faultless. The hand and eye have done their part. There is only a want of taste and genius. It is after we enter upon that enchanted ground that the human mind begins to droop and flag as in a strange road, or in a thick mist, benighted and making little way with many attempts and many failures, and that the best of us only escape with half a triumph. The undefined and the imaginary are the regions that we must pass like Satan, difficult and doubtful, 'half flying, half on foot.' The object in sense is a positive thing, and execution comes with practice.

Cleverness is a certain *knack* or aptitude at doing certain things, which depend more on a particular adroitness and off-hand readiness than on force or perseverance, such as making puns, making epigrams, making extempore verses, mimicking the company, mimicking a style, etc. Cleverness is either liveliness and smartness, or something answering to *sleight of hand*, like letting a glass fall sideways off a table, or else a trick, like knowing the secret spring of a watch. Accomplishments are certain external graces, which are to be learned from others, and which are easily displayed to the admiration of the beholder, viz. dancing, riding, fencing, music, and so on. These ornamental acquirements are only proper to those who are at ease in mind and fortune. I know an individual who, if he had been born to an estate of five thousand a year, would have been the most accomplished gentleman of the age. He would have been the delight and envy of the circle in which he moved—

would have graced by his manners the liberality flowing from the openness of his heart, would have laughed with the women, have argued with the men, have said good things and written agreeable ones, have taken a hand at piquet or the lead at the harpsichord, and have set and sung his own verses—*nugæ canoræ*—with tenderness and spirit; a Rochester without the vice, a modern Surrey. As it is, all these capabilities of excellence stand in his way. He is too versatile for a professional man, not dull enough for a political drudge, too gay to be happy, too thoughtless to be rich. He wants the enthusiasm of the poet, the severity of the prose-writer, and the application of the man of business. Talent is the capacity of doing anything that depends on application and industry, such as writing a criticism, making a speech, studying the law. Talent differs from genius as voluntary differs from involuntary power. Ingenuity is genius in trifles; greatness is genius in undertakings of much pith and moment. A clever or ingenious man is one who can do anything well, whether it is worth doing or not; a great man is one who can do that which when done is of the highest importance. Themistocles said he could not play on the flute, but that he could make of a small city a great one. This gives one a pretty good idea of the distinction in question.

Greatness is great power, producing great effects. It is not enough that a man has great power in himself; he must show it to all the world in a way that cannot be hid or gainsaid. He must fill up a certain idea in the public mind. I have no other notion of greatness than this twofold definition, great results springing from great inherent energy. The great in visible objects has relation to that which extends over space; the great in mental ones has to do with space and time. No man is truly great who is great only in his lifetime. The test of greatness is the page of history. Nothing can be said to be great that has a distinct limit, or that borders on something evidently greater than itself. Besides, what is short-lived and pampered into mere notoriety is of a gross and vulgar quality in itself. A Lord Mayor is hardly a great man. A city orator or patriot of the day only show, by reaching the height of their wishes, the distance they are at from any true ambition. Popularity is neither fame nor greatness. A king (as such) is not a great man. He has great power, but it is not his own. He merely wields the lever of the state, which a child, an idiot, or a madman can do. It is the office, not the man we gaze at. Any one else in the same situation would be just as much an object of abject curiosity. We laugh at the country girl who having seen a king expressed her disappointment by saying, 'Why, he is only a man!' Yet, knowing this, we run to see a king as if he was something more than a man.—To display the greatest powers, unless they are applied to great purposes, makes nothing for the character of greatness. To throw a barleycorn through the eye of a needle, to multiply nine figures by nine in the memory, argues definite dexterity of body and capacity of mind, but nothing comes of either. There is a surprising power at work, but the effects are not proportionate, or such as take hold of the imagination. To impress the idea of power on others, they must be made in some way to feel it. It must be communicated to their understandings in the shape of an increase of knowledge, or it must subdue and overawe them by subjecting their wills. Admiration to be solid and lasting must be founded on proofs from which we have no means of escaping; it is neither a slight nor a voluntary gift. A mathematician who solves a profound problem, a poet who creates an image of beauty in the mind that was not there before, imparts knowledge and power to others, in which his greatness and his fame consists, and on which it reposes. Jedediah Buxton will be forgotten; but Napier's bones will live. Lawgivers, philosophers, founders of religion, conquerors and heroes, inventors and great geniuses in arts and sciences, are great men, for they are great public benefactors, or formidable scourges to mankind. Among ourselves, Shakespeare, Newton, Bacon, Milton, Cromwell, were great men, for they showed great power by acts and thoughts, which have not yet been consigned to oblivion. They must needs be men of lofty stature, whose shadows lengthen out to remote posterity. A great farce-writer may be a great man; for Molière was but a great farce-writer. In my mind, the author of *Don Quixote* was a great man. So have there been many others. A great chess-player is not a great man, for he leaves the world as he found it. No act terminating in itself constitutes greatness. This will apply to all displays of power or trials of skill which are confined to the momentary, individual effort, and construct no permanent image or trophy of themselves without them. Is not an actor then a great man, because 'he dies and leaves the world no copy'? I must make an exception for Mrs. Siddons, or else give up my definition of greatness for her sake. A man at the top of his profession is not therefore a great man. He is great in his way, but that is all, unless he shows the marks of a great moving intellect, so that we trace the master-mind, and can sympathise with the springs that urge him on. The rest is but a craft or *mystery*. John Hunter was a great man—*that* any one might see without the smallest skill in surgery. His style and manner showed the man. He would set about cutting up the carcass of a whale with the same greatness of gusto that Michael Angelo would have hewn a block of marble. Lord Nelson was a great naval commander; but for myself, I have not much opinion of a seafaring life. Sir Humphry Davy is a great chemist, but I am not sure that he is a great man. I am not a bit the wiser for any of his discoveries, nor I never met with any one that was. But it is in the nature of greatness to propagate an idea of itself, as wave impels wave, circle without circle. It is a contradiction in terms for a coxcomb to be a great man. A really great man has always an idea of something greater than himself. I have observed that certain sectaries and polemical writers have no higher compliment to pay their most shining lights than to say that, 'Such a one was a considerable man in his day.' Some new elucidation of a text sets aside the authority of the old interpretation, and a 'great scholar's memory outlives him half a century,' at the utmost. A rich man is not a great man, except to his dependants and his steward. A lord is a great man in the idea we have of his ancestry, and probably of himself, if we know nothing of him but his title. I have heard a story of two bishops, one of whom said (speaking of St. Peter's at Rome) that when he first entered it, he was rather awe-struck, but that as he walked up it, his mind seemed to swell and dilate with it, and at last to fill the whole building: the other said that as he saw more of it, he appeared to himself to grow less and less every step he took, and in the end to dwindle into nothing. This was in some respects a striking picture of a great and little mind; for greatness sympathises with greatness, and littleness shrinks into itself. The one might have become a Wolsey; the other was only fit to become a Mendicant Friar—or there might have been court reasons for making him a bishop. The French have to me a character of littleness in all about them; but they have produced three great men that belong to every country, Molière, Rabelais, and Montaigne.

To return from this digression, and conclude the Essay. A singular instance of manual dexterity was shown in the person of the late John Cavanagh, whom I have several times seen. His death was celebrated at the time in an article in the *Examiner* newspaper (Feb. 7, 1819), written apparently between jest and earnest; but as it is *pat* to our purpose, and falls in with my own way of considering such subjects, I shall here take leave to quote it:—

'Died at his house in Burbage Street, St. Giles's, John Cavanagh, the famous hand fives-player. When a person dies who does any one thing better than any one else in the world, which so many others are trying to do well, it leaves a gap in society. It is not likely that any one will now see the game of fives played in its perfection for many years to come—for Cavanagh is dead, and has not left his peer behind him. It may be said that there are things of more importance than striking a ball against a wall—there are things, indeed, that make more noise and do as little good, such as making war and peace, making speeches and answering them, making verses and blotting them, making money and throwing it away. But the game of fives is what no one despises who has ever played at it. It is the finest exercise for the body, and the best relaxation for the mind. The Roman poet said that "Care mounted behind the horseman and stuck to his skirts." But this remark would not have applied to the fives-player. He who takes to playing at fives is twice young. He feels neither the past nor future "in the instant." Debts, taxes, "domestic treason, foreign levy, nothing can touch him further." He has no other wish, no other thought, from the moment the game begins, but that of striking the ball, of placing it, of *making* it! This Cavanagh was sure to do. Whenever he touched the ball there was an end of the chase. His eye was certain, his hand fatal, his presence of mind complete. He could do what he pleased, and he always knew exactly what to do. He saw the whole game, and played it; took instant advantage of his adversary's weakness, and recovered balls, as if by a miracle and from sudden thought, that every one gave for lost. He had equal power and skill, quickness and judgment. He could either outwit his antagonist by finesse, or beat him by main strength. Sometimes, when he seemed preparing to send the ball with the full swing of his arm, he would by a slight turn of his wrist drop it within an inch of the line. In general, the ball came from his hand, as if from a racket, in a straight, horizontal line; so that it was in vain to attempt to overtake or stop it. As it was said of a great orator that he never was at a loss for a word, and for the properest word, so Cavanagh always could tell the degree of force necessary to be given to a ball, and the precise direction in which it should be sent. He did his work with the greatest ease; never took more pains than was necessary; and while others were fagging themselves to death, was as cool and collected as if he had just entered the court. His style of play was as remarkable as his power of execution. He had no affectation, no trifling. He did not throw away the game to show off an attitude or try an experiment. He was a fine, sensible, manly player, who did what he could, but that was more than any one else could even affect to do. His blows were not undecided and ineffectual—lumbering like Mr. Wordsworth's epic poetry, nor wavering like Mr. Coleridge's lyric prose, nor short of the mark like Mr. Brougham's speeches, nor wide of it like Mr. Canning's wit, nor foul like the *Quarterly*, nor *let* balls like the *Edinburgh Review*. Cobbett and Junius together would have made a Cavanagh. He was the best *up-hill* player in the world; even when his adversary was fourteen, he would play on the same or better, and as he never flung away the game through carelessness and conceit, he never gave it up through laziness or want of heart. The only peculiarity of his play was that he never *volleyed*, but let the balls hop; but if they rose an inch from the ground he never missed having them. There was not only nobody equal, but nobody second to him. It is supposed that he could give any other player half the game, or beat them with his left hand. His service was tremendous. He once played Woodward and Meredith together (two of the best players in England) in the Fives-court, St. Martin's Street, and made seven-and-twenty aces following by services alone—a thing unheard of. He another time played Peru, who was considered a first-rate fives-player, a match of the best out of five games, and in the three first games, which of course decided the match, Peru got only one ace. Cavanagh was an Irishman by birth, and a house-painter by profession. He had once laid aside his working-dress, and walked up, in his smartest clothes, to the Rosemary Branch to have an afternoon's pleasure. A person accosted him, and asked him if he would have a game. So they agreed to play for half-a-crown a game and a bottle of cider. The first game began—it was seven, eight, ten, thirteen, fourteen, all. Cavanagh won it. The next was the same. They played on, and each game was hardly contested. "There," said the unconscious fives-player, "there was a stroke that Cavanagh could not take: I never played better in my life, and yet I can't win a game. I don't know how it is!" However, they played on, Cavanagh winning every game, and the bystanders drinking the cider and laughing all the time. In the twelfth game, when Cavanagh was only four, and the stranger thirteen, a person came in and said, "What! are you here, Cavanagh?" The words were no sooner pronounced than the astonished player let the ball drop from his hand, and saying, "What! have I been breaking my heart all this time to beat Cavanagh?" refused to make another effort. "And yet, I give you my word," said Cavanagh, telling the story with some triumph, "I played all the while with my clenched fist." He used frequently to play matches at Copenhagen House for wagers and dinners. The wall against which they play is the same that supports the kitchen-chimney, and when the wall resounded louder than usual, the cooks exclaimed, "Those are the Irishman's balls," and the joints trembled on the spit! Goldsmith consoled himself that there were places where he too was admired: and Cavanagh was the admiration of all the fives-courts where he ever played. Mr. Powell, when he played matches in the court in St. Martin's Street, used to fill his gallery at half-a-crown a head with amateurs and admirers of talent in whatever department it is shown. He could not have shown himself in any ground in England but he would have been immediately surrounded with inquisitive gazers, trying to find out in what part of his frame his unrivalled skill lay, as politicians wonder to see the balance of Europe suspended in Lord Castlereagh's face, and admire the trophies of the British Navy lurking under Mr. Croker's hanging brow. Now Cavanagh was as good-looking a man as the Noble Lord, and much better looking than the Right Hon. Secretary. He had a clear, open countenance, and did not look sideways or down, like Mr. Murray the bookseller. He was a young fellow of sense, humour, and courage. He once had a quarrel with a waterman at Hungerford Stairs, and, they say, served him out in great style. In a word, there are hundreds at this day who cannot mention his name without admiration, as the best fives-player that perhaps ever lived (the greatest excellence of which they have any notion); and the noisy shout of the ring happily stood him in stead of the unheard voice of posterity!—The only person who seems to have excelled as much in another way as Cavanagh did in his was the late John Davies, the racket-player. It was remarked of him that he did not seem to follow the ball, but the ball seemed to follow him. Give him a foot of wall, and he was sure to make the ball. The four best racket-players of that day were Jack Spines, Jem Harding, Armitage, and Church. Davies could give any one of these two hands a time, that is, half the game, and each of these, at their best, could give the best player now in London the same odds. Such are the gradations in all exertions of human skill and art. He once played four capital players together, and beat them. He was also a first-rate tennis-player, and an excellent fives-player. In the Fleet or King's Bench he would have stood against Powell, who was reckoned the best open-ground player of his time. This last-mentioned player is at present the keeper of the Fives-court, and we might recommend to him for a motto over his door,

"Who enters here, forgets himself, his country, and his friends." And the best of it is, that by the calculation of the odds, none of the three are worth remembering! Cavanagh died from the bursting of a blood-vessel, which prevented him from playing for the last two or three years. This, he was often heard to say, he thought hard upon him. He was fast recovering, however, when he was suddenly carried off, to the regret of all who knew him. As Mr. Peel made it a qualification of the present Speaker, Mr. Manners Sutton, that he was an excellent moral character, so Jack Cavanagh was a zealous Catholic, and could not be persuaded to eat meat on a Friday, the day on which he died. We have paid this willing tribute to his memory.

> Let no rude hand deface it,
> And his forlorn "*Hic Jacet.*"'

ON A LANDSCAPE OF NICOLAS POUSSIN

> And blind Orion hungry for the morn.

ORION, the subject of this landscape, was the classical Nimrod; and is called by Homer, 'a hunter of shadows, himself a shade.' He was the son of Neptune; and having lost an eye in some affray between the Gods and men, was told that if he would go to meet the rising sun he would recover his sight. He is represented setting out on his journey, with men on his shoulders to guide him, a bow in his hand, and Diana in the clouds greeting him. He stalks along, a giant upon earth, and reels and falters in his gait, as if just awakened out of sleep, or uncertain of his way;—you see his blindness, though his back is turned. Mists rise around him, and veil the sides of the green forests; earth is dank and fresh with dews, the 'grey dawn and the Pleiades before him dance,' and in the distance are seen the blue hills and sullen ocean. Nothing was ever more finely conceived or done. It breathes the spirit of the morning; its moisture, its repose, its obscurity, waiting the miracle of light to kindle it into smiles; the whole is, like the principal figure in it, 'a forerunner of the dawn.' The same atmosphere tinges and imbues every object, the same dull light 'shadowy sets off' the face of nature: one feeling of vastness, of strangeness, and of primeval forms pervades the painter's canvas, and we are thrown back upon the first integrity of things. This great and learned man might be said to see nature through the glass of time; he alone has a right to be considered as the painter of classical antiquity. Sir Joshua has done him justice in this respect. He could give to the scenery of his heroic fables that unimpaired look of original nature, full, solid, large, luxuriant, teeming with life and power; or deck it with all the pomp of art, with temples and towers, and mythologic groves. His pictures 'denote a foregone conclusion.' He applies Nature to his purposes, works out her images according to the standard of his thoughts, embodies high fictions; and the first conception being given, all the rest seems to grow out of and be assimilated to it, by the unfailing process of a studious imagination. Like his own Orion, he overlooks the surrounding scene, appears to 'take up the isles as a very little thing, and to lay the earth in a balance.' With a laborious and mighty grasp, he puts Nature into the mould of the ideal and antique; and was among painters (more than any one else) what Milton was among poets. There is in both something of the same pedantry, the same stiffness, the same elevation, the same grandeur, the same mixture of art and nature, the same richness of borrowed materials, the same unity of character. Neither the poet nor the painter lowered the subjects they treated, but filled up the outline in the fancy, and added strength and reality to it; and thus not only satisfied, but surpassed the expectations of the spectator and the reader. This is held for the triumph and the perfection of works of art. To give us nature, such as we see it, is well and deserving of praise; to give us nature, such as we have never seen, but have often wished to see it, is better, and deserving of higher praise. He who can show the world in its first naked glory, with the hues of fancy spread over it, or in its high and palmy state, with the gravity of history stamped on the proud monuments of vanished empire, —who, by his 'so potent art,' can recall time past, transport us to distant places, and join the regions of imagination (a new conquest) to those of reality,—who shows us not only what Nature is, but what she has been, and is capable of,—he who does this, and does it with simplicity, with truth, and grandeur, is lord of Nature and her powers; and his mind is universal, and his art the master-art!

There is nothing in this 'more than natural,' if criticism could be persuaded to think so. The historic painter does not neglect or contravene Nature, but follows her more closely up into her fantastic heights or hidden recesses. He demonstrates what she would be in conceivable circumstances and under implied conditions. He 'gives to airy nothing a local habitation,' not 'a name.' At his touch, words start up into images, thoughts become things. He clothes a dream, a phantom, with form and colour, and the wholesome attributes of reality. *His* art is a second nature; not a different one. There are those, indeed, who think that not to copy nature is the rule for attaining perfection. Because they cannot paint the objects which they have seen, they fancy themselves qualified to paint the ideas which they have not seen. But it is possible to fail in this latter and more difficult style of imitation, as well as in the former humbler one. The detection, it is true, is not so easy, because the objects are not so nigh at hand to compare, and therefore there is more room both for false pretension and for self-deceit. They take an epic motto or subject, and conclude that the spirit is implied as a thing of course. They paint inferior portraits, maudlin lifeless faces, without ordinary expression, or one look, feature, or particle of nature in them, and think that this is to rise to the truth of history. They vulgarise and degrade whatever is interesting or sacred to the mind, and suppose that they thus add to the dignity of their profession. They represent a face that seems as if no thought or feeling of any kind had ever passed through it, and would have you believe that this is the very sublime of expression, such as it would appear in heroes, or demigods of old, when rapture or agony was raised to its height. They show you a landscape that looks as if the sun never shone upon it, and tell you that it is not modern—that so earth looked when Titan first kissed it with his rays. This is not the true *ideal*. It is not to fill the moulds of the imagination, but to deface and injure them; it is not to come up to, but to fall short of the poorest conception in the public mind. Such pictures should not be hung in the same room with that of Orion.[1]

[1] Everything tends to show the manner in which a great artist is formed. If any person could claim an exemption from the careful imitation of individual objects, it was Nicolas Poussin. He studied the antique, but he also studied nature. 'I have often admired,' says Vignuel de Marville, who knew him at a late period of his life, 'the love he had for his art. Old as he was, I frequently saw him among the ruins of ancient Rome, out in the Campagna, or along the banks of the Tyber, sketching a scene that had pleased him; and I often met him with his handkerchief full of stones, moss, or flowers, which he carried home, that he might copy them exactly from nature. One day I asked him how he had attained to such a degree of perfection, as to have gained so high a rank among the great painters of Italy? He answered, "I HAVE NEGLECTED NOTHING." '—*See his Life lately published*. It appears from this account that he had not fallen into a recent error, that Nature puts the man of genius out. As a contrast to the foregoing description, I might mention, that I remember an old gentleman once asking Mr. West in the British Gallery if he had ever been at Athens? To which the President made answer, No; nor did he feel any great desire to go; for that he

Poussin was, of all painters, the most poetical. He was the painter of ideas. No one ever told a story half so well, nor so well knew what was capable of being told by the pencil. He seized on, and struck off with grace and precision, just that point of view which would be likely to catch the reader's fancy. There is a significance, a consciousness in whatever he does (sometimes a vice, but oftener a virtue) beyond any other painter. His Giants sitting on the tops of craggy mountains, as huge themselves, and playing idly on their Pan's-pipes, seem to have been seated there these three thousand years, and to know the beginning and the end of their own story. An infant Bacchus or Jupiter is big with his future destiny. Even inanimate and dumb things speak a language of their own. His snakes, the messengers of fate, are inspired with human intellect. His trees grow and expand their leaves in the air, glad of the rain, proud of the sun, awake to the winds of heaven. In his Plague of Athens, the very buildings seem stiff with horror. His picture of the Deluge is, perhaps, the finest historical landscape in the world. You see a waste of waters, wide, interminable; the sun is labouring, wan and weary, up the sky; the clouds, dull and leaden, lie like a load upon the eye, and heaven and earth seem commingling into one confused mass! His human figures are sometimes 'o'er-informed' with this kind of feeling. Their actions have too much gesticulation, and the set expression of the features borders too much on the mechanical and caricatured style. In this respect they form a contrast to Raphael's, whose figures never appear to be sitting for their pictures, or to be con-

thought he had as good an idea of the place from the Catalogue as he could get by living there for any number of years. What would he have said, if any one had told him, he could get as good an idea of the subject of one of his great works from reading the Catalogue of it, as from seeing the picture itself? Yet the answer was characteristic of the genius of the painter.

scious of a spectator, or to have come from the painter's hand. In Nicolas Poussin, on the contrary, everything seems to have a distinct understanding with the artist; 'the very stones prate of their whereabout'; each object has its part and place assigned, and is in a sort of compact with the rest of the picture. It is this conscious keeping, and, as it were, *internal* design, that gives their peculiar character to the works of this artist. There was a picture of Aurora in the British Gallery a year or two ago. It was a suffusion of golden light. The Goddess wore her saffron-coloured robes, and appeared just risen from the gloomy bed of old Tithonus. Her very steeds, milk-white, were tinged with the yellow dawn. It was a personification of the morning. Poussin succeeded better in classic than in sacred subjects. The latter are comparatively heavy, forced, full of violent contrasts of colour, of red, blue, and black, and without the true prophetic inspiration of the characters. But in his pagan allegories and fables he was quite at home. The native gravity and native levity of the Frenchman were combined with Italian scenery and an antique gusto, and gave even to his colouring an air of learned indifference. He wants, in one respect, grace, form, expression; but he has everywhere sense and meaning, perfect costume and propriety. His personages always belong to the class and time represented, and are strictly versed in the business in hand. His grotesque compositions in particular, his Nymphs and Fauns, are superior (at least, as far as style is concerned) even to those of Rubens. They are taken more immediately out of fabulous history. Rubens' Satyrs and Bacchantes have a more jovial and voluptuous aspect, are more drunk with pleasure, more full of animal spirits and riotous impulses; they laugh and bound along—

Leaping like wanton kids in pleasant spring:

but those of Poussin have more of the intellectual

part of the character, and seem vicious on reflection, and of set purpose. Rubens' are noble specimens of a class; Poussin's are allegorical abstractions of the same class, with bodies less pampered, but with minds more secretly depraved. The Bacchanalian groups of the Flemish painter were, however, his masterpieces in composition. Witness those prodigies of colour, character, and expression at Blenheim. In the more chaste and refined delineation of classic fable, Poussin was without a rival. Rubens, who was a match for him in the wild and picturesque, could not pretend to vie with the elegance and purity of thought in his picture of Apollo giving a poet a cup of water to drink, nor with the gracefulness of design in the figure of a nymph squeezing the juice of a bunch of grapes from her fingers (a rosy wine-press) which falls into the mouth of a chubby infant below. But, above all, who shall celebrate, in terms of fit praise, his picture of the shepherds in the Vale of Tempe going out in a fine morning of the spring, and coming to a tomb with this inscription: ET EGO IN ARCADIA VIXI! The eager curiosity of some, the expression of others who start back with fear and surprise, the clear breeze playing with the branches of the shadowing trees, 'the valleys low, where the mild zephyrs use,' the distant, uninterrupted, sunny prospect speak (and for ever will speak on) of ages past to ages yet to come! [1]

Pictures are a set of chosen images, a stream of pleasant thoughts passing through the mind. It is a luxury to have the walls of our rooms hung round with them, and no less so to have such a gallery in the mind, to con over the relics of ancient art bound

[1] Poussin has repeated this subject more than once, and appears to have revelled in its witcheries. I have before alluded to it, and may again. It is hard that we should not be allowed to dwell as often as we please on what delights us, when things that are disagreeable recur so often against our will.

up 'within the book and volume of the brain, unmixed (if it were possible) with baser matter!' A life passed among pictures, in the study and the love of art, is a happy noiseless dream: or rather, it is to dream and to be awake at the same time; for it has all 'the sober certainty of waking bliss,' with the romantic voluptuousness of a visionary and abstracted being. They are the bright consummate essences of things, and 'he who knows of these delights to taste and interpose them oft, is not unwise!'—The Orion, which I have here taken occasion to descant upon, is one of a collection of excellent pictures, as this collection is itself one of a series from the old masters, which have for some years back embrowned the walls of the British Gallery, and enriched the public eye. What hues (those of nature mellowed by time) breathe around as we enter! What forms are there, woven into the memory! What looks, which only the answering looks of the spectator can express! What intellectual stores have been yearly poured forth from the shrine of ancient art! The works are various, but the names the same—heaps of Rembrandts frowning from the darkened walls, Rubens' glad gorgeous groups, Titians more rich and rare, Claudes always exquisite, sometimes beyond compare, Guido's endless cloying sweetness, the learning of Poussin and the Caracci and Raphael's princely magnificence crowning all. We read certain letters and syllables in the Catalogue, and at the well-known magic sound a miracle of skill and beauty starts to view. One might think that one year's prodigal display of such perfection would exhaust the labours of one man's life; but the next year, and the next to that, we find another harvest reaped and gathered in to the great garner of art, by the same immortal hands—

> Old Genius the porter of them was;
> He letteth in, he letteth out to wend.—

Their works seem endless as their reputation—to be

many as they are complete—to multiply with the desire of the mind to see more and more of them; as if there were a living power in the breath of Fame, and in the very names of the great heirs of glory 'there were propagation too'! It is something to have a collection of this sort to count upon once a year; to have one last, lingering look yet to come. Pictures are scattered like stray gifts through the world; and while they remain, earth has yet a little gilding left, not quite rubbed off, dishonoured, and defaced. There are plenty of standard works still to be found in this country, in the collections at Blenheim, at Burleigh, and in those belonging to Mr. Angerstein, Lord Grosvenor, the Marquis of Stafford, and others, to keep up this treat to the lovers of art for many years; and it is the more desirable to reserve a privileged sanctuary of this sort, where the eye may dote, and the heart take its fill of such pictures as Poussin's Orion, since the Louvre is stripped of its triumphant spoils, and since he who collected it, and wore it as a rich jewel in his Iron Crown, the hunter of greatness and of glory, is himself a shade!

ON GOING A JOURNEY

One of the pleasantest things in the world is going a journey; but I like to go by myself. I can enjoy society in a room; but out of doors, nature is company enough for me. I am then never less alone than when alone.

> The fields his study, nature was his book.

I cannot see the wit of walking and talking at the same time. When I am in the country I wish to vegetate like the country. I am not for criticising hedgerows and black cattle. I go out of town in order to forget the town and all that is in it. There are those who for this purpose go to watering-places, and carry the metropolis with them. I like more elbow-room and fewer encumbrances, I like solitude, when I give myself up to it, for the sake of solitude; nor do I ask for

> a friend in my retreat,
> Whom I may whisper solitude is sweet.

The soul of a journey is liberty, perfect liberty, to think, feel, do just as one pleases. We go a journey chiefly to be free of all impediments and of all inconveniences; to leave ourselves behind, much more to get rid of others. It is because I want a little breathing-space to muse on indifferent matters, where Contemplation

> May plume her feathers and let grow her wings,
> That in the various bustle of resort
> Were all too ruffled, and sometimes impair'd,

that I absent myself from the town for a while, without feeling at a loss the moment I am left by myself. Instead of a friend in a post-chaise or in a Tilbury, to exchange good things with, and vary the same stale topics over again, for once let me have a truce with impertinence. Give me the clear blue sky over my head, and the green turf beneath my feet, a winding road before me, and a three hours' march to dinner—and then to thinking! It is hard if I cannot start some game on these lone heaths. I laugh, I run, I leap, I sing for joy. From the point of yonder rolling cloud I plunge into my past being, and revel there, as the sun-burnt Indian plunges headlong into the wave that wafts him to his native shore. Then long-forgotten things, like 'sunken wrack and sumless treasuries,' burst upon my eager sight, and I begin to feel, think, and be myself again. Instead of an awkward silence, broken by attempts at wit or dull commonplaces, mine is that undisturbed silence of the heart which alone is perfect eloquence. No one likes puns, alliterations, antitheses, argument, and analysis better than I do; but I sometimes had rather be without them. 'Leave, oh, leave me to my repose!' I have just now other business in hand, which would seem idle to you, but is with me 'very stuff o' the conscience.' Is not this wild rose sweet without a comment? Does not this daisy leap to my heart set in its coat of emerald? Yet if I were to explain to you the circumstance that has so endeared it to me, you would only smile. Had I not better then keep it to myself, and let it serve me to brood over, from here to yonder craggy point, and from thence onward to the far-distant horizon? I should be but bad company all that way, and therefore prefer being alone. I have heard it said that you may, when the moody fit comes on, walk or ride on by yourself, and indulge your reveries. But this looks like a breach of manners, a neglect of others, and you are thinking all the time that you ought to rejoin your party. 'Out upon such half-faced fellowship,' say I. I like to be either entirely to myself, or entirely at the disposal of others; to talk or be silent, to walk or sit still, to be sociable or solitary. I was pleased with an observation of Mr. Cobbett's, that 'he thought it a bad French custom to drink our wine with our meals, and that an Englishman ought to do only one thing at a time.' So I cannot talk and think, or indulge in melancholy musing and lively conversation by fits and starts. 'Let me have a companion of my way,' says Sterne, 'were it but to remark how the shadows lengthen as the sun declines.' It is beautifully said; but, in my opinion, this continual comparing of notes interferes with the involuntary impression of things upon the mind, and hurts the sentiment. If you only hint what you feel in a kind of dumb show, it is insipid: if you have to explain it, it is making a toil of a pleasure. You cannot read the book of nature without being perpetually put to the trouble of translating it for the benefit of others. I am for the synthetical method on a journey in preference to the analytical. I am content to lay in a stock of ideas then, and to examine and anatomise them afterwards. I want to see my vague notions float like the down of the thistle before the breeze, and not to have them entangled in the briars and thorns of controversy. For once, I like to have it all my own way; and this is impossible unless you are alone, or in such company as I do not covet. I have no objection to argue a point with any one for twenty miles of measured road, but not for pleasure. If you remark the scent of a bean-field crossing the road, perhaps your fellow-traveller has no smell. If you point to a distant object, perhaps he is short-sighted, and has to take out his glass to look at it. There is a feeling in the air, a tone in the colour of a cloud, which hits your fancy, but the effect of which you are unable to account for. There is then no sympathy, but an uneasy craving after it, and a dissatisfaction which pursues you on the way, and in the end probably produces ill-humour. Now I never quarrel with myself, and take all my own conclusions for granted till I find it necessary to defend them against objections. It is not merely that you may not be of accord on the objects and circumstances that present themselves before you—these may recall a number of objects, and lead to associations too delicate and refined to be possibly communicated to others. Yet these I love to cherish, and sometimes still fondly clutch them, when I can escape from the throng to do so. To give way to our feelings before company seems extravagance or affectation; and, on the other hand, to have to unravel this mystery of our being at every turn, and to make others take an equal interest in it (otherwise the end is not answered), is a task to which few are competent. We must 'give it an understanding, but no tongue.' My old friend Coleridge, however, could do both. He could go on in the most delightful explanatory way over hill and dale, a summer's day, and convert a landscape into a didactic poem or a Pindaric ode. 'He talked far above singing.' If I could so clothe my ideas in sounding and flowing words, I might perhaps wish to have some one with me to admire the swelling theme; or I could be more content, were it possible for me still to hear his echoing voice in the woods of All-Foxden.[1] They had 'that fine madness in them which our first poets had'; and if they could have been caught by some rare instrument, would have breathed such strains as the following:

Here be woods as green
As any, air likewise as fresh and sweet
As when smooth Zephyrus plays on the fleet
Face of the curled stream, with flow'rs as many
As the young spring gives, and as choice as any;
Here be all new delights, cool streams and wells,
Arbours o'ergrown with woodbines, caves and dells;
Choose where thou wilt, whilst I sit by and sing,
Or gather rushes to make many a ring
For thy long fingers; tell thee tales of love,
How the pale Phœbe, hunting in a grove,
First saw the boy Endymion, from whose eyes
She took eternal fire that never dies;
How she convey'd him softly in a sleep,
His temples bound with poppy, to the steep
Head of old Latmos, where she stoops each night,
Gilding the mountain with her brother's light,
To kiss her sweetest.[2]

Had I words and images at command like these, I would attempt to wake the thoughts that lie slumbering on golden ridges in the evening clouds: but at the sight of nature my fancy, poor as it is, droops and closes up its leaves, like flowers at sunset. I can make nothing out on the spot: I must have time to collect myself.

In general, a good thing spoils out-of-door prospects: it should be reserved for Table-talk. Lamb is for this reason, I take it, the worst company in the world out

[1] Near Nether-Stowey, Somersetshire, where the author of this Essay visited Coleridge in 1798. He was there again in 1803.

[2] Fletcher's 'Faithful Shepherdess,' i 3 (Dyce's *Beaumont and Fletcher*, ii. 38, 39).

of doors; because he is the best within. I grant there is one subject on which it is pleasant to talk on a journey, and that is, what one shall have for supper when we get to our inn at night. The open air improves this sort of conversation or friendly altercation, by setting a keener edge on appetite. Every mile of the road heightens the flavour of the viands we expect at the end of it. How fine it is to enter some old town, walled and turreted, just at approach of nightfall, or to come to some straggling village, with the lights streaming through the surrounding gloom; and then, after inquiring for the best entertainment that the place affords, to 'take one's ease at one's inn!' These eventful moments in our lives' history are too precious, too full of solid, heartfelt happiness to be frittered and dribbled away in imperfect sympathy. I would have them all to myself, and drain them to the last drop: they will do to talk of or to write about afterwards. What a delicate speculation it is, after drinking whole goblets of tea—

The cups that cheer, but not inebriate—

and letting the fumes ascend into the brain, to sit considering what we shall have for supper—eggs and a rasher, a rabbit smothered in onions, or an excellent veal cutlet! Sancho in such a situation once fixed on cow-heel; and his choice, though he could not help it, is not to be disparaged. Then, in the intervals of pictured scenery and Shandean contemplation, to catch the preparation and the stir in the kitchen [getting ready for the gentleman in the parlour]. *Procul, O procul este profani!* These hours are sacred to silence and to musing, to be treasured up in the memory, and to feed the source of smiling thoughts hereafter. I would not waste them in idle talk; or if I must have the integrity of fancy broken in upon, I would rather it were by a stranger than a friend. A stranger takes his hue and character from the time and place; he is a part of the furniture and costume of an inn. If he is a Quaker, or from the West Riding of Yorkshire, so much the better. I do not even try to sympathise with him, and he breaks no squares. [How I love to see the camps of the gypsies, and to sigh my soul into that sort of life. If I express this feeling to another, he may qualify and spoil it with some objection.] I associate nothing with my travelling companion but present objects and passing events. in his ignorance of me and my affairs, I in a manner forget myself. But a friend reminds one of other things, rips up old grievances, and destroys the abstraction of the scene. He comes in ungraciously between us and our imaginary character. Something is dropped in the course of conversation that gives a hint of your profession and pursuits; or from having some one with you that knows the less sublime portions of your history, it seems that other people do. You are no longer a citizen of the world; but your 'unhoused free condition is put into circumspection and confine.' The incognito of an inn is one of its striking privileges—'lord of one's self, uncumbered with a name.' Oh! it is great to shake off the trammels of the world and of public opinion—to lose our importunate, tormenting, everlasting personal identity in the elements of nature, and become the creature of the moment, clear of all ties—to hold to the universe only by a dish of sweetbreads, and to owe nothing but the score of the evening—and no longer seeking for applause and meeting with contempt, to be known by no other title than *the Gentleman in the parlour!* One may take one's choice of all characters in this romantic state of uncertainty as to one's real pretensions, and become indefinitely respectable and negatively right worshipful. We baffle prejudice and disappoint conjecture; and from being so to others, begin to be objects of curiosity and wonder even to ourselves. We are no more those hackneyed commonplaces that we appear in the world; an inn restores us to the level of nature, and quits scores with society!

I have certainly spent some enviable hours at inns—sometimes when I have been left entirely to myself, and have tried to solve some metaphysical problem, as once at Witham Common, where I found out the proof that likeness is not a case of the association of ideas—at other times, when there have been pictures in the room, as at St. Neot's (I think it was), where I first met with Gribelin's engravings of the Cartoons, into which I entered at once, and at a little inn on the borders of Wales, where there happened to be hanging some of Westall's drawings, which I compared triumphantly (for a theory that I had, not for the admired artist) with the figure of a girl who had ferried me over the Severn, standing up in a boat between me and the twilight—at other times I might mention luxuriating in books, with a peculiar interest in this way, as I remember sitting up half the night to read *Paul and Virginia*, which I picked up at an inn at Bridgewater, after being drenched in the rain all day; and at the same place I got through two volumes of Madame d'Arblay's *Camilla*. It was on the 10th of April 1798 that I sat down to a volume of the *New Eloise*, at the inn at Llangollen, over a bottle of sherry and a cold chicken. The letter I chose was that in which St. Preux describes his feelings as he first caught a glimpse from the heights of the Jura of the Pays de Vaud, which I had brought with me as a *bon bouche* to crown the evening with. It was my birthday, and I had for the first time come from a place in the neighbourhood to visit this delightful spot. The road to Llangollen turns off between Chirk and Wrexham; and on passing a certain point you come all at once upon the valley, which opens like an amphitheatre, broad, barren hills rising in majestic state on either side, with 'green upland swells that echo to the bleat of flocks below, and the river Dee babbling over its stony bed in the midst of them. The valley at this time 'glittered green with sunny showers,' and a budding ash-tree dipped its tender branches in the chiding stream. How proud, how glad I was to walk along the high road that overlooks the delicious prospect, repeating the lines which I have just quoted from Mr. Coleridge's poems! But besides the prospect which opened beneath my feet, another also opened to my inward sight, a heavenly vision, on which were written in letters large as Hope could make them, these four words, LIBERTY, GENIUS, LOVE, VIRTUE; which have since faded into the light of common day, or mock my idle gaze.

The beautiful is vanished, and returns not.

Still I would return some time or other to this enchanted spot; but I would return to it alone. What other self could I find to share that influx of thoughts, of regret, and delight, the fragments of which I could hardly conjure up to myself, so much have they been broken and defaced. I could stand on some tall rock, and overlook the precipice of years that separates me from what I then was. I was at that time going shortly to visit the poet whom I have above named. Where is he now? Not only I myself have changed; the world, which was then new to me, has become old and incorrigible. Yet will I turn to thee in thought, O sylvan Dee, in joy, in youth and gladness as thou then wert; and thou shalt always be to me the river of Paradise, where I will drink of the waters of life freely!

There is hardly anything that shows the short-sightedness or capriciousness of the imagination more than travelling does. With change of place we change our ideas; nay, our opinions and feelings. We can by an effort indeed transport ourselves to old and long-forgotten scenes, and then the picture of the mind revives again; but we forget those that we have just left. It seems that we can think but of one place at a time. The canvas of the fancy is but of a certain extent, and if we paint one set of objects upon it, they immediately efface every other. We cannot enlarge our conceptions, we only shift our point of view. The landscape bares its bosom to the enraptured eye, we take our fill of it, and seem as if we could form no other image of beauty or grandeur. We pass on, and think no more of it: the horizon that shuts it from our sight also blots it from our memory like a dream. In travelling through a wild barren country I can form no idea of a woody and cultivated one. It appears to me that all the world must be barren, like what I see of it. In the country we forget the town, and in town we despise the country. 'Beyond Hyde Park,' says Sir Fopling Flutter, 'all is a desert.' All that part of the map that we do not see before us is blank. The world in our conceit of it is not much bigger than a nutshell. It is not one prospect expanded into another, county joined to county, kingdom to kingdom, land to seas, making an image voluminous and vast;—the mind can form no larger idea of space than the eye can take in at a single glance. The rest is a name written in a map, a calculation of arithmetic. For instance, what is the true signification of that immense mass of territory and population known by the name of China to us? An inch of pasteboard on a wooden globe, of no more account than a China orange! Things near us are seen of the size of life: things at a distance are diminished to the size of the understanding. We measure the universe by ourselves, and even comprehend the texture of our own being only piecemeal. In this way, however, we remember an infinity of things and places. The mind is like a mechanical instrument that plays a great variety of tunes, but it must play them in succession. One idea recalls another, but it at the same time excludes all others. In trying to renew old recollections, we cannot as it were unfold the whole web of our existence; we must pick out the single threads. So in coming to a place where we have formerly lived, and with which we have intimate associations, every one must have found that the feeling grows more vivid the nearer we approach the spot, from the mere anticipation of the actual impression: we remember circumstances, feelings, persons, faces, names that we had not thought of for years; but for the time all the rest of the world is forgotten!—To return to the question I have quitted above:—

I have no objection to go to see ruins, aqueducts, pictures, in company with a friend or a party, but rather the contrary, for the former reason reversed. They are intelligible matters, and will bear talking about. The sentiment here is not tacit, but communicable and overt. Salisbury Plain is barren of criticism, but Stonehenge will bear a discussion antiquarian, picturesque, and philosophical. In setting out on a party of pleasure, the first consideration always is where we shall go to: in taking a solitary ramble, the question is what we shall meet with by the way. 'The mind is its own place'; nor are we anxious to arrive at the end of our journey. I can myself do the honours indifferently well to works of art and curiosity. I once took a party to Oxford with no mean *éclat*—showed them that seat of the Muses at a distance,

> With glistering spires and pinnacles adorn'd—

descanted on the learned air that breathes from the grassy quadrangles and stone walls of halls and colleges—was at home in the Bodleian; and at Blenheim quite superseded the powdered Cicerone that attended us, and that pointed in vain with his wand to commonplace beauties in matchless pictures. As another exception to the above reasoning, I should not feel confident in venturing on a journey in a foreign country without a companion. I should want at intervals to hear the sound of my own language. There is an involuntary antipathy in the mind of an Englishman to foreign manners and notions that requires the assistance of social sympathy to carry it off. As the distance from home increases, this relief, which was at first a luxury, becomes a passion and an appetite. A person would almost feel stifled to find himself in the deserts of Arabia without friends and countrymen: there must be allowed to be something in the view of Athens or old Rome that claims the utterance of speech; and I own that the Pyramids are too mighty for any single contemplation. In such situations, so opposite to all one's ordinary train of ideas, one seems a species by one's-self, a limb torn off from society, unless one can meet with instant fellowship and support. Yet I did not feel this want or craving very pressing once, when I first set my foot on the laughing shores of France. Calais was peopled with novelty and delight. The confused, busy murmur of the place was like oil and wine poured into my ears; nor did the mariners' hymn, which was sung from the top of an old crazy vessel in the harbour, as the sun went down, send an alien sound into my soul. I only breathed the air of general humanity. I walked over 'the vine-covered hills and gay regions of France,' erect and satisfied; for the image of man was not cast down and chained to the foot of arbitrary thrones: I was at no loss for language, for that of all the great schools of painting was open to me. The whole is vanished like a shade. Pictures, heroes, glory, freedom, all are fled: nothing remains but the Bourbons and the French people!—There is undoubtedly a sensation in travelling into foreign parts that is to be had nowhere else; but it is more pleasing at the time than lasting. It is too remote from our habitual associations to be a common topic of discourse or reference, and, like a dream or another state of existence, does not piece into our daily modes of life. It is an animated but a momentary hallucination. It demands an effort to exchange our actual for our ideal identity; and to feel the pulse of our old transports revive very keenly, we must 'jump' all our present comforts and connections. Our romantic and itinerant character is not to be domesticated. Dr. Johnson remarked how little foreign travel added to the facilities of conversation in those who had been abroad. In fact, the time we have spent there is both delightful, and in one sense instructive; but it appears to be cut out of our substantial, downright existence, and never to join kindly on to it. We are not the same, but another, and perhaps more enviable individual, all the time we are out of our own country. We are lost to ourselves, as well as our friends. So the poet somewhat quaintly sings:

> Out of my country and myself I go.

Those who wish to forget painful thoughts, do well to absent themselves for a while from the ties and objects that recall them; but we can be said only to fulfil our destiny in the place that gave us birth. I should on this account like well enough to spend the whole of my life in travelling abroad, if I could anywhere borrow another life to spend afterwards at home!

ON FAMILIAR STYLE

It is not easy to write a familiar style. Many people mistake a familiar for a vulgar style, and suppose that to write without affectation is to write at random. On the contrary, there is nothing that requires more precision, and, if I may so say, purity of expression, than the style I am speaking of. It utterly rejects not only all unmeaning pomp, but all low, cant phrases, and loose, unconnected, *slipshod* allusions. It is not to take the first word that offers, but the best word in common use; it is not to throw words together in any combinations we please, but to follow and avail ourselves of the true idiom of the language. To write a genuine familiar or truly English style is to write as any one would speak in common conversation who had a thorough command and choice of words, or who could discourse with ease, force, and perspicuity, setting aside all pedantic and oratorical flourishes. Or, to give another illustration, to write naturally is the same thing in regard to common conversation as to read naturally is in regard to common speech. It does not follow that it is an easy thing to give the true accent and inflection to the words you utter, because you do not attempt to rise above the level of ordinary life and colloquial speaking. You do not assume, indeed, the solemnity of the pulpit or the tone of stage-declamation; neither are you at liberty to gabble on at a venture, without emphasis or discretion, or to resort to vulgar dialect or clownish pronunciation. You must steer a middle course. You are tied down to a given and appropriate articulation, which is determined by the habitual associations between sense and sound, and which you can only hit by entering into the author's meaning, as you must find the proper words and style to express yourself by fixing your thoughts on the subject you have to write about. Any one may mouth out a passage with a theatrical cadence, or get upon stilts to tell his thoughts; but to write or speak with propriety and simplicity is a more difficult task. Thus it is easy to affect a pompous style, to use a word twice as big as the thing you want to express: it is not so easy to pitch upon the very word that exactly fits it. Out of eight or ten words equally common, equally intelligible, with nearly equal pretensions, it is a matter of some nicety and discrimination to pick out the very one the preferableness of which is scarcely perceptible, but decisive. The reason why I object to Dr. Johnson's style is that there is no discrimination, no selection, no variety in it. He uses none but 'tall, opaque words,' taken from the 'first row of the rubric'—words with the greatest number of syllables, or Latin phrases with merely English terminations. If a fine style depended on this sort of arbitrary pretension, it would be fair to judge of an author's elegance by the measurement of his words and the substitution of foreign circumlocutions (with no precise associations) for the mother-tongue.[1] How simple is it to be dignified without ease, to be pompous without meaning! Surely it is but a mechanical rule for avoiding what is low, to be always pedantic and affected. It is clear you cannot use a vulgar English word if you never use a common English word at all. A fine tact is shown in adhering to those which are perfectly common, and yet never falling into any expressions which are debased by disgusting circumstances, or which owe their signification and point to technical or professional allusions. A truly natural or familiar style can never be quaint or vulgar, for this reason, that it is of universal force and applicability, and that quaintness and vulgarity arise out of the immediate connection of certain words with coarse and disagreeable or with confined ideas. The last form what we understand by *cant* or *slang* phrases. —To give an example of what is not very clear in the general statement. I should say that the phrase *To cut with a knife*, or *To cut a piece of wood*, is perfectly free from vulgarity, because it is perfectly common; but to *cut an acquaintance* is not quite unexceptionable, because it is not perfectly common or intelligible, and has hardly yet escaped out of the limits of slang phraseology. I should hardly, therefore, use the word in this sense without putting it in italics as a license of expression, to be received *cum grano salis*. All provincial or bye-phrases come under the same mark of reprobation—all such as the writer transfers to the page from his fireside or a particular *coterie*, or that he invents for his own sole use and convenience. I conceive that words are like money, not the worse for being common, but that it is the stamp of custom alone that gives them circulation or value. I am fastidious in this respect,

[1] I have heard of such a thing as an author who makes it a rule never to admit a monosyllable into his vapid verse. Yet the charm and sweetness of Marlowe's lines depended often on their being made up almost entirely of monosyllables.

and would almost as soon coin the currency of the realm as counterfeit the King's English. I never invented or gave a new and unauthorised meaning to any word but one single one (the term *impersonal* applied to feelings), and that was in an abstruse metaphysical discussion to express a very difficult distinction. I have been (I know) loudly accused of revelling in vulgarisms and broken English. I cannot speak to that point; but so far I plead guilty to the determined use of acknowledged idioms and common elliptical expressions. I am not sure that the critics in question know the one from the other, that is, can distinguish any medium between formal pedantry and the most barbarous solecism. As an author I endeavour to employ plain words and popular modes of construction, as, were I a chapman and dealer, I should common weights and measures.

The proper force of words lies not in the words themselves, but in their application. A word may be a fine-sounding word, of an unusual length, and very imposing from its learning and novelty, and yet in the connection in which it is introduced may be quite pointless and irrelevant. It is not pomp or pretension, but the adaptation of the expression to the idea, that clenches a writer's meaning:—as it is not the size or glossiness of the materials, but their being fitted each to its place, that gives strength to the arch; or as the pegs and nails are as necessary to the support of the building as the larger timbers, and more so than the mere showy, unsubstantial ornaments. I hate anything that occupies more space than it is worth. I hate to see a load of bandboxes go along the street, and I hate to see a parcel of big words without anything in them. A person who does not deliberately dispose of all his thoughts alike in cumbrous draperies and flimsy disguises may strike out twenty varieties of familiar everyday language, each coming somewhat nearer to the feeling he wants to convey, and at last not hit upon that particular and only one which may be said to be identical with the exact impression in his mind. This would seem to show that Mr. Cobbett is hardly right in saying that the first word that occurs is always the best. It may be a very good one; and yet a better may present itself on reflection or from time to time. It should be suggested naturally, however, and spontaneously, from a fresh and lively conception of the subject. We seldom succeed by trying at improvement, or by merely substituting one word for another that we are not satisfied with, as we cannot recollect the name of a place or person by merely plaguing ourselves about it. We wander farther from the point by persisting in a wrong scent; but it starts up accidentally in the memory when we least expected it, by touching some link in the chain of previous association.

There are those who hoard up and make a cautious display of nothing but rich and rare phraseology—ancient medals, obscure coins, and Spanish pieces of eight. They are very curious to inspect, but I myself would neither offer nor take them in the course of exchange. A sprinkling of archaisms is not amiss, but a tissue of obsolete expressions is more fit *for keep than wear*. I do not say I would not use any phrase that had been brought into fashion before the middle or the end of the last century, but I should be shy of using any that had not been employed by any approved author during the whole of that time. Words, like clothes, get old-fashioned, or mean and ridiculous, when they have been for some time laid aside. Mr. Lamb is the only imitator of old English style I can read with pleasure; and he is so thoroughly imbued with the spirit of his authors that the idea of imitation is almost done away. There is an inward unction, a marrowy vein, both in the thought and feeling, an intuition, deep and lively, of his subject, that carries off any quaintness or awkwardness arising from an antiquated style and dress. The matter is completely his own, though the manner is assumed. Perhaps his ideas are altogether so marked and individual as to require their point and pungency to be neutralised by the affectation of a singular but traditional form of conveyance. Tricked out in the prevailing costume, they would probably seem more startling and out of the way. The old English authors, Burton, Fuller, Coryate, Sir Thomas Browne, are a kind of mediators between us and the more eccentric and whimsical modern, reconciling us to his peculiarities. I do not, however, know how far this is the case or not, till he condescends to write like one of us. I must confess that what I like best of his papers under the signature of Elia (still I do not presume, amidst such excellence, to decide what is most excellent) is the account of 'Mrs. Battle's Opinions on Whist,' which is also the most free from obsolete allusions and turns of expression—

> A well of native English undefiled.

To those acquainted with his admired prototypes, these *Essays* of the ingenious and highly gifted author have the same sort of charm and relish that Erasmus's *Colloquies* or a fine piece of modern Latin have to the classical scholar. Certainly, I do not know any borrowed pencil that has more power or felicity of execution than the one of which I have here been speaking.

It is as easy to write a gaudy style without ideas as it is to spread a pallet of showy colours or to smear in a flaunting transparency. 'What do you read?' 'Words, words, words.'—'What is the matter?' '*Nothing*,' it might be answered. The florid style is the reverse of the familiar. The last is employed as an unvarnished medium to convey ideas; the first is resorted to as a spangled veil to conceal the want of them. When there is nothing to be set down but words, it costs little to have them fine. Look through the dictionary, and cull out a *florilegium*, rival the *tulippomania*. *Rouge* high enough, and never mind the natural complexion. The vulgar, who are not in the secret, will admire the look of preternatural health and vigour; and the fashionable, who regard only appearances, will be delighted with the imposition. Keep to your sounding generalities, your tinkling phrases, and all will be well. Swell out an unmeaning truism to a perfect tympany of style. A thought, a distinction is the rock on which all this brittle cargo of verbiage splits at once. Such writers have merely *verbal* imaginations, that retain nothing but words. Or their puny thoughts have dragon-wings, all green and gold. They soar far above the vulgar failing of the *Sermo humi obrepens*—their most ordinary speech is never short of an hyperbole, splendid, imposing, vague, incomprehensible, magniloquent, a cento of sounding common-places. If some of us, whose 'ambition is more lowly,' pry a little too narrowly into nooks and corners to pick up a number of 'unconsidered trifles,' they never once direct their eyes or lift their hands to seize on any but the most gorgeous, tarnished, threadbare, patchwork set of phrases, the left-off finery of poetic extravagance, transmitted down through successive generations of barren pretenders. If they criticise actors and actresses, a huddled phantasmagoria of feathers, spangles, floods of light, and oceans of sound float before their morbid sense, which they paint in the style of Ancient Pistol. Not a glimpse can you get of the merits or defects of the performers: they are hidden in a profusion of barbarous epithets and wilful rhodomontade. Our hypercritics are not thinking of these little fantoccini beings—

That strut and fret their hour upon the stage—

but of tall phantoms of words, abstractions, *genera* and *species*, sweeping clauses, periods that unite the Poles, forced alliterations, astounding antitheses—

And on their pens *Fustian* sits plumed.

If they describe kings and queens, it is an Eastern pageant. The Coronation at either House is nothing to it. We get at four repeated images—a curtain, a throne, a sceptre, and a footstool. These are with them the wardrobe of a lofty imagination; and they turn their servile strains to servile uses. Do we read a description of pictures? It is not a reflection of tones and hues which 'nature's own sweet and cunning hand laid on,' but piles of precious stones, rubies, pearls, emeralds, Golconda's mines, and all the blazonry of art. Such persons are in fact besotted with words, and their brains are turned with the glittering but empty and sterile phantoms of things. Personifications, capital letters, seas of sunbeams, visions of glory, shining inscriptions, the figures of a transparency, Britannia with her shield, or Hope leaning on an anchor, make up their stock-in-trade. They may be considered as *hieroglyphical* writers. Images stand out in their minds isolated and important merely in themselves, without any groundwork of feeling—there is no context in their imaginations. Words affect them in the same way, by the mere sound, that is, by their possible, not by their actual application to the subject in hand. They are fascinated by first appearances, and have no sense of consequences. Nothing more is meant by them than meets the ear: they understand or feel nothing more than meets their eye. The web and texture of the universe, and of the heart of man, is a mystery to them: they have no faculty that strikes a chord in unison with it. They cannot get beyond the daubings of fancy, the varnish of sentiment. Objects are not linked to feelings, words to things, but images revolve in splendid mockery, words represent themselves in their strange rhapsodies. The categories of such a mind are pride and ignorance—pride in outside show, to which they sacrifice everything, and ignorance of the true worth and hidden structure both of words and things. With a sovereign contempt for what is familiar and natural, they are the slaves of vulgar affectation—of a routine of high-flown phrases. Scorning to imitate realities, they are unable to invent anything, to strike out one original idea. They are not copyists of nature, it is true; but they are the poorest of all plagiarists, the plagiarists of words. All is far-fetched, dear-bought, artificial, oriental in subject and allusion; all is mechanical, conventional, vapid, formal, pedantic in style and execution. They startle and confound the understanding of the reader by the remoteness and obscurity of their illustrations; they soothe the ear by the monotony of the same everlasting round of circuitous metaphors. They are the *mock-school* in poetry and prose. They flounder about between fustian in expression and bathos in sentiment. They tantalise the fancy, but never reach the head nor touch the heart. Their Temple of Fame is like a shadowy structure raised by Dulness to Vanity, or like Cowper's description of the Empress of Russia's palace of ice, 'as worthless as in show 'twas glittering'—

It smiled, and it was cold!

LEIGH HUNT

1784–1859

ON THE GRACES AND ANXIETIES OF PIG-DRIVING

FROM the perusal of this article we beg leave to warn off vulgar readers of all denominations, whether of the 'great vulgar or the small.' Warn, did we say? We drive them off; for Horace tells us that they, as well as pigs, are to be so treated. *Odi profanum vulgus*, says he, *et arceo*. But do thou lend thine ear, gentle shade of Goldsmith, who didst make thy bear-leader denounce 'everything as is low'; and thou, Steele, who didst humanise upon public-houses and puppet-shows; and Fielding, thou whom the great Richardson, less in that matter (and some others) than thyself, did accuse of vulgarity, because thou didst discern natural gentility in a footman, and yet was not to be taken in by the airs of Pamela and my Lady G.

The title is a little startling; but 'style and sentiment,' as a lady said, 'can do anything.' Remember, then, gentle reader, that talents are not to be despised in the humblest walks of life; we will add, nor in the muddiest. The other day we happened to be among a set of spectators who could not help stopping to admire the patience and address with which a pig-driver huddled and cherished onward his drove of un-accommodating *élèves*, down a street in the suburbs. He was a born genius for a manœuvre. Had he originated in a higher sphere he would have been a general, or a stage-manager, or, at least, the head of a set of monks. Conflicting interests were his forte; pig-headed wills, and proceedings hopeless. To see the *hand* with which he did it! How hovering, yet firm;

how encouraging, yet compelling; how indicative of the space on each side of him, and yet of the line before him; how general, how particular, how perfect! No barber's could quiver about a head with more lightness of apprehension; no cook's pat up and proportion the side of a pasty with a more final eye. The whales, quoth old Chapman, speaking of Neptune,

The whales exulted under him, and knew their mighty king.

The pigs did not exult, but they knew their king. Unwilling was their subjection, but 'more in sorrow than in anger.' They were too far gone for rage. Their case was hopeless. They did not see why they should proceed, but they felt themselves bound to do so; forced, conglomerated, crowded onwards, irresistibly impelled by fate and Jenkins. Often would they have bolted under any other master. They squeaked and grunted as in ordinary; they sidled, they shuffled, they half stopped; they turned an eye to all the little outlets of escape; but in vain. There they stuck (for their very progress was a sort of sticking), charmed into the centre of his sphere of action, laying their heads together, but to no purpose; looking all as if they were shrugging their shoulders, and eschewing the tip-end of the whip of office. Much eye had they to their left leg; shrewd backward glances; not a little anticipative squeak and sudden rush of avoidance. It was a superfluous clutter, and they felt it; but a pig finds it more difficult than any other animal to accommodate himself to circumstances. Being out of his pale, he is in the highest state of wonderment and inaptitude. He is sluggish, obstinate, opinionate, not very social; has no desire of seeing foreign parts. Think of him in a multitude, forced to travel, and wondering what the devil it is that drives him! Judge by this of the talents of his driver.

We beheld a man once, an inferior genius, inducting a pig into the other end of Long Lane, Smithfield.

He had got him thus far towards the market. It was much. His air announced success in nine parts out of ten, and hope for the remainder. It had been a happy morning's work; he had only to look for the termination of it; and he looked (as a critic of an exalted turn of mind would say) in brightness and in joy. Then would he go to the public-house, and indulge in porter and a pleasing security. Perhaps he would not say much at first, being oppressed with the greatness of his success; but by degrees, especially if interrogated, he would open, like Æneas, into all the circumstances of his journey and the perils that beset him. Profound would be his set out; full of tremor his middle course; high and skilful his progress; glorious, though with a quickened pulse, his triumphant entry. Delicate had been his situation in Ducking Pond Row; masterly his turn at Bell Alley. We saw him with the radiance of some such thought on his countenance. He was just entering Long Lane. A gravity came upon him, as he steered his touchy convoy into his last thoroughfare. A dog moved him into a little agitation, darting along; but he resumed his course, not without a happy trepidation, hovering as he was on the borders of triumph. The pig still required care. It was evidently a pig with all the peculiar turn of mind of his species; a fellow that would not move faster than he could help; irritable, retrospective; picking objections, and prone to boggle; a chap with a tendency to take every path but the proper one, and with a sidelong tact for the alleys.

He bolts!

He 's off!—*Evasit! erupit!*

'Oh,' exclaimed the man, dashing his hand against his head, lifting his knee in an agony, and screaming with all the weight of a prophecy which the spectators felt to be too true—'*He'll go up all manner of streets!*'

Poor fellow! we think of him now sometimes, driving up Duke Street, and not to be comforted in Barbican.

A 'NOW'

DESCRIPTIVE OF A HOT DAY

Now the rosy- (and lazy-) fingered Aurora, issuing from her saffron house, calls up the moist vapours to surround her, and goes veiled with them as long as she can; till Phœbus, coming forth in his power, looks everything out of the sky, and holds sharp, uninterrupted empire from his throne of beams. Now the mower begins to make his sweeping cuts more slowly, and resorts oftener to the beer. Now the carter sleeps a-top of his load of hay, or plods with double slouch of shoulder, looking out with eyes winking under his shading hat, and with a hitch upward of one side of his mouth. Now the little girl at her grandmother's cottage-door watches the coaches that go by, with her hand held up over her sunny forehead. Now labourers look well resting in their white shirts at the doors of rural ale-houses. Now an elm is fine there, with a seat under it; and horses drink out of the trough, stretching their yearning necks with loosened collars; and the traveller calls for his glass of ale, having been without one for more than ten minutes; and his horse stands wincing at the flies, giving sharp shivers of his skin, and moving to and fro his ineffectual docked tail; and now Miss Betty Wilson, the host's daughter, comes streaming forth in a flowered gown and ear-rings, carrying with four of her beautiful fingers the foaming glass, for which, after the traveller has drank it, she receives with an indifferent eye, looking another way, the lawful twopence. Now grasshoppers 'fry,' as Dryden says. Now cattle stand in water, and ducks are envied. Now boots, and shoes, and trees by the roadside, are thick with dust; and dogs, rolling in it, after issuing out of the water, into which they have been thrown to fetch sticks, come scattering horror among the legs of the spectators. Now a fellow who finds he has three miles further to go in a pair of tight shoes is in a pretty situation. Now rooms with the sun upon them become intolerable; and the apothecary's apprentice, with a bitterness beyond aloes, thinks of the pond he used to bathe in at school. Now men with powdered heads (especially if thick) envy those that are unpowdered, and stop to wipe them up hill, with countenances that seem to expostulate with destiny. Now boys assemble round the village pump with a ladle to it, and delight to make a forbidden splash and get wet through the shoes. Now also they make suckers of leather, and bathe all day long in rivers and ponds, and make mighty fishings for 'tittle-bats.' Now the bee, as he hums along, seems to be talking heavily of the heat. Now doors and brick-walls are burning to the hand; and a walled lane, with dust and broken bottles in it, near a brick-field, is a thing not to be thought of. Now a green lane, on the contrary, thick-set with hedgerow elms, and having the noise of a brook 'rumbling in pebble-stone,' is one of the pleasantest things in the world.

Now, in town, gossips talk more than ever to one another, in rooms, in doorways, and out of window, always beginning the conversation with saying that the heat is overpowering. Now blinds are let down, and doors thrown open, and flannel waistcoats left off, and cold meat preferred to hot, and wonder expressed why tea continues so refreshing, and people delight to sliver lettuces into bowls, and apprentices water doorways with tin canisters that lay several atoms of dust. Now the water-cart, jumbling along the middle of the street, and jolting the showers out of its box of water, really does something. Now fruiterers' shops and dairies look pleasant, and ices are the only things to those who can get them. Now ladies loiter in baths; and people make presents of flowers; and wine is put into ice; and the after-dinner lounger recreates his head with applications of perfumed water out of long-necked bottles. Now the lounger, who cannot resist riding his new horse, feels his boots burn him. Now buckskins are not the lawn of Cos. Now jockeys, walking in greatcoats to lose flesh, curse inwardly. Now five fat people in a stage-coach hate the sixth fat one who is coming in, and think he has no right to be so large. Now clerks in office do nothing but drink soda-water and spruce-beer, and read the newspaper. Now the old-clothesman drops his solitary cry more deeply into the areas on the hot and forsaken side of the street; and bakers look vicious; and cooks are aggravated; and the steam of a tavern-kitchen catches hold of us like the breath of Tartarus. Now delicate skins are beset with gnats; and boys make their sleeping companion start up, with playing a burning-glass on his hand; and blacksmiths are super-carbonated; and cobblers in their stalls almost feel a wish to be transplanted; and butter is too easy to spread; and the dragoons wonder whether the Romans liked their helmets; and old ladies, with their lappets unpinned, walk along in a state of dilapidation; and the servant maids are afraid they look vulgarly hot; and the author, who has a plate of strawberries brought him, finds that he has come to the end of his writing.

A FEW THOUGHTS ON SLEEP

THIS is an article for the reader to think of when he or she is warm in bed, a little before he goes to sleep, the clothes at his ear, and the wind moaning in some distant crevice.

'Blessings,' exclaimed Sancho, 'on him that first invented sleep! It wraps a man all round like a cloak.' It is a delicious moment certainly—that of being well nestled in bed, and feeling that you shall drop gently to sleep. The good is to come, not past: the limbs have been just tired enough to render the remaining in one posture delightful: the labour of the day is done. A gentle failure of the perceptions comes creeping over one:—the spirit of consciousness disengages itself more and more, with slow and hushing degrees like a mother detaching her hand from that of her sleeping child;—the mind seems to have a balmy lid closing over it, like the eye;—'tis closing;—'tis more closing;—'tis closed. The mysterious spirit has gone to take its airy rounds.

It is said that sleep is best before midnight: and Nature herself, with her darkness and chilling dews, informs us so. There is another reason for going to bed betimes; for it is universally acknowledged that lying late in the morning is a great shortener of life. At least, it is never found in company with longevity. It also tends to make people corpulent. But these matters belong rather to the subject of early rising than of sleep.

Sleep at a late hour in the morning is not half so pleasant as the more timely one. It is sometimes, however, excusable, especially to a watchful or overworked head; neither can we deny the seducing merits of 't' other doze,'—the pleasing wilfulness of nestling in a new posture, when you know you ought to be up, like the rest of the house. But then you cut up the day, and your sleep the next night.

In the course of the day few people think of sleeping, except after dinner; and then it is often rather a hovering and nodding on the borders of sleep than sleep itself. This is a privilege allowable, we think, to none but the old, or the sickly, or the very tired and careworn; and it should be well understood before it is exercised in company. To escape into slumber from an argument; or to take it as an affair of course, only between you and your biliary duct; or to assent with involuntary nods to all that you have just been disputing, is not so well; much less, to sit nodding and tottering beside a lady; or to be in danger of dropping your head into the fruit-plate or your host's face; or of waking up, and saying 'Just so' to the bark of a dog; or 'Yes, madam,' to the black at your elbow.

Care-worn people, however, might refresh themselves oftener with day-sleep than they do; if their bodily state is such as to dispose them to it. It is a mistake to suppose that all care is wakeful. People sometimes sleep, as well as wake, by reason of their sorrow. The difference seems to depend upon the nature of their temperament; though in the *most* excessive cases, sleep is perhaps Nature's never-failing relief, as swooning is upon the rack. A person with jaundice in his blood shall lie down and go to sleep at noonday, when another of a different complexion shall find his eyes as uncloseable as a statue's, though he has had no sleep for nights together. Without meaning to lessen the dignity of suffering, which has quite enough to do with its waking hours, it is this that may often account for the profound sleeps enjoyed the night before hazardous battles, executions, and other demands upon an over-excited spirit.

The most complete and healthy sleep that can be taken in the day is in summer-time, out in a field. There is, perhaps, no solitary sensation so exquisite as that of slumbering on the grass or hay, shaded from the hot sun by a tree, with the consciousness of a fresh but light air running through the wide atmosphere, and the sky stretching far overhead upon all sides. Earth, and heaven, and a placid humanity seem to have the creation to themselves. There is nothing between the slumberer and the naked and glad innocence of nature.

Next to this, but at a long interval, the most relishing snatch of slumber out of bed is the one which a tired person takes before he retires for the night, while lingering in his sitting-room. The consciousness of being very sleepy, and of having the power to go to bed immediately, gives great zest to the unwillingness to move. Sometimes he sits nodding in his chair; but the sudden and leaden jerks of the head, to which a state of great sleepiness renders him liable, are generally too painful for so luxurious a moment; and he gets into a more legitimate posture, sitting sideways with his head on the chair-back, or throwing his legs up at once on another chair, and half reclining. It is curious, however, to find how long an inconvenient posture will be borne for the sake of this foretaste of repose. The worst of it is, that on going to bed the charm sometimes vanishes; perhaps from the colder temperature of the chamber; for a fireside is a great opiate.

Speaking of the painful positions into which a sleepy lounger will get himself, it is amusing to think of the more fantastic attitudes that so often take place in bed. If we could add anything to the numberless things that have been said about sleep by the poets, it would be upon this point. Sleep ever shows himself a greater leveller. A man in his waking moments may look as proud and self-possessed as he pleases. He may walk proudly, he may sit proudly, he may eat his dinner proudly; he may shave himself with an air of infinite superiority; in a word, he may show himself grand and absurd upon the most trifling occasions. But Sleep plays the petrifying magician. He arrests the proudest lord as well as the humblest clown in the most ridiculous postures: so that if you could draw a grandee from his bed without waking him, no limb-twisting fool in a pantomime should create wilder laughter. The toy with the string between his legs is hardly a posture-master more extravagant. Imagine a despot lifted up to the gaze of his valets, with his eyes shut, his mouth open, his left hand under his right ear, his other twisted and hanging helplessly before him like an idiot's, one knee lifted up, and the other leg stretched out, or both knees huddled up together;—what a scarecrow to lodge majestic power in!

But Sleep is kindly even in his tricks; and the poets have treated him with proper reverence. According to the ancient mythologists he had even one of the Graces to wife. He had a thousand sons, of whom the chief were Morpheus, or the Shaper; Icelos, or the Likely; Phantasus, the Fancy; and Phobetor, the Terror. His dwelling some writers place in a dull and darkling part of the earth; others, with greater compliment, in heaven; and others, with another kind of propriety, by the sea-shore. There is a good description of it in Ovid; but in these abstracted tasks of poetry the moderns outvie the ancients; and there is nobody who has built his bower for him so finely as Spenser. Archimago, in the first book of the *Faerie Queene* (canto I. st. 39), sends a little spirit down to Morpheus to fetch him a Dream:

He, making speedy way through spersed ayre,
And through the world of waters, wide and deepe,
To Morpheus' house doth hastily repaire.
Amid the bowels of the earth full steepe
And low, where dawning day doth never peepe,
His dwelling is. There, Tethys his wet bed
Doth ever wash: and Cynthia still doth steepe
In silver dew his ever-drooping head,
Whiles sad Night over him her mantle black doth spred.

And more to lull him in his slumber soft
A trickling streame from high rocke tumbling downe,
And ever-drizzling rain upon the loft,
Mixed with a murmuring winde, much like the soune
Of swarming bees, did cast him in a swoune.
No other noise, nor people's troublous cryes,
As still are wont to annoy the wallèd towne,
Might there be heard; but careless Quiet lyes,
Wrapt in eternall silence, far from enimyes.

Chaucer has drawn the cave of the same god with greater simplicity; but nothing can have a more deep and sullen effect than his cliffs and cold running waters. It seems as real as an actual solitude, or some quaint old picture in a book of travels in Tartary. He is telling the story of Ceyx and Alcyone in the poem called his Dream. Juno tells a messenger to go to Morpheus and 'bid him creep into the body' of the drowned king, to let his wife know the fatal event by his apparition.

This messenger tooke leave, and went
Upon his way; and never he stent

Till he came to the dark valley,
That stant betweene rockes twey.
There never yet grew corne, ne gras.
Ne tree, ne nought that aught was.
Beast, ne man, ne naught else;
Save that there were a few wells
Came running fro the cliffs adowne,
That made a deadly sleeping soune,
And runnen downe right by a cave,
That was under a rocky grave,
Amid the valley, wonder-deepe.
There these goddis lay asleepe,
Morpheus and Eclympasteire,
That was the god of Sleepis heire,
That slept and did none other worke.

Where the credentials of this new son and heir, Eclympasteire, are to be found, we know not; but he acts very much, it must be allowed, like an heir-presumptive, in sleeping and doing 'none other work.'

We dare not trust ourselves with many quotations upon sleep from the poets; they are so numerous as well as beautiful. We must content ourselves with mentioning that our two most favourite passages are one in the *Philoctetes* of Sophocles, admirable for its contrast to a scene of terrible agony, which it closes; and the other the following address in Beaumont and Fletcher's tragedy of *Valentinian*, the hero of which is also a sufferer under bodily torment. He is in a chair, slumbering; and these most exquisite lines are gently sung with music:—

Care-charming Sleep, thou easer of all woes,
Brother to Death, sweetly thyself dispose
On this afflicted prince. Fall like a cloud
In gentle showers: give nothing that is loud
Or painful to his slumbers: easy, sweet,
And as a purling stream, thou son of Night,
Pass by his troubled senses; sing his pain
Like hollow murmuring wind, or silver rain:
Into this prince, gently, oh gently slide,
And kiss him into slumbers, like a bride.

How earnest and prayer-like are these pauses! How lightly sprinkled, and yet how deeply settling, like rain, the fancy! How quiet, affectionate, and perfect the conclusion!

Sleep is most graceful in an infant; soundest, in one who has been tired in the open air; completest, to the seaman after a hard voyage; most welcome, to the mind haunted with one idea; most touching to look at, in the parent that has wept; lightest, in the playful child; proudest, in the bride adored.

ON GETTING UP ON COLD MORNINGS

An Italian author—Giulio Cordara, a Jesuit—has written a poem upon insects, which he begins by insisting, that those troublesome and abominable little animals were created for our annoyance, and that they were certainly not inhabitants of Paradise. We of the north may dispute this piece of theology; but on the other hand, it is as clear as the snow on the house-tops, that Adam was not under the necessity of shaving; and that when Eve walked out of her delicious bower, she did not step upon ice three inches thick.

Some people say it is a very easy thing to get up of a cold morning. You have only, they tell you, to take the resolution; and the thing is done. This may be very true; just as a boy at school has only to take a flogging, and the thing is over. But we have not at all made up our minds upon it; and we find it a very pleasant exercise to discuss the matter, candidly, before we get up. This, at least, is not idling, though it may be lying. It affords an excellent answer to those who ask how lying in bed can be indulged in by a reasoning being,—a rational creature. How? Why, with the argument calmly at work in one's head, and the clothes over one's shoulder. Oh—it is a fine way of spending a sensible, impartial half-hour.

If these people would be more charitable they would

get on with their argument better. But they are apt to reason so ill, and to assert so dogmatically, that one could wish to have them stand round one's bed, of a bitter morning, and *lie* before their faces. They ought to hear both sides of the bed, the inside and out. If they cannot entertain themselves with their own thoughts for half-an-hour or so, it is not the fault of those who can.

Candid inquiries into one's decumbency, besides the greater or less privileges to be allowed a man in proportion to his ability of keeping early hours, the work given his faculties, etc., will at least concede their due merits to such representations as the following. In the first place, says the injured but calm appealer, I have been warm all night, and find my system in a state perfectly suitable to a warm-blooded animal. To get out of this state into the cold, besides the inharmonious and uncritical abruptness of the transition, is so unnatural to such a creature, that the poets, refining upon the tortures of the damned, make one of their greatest agonies consist in being suddenly transported from heat to cold,—from fire to ice. They are 'haled' out of their 'beds,' says Milton, by 'harpy-footed furies,'—fellows who come to call them. On my first movement towards the anticipation of getting up I find that such parts of the sheets and bolster as are exposed to the air of the room are stone-cold. On opening my eyes, the first thing that meets them is my own breath rolling forth, as if in the open air, like smoke out of a chimney. Think of this symptom. Then I turn my eyes sideways and see the window all frozen over. Think of that. Then the servant comes in. 'It is very cold this morning, is it not?'—'Very cold, sir.'—'Very cold indeed, isn't it?'—'Very cold indeed, sir.'—'More than usually so, isn't it, even for this weather?' (Here the servant's wit and good-nature are put to a considerable test, and the inquirer lies on thorns for the answer.) 'Why, sir . . . I think it *is*.' (Good creature! There is not a better or more truth-telling servant going.) 'I must rise, however—get me some warm water.'—Here comes a fine interval between the departure of the servant and the arrival of the hot water; during which, of course, it is of 'no use?' to get up. The hot water comes. 'Is it quite hot?'—'Yes, sir.'—'Perhaps too hot for shaving; I must wait a little?'—'No, sir; it will just do.' (There is an over-nice propriety sometimes, an officious zeal of virtue, a little troublesome.) 'Oh—the shirt—you must air my clean shirt;—linen gets very damp this weather.'—'Yes, sir.' Here another delicious five minutes. A knock at the door. 'Oh, the shirt—very well. My stockings—I think the stockings had better be aired too.'—'Very well, sir.' Here another interval. At length everything is ready, except myself. I now, continues our incumbent (a happy word, by-the-by, for a country vicar)—I now cannot help thinking a good deal—who can?—upon the unnecessary and villainous custom of shaving: it is a thing so unmanly (here I nestle closer)—so effeminate (here I recoil from an unlucky step into the colder part of the bed).—No wonder that the Queen of France took part with the rebels against that degenerate king, her husband, who first affronted her smooth visage with a face like her own. The Emperor Julian never showed the luxuriancy of his genius to better advantage than in reviving the flowing beard. Look at Cardinal Bembo's picture—at Michael Angelo's—at Titian's—at Shakespeare's—at Fletcher's—at Spenser's—at Chaucer's—at Alfred's—at Plato's—I could name a great man for every tick of my watch.—Look at the Turks, a grave and otiose people.—Think of Haroun Al Raschid and Bed-ridden Hassan.—Think of Wortley Montague, the worthy son of his mother, above the prejudice of his time.—Look at the Persian gentlemen, whom one is ashamed of meeting about the suburbs, their dress and appearance are so much finer than our own.—Lastly, think of the razor itself—how totally opposed to every sensation of bed—how cold, how edgy, how hard! how utterly different from anything like the warm and circling amplitude, which

> Sweetly recommends itself
> Unto our gentle senses.

Add to this, benumbed fingers, which may help you to cut yourself, a quivering body, a frozen towel, and a ewer full of ice; and he that says there is nothing to oppose in all this, only shows that he has no merit in opposing it.

Thomson the poet, who exclaims in his *Seasons*—

> Falsely luxurious! Will not man awake?

used to lie in bed till noon, because he said he had no motive in getting up. He could imagine the good of rising; but then he could also imagine the good of lying still; and his exclamation, it must be allowed, was made upon summer-time, not winter. We must proportion the argument to the individual character. A money-getter may be drawn out of his bed by three or four pence; but this will not suffice for a student. A proud man may say, 'What shall I think of myself, if I don't get up?' but the more humble one will be content to waive this prodigious notion of himself, out of respect to his kindly bed. The mechanical man shall get up without any ado at all; and so shall the barometer. An ingenious lier in bed will find hard matter of discussion even on the score of health and longevity. He will ask us for our proofs and precedents of the ill effects of lying later in cold weather; and sophisticate much on the advantages of an even temperature of body; of the natural propensity (pretty universal) to have one's way; and of the animals that roll themselves up and sleep all the winter. As to longevity, he will ask whether the longest is of necessity the best; and whether Holborn is the handsomest street in London.

DEATHS OF LITTLE CHILDREN

A Grecian philosopher being asked why he wept for the death of his son, since the sorrow was in vain, replied, 'I weep on that account.' And his answer became his wisdom. It is only for sophists to contend that we, whose eyes contain the fountain of tears, need never give way to them. It would be unwise not to do so on some occasions. Sorrow unlocks them in her balmy moods. The first bursts may be bitter and overwhelming; but the soil on which they pour would be worse without them. They refresh the fever of the soul—the dry misery which parches the countenance into furrows, and renders us liable to our most terrible 'flesh-quakes.'

There are sorrows, it is true, so great, that to give them some of the ordinary vents is to run a hazard of being overthrown. These we must rather strengthen ourselves to resist, or bow quietly and drily down, in order to let them pass over us, as the traveller does the wind of the desert. But where we feel that tears would relieve us, it is false philosophy to deny ourselves at least that first refreshment; and it is always false consolation to tell people that because they cannot help a thing, they are not to mind it. The true way is, to let them grapple with the unavoidable sorrow, and try to win it into gentleness by a reasonable yielding. There are griefs so gentle in their very nature that it would be worse than false heroism to refuse them a tear. Of this kind are the deaths of infants. Particular circumstances may render it more or less advisable to indulge in grief for the loss of a little child; but, in general, parents should be no more advised to repress their first tears on such an occasion, than to repress their smiles towards a child surviving, or to indulge in any other sympathy. It is an appeal to the same gentle tenderness; and such appeals are never made in vain. The end of them is an acquittal from the harsher bonds of affliction—from the tying down of the spirit to one melancholy idea.

It is the nature of tears of this kind, however strongly they may gush forth, to run into quiet waters at last. We cannot easily, for the whole course of our lives, think with pain of any good and kind person whom we have lost. It is the divine nature of their qualities to conquer pain and death itself; to turn the memory of them into pleasure; to survive with a placid aspect in our imaginations. We are writing at this moment just opposite a spot which contains the grave of one inexpressibly dear to us. We see from our window the trees about it, and the church spire. The green fields lie around. The clouds are travelling overhead, alternately taking away the sunshine and restoring it. The vernal winds, piping of the flowery summer-time, are nevertheless calling to mind the far-distant and dangerous ocean, which the heart that lies in that grave had many reasons to think of. And yet the sight of this spot does not give us pain. So far from it, it is the existence of that grave which doubles every charm of the spot; which links the pleasures of our childhood and manhood together; which puts a hushing tenderness in the winds, and a patient joy upon the landscape; which seems to unite heaven and earth, mortality and immortality, the grass of the tomb and the grass of the green field; and gives a more maternal aspect to the whole kindness of nature. It does not hinder gaiety itself. Happiness was what its tenant, through all her troubles, would have diffused. To diffuse happiness, and to enjoy it, is not only carrying on her wishes, but realising her hopes; and gaiety, freed from its only pollutions, malignity and want of sympathy, is but a child playing about the knees of its mother.

The remembered innocence and endearments of a child stand us instead of virtues that have died older. Children have not exercised the voluntary offices of friendship; they have not chosen to be kind and good to us; nor stood by us, from conscious will, in the hour of adversity. But they have shared their pleasures and pains with us as well as they could; the interchange of good offices between us has, of necessity, been less mingled with the troubles of the world; the sorrow arising from their death is the only one which we can associate with their memories. These are happy thoughts that cannot die. Our loss may always render them pensive; but they will not always be painful. It is a part of the benignity of Nature that pain does not survive like pleasure, at any time, much less where the cause of it is an innocent one. The smile will remain reflected by memory, as the moon reflects the light upon us when the sun has gone into heaven.

When writers like ourselves quarrel with earthly pain (we mean writers of the same intentions, without implying, of course, anything about abilities or otherwise), they are misunderstood if they are supposed to quarrel with pains of every sort. This would be idle and effeminate. They do not pretend, indeed, that humanity might not wish, if it could, to be entirely free from pain; for it endeavours, at all times, to turn pain into pleasure: or at least to set off the one with the other, to make the former a zest and the latter a refreshment. The most unaffected dignity of suffering does this, and, if wise, acknowledges it. The greatest benevolence towards others, the most unselfish relish of their pleasures, even at its own expense, does not look to increasing the general stock of happiness, though content, if it could, to have its identity swallowed up in that splendid contemplation. We are far from meaning that this is to be called selfishness. We are far, indeed, from thinking so, or of so confounding words. But neither is it to be called pain when most unselfish, if disinterestedness be truly understood. The pain that is in it softens into pleasure, as the darker hue of the rainbow melts into the brighter. Yet even if a harsher line is to be drawn between the pain and pleasure of the most unselfish mind (and ill-health, for instance, may draw it), we should not quarrel with it if it contributed to the general mass of comfort, and were of a nature which general kindliness could not avoid. Made as we are, there are certain pains without which it would be difficult to conceive certain great and overbalancing pleasures. We may conceive it possible for beings to be made entirely happy; but in our composition something of pain seems to be a necessary ingredient, in order that the materials may turn to as fine account as possible, though our clay, in the course of ages and experience, may be refined more and more. We may get rid of the worst earth, though not of earth itself.

Now the liability to the loss of children—or rather what renders us sensible of it, the occasional loss itself—seems to be one of these necessary bitters thrown into the cup of humanity. We do not mean that every one must lose one of his children in order to enjoy the rest; or that every individual loss afflicts us in the same proportion. We allude to the deaths of infants in general. These might be as few as we could render them. But if none at all ever took place, we should regard every little child as a man or woman secured; and it will easily be conceived what a world of endearing cares and hopes this security would endanger. The very idea of infancy would lose its continuity with us. Girls and boys would be future men and women, not present children. They would have attained their full growth in our imaginations, and might as well have been men and women at once. On the other hand, those who have lost an infant, are never, as it were, without an infant child. They are the only persons who, in one sense, retain it always, and they furnish their neighbours with the same idea. The other children grow up to manhood and womanhood, and suffer all the changes of mortality. This one alone is rendered an immortal child. Death has arrested it with his kindly harshness, and blessed it into an eternal image of youth and innocence.

Of such as these are the pleasantest shapes that visit our fancy and our hopes. They are the ever-smiling emblems of joy; the prettiest pages that wait upon imagination. Lastly, 'Of these are the kingdom of heaven.' Wherever there is a province of that benevolent and all-accessible empire, whether on earth or elsewhere, such are the gentle spirits that must inhabit it. To such simplicity, or the resemblance of it, must they come. Such must be the ready confidence of their hearts and creativeness of their fancy. And so ignorant must they be of the 'knowledge of good and evil,' losing their discernment of that self-created trouble, by enjoying the garden before them, and not being ashamed of what is kindly and innocent.

THOMAS DE QUINCEY

1785–1859

ON MURDER CONSIDERED AS ONE OF THE FINE ARTS

To the Editor of 'Blackwood's Magazine'

SIR,—We have all heard of a Society for the Promotion of Vice, of the Hell-Fire Club, etc. At Brighton I think it was that a Society was formed for the Suppression of Virtue. That Society was itself suppressed—but I am sorry to say that another exists in London, of a character still more atrocious. In tendency, it may be denominated a Society for the Encouragement of Murder; but, according to their own delicate εὐφημισμὸς, it is styled—The Society of Connoisseurs in Murder. They profess to be curious in homicide; amateurs and dilettanti in the various modes of bloodshed; and, in short, Murder-Fanciers. Every fresh atrocity of that class, which the police annals of Europe bring up, they meet and criticise as they would a picture, statue, or other work of art. But I need not trouble myself with any attempt to describe the spirit of their proceedings, as you will collect *that* much better from one of the Monthly Lectures read before the Society last year. This has fallen into my hands accidentally, in spite of all the vigilance exercised to keep their transactions from the public eye. The publication of it will alarm them; and my purpose is that it should. For I would much rather put them down quietly, by an appeal to public opinion through you, than by such an exposure of names as would follow an appeal to Bow Street; which last appeal, however, if this should fail, I must positively resort to. For it is scandalous that such things should go on in a Christian land. Even in a heathen land, the public toleration of murder was felt by a

Christian writer to be the most crying reproach of the public morals. This writer was Lactantius; and with his words, as singularly applicable to the present occasion, I shall conclude:—'Quid tam horribile,' says he, 'tam tetrum, quam hominis trucidatio? Ideo severissimis legibus vita nostra munitur; ideo bella execrabilia sunt. Invenit tamen consuetudo quatenus homicidium sine bello ac sine legibus faciat: et hoc sibi voluptas quod scelus vindicavit. Quod si interesse homicidio sceleris conscientia est,—et eidem facinori spectator obstrictus est cui et admissor; ergo et in his gladiatorum cædibus non minus cruore profunditur qui spectat, quam ille qui facit: nec potest esse immunis à sanguine qui voluit effundi; aut videri non interfecisse, qui interfectori et favit et præmium postulavit.' 'Human life,' says he, 'is guarded by laws of the uttermost rigour, yet custom has devised a mode of evading them in behalf of murder; and the demands of taste (voluptas) are now become the same as those of abandoned guilt.' Let the Society of Gentlemen Amateurs consider this; and let me call their especial attention to the last sentence, which is so weighty, that I shall attempt to convey it in English:—'Now, if merely to be present at a murder fastens on a man the character of an accomplice,—if barely to be a spectator involves us in one common guilt with the perpetrator; it follows of necessity, that in these murders of the amphitheatre, the hand which inflicts the fatal blow is not more deeply imbrued in blood than his who sits and looks on; neither can *he* be clear of blood who has countenanced its shedding; nor that man seem other than a participator in murder who gives his applause to the murderer, and calls for prizes in his behalf.' The '*præmia postulavit*' I have not yet heard charged upon the Gentlemen Amateurs of London, though undoubtedly their proceedings tend to that; but the '*interfectori favit*' is implied in the very title of this association, and expressed in every line of the lecture which I send you.—I am, etc. X. Y. Z.

[*Note of the Editor.*—We thank our correspondent for his communication, and also for the quotation from Lactantius, which is very pertinent to *his* view of the case; our own, we confess, is different. We cannot suppose the lecturer to be in earnest, any more than Erasmus in his Praise of Folly, or Dean Swift in his proposal for eating children. However, either on his view or on ours, it is equally fit that the lecture should be made public.]

LECTURE

GENTLEMEN,—I have had the honour to be appointed by your committee to the trying task of reading the Williams' Lecture on Murder, considered as one of the Fine Arts—a task which might be easy enough three or four centuries ago, when the art was little understood, and few great models had been exhibited; but in this age, when masterpieces of excellence have been executed by professional men, it must be evident, that in the style of criticism applied to them, the public will look for something of a corresponding improvement. Practice and theory must advance *pari passu.* People begin to see that something more goes to the composition of a fine murder than two blockheads to kill and be killed—a knife—a purse—and a dark lane. Design, gentlemen, grouping, light and shade, poetry, sentiment, are now deemed indispensable to attempts of this nature. Mr. Williams has exalted the ideal of murder to all of us; and to me, therefore, in particular, has deepened the arduousness of my task. Like Æschylus or Milton in poetry, like Michael Angelo in painting, he has carried his art to a point of colossal sublimity; and as Mr. Wordsworth observes, has in a manner 'created the taste by which he is to be enjoyed.' To sketch the history of the art, and to examine its principles critically, now remains as a duty for the connoisseur, and for judges of quite another stamp from His Majesty's Judges of Assize.

Before I begin, let me say a word or two to certain

prigs, who affect to speak of our society as if it were in some degree immoral in its tendency. Immoral!—God bless my soul, gentlemen, what is it that people mean? I am for morality, and always shall be, and for virtue and all that; and I do affirm, and always shall (let what will come of it), that murder is an improper line of conduct—highly improper; and I do not stick to assert, that any man who deals in murder, must have very incorrect ways of thinking, and truly inaccurate principles; and so far from aiding and abetting him by pointing out his victim's hiding-place, as a great moralist[1] of Germany declared it to be every good man's duty to do, I would subscribe one shilling and sixpence to have him apprehended, which is more by eighteenpence than the most eminent moralists have subscribed for that purpose. But what then? Everything in this world has two handles. Murder, for instance, may be laid hold of by its moral handle (as it generally is in the pulpit, and at the Old Bailey); and *that*, I confess, is its weak side; or it may also be treated *æsthetically*, as the Germans call it, that is, in relation to good taste.

To illustrate this, I will urge the authority of three eminent persons, viz., S. T. Coleridge, Aristotle, and Mr. Howship the surgeon. To begin with S. T. C.—One night, many years ago, I was drinking tea with him in Berners Street (which by the way, for a short street, has been uncommonly fruitful in men of genius). Others were there besides myself; and amidst some

[1] Kant—who carried his demands of unconditional veracity to so extravagant a length as to affirm, that, if a man were to see an innocent person escape from a murderer, it would be his duty, on being questioned by the murderer, to tell the truth, and to point out the retreat of the innocent person, under any certainty of causing murder. Lest this doctrine should be supposed to have escaped him in any heat of dispute, on being taxed with it by a celebrated French writer, he solemnly reaffirmed it, with his reasons.

carnal considerations of tea and toast, we were all imbibing a dissertation on Plotinus from the Attic lips of S. T. C. Suddenly a cry arose of '*Fire—fire!*'—upon which all of us, master and disciples, Plato and *οἱ περὶ τὸν Πλάτωνα*, rushed out, eager for the spectacle. The fire was in Oxford Street, at a pianoforte maker's; and, as it promised to be a conflagration of merit, I was sorry that my engagements forced me away from Mr. Coleridge's party before matters were come to a crisis. Some days after, meeting with my Platonic host, I reminded him of the case, and begged to know how that very promising exhibition had terminated. 'Oh, sir,' said he, 'it turned out so ill, that we damned it unanimously.' Now, does any man suppose that Mr. Coleridge,—who, for all he is too fat to be a person of active virtue, is undoubtedly a worthy Christian,—that this good S. T. C., I say, was an incendiary, or capable of wishing any ill to the poor man and his pianofortes (many of them, doubtless, with the additional keys)? On the contrary, I know him to be that sort of man that I durst stake my life upon it he would have worked an engine in a case of necessity, although rather of the fattest for such fiery trials of his virtue. But how stood the case? Virtue was in no request. On the arrival of the fire-engines, morality had devolved wholly on the insurance office. This being the case, he had a right to gratify his taste. He had left his tea. Was he to have nothing in return?

I contend that the most virtuous man, under the premises stated, was entitled to make a luxury of the fire, and to hiss it, as he would any other performance that raised expectations in the public mind, which afterwards it disappointed. Again, to cite another great authority, what says the Stagyrite? He (in the Fifth Book, I think it is, of his Metaphysics) describes what he calls *κλέπτην τέλειον*, i.e. *perfect thief*; and, as to Mr. Howship, in a work of his on Indigestion, he makes no scruple to talk with admiration of a certain ulcer which he had seen, and which he styles 'a beautiful ulcer.' Now will any man pretend, that, abstractedly considered, a thief could appear to Aristotle a perfect character, or that Mr. Howship could be enamoured of an ulcer? Aristotle, it is well known, was himself so very moral a character, that, not content with writing his Nichomachéan Ethics, in one volume octavo, he also wrote another system, called *Magna Moralia*, or Big Ethics. Now, it is impossible that a man who composes any ethics at all, big or little, should admire a thief *per se*, and, as to Mr. Howship, it is well known that he makes war upon all ulcers; and, without suffering himself to be seduced by their charms, endeavours to banish them from the county of Middlesex. But the truth is, that, however objectionable *per se*, yet, relatively to others of their class, both a thief and an ulcer may have infinite degrees of merit. They are both imperfections, it is true; but to be imperfect being their essence, the very greatness of their imperfection becomes their perfection. *Spartam nactus es, hanc exorna.* A thief like Autolycus or Mr. Barrington, and a grim phagedænic ulcer, superbly defined, and running regularly through all its natural stages, may no less justly be regarded as ideals after *their* kind, than the most faultless moss-rose amongst flowers, in its progress from bud to 'bright consummate flower'; or, amongst human flowers, the most magnificent young female, apparelled in the pomp of womanhood. And thus not only the ideal of an inkstand may be imagined (as Mr. Coleridge demonstrated in his celebrated correspondence with Mr. Blackwood), in which, by the way, there is not so much, because an inkstand is a laudable sort of thing, and a valuable member of society; but even imperfection itself may have its ideal or perfect state.

Really, gentlemen, I beg pardon for so much philosophy at one time, and now, let me apply it. When a murder is in the paulo-post-futurum tense, and a rumour of it comes to our ears, by all means let us treat it morally. But suppose it over and done, and that you can say of it, τετέλεσται, or (in that adamantine molossus of Medea) εἴργασται; suppose the poor murdered man to be out of his pain, and the rascal that did it off like a shot, nobody knows whither; suppose, lastly, that we have done our best, by putting out our legs to trip up the fellow in his flight, but all to no purpose—'abiit, evasit,' etc.—why, then, I say, what 's the use of any more virtue? Enough has been given to morality; now comes the turn of Taste and the Fine Arts. A sad thing it was, no doubt, very sad; but *we* can't mend it. Therefore let us make the best of a bad matter; and, as it is impossible to hammer anything out of it for moral purposes, let us treat it æsthetically, and see if it will turn to account in that way. Such is the logic of a sensible man, and what follows? We dry up our tears, and have the satisfaction perhaps to discover, that a transaction, which, morally considered, was shocking, and without a leg to stand upon, when tried by principles of Taste, turns out to be a very meritorious performance. Thus all the world is pleased; the old proverb is justified, that it is an ill wind which blows nobody good; the amateur, from looking bilious and sulky, by too close an attention to virtue, begins to pick up his crumbs, and general hilarity prevails. Virtue has had her day; and henceforward, *Vertu* and Connoisseurship have leave to provide for themselves. Upon this principle, gentlemen, I propose to guide your studies, from Cain to Mr. Thurtell. Through this great gallery of murder, therefore, together let us wander hand in hand, in delighted admiration, while I endeavour to point your attention to the objects of profitable criticism.

The first murder is familiar to you all. As the inventor of murder, and the father of the art, Cain must have been a man of first-rate genius. All the Cains were men of genius. Tubal Cain invented tubes, I think, or some such thing. But, whatever were the originality and genius of the artist, every art was then in its infancy; and the works must be criticised with a recollection of that fact. Even Tubal's work would probably be little approved at this day in Sheffield; and therefore of Cain (Cain senior, I mean), it is no disparagement to say, that his performance was but so so. Milton, however, is supposed to have thought differently. By his way of relating the case, it should seem to have been rather a pet murder with him, for he retouches it with an apparent anxiety for its picturesque effect:

> Whereat he inly raged; and, as they talk'd,
> Smote him into the midriff with a stone
> That beat out life: he fell; and, deadly pale,
> Groan'd out his soul *with gushing blood effus'd.*
>
> *Paradise Lost*, B. XI.

Upon this, Richardson the painter, who had an eye for effect, remarks as follows, in his Notes on *Paradise Lost*, p. 497:—'It has been thought,' says he, 'that Cain beat (as the common saying is) the breath out of his brother's body with a great stone; Milton gives in to this, with the addition, however, of a large wound.' In this place it was a judicious addition; for the rudeness of the weapon, unless raised and enriched by a warm, sanguinary colouring, has too much of the naked air of the savage school; as if the deed were perpetrated by a Polypheme without science, premeditation, or anything but a mutton bone. However, I am chiefly pleased with the improvement, as it implies that Milton was an amateur. As to Shakespeare, there never was a better; as his description of the murdered Duke of Gloucester, in Henry VI., of Duncan's, Banquo's etc., sufficiently proves.

The foundation of the art having been once laid, it is pitiable to see how it slumbered without improvement for ages. In fact, I shall now be obliged to leap over all murders, sacred and profane, as utterly unworthy of notice until long after the Christian era. Greece, even in the age of Pericles, produced no murder of the slightest merit; and Rome had too little originality of genius in any of the arts to succeed, where her model failed her. In fact, the Latin language sinks under the very idea of murder. 'The man was murdered'; how will this sound in Latin? *Interfectus est*, *interemptus est*—which simply expresses a homicide; and hence the Christian Latinity of the middle ages was obliged to introduce a new word, such as the feebleness of classic conceptions never ascended to. *Murdratus est*, said the sublimer dialect of Gothic ages. Meantime, the Jewish school of murder kept alive whatever was yet known in the art, and gradually transferred it to the Western World. Indeed the Jewish school was always respectable, even in the dark ages, as the case of Hugh of Lincoln shows, which was honoured with the approbation of Chaucer, on occasion of another performance from the same school, which he puts into the mouth of the Lady Abbess.

Recurring, however, for one moment to classical antiquity, I cannot but think that Catiline, Clodius, and some of that coterie, would have made first-rate artists; and it is on all accounts to be regretted, that the priggism of Cicero robbed his country of the only chance she had for distinction in this line. As the *subject* of a murder, no person could have answered better than himself. Lord! how he would have howled with panic, if he had heard Cethegus under his bed. It would have been truly diverting to have listened to him; and satisfied I am, gentlemen, that he would have preferred the *utile* of creeping into a closet, or even into a *cloaca*, to the *honestum* of facing the bold artist.

To come now to the dark ages—(by which we, that speak with precision, mean, *par excellence*, the tenth century, and the times immediately before and after)—these ages ought naturally to be favourable to the art of murder, as they were to church-architecture, to stained-glass, etc.; and, accordingly, about the latter end of this period, there arose a great character in our art, I mean the Old Man of the Mountains. He was a shining light, indeed, and I need not tell you, that the very word 'assassin' is deduced from him. So keen an amateur was he, that on one occasion, when his own life was attempted by a favourite assassin, he was so much pleased with the talent shown, that notwithstanding the failure of the artist, he created him a duke upon the spot, with remainder to the female line, and settled a pension on him for three lives. Assassination is a branch of the art which demands a separate notice; and I shall devote an entire lecture to it. Meantime, I shall only observe how odd it is, that this branch of the art has flourished by fits. It never rains, but it pours. Our own age can boast of some fine specimens; and, about two centuries ago, there was a most brilliant constellation of murders in this class. I need hardly say, that I allude especially to those five splendid works,—the assassinations of William I. of Orange, of Henry IV. of France, of the Duke of Buckingham (which you will find excellently described in the letters published by Mr. Ellis, of the British Museum), of Gustavus Adolphus, and of Wallenstein. The King of Sweden's assassination, by-the-by, is doubted by many writers, Harte amongst others; but they are wrong. He was murdered; and I consider his murder unique in its excellence; for he was murdered at noonday, and on the field of battle,—a feature of original conception, which occurs in no other work of art that I remember. Indeed, all of these assassinations may be studied with profit by the advanced connoisseur. They are all of them *exemplaria*, of which one may say,—

Nocturnâ versate manu, versate diurnâ:

Especially *nocturnâ*.

In these assassinations of princes and statesmen, there is nothing to excite our wonder: important changes often depend on their deaths; and from the eminence on which they stand, they are peculiarly exposed to the aim of every artist who happens to be possessed by the craving for scenical effect. But there is another class of assassinations, which has prevailed from an early period of the seventeenth century, that really *does* surprise me; I mean the assassination of philosophers. For, gentlemen, it is a fact, that every philosopher of eminence for the two last centuries has either been murdered, or, at the least, been very near it; insomuch, that if a man calls himself a philosopher, and never had his life attempted, rest assured there is nothing in him; and against Locke's philosophy in particular, I think it an unanswerable objection (if we needed any) that, although he carried his throat about with him in this world for seventy-two years, no man ever condescended to cut it. As these cases of philosophers are not much known, and are generally good and well composed in their circumstances, I shall here read an excursus on that subject, chiefly by way of showing my own learning.

The first great philosopher of the seventeenth century (if we except Galileo) was Des Cartes; and if ever one could say of a man that he was all *but* murdered—murdered within an inch, one must say it of him. The case was this, as reported by Baillet in his *Vie de M. Des Cartes*, tom. i. p. 102–3. In the year 1621, when Des Cartes might be about twenty-six years old, he was touring about as usual (for he was as restless as a hyæna), and, coming to the Elbe, either at Glückstadt or at Hamburgh, he took shipping for East Friezland: what he could want in East Friezland no man has ever discovered; and perhaps he took this into consideration himself; for, on reaching Embden, he resolved to sail instantly for *West* Friezland; and being very impatient of delay, he hired a bark, with a few mariners to navigate it. No sooner had he got out to sea than he made a pleasing discovery, viz., that he had shut himself up in a den of murderers. His crew, says M. Baillet, he soon found out to be 'des scélérats,' —not *amateurs*, gentlemen, as we are, but professional men—the height of whose ambition at that moment was to cut his throat. But the story is too pleasing to be abridged—I shall give it, therefore, accurately, from the French of his biographer: 'M. Des Cartes had no company but that of his servant, with whom he was conversing in French. The sailors, who took him for a foreign merchant, rather than a cavalier, concluded that he must have money about him. Accordingly they came to a resolution by no means advantageous to his purse. There is this difference, however, between sea-robbers and the robbers in forests, that the latter may, without hazard, spare the lives of their victims; whereas the other cannot put a passenger on shore in such a case without running the risk of being apprehended. The crew of M. Des Cartes arranged their measures with a view to evade any danger of that sort. They observed that he was a stranger from a distance, without acquaintance in the country, and that nobody would take any trouble to inquire about him, in case he should never come to hand (*quand il viendroit à manquer*).' Think, gentlemen, of these Friezland dogs discussing a philosopher as if he were a puncheon of rum. 'His temper, they remarked, was very mild and patient; and judging from the gentleness of his deportment, and the courtesy with which he treated themselves, that he could be nothing more than some green young man, they concluded that they should have all the easier task in disposing of his life. They made no scruple to discuss the whole matter in his presence, as not supposing that he understood any other language than that in which he conversed with his servant; and the amount of their deliberation was—to murder him, then to throw him into the sea, and to divide his spoils.'

Excuse my laughing, gentlemen, but the fact is, I always *do* laugh when I think of this case—two things about it seem so droll. One is, the horrid panic or 'funk' (as the men of Eton call it), in which Des Cartes must have found himself upon hearing this regular drama sketched for his own death—funeral—succession and administration to his effects. But another thing, which seems to me still more funny, about this affair is, that if these Friezland hounds had been 'game,' we should have no Cartesian philosophy; and how we could have done without *that*, considering the world of books it has produced, I leave to any respectable trunk-maker to declare.

However, to go on; spite of his enormous funk, Des Cartes showed fight, and by that means awed these Anti-Cartesian rascals. 'Finding,' says M. Baillet, 'that the matter was no joke, M. Des Cartes leaped upon his feet in a trice, assumed a stern countenance that these cravens had never looked for, and addressing them in their own language, threatened to run them through on the spot if they dared to offer him any insult.' Certainly, gentlemen, this would have been an honour far above the merits of such inconsiderable rascals—to be spitted like larks upon a Cartesian sword; and therefore I am glad M. Des Cartes did not rob the gallows by executing his threat, especially as he could not possibly have brought his vessel to port, after he had murdered his crew; so that he must have continued to cruise for ever in the Zuyder Zee, and would probably have been mistaken by sailors for the *Flying Dutchman*, homeward-bound. 'The spirit which M. Des Cartes manifested,' says his biographer, 'had the effect of magic on these wretches. The suddenness of their consternation struck their minds with a confusion which blinded them to their advantage, and they conveyed him to his destination as peaceably as he could desire.'

Possibly, gentlemen, you may fancy that, on the model of Cæsar's address to his poor ferryman,—'*Cæsarem vehis et fortunas ejus*,'—M. Des Cartes needed only to have said,—'Dogs, you cannot cut my throat, for you carry Des Cartes and his philosophy,' and might safely have defied them to do their worst. A German emperor had the same notion, when, being cautioned to keep out of the way of a cannonading, he replied, 'Tut! man. Did you ever hear of a cannon-ball that killed an emperor?' As to an emperor I cannot say, but a less thing has sufficed to smash a philosopher; and the next great philosopher of Europe undoubtedly *was* murdered. This was Spinosa.

I know very well the common opinion about him is, that he died in his bed. Perhaps he did, but he was murdered for all that; and this I shall prove by a book published at Brussels, in the year 1731, entitled, *La Vie de Spinosa; par M. Jean Colerus*, with many additions, from a MS. life, by one of his friends. Spinosa died on the 21st February 1677, being then little more than forty-four years old. This of itself looks suspicious; and M. Jean admits, that a certain expression in the MS. life of him would warrant the conclusion, 'que sa mort n'a pas été tout-à-fait naturelle.' Living in a damp country, and a sailor's country, like Holland, he may be thought to have indulged a good deal in grog, especially in punch,[1] which was then newly discovered. Undoubtedly he might have done so; but the fact is that he did not. M. Jean calls him 'extrêmement sobre en son boire et son manger.' And though some wild stories were afloat about his using the juice of mandragora (p. 140), and opium (p. 144), yet neither of these articles appeared in his druggist's bill. Living, therefore, with such sobriety, how was it possible that he should die a natural death at forty-four? Hear his biographer's account:—

[1] 'June 1, 1675.—Drinke part of 3 boules of punch (a liquor very strainge to me),' says the Rev. Mr. Henry Teonge, in his Diary lately published. In a note on this passage, a reference is made to Fryer's Travels to the East Indies, 1672, who speaks of 'that enervating liquor called *Paunch* (which is Hindostanee for five), from five ingredients.' Made thus, it seems the medical men called it Diapente; if with four only, Diatessaron. No doubt, it was its Evangelical name that recommended it to the Rev. Mr. Teonge.

'Sunday morning the 21st of February, before it was church-time, Spinosa came downstairs and conversed with the master and mistress of the house.' At this time, therefore, perhaps ten o'clock on Sunday morning, you see that Spinosa was alive, and pretty well. But it seems 'he had summoned from Amsterdam a certain physician, whom,' says the biographer, 'I shall not otherwise point out to notice than by these two letters, L. M. This L. M. had directed the people of the house to purchase an ancient cock, and to have him boiled forthwith, in order that Spinosa might take some broth about noon, which in fact he did, and ate some of the *old cock* with a good appetite, after the landlord and his wife had returned from church.

'In the afternoon, L. M. stayed alone with Spinosa, the people of the house having returned to church; on coming out from which they learnt, with much surprise, that Spinosa had died about three o'clock, in the presence of L. M., who took his departure for Amsterdam the same evening, by the night-boat, without paying the least attention to the deceased. No doubt he was the readier to dispense with these duties, as he had possessed himself of a ducatoon and a small quantity of silver, together with a silver-hafted knife, and had absconded with his pillage.' Here you see, gentlemen, the murder is plain, and the manner of it. It was L.M. who murdered Spinosa for his money. Poor S. was an invalid, meagre, and weak: as no blood was observed, L.M., no doubt, threw him down and smothered him with pillows,—the poor man being already half-suffocated by his infernal dinner.—But who was L.M.? It surely never could be Lindley Murray; for I saw him at York in 1825; and besides, I do not think he would do such a thing; at least, not to a brother grammarian: for you know, gentlemen, that Spinosa wrote a very respectable Hebrew grammar.

Hobbes, but why, or on what principle, I never could understand, was not murdered. This was a capital oversight of the professional men in the seventeenth century; because in every light he was a fine subject for murder, except, indeed, that he was lean and skinny; for I can prove that he had money, and (what is very funny) he had no right to make the least resistance; for, according to himself, irresistible power creates the very highest species of right, so that it is rebellion of the blackest dye to refuse to be murdered, when a competent force appears to murder you. However, gentlemen, though he was not murdered, I am happy to assure you that (by his own account) he was three times very near being murdered.—The first time was in the spring of 1640, when he pretends to have circulated a little MS. on the king's behalf, against the Parliament; he never could produce this MS., by-the-by; but he says that, 'Had not His Majesty dissolved the Parliament' (in May), 'it had brought him into danger of his life.' Dissolving the Parliament, however, was of no use; for, in November of the same year, the Long Parliament assembled, and, Hobbes, a second time, fearing he should be murdered, ran away to France. This looks like the madness of John Dennis, who thought that Louis XIV. would never make peace with Queen Anne, unless he were given up to his vengeance; and actually ran away from the sea-coast in that belief. In France, Hobbes managed to take care of his throat pretty well for ten years; but at the end of that time, by way of paying court to Cromwell, he published his Leviathan. The old coward now began to 'funk' horribly for the third time; he fancied the swords of the cavaliers were constantly at his throat, recollecting how they had served the Parliament ambassadors at the Hague and Madrid. 'Tum,' says he, in his dog-Latin life of himself—

> Tum venit in mentem mihi Dorislaus et Ascham;
> Tamquam proscripto terror ubique aderat.

And accordingly he ran home to England. Now, certainly, it is very true that a man deserved a cudgelling for writing Leviathan; and two or three cudgellings for writing a pentameter ending so villainously as—'terror ubique aderat'! But no man ever thought him worthy of anything beyond cudgelling. And, in fact, the whole story is a bounce of his own. For, in a most abusive letter which he wrote 'to a learned person' (meaning Wallis the mathematician), he gives quite another account of the matter, and says (p. 8), he ran home 'because he would not trust his safety with the French clergy'; insinuating that he was likely to be murdered for his religion, which would have been a high joke indeed—Tom's being brought to the stake for religion.

Bounce or not bounce, however, certain it is, that Hobbes, to the end of his life, feared that somebody would murder him. This is proved by the story I am going to tell you: it is not from a manuscript, but (as Mr. Coleridge says) it is as good as manuscript; for it comes from a book now entirely forgotten, viz.—'The Creed of Mr. Hobbes examined; in a Conference between him and a Student in Divinity' (published about ten years before Hobbes' death). The book is anonymous, but it was written by Tennison, the same who, about thirty years after, succeeded Tillotson as Archbishop of Canterbury. The introductory anecdote is as follows:—'A certain divine, it seems (no doubt Tennison himself), took an annual tour of one month to different parts of the island. In one of these excursions (1670) he visited the Peak in Derbyshire, partly in consequence of Hobbes' description of it. Being in that neighbourhood, he could not but pay a visit to Buxton; and at the very moment of his arrival, he was fortunate enough to find a party of gentlemen dismounting at the inn door, amongst whom was a long thin fellow, who turned out to be no less a person than Mr. Hobbes, who probably had ridden over from Chatsworth.' Meeting so great a lion,—a tourist, in search of the picturesque, could do no less than present himself in the character of bore. And luckily for this scheme, two of Mr. Hobbes' companions were suddenly summoned away by express; so that, for the rest of his stay at Buxton, he had Leviathan entirely to himself, and had the honour of bowsing with him in the evening. Hobbes, it seems, at first showed a good deal of stiffness, for he was shy of divines; but this wore off, and he became very sociable and funny, and they agreed to go into the bath together. How Tennison could venture to gambol in the same water with Leviathan, I cannot explain; but so it was: they frolicked about like two dolphins, though Hobbes must have been as old as the hills; and 'in those intervals wherein they abstained from swimming and plunging themselves' [*i.e.* diving], 'they discoursed of many things relating to the Baths of the Ancients, and the Origin of Springs. When they had in this manner passed away an hour, they stepped out of the bath; and, having dried and clothed themselves, they sate down in expectation of such a supper as the place afforded; designing to refresh themselves like the *Deipnosophistæ*, and rather to reason than to drink profoundly. But in this innocent intention they were interrupted by the disturbance arising from a little quarrel, in which some of the ruder people in the house were for a short time engaged. At this Mr. Hobbes seemed much concerned, though he was at some distance from the persons.'—And why was he concerned, gentlemen? No doubt you fancy, from some benign and disinterested love of peace and harmony, worthy of an old man and a philosopher. But listen—'For a while he was not composed, but related it once or twice as to himself, with a low and careful tone, how Sextus Roscius was murthered after supper by the Balneæ Palatinæ. Of such general extent is that remark of Cicero, in relation to Epicurus the Atheist, of whom he observed that he of all men dreaded most those things which he contemned—Death and the Gods.'—Merely because it was supper-time, and in the neighbourhood of a bath, Mr. Hobbes must have the fate of Sextus Roscius. What logic was there in this, unless to a man who was always dreaming of murder?—Here was Leviathan, no longer afraid of the daggers of English cavaliers or French clergy, but 'frightened from his propriety' by a row in an alehouse between some honest clod-hoppers of Derbyshire whom his own gaunt scarecrow of a person, that belonged to quite another century, would have frightened out of their wits.

Malebranche, it will give you pleasure to hear, was murdered. The man who murdered him is well known: it was Bishop Berkeley. The story is familiar, though hitherto not put in a proper light. Berkeley, when a young man, went to Paris and called on Père Malebranche. He found him in his cell cooking. Cooks have ever been a *genus irritabile*; authors still more so: Malebranche was both: a dispute arose; the old Father, warm already, became warmer; culinary and metaphysical irritations united to derange his liver; he took to his bed, and died. Such is the common version of the story: 'So the whole ear of Denmark is abused.'—The fact is, that the matter was hushed up, out of consideration for Berkeley, who (as Pope remarked) had 'every virtue under heaven': else it was well known that Berkeley, feeling himself nettled by the waspishness of the old Frenchman, squared at him; a *turn-up* was the consequence: Malebranche was floored in the first round; the conceit was wholly taken out of him; and he would perhaps have given in; but Berkeley's blood was now up, and he insisted on the old Frenchman's retracting his doctrine of Occasional Causes. The vanity of the man was too great for this; and he fell a sacrifice to the impetuosity of Irish youth, combined with his own absurd obstinacy.

Leibnitz, being every way superior to Malebranche, one might, *a fortiori*, have counted on *his* being murdered; which, however, was not the case. I believe he was nettled at this neglect, and felt himself insulted by the security in which he passed his days. In no other way can I explain his conduct at the latter end of his life, when he chose to grow very avaricious, and to hoard up large sums of gold, which he kept in his own house. This was at Vienna, where he died; and letters are still in existence, describing the immeasurable anxiety which he entertained for his throat. Still his ambition, for being *attempted* at least, was so great, that he would not forego the danger. A late English pedagogue, of Birmingham manufacture, viz., Dr. Parr, took a more selfish course, under the same circumstances. He had amassed a considerable quantity of gold and silver plate, which was for some time deposited in his bedroom at his parsonage house, Hatton. But growing every day more afraid of being murdered, which he knew that he could not stand (and to which, indeed, he never had the slightest pretension), he transferred the whole to the Hatton blacksmith; conceiving, no doubt, that the murder of a blacksmith would fall more lightly on the *salus reipublicæ*, than that of a pedagogue. But I have heard this greatly disputed; and it seems now generally agreed, that one good horse-shoe is worth about 2½ Spital sermons.

As Leibnitz, though not murdered, may be said to have died, partly of the fear that he should be murdered, and partly of vexation that he was not,—Kant, on the other hand—who had no ambition in that way—had a narrower escape from a murderer than any man we read of, except Des Cartes. So absurdly does Fortune throw about her favours! The case is told, I think, in an anonymous life of this very great man. For health's sake, Kant imposed upon himself, at one time, a walk of six miles every day along a highroad. This fact becoming known to a man who had his private reasons for committing murder, at the third milestone from Königsberg, he waited for his 'intended,' who came up to time as duly as a mail-coach. But for an accident, Kant was a dead man. However, on considerations of 'morality,' it happened that the murderer preferred a little child, whom he saw playing in the road, to the old transcendentalist: this child he murdered; and thus it happened that Kant escaped. Such is the German account of the matter; but my opinion is—that the murderer was an amateur, who felt how little would be gained to the cause of good taste by murdering an old, arid, and adust metaphysician; there was no room for display, as the man could not possibly look more like a mummy when dead, than he had done alive.

Thus, gentlemen, I have traced the connection between philosophy and our art, until insensibly I find that I have wandered into our own era. This I shall not take any pains to characterise apart from that which preceded it, for, in fact, they have no distinct character. The seventeenth and eighteenth centuries, together with so much of the nineteenth as we have yet seen, jointly compose the Augustan age of murder. The finest work of the seventeenth century is, unquestionably, the murder of Sir Edmondbury Godfrey, which has my entire approbation. At the same time, it must be observed, that the quantity of murder was not great in this century, at least amongst our own artists; which, perhaps, is attributable to the want of enlightened patronage. *Sint Mæcenates, non deerunt, Flacce, Marones.* Consulting Grant's 'Observations on the Bills of Mortality' (4th edition, Oxford, 1665), I find, that out of 229,250, who died in London during one period of twenty years in the seventeenth century, not more than eighty-six were murdered; that is, about four three-tenths per annum. A small number this, gentlemen, to found an academy upon; and certainly, where the quantity is so small, we have a right to expect that the quality should be first-rate. Perhaps it was; yet, still I am of opinion that the best artist in this century was not equal to the best in that which followed. For instance, however praiseworthy the case of Sir Edmondbury Godfrey may be (and nobody can be more sensible of its merits than I am), still I cannot consent to place it on a level with that of Mrs. Ruscombe of Bristol, either as to originality of design, or boldness and breadth of style. This good lady's murder took place early in the reign of George III.—a reign which was notoriously favourable to the arts generally. She lived in College Green, with a single maid-servant, neither of them having any pretension to the notice of history but what they derived from the great artist whose workmanship I am recording. One fine morning, when all Bristol was alive and in motion, some suspicion arising, the neighbours forced an entrance into the house, and found Mrs. Ruscombe murdered in her bedroom, and the servant murdered on the stairs: this was at noon; and, not more than two hours before, both mistress and servant had been seen alive. To the best of my remembrance, this was in 1764; upwards of sixty years, therefore, have now elapsed, and yet the artist is still undiscovered. The suspicions of posterity have settled upon two pretenders—a baker and a chimney-sweeper. But posterity is wrong; no unpractised artist could have conceived so bold an idea as that of a noonday murder in the heart of a great city. It was no obscure baker, gentlemen, or anonymous chimney-sweeper, be assured, that executed this work. I know who it was. (*Here there was a general buzz, which at length broke out into open applause; upon which the lecturer blushed, and went on with much earnestness.*) For Heaven's sake, gentlemen, do not mistake me; it was not I that did it. I have not the vanity to think myself equal to any such achievement; be assured that you greatly overrate my poor talents; Mrs. Ruscombe's affair was far beyond my slender abilities. But I came to know who the artist was, from a celebrated surgeon, who assisted at his dissection. This gentleman had a private museum in the way of his profession, one corner of which was occupied by a cast from a man of remarkably fine proportions.

'That,' said the surgeon, 'is a cast from the celebrated

Lancashire highwayman, who concealed his profession for some time from his neighbours, by drawing woollen stockings over his horse's legs, and in that way muffling the clatter which he must else have made in riding up a flagged alley that led to his stable. At the time of his execution for highway robbery, I was studying under Cruickshank: and the man's figure was so uncommonly fine, that no money or exertion was spared to get into possession of him with the least possible delay. By the connivance of the under-sheriff he was cut down within the legal time, and instantly put into a chaise and four; so that, when he reached Cruickshank's, he was positively not dead. Mr. ——, a young student at that time, had the honour of giving him the *coup de grâce*—and finishing the sentence of the law.' This remarkable anecdote, which seemed to imply that all the gentlemen in the dissecting-room were amateurs of our class, struck me a good deal; and I was repeating it one day to a Lancashire lady, who thereupon informed me, that she had herself lived in the neighbourhood of that highwayman, and well remembered two circumstances, which combined, in the opinion of all his neighbours, to fix upon him the credit of Mrs. Ruscombe's affair. One was, the fact of his absence for a whole fortnight at the period of that murder; the other, that, within a very little time after, the neighbourhood of this highwayman was deluged with dollars: now Mrs. Ruscombe was known to have hoarded about two thousand of that coin. Be the artist, however, who he might, the affair remains a durable monument of his genius; for such was the impression of awe, and the sense of power left behind, by the strength of conception manifested in this murder, that no tenant (as I was told in 1810) had been found up to that time for Mrs. Ruscombe's house.

But while I thus eulogise the Ruscombian case, let me not be supposed to overlook the many other specimens of extraordinary merit spread over the face of this century. Such cases, indeed, as that of Miss

Bland, or of Captain Donnellan, and Sir Theophilus Boughton, shall never have any countenance from me. Fie on these dealers in poison, say I: can they not keep to the old honest way of cutting throats, without introducing such abominable innovations from Italy? I consider all these poisoning cases, compared with the legitimate style, as no better than waxwork by the side of sculpture, or a lithographic print by the side of a fine Volpato. But, dismissing these, there remain many excellent works of art in a pure style, such as nobody need be ashamed to own, as every candid connoisseur will admit. *Candid*, observe, I say; for great allowances must be made in these cases; no artist can ever be sure of carrying through his own fine preconception. Awkward disturbances will arise; people will not submit to have their throats cut quietly; they will run, they will kick, they will bite; and, whilst the portrait painter often has to complain of too much torpor in his subject, the artist, in our line, is generally embarrassed by too much animation. At the same time, however disagreeable to the artist, this tendency in murder to excite and irritate the subject, is certainly one of its advantages to the world in general, which we ought not to overlook, since it favours the development of latent talent. Jeremy Taylor notices with admiration, the extraordinary leaps which people will take under the influence of fear. There was a striking instance of this in the recent case of the M'Keans; the boy cleared a height, such as he will never clear again to his dying day. Talents also of the most brilliant description for thumping, and indeed for all the gymnastic exercises, have sometimes been developed by the panic which accompanies our artists; talents else buried and hid under a bushel to the possessors, as much as to their friends. I remember an interesting illustration of this fact, in a case which I learned in Germany.

Riding one day in the neighbourhood of Munich, I overtook a distinguished amateur of our society, whose name I shall conceal. This gentleman informed me that, finding himself wearied with the frigid pleasures (so he called them) of mere amateurship, he had quitted England for the continent—meaning to practise a little professionally. For this purpose he resorted to Germany, conceiving the police in that part of Europe to be more heavy and drowsy than elsewhere. His *début* as a practitioner took place at Mannheim; and, knowing me to be a brother amateur, he freely communicated the whole of his maiden adventure. 'Opposite to my lodging,' said he, 'lived a baker: he was somewhat of a miser, and lived quite alone. Whether it were his great expanse of chalky face, or what else, I know not—but the fact was, I "fancied" him, and resolved to commence business upon his throat, which, by the way, he always carried bare—a fashion which is very irritating to my desires. Precisely at eight o'clock in the evening, I observed that he regularly shut up his windows. One night I watched him when thus engaged—bolted in after him—locked the door—and, addressing him with great suavity, acquainted him with the nature of my errand; at the same time advising him to make no resistance, which would be mutually unpleasant. So saying I drew out my tools; and was proceeding to operate. But at this spectacle, the baker, who seemed to have been struck by catalepsy at my first announcement, awoke into tremendous agitation. "I will *not* be murdered!" he shrieked aloud; "what for will I lose my precious throat?"—"What for?" said I; "if for no other reason, for this—that you put alum into your bread. But no matter, alum or no alum (for I was resolved to forestall any argument on that point), know that I am a virtuoso in the art of murder—am desirous of improving myself in its details—and am enamoured of your vast surface of throat, to which I am determined to be a customer." "Is it so?" said he, "but I'll find you custom in another line"; and so saying he threw himself into a boxing attitude.

The very idea of his boxing struck me as ludicrous. It is true, a London baker had distinguished himself in the ring, and became known to fame under the title of the Master of the Rolls; but he was young and unspoiled; whereas this man was a monstrous feather-bed in person, fifty years old, and totally out of condition. Spite of all this, however, and contending against me, who am a master in the art, he made so desperate a defence, that many times I feared he might turn the tables upon me; and that I, an amateur, might be murdered by a rascally baker. What a situation! Minds of sensibility will sympathise with my anxiety. How severe it was, you may understand by this, that for the first thirteen rounds the baker had the advantage. Round the fourteenth, I received a blow on the right eye, which closed it up; in the end, I believe this was my salvation: for the anger it roused in me was so great that, in this and every one of the three following rounds, I floored the baker.

'Round eighteenth.—The baker came up piping, and manifestly the worse for wear. His geometrical exploits in the four last rounds had done him no good. However, he showed some skill in stopping a message which I was sending to his cadaverous mug; in delivering which, my foot slipped, and I went down.

'Round nineteenth.—Surveying the baker, I became ashamed of having been so much bothered by a shapeless mass of dough; and I went in fiercely, and administered some severe punishment. A rally took place—both went down—Baker undermost—ten to three on Amateur.

'Round twentieth.—The baker jumped up with surprising agility; indeed, he managed his pins capitally, and fought wonderfully, considering that he was drenched in perspiration; but the shine was now taken out of him, and his game was the mere effect of panic. It was now clear that he could not last much longer. In the course of this round we tried the weaving system, in which I had greatly the advantage, and hit him repeatedly on the conk. My reason for this was, that his conk was covered with carbuncles; and I thought I should vex him by taking such liberties with his conk, which in fact I did.

'The three next rounds, the master of the rolls staggered about like a cow on the ice. Seeing how matters stood, in round twenty-fourth I whispered something into his ear, which sent him down like a shot. It was nothing more than my private opinion of the value of his throat at an annuity office. This little confidential whisper affected him greatly; the very perspiration was frozen on his face, and for the next two rounds I had it all my own way. And when I called *time* for the twenty-seventh round, he lay like a log on the floor.'

After which, said I to the amateur, 'It may be presumed that you accomplished your purpose.'—'You are right,' said he mildly, 'I did; and a great satisfaction, you know, it was to my mind, for by this means I killed two birds with one stone'; meaning that he had both thumped the baker and murdered him. Now, for the life of me, I could not see *that*; for, on the contrary, to my mind it appeared that he had taken two stones to kill one bird, having been obliged to take the conceit out of him first with his fists, and then with his tools. But no matter for his logic. The moral of his story was good, for it showed what an astonishing stimulus to latent talent is contained in any reasonable prospect of being murdered. A pursy, unwieldy, half cataleptic baker of Mannheim had absolutely fought six-and-twenty rounds with an accomplished English boxer merely upon this inspiration; so greatly was natural genius exalted and sublimed by the genial presence of his murderer.

Really, gentlemen, when one hears of such things as these, it becomes a duty, perhaps, a little to soften that extreme asperity with which most men speak of murder. To hear people talk, you would suppose that all the disadvantages and inconveniences were on the side of being murdered, and that there were none at all in *not* being murdered. But considerate men think otherwise. 'Certainly,' says Jeremy Taylor, 'it is a less temporal evil to fall by the rudeness of a sword than the violence of a fever: and the axe' (to which he might have added the ship-carpenter's mallet and a crowbar) 'a much less affliction than a strangury.' Very true; the Bishop talks like a wise man and an amateur, as he is; and another great philosopher, Marcus Aurelius, was equally above the vulgar prejudices on this subject. He declares it to be one of 'the noblest functions of reason to know whether it is time to walk out of the world or not.' (Book III. Collier's translation.) No sort of knowledge being rarer than this, surely *that* man must be a most philanthropic character, who undertakes to instruct people in this branch of knowledge gratis, and at no little hazard to himself. All this, however, I throw out only in the way of speculation to future moralists; declaring in the meantime my own private conviction, that very few men commit murder upon philanthropic or patriotic principles, and repeating what I have already said once at least—that, as to the majority of murderers, they are very incorrect characters.

With respect to Williams's murders, the sublimest and most entire in their excellence that ever were committed, I shall not allow myself to speak incidentally. Nothing less than an entire lecture, or even an entire course of lectures, would suffice to expound their merits. But one curious fact, connected with his case, I shall mention, because it seems to imply that the blaze of his genius absolutely dazzled the eye of criminal justice. You all remember, I doubt not, that the instruments with which he executed his first great work (the murder of the Marrs), were a ship-carpenter's mallet and a knife. Now the mallet belonged to an old Swede, one John Petersen, and bore his initials. This instrument Williams left behind him, in Marr's house, and it fell into the hands of the Magistrates. Now, gentlemen, it is a fact that the publication of this circumstance of the initials led immediately to the apprehension of Williams, and, if made earlier, would have prevented his second great work (the murder of the Williamsons), which took place precisely twelve days after. But the Magistrates kept back this fact from the public for the entire twelve days, and until that second work was accomplished. That finished, they published it, apparently feeling that Williams had now done enough for his fame, and that his glory was at length placed beyond the reach of accident.

As to Mr. Thurtell's case, I know not what to say. Naturally, I have every disposition to think highly of my predecessor in the chair of this society; and I acknowledge that his lectures were unexceptionable. But, speaking ingenuously, I do really think that his principal performance, as an artist, has been much overrated. I admit that at first I was myself carried away by the general enthusiasm. On the morning when the murder was made known in London, there was the fullest meeting of amateurs that I have ever known since the days of Williams; old bed-ridden connoisseurs, who had got into a peevish way of sneering and complaining 'that there was nothing doing,' now hobbled down to our club-room: such hilarity, such benign expression of general satisfaction, I have rarely witnessed. On every side you saw people shaking hands, congratulating each other, and forming dinner-parties for the evening; and nothing was to be heard but triumphant challenges of—'Well! will *this* do?' 'Is *this* the right thing?' 'Are you satisfied at last?' But, in the midst of this, I remember we all grew silent on hearing the old cynical amateur, L. S——, that *laudator temporis acti*, stumping along with his wooden leg; he entered the room with his usual scowl, and, as he advanced, he continued to growl and stutter the whole way—'Not an original idea in the whole piece—mere plagiarism,—base plagiarism from hints that I threw out! Besides, his style is as hard as Albert Durer, and as coarse as Fuseli.' Many thought that this was mere jealousy, and general waspishness; but I confess that, when the first glow of enthusiasm had subsided, I have found most judicious critics to agree that there was something *falsetto* in the style of Thurtell. The fact is, he was a member of our society, which naturally gave a friendly bias to our judgments; and his person was universally familiar to the Cockneys, which gave him, with the whole London public, a temporary popularity, that his pretensions are not capable of supporting; for *opinionum commenta delet dies, naturæ judicia confirmat.*—There was, however, an unfinished design of Thurtell's for the murder of a man with a pair of dumb-bells, which I admired greatly; it was a mere outline that he never completed; but to my mind it seemed every way superior to his chief work. I remember that there was great regret expressed by some amateurs that this sketch should have been left in an unfinished state: but there I cannot agree with them; for the fragments and first bold outlines of original artists have often a felicity about them which is apt to vanish in the management of the details.

The case of the M'Keans I consider far beyond the vaunted performance of Thurtell,—indeed above all praise; and bearing that relation, in fact, to the immortal works of Williams, which the *Æneid* bears to the *Iliad*.

But it is now time that I should say a few words about the principles of murder, not with a view to regulate your practice, but your judgment: as to old women, and the mob of newspaper readers, they are pleased with anything, provided it is bloody enough. But the mind of sensibility requires something more. *First*, then, let us speak of the kind of person who is adapted to the purpose of the murderer; *secondly*, of the place where; *thirdly*, of the time when, and other little circumstances.

As to the person, I suppose it is evident that he ought to be a good man; because, if he were not, he might himself, by possibility, be contemplating murder at the very time; and such 'diamond-cut-diamond' tussles, though pleasant enough where nothing better is stirring, are really not what a critic can allow himself to call murders. I could mention some people (I name no names) who have been murdered by other people in a dark lane; and so far all seemed correct enough; but, on looking farther into the matter, the public have become aware that the murdered party was himself, at the moment, planning to rob his murderer, at the least, and possibly to murder him, if he had been strong enough. Whenever that is the case, or may be thought to be the case, farewell to all the genuine effects of the art. For the final purpose of murder, considered as a fine art, is precisely the same as that of Tragedy, in Aristotle's account of it, viz., 'to cleanse the heart by means of pity and terror.' Now, terror there may be, but how can there be any pity for one tiger destroyed by another tiger?

It is also evident that the person selected ought not to be a public character. For instance, no judicious artist would have attempted to murder Abraham Newland. For the case was this: everybody read so much about Abraham Newland, and so few people ever saw him, that there was a fixed belief that he was an abstract idea. And I remember that once, when I happened to mention that I had dined at a coffee-house in company with Abraham Newland, everybody looked scornfully at me, as though I had pretended to have played at billiards with Prester John, or to have had an affair of honour with the Pope. And, by the way, the Pope would be a very improper person to murder: for he has such a virtual ubiquity as the Father of Christendom, and, like the cuckoo, is so often heard but never seen, that I suspect most people regard *him* also as an abstract idea. Where, indeed, a public character is in the habit of giving dinners, 'with every delicacy of the season,' the case is very different: every person is satisfied that *he* is no abstract idea; and, therefore, there can be no impropriety in murdering him; only that his murder will fall into the class of assassinations which I have not yet treated.

Thirdly, The subject chosen ought to be in good health: for it is absolutely barbarous to murder a sick person, who is usually quite unable to bear it. On this principle, no Cockney ought to be chosen who is above twenty-five, for after that age he is sure to be dyspeptic. Or at least, if a man will hunt in that warren, he ought to murder a couple at one time; if the Cockneys chosen should be tailors, he will of course think it his duty, on the old established equation, to murder eighteen—And, here, in this attention to the comfort of sick people, you will observe the usual effect of a fine art to soften and refine the feelings. The world in general, gentlemen, are very bloody-minded; and all they want in a murder is a copious effusion of blood; gaudy display in this point is enough for *them*. But the enlightened connoisseur is more refined in his taste; and from our art, as from all the other liberal arts when thoroughly cultivated, the result is—to improve and to humanise the heart; so true is it, that—

> Ingenuas didicisse fideliter artes,
> Emollit mores, nec sinit esse feros.

A philosophic friend, well known for his philanthropy and general benignity, suggests that the subject chosen ought also to have a family of young children wholly dependent on his exertions, by way of deepening the pathos. And, undoubtedly, this is a judicious caution. Yet I would not insist too keenly on this condition. Severe good taste unquestionably demands it; but still, where the man was otherwise unobjectionable in point of morals and health, I would not look with too curious a jealousy to a restriction which might have the effect of narrowing the artist's sphere.

So much for the person. As to the time, the place, and the tools, I have many things to say, which at present I have no room for. The good sense of the practitioner has usually directed him to night and privacy. Yet there have not been wanting cases where this rule was departed from with excellent effect. In respect to time, Mrs. Ruscombe's case is a beautiful exception, which I have already noticed; and in respect both to time and place, there is a fine exception in the Annals of Edinburgh (year 1805), familiar to every child in Edinburgh, but which has unaccountably been defrauded of its due portion of fame amongst English amateurs. The case I mean is that of a porter to one of the Banks, who was murdered whilst carrying a bag of money, in broad daylight, on turning out of the High Street, one of the most public streets in Europe, and the murderer is to this hour undiscovered.

> Sed fugit interea, fugit irreparabile tempus,
> Singula dum capti circumvectamur amore.

And now, gentlemen, in conclusion, let me again solemnly disclaim all pretensions on my own part to the character of a professional man. I never attempted any murder in my life, except in the year 1801, upon the body of a tom-cat; and *that* turned out differently from my intention. My purpose, I own, was downright murder. 'Semper ego auditor tantum?' said I, 'nunquamne reponam?' And I went downstairs in search of Tom at one o'clock on a dark night, with the 'animus,' and no doubt with the fiendish looks, of a murderer. But when I found him, he was in the act of plundering the pantry of bread and other things. Now this gave a new turn to the affair; for the time being one of general scarcity, when even Christians were reduced to the use of potato-bread, rice-bread, and all sorts of things, it was downright treason in a tom-cat to be wasting good wheaten-bread in the way he was doing. It instantly became a patriotic duty to put him to death; and as I raised aloft and shook the glittering steel, I fancied myself rising like Brutus, effulgent from a crowd of patriots, and, as I stabbed him, I

> called aloud on Tully's name,
> And bade the father of his country hail!

Since then, what wandering thoughts I may have had of attempting the life of an ancient ewe, of a superannuated hen, and such 'small deer,' are locked up in the secrets of my own breast; but for the higher departments of the art, I confess myself to be utterly unfit. My ambition does not rise so high. No, gentlemen, in the words of Horace,

> fungar vice cotis, acutum
> Reddere quæ ferrum valet, exsors ipsa secandi.

II

DOCTOR NORTH,—You are a liberal man: liberal in the true classical sense, not in the slang sense of modern politicians and education-mongers. Being so, I am sure that you will sympathise with my case. I am an ill-used man, Dr. North—particularly ill-used; and, with your permission, I will briefly explain how. A black scene of calumny will be laid open; but you, Doctor, will make all things square again. One frown from you, directed to the proper quarter, or a warning shake of the crutch, will set me right in public opinion, which at present, I am sorry to say, is rather hostile to me and mine—all owing to the wicked arts of slanderers. But you shall hear.

A good many years ago you may remember that I came forward in the character of a *dilettante* in murder. Perhaps *dilettante* may be too strong a word. *Connoisseur* is better suited to the scruples and infirmity of public taste. I suppose there is no harm in *that* at least. A man is not bound to put his eyes, ears, and understanding into his breeches pocket when he meets with a murder. If he is not in a downright comatose state, I suppose he must see that one murder is better or worse than another in point of good taste. Murders have their little differences and shades of merit as well as statues, pictures, oratorios, cameos, intaglios, or what not. You may be angry with the man for talking too much, or too publicly (as to the too much, that I deny—a man can never cultivate his taste too highly); but you must allow him to think, at any rate; and you, Doctor—you think, I am sure, both deeply and correctly on the subject. Well, would you believe it? all my neighbours came to hear of that little æsthetic essay which you had published; and, unfortunately, hearing at the very same time of a Club that I was connected with, and a Dinner at which I presided—both tending to the same little object as the essay, viz., the diffusion of a just taste among her Majesty's subjects, they got up the most barbarous calumnies against me. In particular, they said that I, or that the Club, which comes to the same thing, had offered bounties on well-conducted homicides—with a scale of drawbacks, in case of any one defect or flaw, according to a table issued to private friends. Now, Doctor, I'll tell you the whole truth about the Dinner and the Club, and you'll see how malicious the world is. But first let me tell you, confidentially, what my real principles are upon the matters in question.

As to murder, I never committed one in my life. It 's a well-known thing amongst all my friends. I can get a paper to certify as much, signed by lots of people. Indeed, if you come to that, I doubt whether many people could produce as strong a certificate. Mine would be as big as a tablecloth. There is indeed one member of the Club, who pretends to say that he caught me once making too free with his throat on a club night, after everybody else had retired. But, observe, he shuffles in his story according to his state of civilization. When not far gone, he contents himself with saying that he caught me ogling his throat; and that I was melancholy for some weeks after, and that my voice sounded in a way expressing, to the nice ear of a connoisseur, *the sense of opportunities lost*—but the Club all know that he 's a disappointed man himself, and that he speaks querulously at times about the fatal neglect of a man's coming abroad without his tools. Besides, all this is an affair between two amateurs, and everybody makes allowances for little asperities and sorenesses in such a case. 'But,' say you, 'if no murderer, my correspondent may have encouraged, or even have bespoke, a murder.' No, upon my honour—nothing of the kind. And that was the very point I wished to argue for your satisfaction. The truth is, I am a very particular man in everything relating to murder; and perhaps I carry my delicacy too far. The Stagyrite most justly, and possibly with a view to my case, placed virtue in the τὸ μέσον or middle point between two extremes. A golden mean is certainly what every man should aim at. But it is easier talking than doing: and, my infirmity being notoriously too much milkiness of heart, I find it difficult to maintain that steady equatorial line between the two poles of too much murder on the one hand, and too little on the other. I am too soft—Doctor, too soft; and people get excused through me—nay, go through life without an attempt made upon them, that ought not to be excused. I believe if I had the management of things there would hardly be a murder from year's end to year's end. In fact I'm for virtue, and goodness, and all that sort of thing. And two instances I'll give you to what an extremity I carry my virtue. The first may seem a trifle; but not if you knew my nephew, who was certainly born to be hanged, and would have been so long ago, but for my restraining voice. He is horribly ambitious, and thinks himself a man of cultivated taste in most branches of murder, whereas, in fact, he has not one idea on the subject, but such as he has stolen from me. This is so well known, that the Club has twice blackballed him, though every indulgence was shown to him as my relative. People came to me and said—'Now really, President, we would do much to serve a relative of yours. But still, what can be said? You know yourself that he'll disgrace us. If we were to elect him, why, the next thing we should hear of would be some vile butcherly murder, by way of justifying our choice. And what sort of a concern would it be? You know, as well as we do, that it would be a disgraceful affair, more worthy of the shambles than of an artist's *atelier*. He would fall upon some great big man, some huge farmer returning drunk from a fair. There would be plenty of blood, and *that* he would expect us to take in lieu of taste, finish, scenical grouping. Then, again, how would he tool? Why, most probably with a cleaver and a couple of paving stones: so that the whole *coup d'œil* would remind you rather of some hideous Ogre or Cyclops, than of the delicate operator of the nineteenth century.' The picture was drawn with the hand of truth; *that* I could not but allow, and, as to personal feelings in the matter, I dismissed them from the first. The next morning I spoke to my nephew—I was delicately situated, as you see, but I determined that no consideration should induce me to flinch from my duty. 'John,' said I, 'you seem to me to have taken an erroneous view of life and its duties. Pushed on by ambition, you are dreaming rather of what it might be glorious to attempt than what it would be possible for you to accomplish. Believe me, it is not necessary to a man's respectability that he should commit a murder. Many a man has passed through life most respectably, without attempting any species of homicide—good, bad, or indifferent. It is your first duty to ask yourself, *quid valeant humeri, quid ferre recusent?* we cannot all be brilliant men in this life. And it is for your interest to be contented rather with a humble station well filled, than to shock everybody with failures, the more conspicuous by contrast with the ostentation of their promises.' John made no answer, he looked very sulky at the moment, and I am in high hopes that I have saved a near relation from making a fool of himself by attempting what is as much beyond his capacity as an epic poem. Others, however, tell me that he is meditating a revenge upon me and the whole Club. But let this be as it may, *liberavi animam meam*; and, as you see, have run some risk with a wish to diminish the amount of homicide. But the other case still more forcibly illustrates my virtue. A man came to me as a candidate for the place of my servant, just then vacant. He had the reputation of having dabbled a little in our art; some said not without merit. What startled me, however, was, that he supposed this art to be part of his regular duties in my service. Now that was a thing I would not allow; so I said at once, 'Richard (or James, as the case might be), you misunderstand my character. If a man will and must practise this difficult (and allow me to add, dangerous) branch of art—if he has an overruling genius for it, why, he might as well pursue his studies whilst living in my service as in another's. And also, I may observe, that it can do no harm, either to himself or to the subject on whom he operates, that he should be guided by men of more taste than himself. Genius may do much, but long study of the art must always entitle a man to offer advice. So far I will go—general principles I will suggest. But, as to any particular case, once for all I will have nothing to do with it. Never tell me of any special work of art you are meditating—I set my face against it *in toto.* For if once a man indulges himself in murder, very soon he comes to think little of robbing; and from robbing he comes next to drinking and Sabbath-breaking, and from that to incivility and procrastination. Once begin upon this downward path, you never know where you are to stop. Many a man has dated his ruin from some murder or other that perhaps he thought little of at the time. *Principiis obsta*—that 's my rule.' Such was my speech, and I have always acted up to it; so if that is not being virtuous, I should be glad to know what is. But now about the Dinner and the Club. The Club was not particularly of my creation; it arose pretty much as other similar associations, for the propagation of truth and the communication of new ideas, rather from the necessities of things than upon any one man's suggestion. As to the Dinner, if any man more than another could be held responsible for that, it was a member known amongst us by the name of *Toad-in-the-hole.* He was so called from his gloomy misanthropical disposition, which led him into constant disparagements of all modern murders as vicious abortions, belonging to no authentic school of art. The finest performances of our own age he snarled at cynically; and at length this querulous humour grew upon him so much, and he became so notorious as a *laudator temporis acti*, that few people cared to seek his society. This made him still more fierce and truculent. He went about muttering and growling; wherever you met him he was soliloquising and saying, 'despicable pretender—without grouping—without two ideas upon handling—without'—and there you lost him. At length existence seemed to be painful to him; he rarely spoke, he seemed conversing with phantoms in the air, his housekeeper informed us that his reading was nearly confined to *God's Revenge upon Murder* by Reynolds, and a more ancient book of the same title, noticed by Sir Walter Scott in his *Fortunes of Nigel.* Sometimes, perhaps, he might read in the Newgate Calendar down to the year 1788, but he never looked into a book more recent. In fact, he had a theory with regard to the French Revolution, as having been the great cause of degeneration in murder. 'Very soon, sir,' he used to say, 'men will have lost the art of killing poultry: the very rudiments of the art will have perished!' In the year 1811 he retired from general society. Toad-in-the-hole was no more seen in any public resort. We missed him from his wonted haunts

—nor up the lawn, nor at the wood was he. By the side of the main conduit his listless length at noontide he would stretch, and pore upon the filth that muddled by. 'Even dogs are not what they were, sir—not what they should be. I remember in my grandfather's time that some dogs had an idea of murder. I have known a mastiff lie in ambush for a rival, sir, and murder him with pleasing circumstances of good taste. Yes, sir, I knew a tom-cat that was an assassin. But now——' and then, the subject growing too painful, he dashed his hand to his forehead, and went off abruptly in a homeward direction towards his favourite conduit, where he was seen by an amateur in such a state that he thought it dangerous to address him. Soon after he shut himself entirely up; it was understood that he had resigned himself to melancholy; and at length the prevailing notion was—that Toad-in-the-hole had hanged himself.

The world was wrong *there*, as it has been on some other questions. Toad-in-the-hole might be sleeping, but dead he was not; and of that we soon had ocular proof. One morning in 1812 an amateur surprised us with the news that he had seen Toad-in-the-hole brushing with hasty steps the dews away to meet the postman by the conduit side. Even that was something: how much more, to hear that he had shaved his beard—had laid aside his sad-coloured clothes, and was adorned like a bridegroom of ancient days. What could be the meaning of all this? Was Toad-in-the-hole mad? or how? Soon after the secret was explained—in more than a figurative sense 'the murder was out.' For in came the London morning papers, by which it appeared that but three days before a murder, the most superb of the century by many degrees, had occurred in the heart of London. I need hardly say, that this was the great exterminating *chef-d'œuvre* of Williams at Mr. Marr's, No. 29 Ratcliffe Highway. That was the *début* of the artist; at least for anything the public knew. What occurred at Mr.

Williamson's, twelve nights afterwards—the second work turned out from the same chisel—some people pronounced even superior. But Toad-in-the-hole always 'reclaimed'—he was even angry at comparisons. 'This vulgar *goût de comparaison*, as La Bruyère calls it,' he would often remark, 'will be our ruin; each work has its own separate characteristics—each in and for itself is incomparable. One, perhaps, might suggest the *Iliad*—the other the *Odyssey*: what do you get by such comparisons? Neither ever was, or will be surpassed; and when you've talked for hours, you must still come back to that.' Vain, however, as all criticism might be, he often said that volumes might be written on each case for itself; and he even proposed to publish in quarto on the subject.

Meantime, how had Toad-in-the-hole happened to hear of this great work of art so early in the morning? He had received an account by express, dispatched by a correspondent in London, who watched the progress of art on *Toady's* behalf, with a general commission to send off a special express, at whatever cost, in the event of any estimable works appearing—how much more upon occasion of a *ne plus ultra* in art! The express arrived in the night-time; Toad-in-the-hole was then gone to bed; he had been muttering and grumbling for hours, but of course he was called up. On reading the account, he threw his arms round the express, called him his brother and his preserver; settled a pension upon him for three lives, and expressed his regret at not having it in his power to knight him. We, on our part—we amateurs, I mean—having heard that he was abroad, and therefore had *not* hanged himself, made sure of soon seeing him amongst us. Accordingly he soon arrived, knocked over the porter on his road to the reading-room, seized every man's hand as he passed him—wrung it almost frantically, and kept ejaculating, 'Why, now, here's something like a murder!—this is the real thing—this is genuine—this is what you can approve, can recommend to a friend: this—says every man, on reflection—this is the thing that ought to be!' Then, looking at particular friends, he said—'Why, Jack, how are you? Why, Tom, how are you?—bless me, you look ten years younger than when I last saw you.' 'No, sir,' I replied, 'it is you who look ten years younger.' 'Do I?—well, I shouldn't wonder if I did; such works are enough to make us all young.' And in fact the general opinion is, that Toad-in-the-hole would have died but for this regeneration of art, which he called a second age of Leo the Tenth; and it was our duty, he said solemnly, to commemorate it. At present, and *en attendant*—rather as an occasion for a public participation in public sympathy, than as in itself any commensurate testimony of our interest—he proposed that the Club should meet and dine together. A splendid public Dinner, therefore, was given by the Club; to which all amateurs were invited from a distance of one hundred miles.

Of this Dinner there are ample shorthand notes amongst the archives of the Club. But they are not 'extended,' to speak diplomatically; and the reporter is missing—I believe, murdered. Meantime, in years long after that day, and on an occasion perhaps equally interesting, viz., the turning up of Thugs and Thuggism, another Dinner was given. Of this I myself kept notes, for fear of another accident to the shorthand reporter. And I here subjoin them. Toad-in-the-hole, I must mention, was present at this Dinner. In fact, it was one of its sentimental incidents. Being as old as the valleys at the Dinner of 1812; naturally, he was as old as the hills at the Thug Dinner of 1838. He had taken to wearing his beard again; why, or with what view, it passes my persimmon to tell you. But so it was. And his appearance was most benign and venerable. Nothing could equal the angelic radiance of his smile as he inquired after the unfortunate reporter (whom, as a piece of private scandal, I should tell you that he was himself supposed to have murdered, in a rapture of creative art): the answer was, with roars of laughter, from the under-sheriff of our country—'non est inventus.' Toad-in-the-hole laughed outrageously at this: in fact, we all thought he was choking; and, at the earnest request of the company, a musical composer furnished a most beautiful glee upon the occasion, which was sung five times after dinner, with universal applause and inextinguishable laughter, the words being these (and the chorus so contrived, as most beautifully to mimic the peculiar laughter of Toad-in-the-hole):

Et interrogatum est à Toad-in-the-hole—Ubi est ille reporter?
Et responsum est cum cachinno—Non est inventus.

CHORUS

Deinde iteratum est ab omnibus, cum cachinnatione undulante—Non est inventus.

Toad-in-the-hole, I ought to mention, about nine years before, when an express from Edinburgh brought him the earliest intelligence of the Burke-and-Hare revolution in the art, went mad upon the spot; and, instead of a pension to the express for even one life, or a knighthood, endeavoured to burke him; in consequence of which he was put into a strait-waistcoat. And that was the reason we had no dinner then. But now all of us were alive and kicking, strait-waistcoaters and others; in fact, not one absentee was reported upon the entire roll. There were also many foreign amateurs present.

Dinner being over, and the cloth drawn, there was a general call made for the new glee of *Non est inventus*; but, as this would have interfered with the requisite gravity of the company during the earlier toasts, I overruled the call. After the national toasts had been given, the first official toast of the day was—*The Old Man of the Mountains*—drunk in solemn silence.

Toad-in-the-hole returned thanks in a neat speech. He likened himself to the Old Man of the Mountains, in a few brief allusions, that made the company absolutely yell with laughter; and he concluded with giving the health of

Mr. Von Hammer, with many thanks to him for his learned History of the Old Man and his subjects the Assassins.

Upon this I rose and said, that doubtless most of the company were aware of the distinguished place assigned by orientalists to the very learned Turkish scholar Von Hammer the Austrian; that he had made the profoundest researches into our art as connected with those early and eminent artists the Syrian assassins in the period of the Crusaders; that his work had been for several years deposited, as a rare treasure of art, in the library of the Club. Even the author's name, gentlemen, pointed him out as the historian of our art—Von Hammer——

'Yes, yes,' interrupted Toad-in-the-hole, who never can sit still—'Yes, yes, Von Hammer—he 's the man for a *malleus hæreticorum*: think rightly of our art, or he 's the man to tickle your catastrophes. You all know what consideration Williams bestowed on the hammer, or the ship-carpenter's mallet, which is the same thing. Gentlemen, I give you another great hammer—Charles the Hammer, the Marteau, or, in old French, the Martel—he hammered the Saracens till they were all as dead as door-nails:—he did, believe me.'

'*Charles Martel*, with all the honours.'

But the explosion of Toad-in-the-hole, together with the uproarious cheers for the grandpapa of Charlemagne, had now made the company unmanageable. The orchestra was again challenged with shouts the stormiest for the new glee. I made again a powerful effort to overrule the challenge. I might as well have talked to the winds. I foresaw a tempestuous evening; and I ordered myself to be strengthened with three waiters on each side; the vice-president with as many. Symptoms of unruly enthusiasm were beginning to show out; and I own that I myself was considerably excited as the orchestra opened with its storm of music, and the impassioned glee began—'*Et interrogatum est à Toad-in-the-hole—Ubi est ille Reporter?*' And the frenzy of the passion became absolutely convulsing, as the full chorus fell in—'*Et iteratum est ab omnibus—Non est inventus.*'

By this time I saw how things were going: wine and music were making most of the amateurs wild. Particularly Toad-in-the-hole, though considerably above a hundred years old, was getting as vicious as a young leopard. It was a fixed impression with the company that he had murdered the reporter in the year 1812; since which time (viz., twenty-six years) 'ille reporter' had been constantly reported 'non est inventus.' Consequently the glee about himself, which of itself was most tumultuous and jubilant, carried him off his feet. Like the famous choral songs amongst the citizens of Abdera, nobody could hear it without a contagious desire for falling back into the agitating music of 'Et interrogatum est à Toad-in-the-hole,' etc. I enjoined vigilance upon my assessors, and the business of the evening proceeded.

The next toast was—*The Jewish Sicarii.*

Upon which I made the following explanation to the company:—'Gentlemen, I am sure it will interest you all to hear that the assassins, ancient as they were, had a race of predecessors in the very same country. All over Syria, but particularly in Palestine, during the early years of the Emperor Nero, there was a band of murderers, who prosecuted their studies in a very novel manner. They did not practise in the night-time, or in lonely places; but justly considering that great crowds are in themselves a sort of darkness by means of the dense pressure and the impossibility of finding out who it was that gave the blow, they mingled with mobs everywhere; particularly at the great paschal feast in Jerusalem; where they actually had the audacity, as Josephus assures us, to press into the temple,—and whom should they choose for operating upon but Jonathan himself, the Pontifex Maximus? They murdered him, gentlemen, as beautifully as if they had had him alone on a moonless night in a dark lane. And when it was asked, who was the murderer, and where he was——'

'Why, then, it was answered,' interrupted Toad-in-the-hole, '*non est inventus*.' And then, in spite of all I could do or say, the orchestra opened, and the whole company began—'Et interrogatum est à Toad-in-the-hole—Ubi est ille Sicarius? Et responsum est ab omnibus—*Non est inventus*.'

When the tempestuous chorus had subsided, I began again:—'Gentlemen, you will find a very circumstantial account of the Sicarii in at least three different parts of Josephus; once in Book xx. sect. v. c. 8 of his *Antiquities*; once in Book I. of his *Wars*: but in sect. x. of the chapter first cited you will find a particular description of their tooling. This is what he says—"They tooled with small scimitars not much different from the Persian *acinacæ*, but more curved, and for all the world most like the Roman sickles or *sicæ*." It is perfectly magnificent, gentlemen, to hear the sequel of their history. Perhaps the only case on record where a regular army of murderers was assembled, a *justus exercitus*, was in the case of these *Sicarii*. They mustered in such strength in the wilderness, that Festus himself was obliged to march against them with the Roman legionary force.'

Upon which Toad-in-the-hole, that cursed interrupter, broke out a-singing—'Et interrogatum est à Toad-in-the-hole—Ubi est ille exercitus? Et responsum est ab omnibus—Non est inventus.'

'No, no, Toad—you are wrong for once; that army *was* found, and was all cut to pieces in the desert. Heavens, gentlemen, what a sublime picture! The Roman legions—the wilderness—Jerusalem in the distance—an army of murderers in the foreground!'

Mr. R., a member, now gave the next toast:—'To

the further improvement of Tooling, and thanks to the Committee for their services.'

Mr. L., on behalf of the Committee who had reported on that subject, returned thanks. He made an interesting extract from the Report, by which it appeared how very much stress had been laid formerly on the mode of Tooling by the Fathers, both Greek and Latin. In confirmation of this pleasing fact, he made a very striking statement in reference to the earliest work of antediluvian art. Father Mersenne, that learned Roman Catholic, in page one thousand four hundred and thirty-one[1] of his operose Commentary on Genesis, mentions, on the authority of several Rabbis, that the quarrel of Cain with Abel was about a young woman; that, by various accounts, Cain had tooled with his teeth [Abelem fuisse *morsibus* dilaceratum à Cain]; by many others, with the jaw-bone of an ass; which is the tooling adopted by most painters. But it is pleasing to the mind of sensibility to know that, as science expanded, sounder views were adopted. One author contends for a pitchfork, St. Chrysostom for a sword, Irenæus for a scythe, and Prudentius for a hedging-bill. This last writer delivers his opinion thus:

> Frater, probatæ sanctitatis æmulus,
> Germana curvo colla frangit sarculo.

i.e. his brother, jealous of his attested sanctity, fractures his brotherly throat with a curved hedging-bill. 'All which is respectfully submitted by your Committee, not so much as decisive of the question (for it is not), but in order to impress upon the youthful mind the importance which has ever been attached to the quality of the tooling by such men as Chrysostom and Irenæus.'

'Dang Irenæus!' said Toad-in-the-hole, who now rose impatiently to give the next toast:—'Our Irish

[1] 'Page one thousand four hundred and thirty-one'—*literally*, good reader, and no joke at all.

friends—and a speedy revolution in their mode of Tooling, as well as everything else connected with the art!'

'Gentlemen, I'll tell you the plain truth. Every day of the year we take up a paper, we read the opening of a murder. We say, this is good—this is charming—this is excellent! But, behold you! scarcely have we read a little farther before the word Tipperary or Ballina-something betrays the Irish manufacture. Instantly we loathe it: we call to the waiter; we say, "Waiter, take away this paper; send it out of the house; it is absolutely offensive to all just taste." I appeal to every man whether, on finding a murder (otherwise perhaps promising enough) to be Irish, he does not feel himself as much insulted as when, Madeira being ordered, he finds it to be Cape; or when, taking up what he believes to be a mushroom, it turns out what children call a toadstool. Tithes, politics, or something wrong in principle, vitiate every Irish murder. Gentlemen, this must be reformed, or Ireland will not be a land to live in; at least, if we do live there, we must import all our murders, that 's clear.' Toad-in-the-hole sat down growling with suppressed wrath, and the universal 'Hear, hear!' sufficiently showed that he spoke the general feeling.

The next toast was—'The sublime epoch of Burkism and Harism!'

This was drunk with enthusiasm; and one of the members, who spoke to the question, made a very curious communication to the company:—'Gentlemen, we fancy Burkism to be a pure invention of our own times; and in fact no Pancirollus has ever enumerated this branch of art when writing *de rebus deperditis*. Still I have ascertained that the essential principle of the art *was* known to the ancients, although, like the art of painting upon glass, of making the myrrhine cups, etc., it was lost in the dark ages for want of encouragement. In the famous collection of Greek epigrams made by Planudes is one upon a very charming little case of Burkism; it is a perfect little gem of art. The epigram itself I cannot lay my hand upon at this moment: but the following is an abstract of it by Salmasius, as I find it in his notes on Vopiscus: "Est et elegans epigramma Lucilii (well might he call it "elegans!"), ubi medicus et pollinctor de compacto sic egerunt, ut medicus ægros omnes curæ suæ commissos occideret"—this was the basis of the contract, you see, that on the one part the doctor for himself and his assigns doth undertake and contract duly and truly to murder all the patients committed to his charge: but why? There lies the beauty of the case—"Et ut pollinctori amico suo traderet pollingendos." The *pollinctor*, you are aware, was a person whose business it was to dress and prepare dead bodies for burial. The original ground of the transaction appears to have been sentimental: "he was my friend," says the murderous doctor—"he was dear to me," in speaking of the pollinctor. But the law, gentlemen, is stern and harsh: the law will not hear of these tender motives: to sustain a contract of this nature in law, it is essential that a "consideration" should be given. Now, what *was* the consideration? For thus far all is on the side of the pollinctor: he will be well paid for his services; but meantime, the generous, the noble-minded doctor gets nothing. What *was* the little consideration, again I ask, which the law would insist on the doctor's taking? You shall hear: "Et ut pollinctor vicissim τελαμῶνας quos furabatur de pollinctione mortuorum medico mitteret donis ad alliganda vulnera eorum quos curabat." Now, the case is clear: the whole went on a principle of reciprocity which would have kept up the trade for ever. The doctor was also a surgeon; he could not murder *all* his patients: some of the surgical patients must be retained intact; *re infectâ*. For these he wanted linen bandages. But unhappily the Romans wore woollen, on which account they bathed so often. Meantime, there *was* linen to be had in Rome: but it was monstrously dear:

and the τελαμῶνες or linen swathing bandages in which superstition obliged them to bind up corpses, would answer capitally for the surgeon. The doctor, therefore, contracts to furnish his friend with a constant succession of corpses, provided, and be it understood always, that his said friend in return should supply him with one-half of the articles he would receive from the friends of the parties murdered or to be murdered. The doctor invariably recommended his invaluable friend the pollinctor (whom let us call the undertaker); the undertaker, with equal regard to the sacred rights of friendship, uniformly recommended the doctor. Like Pylades and Orestes, they were models of a perfect friendship: in their lives they were lovely; and on the gallows, it is to be hoped, they were not divided.

'Gentlemen, it makes me laugh horribly when I think of those two friends drawing and redrawing on each other: "Pollinctor in account with Doctor, debtor by sixteen corpses; creditor by forty-five bandages, two of which damaged." Their names unfortunately are lost; but I conceive they must have been Quintus Burkius and Publius Harius. By the way, gentlemen, has anybody heard lately of Hare? I understand he is comfortably settled in Ireland, considerably to the west, and does a little business now and then; but, as he observes with a sigh, only as a retailer—nothing like the fine thriving wholesale concern so carelessly blown up at Edinburgh. "You see what comes of neglecting business,"—is the chief moral, the ἐπιμύθιον, as Æsop would say, which he draws from his past experience.'

At length came the toast of the day—*Thugdom in all its branches.*

The speeches *attempted* at this crisis of the Dinner were past all counting. But the applause was so furious, the music so stormy, and the crashing of glasses so incessant, from the general resolution never again to drink an inferior toast from the same glass, that my power is not equal to the task of reporting. Besides which, Toad-in-the-hole now became quite ungovernable. He kept firing pistols in every direction; sent his servant for a blunderbuss, and talked of loading with ball-cartridge. We conceived that his former madness had returned at the mention of Burke and Hare; or that, being again weary of life, he had resolved to go off in a general massacre. This we could not think of allowing; it became indispensable, therefore, to kick him out, which we did with universal consent, the whole company lending their toes *uno pede*, as I may say, though pitying his grey hairs and his angelic smile. During the operation, the orchestra poured in their old chorus. The universal company sang, and (what surprised us most of all) Toad-in-the-hole joined us furiously in singing:

Et interrogatum est ab omnibus—Ubi est ille Toad-in-the-hole?
Et responsum est ab omnibus—Non est inventus.[1]

[1] The foregoing is a reprint of the shorter version of the essay—the form in which it originally appeared.

PERCY BYSSHE SHELLEY

1792–1822

ON LOVE

WHAT is love? Ask him who lives, what is life? ask him who adores, what is God?

I know not the internal constitution of other men, nor even thine, whom I now address. I see that in some external attributes they resemble me, but when, misled by that appearance, I have thought to appeal to something in common, and unburthen my inmost soul to them, I have found my language misunderstood, like one in a distant and savage land. The more opportunities they have afforded me for experience, the wider has appeared the interval between us, and to a greater distance have the points of sympathy been withdrawn. With a spirit ill fitted to sustain such proof, trembling and feeble through its tenderness, I have everywhere sought sympathy, and have found only repulse and disappointment.

Thou demandest what is love? It is that powerful attraction towards all that we conceive, or fear, or hope beyond ourselves, when we find within our own thoughts the chasm of an insufficient void, and seek to awaken in all things that are, a community with what we experience within ourselves. If we reason, we would be understood; if we imagine, we would that the airy children of our brain were born anew within another's; if we feel, we would that another's nerves should vibrate to our own, that the beams of their eyes should kindle at once and mix and melt into our own, that lips of motionless ice should not reply to lips quivering and burning with the heart's best blood. This is Love. This is the bond and the sanction which connects not only man with man, but with everything which exists. We are born into the world, and there is something within us which, from the instant that we live, more and more thirsts after its likeness. It is probably in correspondence with this law that the infant drains milk from the bosom of its mother; this propensity develops itself with the development of our nature. We dimly see within our intellectual nature a miniature as it were of our entire self yet deprived of all that we condemn or despise, the ideal prototype of everything excellent or lovely that we are capable of conceiving as belonging to the nature of man. Not only the portrait of our external being, but an assemblage of the minutest particles of which our nature is composed[1]; a mirror whose surface reflects only the forms of purity and brightness; a soul within our soul that describes a circle around its proper paradise, which pain, and sorrow, and evil dare not overleap. To this we eagerly refer all sensations, thirsting that they should resemble or correspond with it. The discovery of its antitype; the meeting with an understanding capable of clearly estimating our own; an imagination which should enter into and seize upon the subtle and delicate peculiarities which we have delighted to cherish and unfold in secret; with a frame whose nerves, like the chords of two exquisite lyres, strung to the accompaniment of one delightful voice, vibrate with the vibrations of our own; and of a combination of all these in such proportion as the type within demands; this is the invisible and unattainable point to which Love tends: and to attain which, it urges forth the powers of man to arrest the faintest shadow of that, without the possession of which there is no rest nor respite to the heart over which it rules. Hence in solitude, or in that deserted state when we are surrounded by human beings, and yet they sympathise not with us, we love the flowers, the grass, and the waters, and the sky. In the motion of the very leaves of spring, in the blue

[1] These words are ineffectual and metaphorical. Most words are so—No help!

air, there is then found a secret correspondence with our heart. There is eloquence in the tongueless wind, and a melody in the flowing brooks and the rustling of the reeds beside them, which by their inconceivable relation to something within the soul, awaken the spirits to a dance of breathless rapture, and bring tears of mysterious tenderness to the eyes, like the enthusiasm of patriotic success, or the voice of one beloved singing to you alone. Sterne says that, if he were in a desert, he would love some cypress. So soon as this want of power is dead, man becomes the living sepulchre of himself, and what yet survives is the mere husk of what once he was.

THOMAS CARLYLE

1795–1881

THE HERO AS POET. DANTE; SHAKESPEARE

A LECTURE, 1840

THE Hero as Divinity, the Hero as Prophet, are productions of old ages; not to be repeated in the new. They presuppose a certain rudeness of conception, which the progress of mere scientific knowledge puts an end to. There needs to be, as it were, a world vacant, or almost vacant of scientific forms, if men in their loving wonder are to fancy their fellow-man either a god or one speaking with the voice of a god. Divinity and Prophet are past. We are now to see our Hero in the less ambitious, but also less questionable, character of Poet; a character which does not pass. The Poet is a heroic figure belonging to all ages; whom all ages possess, when once he is produced, whom the newest age as the oldest may produce;—and will produce, always when Nature pleases. Let Nature send a Hero-soul; in no age is it other than possible that he may be shaped into a Poet.

Hero, Prophet, Poet,—many different names, in different times and places, do we give to Great Men; according to varieties we note in them, according to the sphere in which they have displayed themselves! We might give many more names, on this same principle. I will remark again, however, as a fact not unimportant to be understood, that the different *sphere* constitutes the grand origin of such distinction; that the Hero can be Poet, Prophet, King, Priest or what you will, according to the kind of world he finds himself born into. I confess, I have no notion of a truly great man that could not be *all* sorts of men. The Poet who could merely sit on a chair, and compose stanzas, would never make a stanza worth much. He could not sing the Heroic warrior, unless he himself were at least a Heroic warrior too. I fancy there is in him the Politician, the Thinker, Legislator, Philosopher;—in one or the other degree, he could have been, he is all these. So too I cannot understand how a Mirabeau, with that great glowing heart, with the fire that was in it, with the bursting tears that were in it, could not have written verses, tragedies, poems, touched all hearts in that way, had his course of life and education led him thitherward. The grand fundamental character is that of Great Man; that the man be great. Napoleon has words in him which are like Austerlitz Battles. Louis Fourteenth's Marshals are a kind of poetical men withal; the things Turenne says are full of sagacity and geniality, like sayings of Samuel Johnson. The great heart, the clear deep-seeing eye: there it lies; no man whatever, in what province soever, can prosper at all without these. Petrarch and Boccaccio did diplomatic messages, it seems, quite well: one can easily believe it; they had done things a little harder than these! Burns, a gifted song-writer, might have made a still better Mirabeau. Shakespeare,—one knows not what *he* could not have made, in the supreme degree.

True, there are aptitudes of Nature too. Nature does not make all great men, more than all other men, in the self-same mould. Varieties of aptitude doubtless; but infinitely more of circumstance; and far oftenest it is the *latter* only that are looked to. But it is as with common men in the learning of trades. You take any man, as yet a vague capability of a man, who could be any kind of craftsman; and make him into a smith, a carpenter, a mason: he is then and thenceforth that and nothing else. And if, as Addison complains, you sometimes see a street-porter staggering under his load on spindle-shanks, and near at hand a tailor with the frame of a Samson handling a bit of cloth and small Whitechapel needle,—it cannot be considered that aptitude of Nature alone has been consulted here either!—The Great Man also, to what shall he be bound apprentice? Given your Hero, is he to become Conqueror, King, Philosopher, Poet? It is an inexplicably complex controversial-calculation between the world and him! He will read the world and its laws; the world with its laws will be there to be read. What the world, on *this* matter, shall permit and bid is, as we said, the most important fact about the world.

Poet and Prophet differ greatly in our loose modern notions of them. In some old languages, again, the titles are synonymous; *Vates* means both Prophet and Poet: and indeed at all times, Prophet and Poet, well understood, have much kindred of meaning. Fundamentally indeed they are still the same; in this most important respect especially, That they have penetrated both of them into the sacred mystery of the Universe; what Goethe calls 'the open secret.' 'Which is the great secret?' asks one.—'The *open* secret,'—open to all, seen by almost none! That divine mystery, which lies everywhere in all Beings, 'the Divine Idea of the World, that which lies at the bottom of Appearance,' as Fichte styles it; of which all Appearance, from the starry sky to the grass of the field, but especially the Appearance of Man and his work, is but the *vesture*, the embodiment that renders it visible. This divine mystery *is* in all times and in all places; veritably is. In most times and places it is greatly overlooked; and the Universe, definable always in one or the other dialect, as the realised Thought of God, is considered a trivial, inert, commonplace matter,—as if, says the Satirist, it were a dead thing, which some upholsterer had put together! It could do no good at present, to *speak* much about this; but it is a pity for every one of us if we do not know it, live ever in the knowledge of it. Really a most mournful pity;—a failure to live at all, if we live otherwise!

But now, I say, whoever may forget this divine mystery, the *Vates*, whether Prophet or Poet, has penetrated into it; is a man sent hither to make it more impressively known to us. That always is his message; he is to reveal that to us,—that sacred mystery which he more than others lives ever present with. While others forget it, he knows it;—I might say, he has been driven to know it; without consent asked of *him*, he finds himself living in it, bound to live in it. Once more, here is no Hearsay, but a direct Insight and Belief; this man too could not help being a sincere man! Whosoever may live in the shows of things, it is for him a necessity of nature to live in the very fact of things. A man once more, in earnest with the Universe, though all others were but toying with it. He is a *Vates*, first of all, in virtue of being sincere. So far Poet and Prophet, participators in the 'open secret,' are one.

With respect to their distinction again: The *Vates* Prophet, we might say, has seized that sacred mystery rather on the moral side, as Good and Evil, Duty and Prohibition; the *Vates* Poet on what the Germans call the æsthetic side, as Beautiful, and the like. The one we may call a revealer of what we are to do, the other of what we are to love. But indeed these two provinces run into one another, and cannot be disjoined. The Prophet too has his eye on what we are to love: how else shall he know what it is we are to do? The highest Voice ever heard on this earth said withal, 'Consider the lilies of the field; they toil not, neither do they spin: yet Solomon in all his glory was not arrayed like one of these.' A glance, that, into the deepest deep of Beauty. 'The lilies of the field,'—dressed finer than earthly princes, springing-up there in the humble furrow-field; a beautiful *eye* looking-out on you, from the great inner Sea of Beauty! How could the rude Earth make these, if her Essence, rugged as she looks and is, were not inwardly Beauty? In this point of view, too, a saying of Goethe's, which has staggered several, may have meaning: 'The Beautiful,' he intimates, 'is higher than the Good: the Beautiful includes in it the Good.' The *true* Beautiful; which, however, I have said somewhere, 'differs from the *false* as Heaven does from Vauxhall!' So much for the distinction and identity of Poet and Prophet.

In ancient and also in modern periods we find a few Poets who are accounted perfect; whom it were a kind of treason to find fault with. This is noteworthy; this is right: yet in strictness it is only an illusion. At bottom, clearly enough, there is no perfect Poet! A vein of Poetry exists in the hearts of all men; no man is made altogether of Poetry. We are all poets when we *read* a poem well. The 'imagination that shudders at the Hell of Dante,' is not that the same faculty, weaker in degree, as Dante's own? No one but Shakespeare can embody, out of *Saxo Grammaticus*, the story of *Hamlet* as Shakespeare did: but every one models some kind of story out of it; every one embodies it better or worse. We need not spend time in defining. Where there is no specific difference, as between round and square, all definition must be more or less arbitrary. A man that has *so* much more of the poetic element developed in him as to have become noticeable, will be called Poet by his neighbours. World-Poets too, those whom we are to take for perfect Poets, are settled by critics in the same way. One who rises *so* far above the general level of Poets will, to such and such critics, seem a Universal Poet; as he ought to do. And yet it is, and must be, an arbitrary distinction. All Poets, all men, have some touches of the Universal; no man is wholly made of that. Most Poets are very soon forgotten: but not the noblest Shakespeare or Homer of them can be remembered *forever*;—a day comes when he too is not!

Nevertheless, you will say, there must be a difference between true Poetry and true Speech not poetical: what is the difference? On this point many things have been written, especially by late German Critics, some of which are not very intelligible at first. They say, for example, that the Poet has an *infinitude* in him; communicates an *Unendlichkeit*, a certain character of 'infinitude,' to whatsoever he delineates. This, though not very precise, yet on so vague a matter is worth remembering: if well meditated, some meaning will gradually be found in it. For my own part, I find considerable meaning in the old vulgar distinction of Poetry being *metrical*, having music in it, being a Song. Truly, if pressed to give a definition, one might say this as soon as anything else: If your delineation be authentically *musical*, musical, not in word only, but in heart and substance, in all the thoughts and utterances of it, in the whole conception of it, then it will be poetical; if not, not.—Musical: how much lies in that! A *musical* thought is one spoken by a mind that has penetrated into the inmost heart of the thing; detected the inmost mystery of it, namely the *melody* that lies hidden in it; the inward harmony of coherence which is its soul, whereby it exists, and has a right to be, here in this world. All inmost things, we may say, are melodious; naturally utter themselves in Song. The meaning of Song goes deep. Who is there that, in logical words, can express the effect music has on us? A kind of inarticulate unfathomable speech, which leads us to the edge of the Infinite, and lets us for moments gaze into that!

Nay, all speech, even the commonest speech, has something of song in it: not a parish in the world but has its parish-accent;—the rhythm or *tune* to which the people there *sing* what they have to say! Accent is a kind of chanting; all men have accent of their own, —though they only *notice* that of others. Observe too how all passionate language does of itself become musical,—with a finer music than the mere accent; the speech of a man even in zealous anger becomes a chant, a song. All deep things are Song. It seems somehow the very central essence of us, Song; as if all the rest were but wrappages and hulls! The primal element of us; of us, and of all things. The Greeks fabled of Sphere-Harmonies; it was the feeling they had of the inner structure of Nature; that the soul of all her voices and utterances was perfect music. Poetry, therefore, we will call *musical Thought.* The Poet is he who *thinks* in that manner. At bottom, it turns still on power of intellect; it is a man's sincerity and depth of vision that makes him a Poet. See deep enough, and you see musically; the heart of Nature *being* everywhere music, if you can only reach it.

The *Vates* Poet, with his melodious Apocalypse of Nature, seems to hold a poor rank among us, in comparison with the *Vates* Prophet; his function, and our esteem of him for his function, alike slight. The Hero taken as Divinity; the Hero taken as Prophet; then next the Hero taken only as Poet: does it not look as if our estimate of the Great Man, epoch after epoch, were continually diminishing? We take him first for a god, then for one god-inspired; and now in the next stage of it, his most miraculous word gains from us only the recognition that he is a Poet, beautiful verse-maker, man of genius, or suchlike!—It looks so; but I persuade myself that intrinsically it is not so. If we consider well, it will perhaps appear that in man still there is the *same* altogether peculiar admiration for the Heroic Gift, by what name soever called, that there at any time was.

I should say, if we do not now reckon a Great Man literally divine, it is that our notions of God, of the supreme unattainable Fountain of Splendour, Wisdom and Heroism, are ever rising *higher*; not altogether that our reverence for these qualities, as manifested in our like, is getting lower. This is worth taking thought of. Sceptical Dilettantism, the curse of these ages, a curse which will not last forever, does indeed in this the highest province of human things, as in all provinces, make sad work; and our reverence for great men, all crippled, blinded, paralytic as it is, comes out in poor plight, hardly recognisable. Men worship the shows of great men; the most disbelieve that there is any reality of great men to worship. The dreariest, fatalest faith; believing which, one would literally despair of human things. Nevertheless look, for example, at Napoleon! A Corsican lieutenant of artillery; that is the show of *him*: yet is he not obeyed, *worshipped* after his sort, as all the Tiaraed and Diademed of the world put together could not be? High Duchesses, and ostlers of inns, gather round the Scottish rustic, Burns;—a strange feeling dwelling in each that they had never heard a man like this; that, on the whole, this is the man! In the secret heart of these people it still dimly reveals itself, though there is no accredited way of uttering it at present, that this rustic, with his black brows and flashing sun-eyes, and strange words moving laughter and tears, is of a dignity far beyond all others, incommensurable with all others. Do not we feel it so? But now, were Dilettantism, Scepticism, Triviality, and all that sorrowful brood, cast-out of us,—as, by God's blessing, they shall one day be; were faith in the shows of things entirely swept-out, replaced by clear faith in the *things*, so that a man acted on the impulse of that only, and counted the other non-extant; what a new livelier feeling towards this Burns were it!

Nay here in these pages, such as they are, have we not two mere Poets, if not deified, yet we may say beatified? Shakespeare and Dante are Saints of Poetry; really, if we will think of it, *canonised*, so that it is impiety to meddle with them. The unguided instinct of the world, working across all these perverse impediments, has arrived at such result. Dante and Shakespeare are a peculiar Two. They dwell apart, in a kind of royal solitude; none equal, none second to them: in the general feeling of the world, a certain transcendentalism, a glory as of complete perfection, invests these two. They *are* canonised, though no Pope or Cardinals took hand in doing it! Such, in spite of every perverting influence, in the most unheroic times, is still our indestructible reverence for heroism.—We will look a little at these Two, the Poet Dante and the Poet Shakespeare: what little it is permitted us to say here of the Hero as Poet will most fitly arrange itself in that fashion.

Many volumes have been written by way of commentary on Dante and his Book; yet, on the whole, with no great result. His Biography is, as it were, irrecoverably lost for us. An unimportant, wandering, sorrowstricken man, not much note was taken of him while he lived; and the most of that has vanished, in the long space that now intervenes. It is five centuries since he ceased writing and living here. After all commentaries, the Book itself is mainly what we know of him. The Book;—and one might add that Portrait commonly attributed to Giotto, which, looking on it, you cannot help inclining to think genuine, whoever did it. To me it is a most touching face; perhaps of all faces that I know, the most so. Lonely there, painted as on vacancy, with the simple laurel wound round it; the deathless sorrow and pain, the known victory which is also deathless; significant of the whole history of Dante! I think it is the mournfulest face that ever was painted from reality; an altogether tragic, heart-affecting face. There is in it, as foundation of it, the softness, tenderness, gentle affection as of a child; but all this is as if congealed into sharp contradiction, into abnegation, isolation, proud hopeless pain. A soft ethereal soul looking-out so stern, implacable, grim-trenchant, as from imprisonment of thick-ribbed ice! Withal it is a silent pain too, a silent scornful one: the lip is curled,in a kind of godlike disdain of the thing that is eating-out his heart,—as if it were withal a mean insignificant thing, as if he whom it had power to torture and strangle were greater than it. The face of one wholly in protest, and life-long unsurrendering battle, against the world. Affection all converted into indignation: an implacable indignation; slow, equable, silent, like that of a god! The eye too, it looks-out as in a kind of *surprise*, a kind of inquiry, Why the world was of such a sort? This is Dante: so he looks, this 'voice of ten silent centuries,' and sings us 'his mystic unfathomable song.'

The little that we know of Dante's Life corresponds well enough with this Portrait and this Book. He was born at Florence, in the upper class of society, in the year 1265. His education was the best then going; much school-divinity, Aristotelean logic, some Latin classics,—no inconsiderable insight into certain provinces of things: and Dante, with his earnest intelligent nature, we need not doubt, learned better than most all that was learnable. He has a clear cultivated understanding, and of great subtlety; the best fruit of education he had contrived to realise from these scholastics. He knows accurately and well what lies close to him; but, in such a time, without printed books or free intercourse, he could not know well what was distant: the small clear light, most luminous for what is near, breaks itself into singular *chiaroscuro* striking on what is far off. This was Dante's learning from the schools. In life, he had gone through the usual destinies; been twice out campaigning as a soldier for the Florentine State, been on embassy; had in his thirty-fifth year, by natural gradation of talent and service, become one of the Chief Magistrates of Florence. He had met in boyhood a certain Beatrice Portinari, a beautiful little girl of his own age and rank, and grown-up thenceforth in partial sight of her, in some distant intercourse with her. All readers know his graceful affecting account of this; and then of their being parted; of her being wedded to another, and of her death soon after. She makes a great figure in Dante's Poem; seems to have made a great figure in his life. Of all beings it might seem as if she, held apart from him, far apart at last in the dim Eternity, were the only one he had ever with his whole strength of affection loved. She died: Dante himself was wedded; but it seems not happily, far from happily. I fancy, the rigorous earnest man, with his keen excitabilities, was not altogether easy to make happy.

We will not complain of Dante's miseries: had all gone right with him as he wished it, he might have been Prior, Podestà, or whatsoever they call it, of Florence, well accepted among neighbours,—and the world had wanted one of the most notable works ever spoken or sung. Florence would have had another prosperous Lord Mayor; and the ten dumb centuries continued voiceless, and the ten other listening centuries (for there will be ten of them and more) had no *Divina Commedia* to hear! We will complain of nothing. A nobler destiny was appointed for this Dante; and he, struggling like a man led towards death and crucifixion, could not help fulfilling it. Give *him* the choice of his happiness! He knew not, more than we do, what was really happy, what was really miserable.

In Dante's Priorship, the Guelf-Ghibelline, Bianchi-Neri, or some other confused disturbance rose to such a height, that Dante, whose party had seemed the stronger, was with his friends cast unexpectedly forth into banishment; doomed thenceforth to a life of woe and wandering. His property was all confiscated and more; he had the fiercest feeling that it was entirely unjust, nefarious in the sight of God and man. He tried what was in him to get reinstated; tried even by warlike surprisal, with arms in his hand: but it would not do; bad only had become worse. There is a record, I believe, still extant in the Florence Archives, dooming this Dante, wheresoever caught, to be burnt alive. Burnt alive; so it stands, they say: a very curious civic document. Another curious document, some considerable number of years later, is a Letter of Dante's to the Florentine Magistrates, written in answer to a milder proposal of theirs, that he should return on condition of apologising and paying a fine.

He answers, with fixed stern pride: 'If I cannot return without calling myself guilty, I will never return, *nunquam revertar*.'

For Dante there was now no home in this world. He wandered from patron to patron, from place to place; proving in his own bitter words, 'How hard is the path, *Come è duro calle*.' The wretched are not cheerful company. Dante, poor and banished, with his proud earnest nature, with his moody humours, was not a man to conciliate men. Petrarch reports of him that being at Can della Scala's court, and blamed one day for his gloom and taciturnity, he answered in no courtier-like way. Della Scala stood among his courtiers, with mimes and buffoons (*nebulones ac histriones*) making him heartily merry; when turning to Dante, he said: 'Is it not strange, now, that this poor fool should make himself so entertaining; while you, a wise man, sit there day after day, and have nothing to amuse us with at all?' Dante answered bitterly: 'No, not strange; your Highness is to recollect the Proverb, *Like to Like*';—given the amuser, the amusee must also be given! Such a man, with his proud silent ways, with his sarcasms and sorrows, was not made to succeed at court. By degrees it came to be evident to him that he had no longer any resting-place, or hope of benefit, in this earth. The earthly world had cast him forth, to wander, wander; no living heart to love him now; for his sore miseries there was no solace here.

The deeper naturally would the Eternal World impress itself on him; that awful reality over which, after all, this Time-world, with its Florences and banishments, only flutters as an unreal shadow. Florence thou shalt never see: but Hell and Purgatory and Heaven thou shalt surely see! What is Florence, Can della Scala, and the World and Life altogether? ETERNITY: thither, of a truth, not else-whither, art thou and all things bound! The great soul of Dante, homeless on earth, made its home more and more in that awful other world. Naturally his thoughts brooded on that, as on the one fact important for him. Bodied or bodiless, it is the one fact important for all men:—but to Dante, in that age, it was bodied in fixed certainty of scientific shape; he no more doubted of that *Malebolge* Pool, that it all lay there with its gloomy circles, with its *alti guai*, and that he himself should see it, than we doubt that we should see Constantinople if we went thither. Dante's heart, long filled with this, brooding over it in speechless thought and awe, bursts forth at length into 'mystic unfathomable song'; and this his *Divine Comedy*, the most remarkable of all modern Books, is the result.

It must have been a great solacement to Dante, and was, as we can see, a proud thought for him at times, That he, here in exile, could do this work; that no Florence, nor no man or men, could hinder him from doing it, or even much help him in doing it. He knew too, partly, that it was great; the greatest a man could do. 'If thou follow thy star, *Se tu segui tua stella*,'—so could the Hero, in his forsakenness, in his extreme need, still say to himself: 'Follow thou thy star, thou shalt not fail of a glorious haven!' The labour of writing, we find, and indeed could know otherwise, was great and painful for him; he says, This Book, 'which has made me lean for many years.' Ah yes, it was won, all of it, with pain and sore toil, not in sport, but in grim earnest. His Book, as indeed most good Books are, has been written, in many senses, with his heart's blood. It is his whole history, this Book. He died after finishing it; not yet very old, at the age of fifty-six; broken-hearted rather, as is said. He lies buried in his death-city Ravenna: *Hic claudor Dantes patriis extorris ab oris*. The Florentines begged back his body, in a century after; the Ravenna people would not give it. 'Here am I Dante laid, shut-out from my native shores.'

I said, Dante's Poem was a Song: it is Tieck who calls it 'a mystic unfathomable Song'; and such is literally the character of it. Coleridge remarks very pertinently somewhere, that wherever you find a sentence musically worded, of true rhythm and melody in the words, there is something deep and good in the meaning too. For body and soul, word and idea, go strangely together here as everywhere. Song: we said before, it was the Heroic of Speech! All *old* Poems, Homer's and the rest, are authentically Songs. I would say, in strictness, that all right Poems are; that whatsoever is not *sung* is properly no Poem, but a piece of Prose cramped into jingling lines,—to the great injury of the grammar, to the great grief of the reader, for most part! What we want to get at is the *thought* the man had, if he had any: why should he twist it into jingle, if he *could* speak it out plainly? It is only when the heart of him is rapt into true passion of melody, and the very tones of him, according to Coleridge's remark, become musical by the greatness, depth and music of his thoughts, that we can give him right to rhyme and sing; that we call him a Poet, and listen to him as the Heroic of Speakers,—whose speech *is* Song. Pretenders to this are many; and to an earnest reader, I doubt, it is for most part a very melancholy, not to say an insupportable business, that of reading rhyme! Rhyme that had no inward necessity to be rhymed;—it ought to have told us plainly, without any jingle, what it was aiming at. I would advise all men who *can* speak their thought, not to sing it; to understand that, in a serious time, among serious men, there is no vocation in them for singing it. Precisely as we love the true song, and are charmed by it as by something divine, so shall we hate the false song, and account it a mere wooden noise, a thing hollow, superfluous, altogether an insincere and offensive thing.

I give Dante my highest praise when I say of his *Divine Comedy* that it is, in all senses, genuinely a Song. In the very sound of it there is a *canto fermo*; it proceeds as by a chant. The language, his simple *terza rima*, doubtless helped him in this. One reads along naturally with a sort of *lilt.* But I add, that it could not be otherwise; for the essence and material of the work are themselves rhythmic. Its depth, and rapt passion and sincerity, make it musical;—go *deep* enough, there is music everywhere. A true inward symmetry, what one calls an architectural harmony, reigns in it, proportionates it all: architectural; which also partakes of the character of music. The three kingdoms, *Inferno*, *Purgatorio*, *Paradiso*, look-out on one another like compartments of a great edifice; a great supernatural world-cathedral, piled-up there, stern, solemn, awful; Dante's World of Souls! It is, at bottom, the *sincerest* of all Poems; sincerity, here too, we find to be the measure of worth. It came deep out of the author's heart of hearts; and it goes deep, and through long generations, into ours. The people of Verona, when they saw him on the streets, used to say, '*Eccovi l' uom ch' è stato all' Inferno*, See, there is the man that was in Hell!' Ah yes, he had been in Hell;—in Hell enough, in long severe sorrow and struggle; as the like of him is pretty sure to have been. Commedias that come-out *divine* are not accomplished otherwise. Thought, true labour of any kind, highest virtue itself, is it not the daughter of Pain? Born as out of the black whirlwind;—true *effort*, in fact, as of a captive struggling to free himself: that is Thought. In all ways we are 'to become perfect through *suffering*.'—But, as I say, no work known to me is so elaborated as this of Dante's. It has all been as if molten, in the hottest furnace of his soul. It had made him 'lean' for many years. Not the general whole only; every compartment of it is worked-out, with intense earnestness, into truth, into clear visuality. Each answers to the other; each fits in its place, like a marble stone accurately hewn and polished. It is the soul of Dante, and in this the soul of the middle ages, rendered forever rhythmically visible there. No light task; a right intense one: but a task which is *done*.

Perhaps one would say, *intensity*, with the much that depends on it, is the prevailing character of Dante's genius. Dante does not come before us as a large catholic mind; rather as a narrow and even sectarian mind: it is partly the fruit of his age and position, but partly too of his own nature. His greatness has, in all senses, concentered itself into fiery emphasis and depth. He is world-great not because he is world-wide, but because he is world-deep. Through all objects he pierces as it were down into the heart of Being. I know nothing so intense as Dante. Consider, for example, to begin with the outermost development of his intensity, consider how he paints. He has a great power of vision; seizes the very type of a thing; presents that and nothing more. You remember that first view he gets of the Hall of Dite: *red* pinnacle, redhot cone of iron glowing through the dim immensity of gloom;—so vivid, so distinct, visible at once and forever! It is as an emblem of the whole genius of Dante. There is a brevity, an abrupt precision in him: Tacitus is not briefer, more condensed; and then in Dante it seems a natural condensation, spontaneous to the man. One smiting word; and then there is silence, nothing more said. His silence is more eloquent than words. It is strange with what a sharp decisive grace he snatches the true likeness of a matter: cuts into the matter as with a pen of fire. Plutus, the blustering giant, collapses at Virgil's rebuke; it is 'as the sails sink, the mast being suddenly broken.' Or that poor Brunetto Latini, with the *cotto aspetto*, 'face *baked*,' parched brown and lean; and the 'fiery snow,' that falls on them there, a 'fiery snow without wind,' slow, deliberate, never-ending! Or the lids of those Tombs; square sarcophaguses, in that silent dim-burning Hall, each with its Soul in torment; the lids laid open there; they are to be shut at the Day of Judgment, through Eternity. And how Farinata rises; and how Cavalcante falls—at hearing of his Son, and the past tense '*fue*'! The very movements in Dante have something brief; swift, decisive, almost military. It is of the inmost essence of his genius this sort of painting. The fiery, swift Italian nature of the man, so silent, passionate, with its quick abrupt movements, its silent 'pale rages,' speaks itself in these things.

For though this of painting is one of the outermost developments of a man, it comes like all else from the essential faculty of him; it is physiognomical of the whole man. Find a man whose words paint you a likeness, you have found a man worth something; mark his manner of doing it, as very characteristic of him. In the first place, he could not have discerned the object at all, or seen the vital type of it, unless he had, what we may call, *sympathised* with it—had sympathy in him to bestow on objects. He must have been *sincere* about it too; sincere and sympathetic: a man without worth cannot give you the likeness of any object; he dwells in vague outwardness, fallacy and trivial hearsay, about all objects. And indeed may we not say that intellect altogether expresses itself in this power of discerning what an object is? Whatsoever of faculty a man's mind may have will come out here. Is it even of business, a matter to be done? The gifted man is he who *sees* the essential point, and leaves all the rest aside as surplusage: it is his faculty too, the man of business's faculty, that he discern the true *likeness*, not the false superficial one, of the thing, he has got to work in. And how much of *morality* is in the kind of insight we get of anything; 'the eye seeing in all things what it brought with it the faculty of seeing!' To the mean eye all things are trivial, as certainly as to the jaundiced they are yellow. Raphael, the Painters tell us, is the best of all Portrait-painters withal. No most gifted eye can exhaust the significance of any object. In the commonest human face there lies more than Raphael will take away with him.

Dante's painting is not graphic only, brief, true, and

of a vividness as of fire in dark night; taken on the wider scale, it is everyway noble, and the outcome of a great soul. Francesca and her Lover, what qualities in that! A thing woven as out of rainbows, on a ground of eternal black. A small flute-voice of infinite wail speaks there, into our very heart of hearts. A touch of womanhood in it too; *della bella persona, che mi fu tolta*; and how, even in the Pit of woe, it is a solace that *he* will never part from her! Saddest tragedy in these *alti guai*. And the racking winds, in that *aer bruno*, whirl them away again, to wail forever!—Strange to think: Dante was the friend of this poor Francesca's father; Francesca herself may have sat upon the Poet's knee, as a bright innocent little child. Infinite pity, yet also infinite rigour of law: it is so Nature is made; it is so Dante discerned that she was made. What a paltry notion is that of his *Divine Comedy's* being a poor splenetic impotent terrestrial libel; putting those into Hell whom he could not be avenged-upon on earth! I suppose if ever pity, tender as a mother's, was in the heart of any man, it was in Dante's. But a man who does not know rigour cannot pity either. His very pity will be cowardly, egoistic,—sentimentality, or little better. I know not in the world an affection equal to that of Dante. It is a tenderness, a trembling, longing, pitying love: like the wail of Æolean harps, soft, soft; like a child's young heart;—and then that stern, sore-saddened heart! These longings of his towards his Beatrice; their meeting together in the *Paradiso*; his gazing in her pure transfigured eyes, her that had been purified by death so long, separated from him so far:—one likens it to the song of angels; it is among the purest utterances of affection, perhaps the very purest, that ever came out of a human soul.

For the *intense* Dante is intense in all things; he has got into the essence of all. His intellectual insight as painter, on occasion too as reasoner, is but the result of all other sorts of intensity. Morally great, above all, we must call him; it is the beginning of all. His scorn, his grief are as transcendent as his love;—as indeed, what are they but the *inverse* or *converse* of his love? '*A Dio spiacenti ed a' nemici sui*, Hateful to God and to the enemies of God': lofty scorn, unappeasable silent reprobation and aversion; '*Non ragionam di lor*, We will not speak of *them*, look only and pass.' Or think of this; 'They have not the *hope* to die, *Non han speranza di morte*.' One day, it had risen sternly benign on the scathed heart of Dante, that he, wretched, never-resting, worn as he was, would full surely *die*; 'that Destiny itself could not doom him not to die.' Such words are in this man. For rigour, earnestness and depth, he is not to be paralleled in the modern world; to seek his parallel we must go into the Hebrew Bible, and live with the antique Prophets there.

I do not agree with much modern criticism, in greatly preferring the *Inferno* to the two other parts of the Divine *Commedia*. Such preference belongs, I imagine, to our general Byronism of taste, and is like to be a transient feeling. The *Purgatorio* and *Paradiso*, especially the former, one would almost say, is even more excellent than it. It is a noble thing that *Purgatorio*, 'Mountain of Purification'; an emblem of the noblest conception of that age. If Sin is so fatal, and Hell is and must be so rigorous, awful, yet in Repentance too is man purified; Repentance is the grand Christian act. It is beautiful how Dante works it out. The *tremolar dell' onde*, that 'trembling' of the ocean-waves, under the first pure gleam of morning, dawning afar on the wandering Two, is as the type of an altered mood. Hope has now dawned; never-dying Hope, if in company still with heavy sorrow. The obscure sojourn of dæmons and reprobate is underfoot; a soft breathing of penitence mounts higher and higher, to the Throne of Mercy itself. 'Pray for me,' the denizens of that Mount of Pain all say to him. 'Tell my Giovanna to pray for me,' my daughter Giovanna; 'I think her mother loves me no more!' They toil painfully up by that winding steep, 'bent-down like corbels of a building,' some of them—crushed-together so 'for the sin of pride'; yet nevertheless in years, in ages and æons, they shall have reached the top, which is Heaven's gate, and by Mercy shall have been admitted in. The joy too of all, when one has prevailed; the whole Mountain shakes with joy, and a psalm of praise rises, when one soul has perfected repentance and got its sin and misery left behind! I call all this a noble embodiment of a true noble thought.

But indeed the Three compartments mutually support one another, are indispensable to one another. The *Paradiso*, a kind of inarticulate music to me, is the redeeming side of the *Inferno*; the *Inferno* without it were untrue. All three make-up the true Unseen World, as figured in the Christianity of the Middle Ages; a thing forever memorable, forever true in the essence of it, to all men. It was perhaps delineated in no human soul with such depth of veracity as in this of Dante's; a man *sent* to sing it, to keep it long memorable. Very notable with what brief simplicity he passes out of the every-day reality, into the Invisible one; and in the second or third stanza, we find ourselves in the World of Spirits; and dwell there, as among things palpable, indubitable! To Dante they *were* so; the real world, as it is called, and its facts, was but the threshold to an infinitely higher Fact of a World. At bottom, the one was as *preter*-natural as the other. Has not each man a soul? He will not only be a spirit, but is one. To the earnest Dante it is all one visible Fact; he believes it, sees it; is the Poet of it in virtue of that. Sincerity, I say again, is the saving merit, now as always.

Dante's Hell, Purgatory, Paradise, are a symbol withal, an emblematic representation of his Belief about this Universe:—some Critic in a future age, like those Scandinavian ones the other day, who has ceased altogether to think as Dante did, may find this too all an 'Allegory,' perhaps an idle Allegory! It is a sublime embodiment, or sublimest, of the soul of Christianity. It expresses, as in huge worldwide architectural emblems, how the Christian Dante felt Good and Evil to be the two polar elements of this Creation, on which it all turns; that these two differ not by *preferability* of one to the other, but by incompatibility absolute and infinite; that the one is excellent and high as light and Heaven, the other hideous, black as Gehenna and the Pit of Hell! Everlasting Justice, yet with Penitence, with everlasting Pity,—all Christianism, as Dante and the Middle Ages had it, is emblemed here. Emblemed: and yet, as I urged the other day, with what entire truth of purpose; how unconscious of any embleming! Hell, Purgatory, Paradise: these things were not fashioned as emblems; was there, in our Modern European Mind, any thought at all of their being emblems? Were they not indubitable awful facts; the whole heart of man taking them for practically true, all Nature everywhere confirming them? So is it always in these things. Men do not believe an Allegory. The future Critic, whatever his new thought may be, who considers this of Dante to have been all got-up as an Allegory, will commit one sore mistake!—Paganism we recognised as a veracious expression of the earnest awe-struck feeling of man towards the Universe; veracious, true once, and still not without worth for us. But mark here the difference of Paganism and Christianism; one great difference. Paganism emblemed chiefly the Operations of Nature; the destinies, efforts, combinations, vicissitudes of things and men in this world; Christianism emblemed the Law of Human Duty, the Moral Law of Man. One was for the sensuous nature: a rude helpless utterance of the *first* Thought of men—the chief recognised virtue, Courage, Superiority to Fear. The other was not for the sensuous nature, but for the moral. What a progress is here, if in that one respect only!—

And so in this Dante, as we said, had ten silent

centuries, in a very strange way, found a voice. The *Divina Commedia* is of Dante's writing; yet in truth *it* belongs to ten Christian centuries, only the finishing of it is Dante's. So always. The craftsman there, the smith with that metal of his, with these tools, with these cunning methods,—how little of all he does is properly *his* work! All past inventive men work there with him;—as indeed with all of us, in all things. Dante is the spokesman of the Middle Ages; the Thought they lived by stands here in everlasting music. These sublime ideas of his, terrible and beautiful, are the fruit of the Christian Meditation of all the good men who had gone before him. Precious they; but also is not he precious? Much, had not he spoken, would have been dumb; not dead, yet living voiceless.

On the whole, is it not an utterance, this Mystic Song, at once of one of the greatest human souls, and of the highest thing that Europe had hitherto realised for itself? Christianism, as Dante sings it, is another than Paganism in the rude Norse mind; another than 'Bastard Christianism' half articulately spoken in the Arab Desert seven-hundred years before!—The noblest *idea* made *real* hitherto among men, is sung, and emblemed-forth abidingly, by one of the noblest men. In the one sense and in the other, are we not right glad to possess it? As I calculate, it may last yet for long thousands of years. For the thing that is uttered from the inmost parts of a man's soul, differs altogether from what is uttered by the outer part. The outer is of the day, under the empire of mode; the outer passes away, in swift endless changes; the inmost is the same yesterday, to-day and forever. True souls, in all generations of the world, who look on this Dante, will find a brotherhood in him; the deep sincerity of his thoughts, his woes and hopes, will speak likewise to their sincerity; they will feel that this Dante too was a brother. Napoleon in Saint-Helena is charmed with the genial veracity of old Homer. The oldest Hebrew

Prophet, under a vesture the most diverse from ours, does yet, because he speaks from the heart of man, speak to all men's hearts. It is the one sole secret of continuing long memorable. Dante, for depth of sincerity, is like an antique Prophet too; his words, like theirs, come from his very heart. One need not wonder if it were predicted that his Poem might be the most enduring thing our Europe has yet made; for nothing so endures as a truly spoken word. All cathedrals, pontificalities, brass and stone, and outer arrangement never so lasting, are brief in comparison to an unfathomable heart-song like this: one feels as if it might survive, still of importance to men, when these had all sunk into new irrecognisable combinations, and had ceased individually to be. Europe has made much; great cities, great empires, encyclopædias, creeds, bodies of opinion and practice: but it has made little of the class of Dante's Thought. Homer yet *is*, veritably present face to face with every open soul of us; and Greece, where is *it*? Desolate for thousands of years; away, vanished; a bewildered heap of stones and rubbish, the life and existence of it all gone. Like a dream; like the dust of King Agamemnon! Greece was; Greece, except in the *words* it spoke, is not.

The uses of this Dante? We will not say much about his 'uses.' A human soul who has once got into that primal element of *Song*, and sung-forth fitly somewhat therefrom, has worked in the *depths* of our existence; feeding through long times the life-*roots* of all excellent human things whatsoever,—in a way that 'utilities' will not succeed well in calculating! We will not estimate the Sun by the quantity of gaslight it saves us; Dante shall be invaluable, or of no value. One remark I may make: the contrast in this respect between the Hero-Poet and the Hero-Prophet. In a hundred years, Mahomet, as we saw, had his Arabians at Grenada and at Delhi; Dante's Italians seem to be yet very much where they were. Shall we say, then, Dante's effect on the world was small in comparison?

Not so: his arena is far more restricted: but also it is far nobler, clearer;—perhaps not less but more important. Mahomet speaks to great masses of men, in the coarse dialect adapted to such; a dialect filled with inconsistencies, crudities, follies: on the great masses alone can he act, and there with good and with evil strangely blended. Dante speaks to the noble, the pure and great, in all times and places. Neither does he grow obsolete, as the other does. Dante burns as a pure star, fixed there in the firmament, at which the great and the high of all ages kindle themselves: he is the possession of all the chosen of the world for uncounted time. Dante, one calculates, may long survive Mahomet. In this way the balance may be made straight again.

But, at any rate, it is not by what is called their effect on the world, by what *we* can judge of their effect there, that a man and his work are measured. Effect? Influence? Utility? Let a man *do* his work; the fruit of it is the care of Another than he. It will grow its own fruit; and whether embodied in Caliph Thrones and Arabian Conquests, so that it 'fills all Morning and Evening Newspapers,' and all Histories, which are a kind of distilled Newspapers; or not embodied so at all;—what matters that? That is not the real fruit of it! The Arabian Caliph, in so far only as he did something, was something. If the great Cause of Man, and Man's work in God's Earth, got no furtherance from the Arabian Caliph, then no matter how many scimitars he drew, how many gold piasters pocketed, and what uproar and blaring he made in this world—*he* was but a loud-sounding inanity and futility; at bottom, he *was* not at all. Let us honour the great empire of *Silence*, once more! The boundless treasury which we do *not* jingle in our pockets, or count up and present before men! It is perhaps, of all things, the usefulest for each of us to do, in these loud times.——

As Dante, the Italian man, was sent into our world

to embody musically the Religion of the Middle Ages, the Religion of our Modern Europe, its Inner Life; so Shakespeare, we may say, embodies for us the Outer Life of our Europe as developed then, its chivalries, courtesies, humours, ambitions, what practical way of thinking, acting, looking at the world, men then had. As in Homer we may still construe Old Greece, so in Shakespeare and Dante, after thousands of years, what our modern Europe was, in Faith and Practice, will still be legible. Dante has given us the Faith or soul; Shakespeare, in a not less noble way, has given us the Practice or body. This latter also we were to have: a man was sent for it, the man Shakespeare. Just when that chivalry way of life had reached its last finish, and was on the point of breaking down into slow or swift dissolution, as we now see it everywhere, this other sovereign Poet, with his seeing eye, with his perennial singing voice, was sent to take note of it, to give long-enduring record of it. Two fit men: Dante, deep, fierce as the central fire of the world; Shakespeare, wide, placid, far-seeing, as the Sun, the upper light of the world. Italy produced the one world-voice; we English had the honour of producing the other.

Curious enough how, as it were by mere accident, this man came to us. I think always, so great, quiet, complete and self-sufficing is this Shakespeare, had the Warwickshire Squire not prosecuted him for deer-stealing, we had perhaps never heard of him as a Poet! The woods and skies, the rustic Life of Man in Stratford there, had been enough for this man! But indeed that strange outbudding of our whole English Existence, which we call the Elizabethan Era, did not it too come as of its own accord? The 'Tree Igdrasil' buds and withers by its own laws,—too deep for our scanning. Yet it does bud and wither, and every bough and leaf of it is there, by fixed eternal laws; not a Sir Thomas Lucy but comes at the hour fit for him. Curious, I say, and not sufficiently considered: how every thing does co-operate with all; not a leaf rotting on the highway but is indissoluble portion of solar and stellar systems, no thought, word or act of man but has sprung withal out of all men, and works sooner or later, recognisably or irrecognisably, on all men! It is all a Tree: circulation of sap and influences, mutual communication of every minutest leaf with the lowest talon of a root, with every other greatest and minutest portion of the whole. The Tree Igdrasil, that has its roots down in the Kingdoms of Hela and Death, and whose boughs overspread the highest Heaven!—

In some sense it may be said that this glorious Elizabethan Era with its Shakespeare, as the outcome and flowerage of all which had preceded it, is itself attributable to the Catholicism of the Middle Ages. The Christian Faith, which was the theme of Dante's Song, had produced this Practical Life which Shakespeare was to sing. For Religion then, as it now and always is, was the soul of Practice; the primary vital fact in men's life. And remark here, as rather curious, the Middle-Age Catholicism was abolished, so far as Acts of Parliament could abolish it, before Shakespeare, the noblest product of it, made his appearance. He did make his appearance nevertheless. Nature at her own time, with Catholicism or what else might be necessary, sent him forth; taking small thought of Acts of Parliament. King-Henrys, Queen-Elizabeths go their way; and Nature too goes hers. Acts of Parliament, on the whole, are small, notwithstanding the noise they make. What Act of Parliament, debate at St. Stephen's, on the hustings or elsewhere, was it that brought this Shakespeare into being? No dining at Freemasons' Tavern, opening subscription-lists, selling of shares, and infinite other jangling and true or false endeavouring! This Elizabethan Era, and all its nobleness and blessedness, came without proclamation, preparation of ours. Priceless Shakespeare was the free gift of Nature; given altogether silently;—

received altogether silently, as if it had been a thing of little account. And yet, very literally, it is a priceless thing. One should look at that side of matters too.

Of this Shakespeare of ours, perhaps the opinion one sometimes hears a little idolatrously expressed is, in fact, the right one; I think the best judgment not of this country only, but of Europe at large, is slowly pointing to the conclusion, That Shakespeare is the chief of all Poets hitherto; the greatest intellect who, in our recorded world, has left record of himself in the way of Literature. On the whole, I know not such a power of vision, such a faculty of thought, if we take all the characters of it, in any other man. Such a calmness of depth; placid joyous strength; all things imaged in that great soul of his so true and clear, as in a tranquil unfathomable sea! It has been said, that in the constructing of Shakespeare's Dramas there is, apart from all other 'faculties' as they are called, an understanding manifested, equal to that in Bacon's *Novum Organum.* That is true; and it is not a truth that strikes every one. It would become more apparent if we tried, any of us for himself, how, out of Shakespeare's dramatic materials, *we* could fashion such a result! The built house seems all so fit,—everyway as it should be, as if it came there by its own law and the nature of things,—we forget the rude disorderly quarry it was shaped from. The very perfection of the house, as if Nature herself had made it, hides the builder's merit. Perfect, more perfect than any other man, we may call Shakespeare in this: he discerns, knows as by instinct, what condition he works under, what his materials are, what his own force and its relation to them is. It is not a transitory glance of insight that will suffice; it is deliberate illumination of the whole matter; it is a calmly *seeing* eye; a great intellect, in short. How a man, of some wide thing that he has witnessed, will construct a narrative, what kind of picture and delineation he will give of it,—is the best measure you could get of what intellect is in the man. Which circumstance is vital and shall stand prominent; which unessential, fit to be suppressed; where is the true *beginning*, the true sequence and ending? To find out this, you task the whole force of insight that is in the man. He must *understand* the thing; according to the depth of his understanding, will the fitness of his answer be. You will try him so. Does like join itself to like; does the spirit of method stir in that confusion, so that its embroilment becomes order? Can the man say, *Fiat lux*, Let there be light; and out of chaos make a world? Precisely as there is *light* in himself, will he accomplish this.

Or indeed we may say again, it is in what I called Portrait-painting, delineating of men and things, especially of men, that Shakespeare is great. All the greatness of the man comes out decisively here. It is unexampled, I think, that calm creative perspicacity of Shakespeare. The thing he looks at reveals not this or that face of it, but its inmost heart, and generic secret: it dissolves itself as in light before him, so that he discerns the perfect structure of it. Creative, we said: poetic creation, what is this too but *seeing* the thing sufficiently? The *word* that will describe the thing, follows of itself from such clear intense sight of the thing. And is not Shakespeare's *morality*, his valour, candour, tolerance, truthfulness; his whole victorious strength and greatness, which can triumph over such obstructions, visible there too? Great as the world! No *twisted*, poor convex-concave mirror, reflecting all objects with its own convexities and concavities; a perfectly *level* mirror;—that is to say withal, if we will understand it, a man justly related to all things and men, a good man. It is truly a lordly spectacle how this great soul takes-in all kinds of men and objects, a Falstaff, an Othello, a Juliet, a Coriolanus; sets them all forth to us in their round completeness; loving, just, the equal brother of all. *Novum*

Organum, and all the intellect you will find in Bacon, is of a quite secondary order; earthly, material, poor in comparison with this. Among modern men, one finds, in strictness, almost nothing of the same rank. Goethe alone, since the days of Shakespeare, reminds me of it. Of him too you say that he *saw* the object; you may say what he himself says of Shakespeare: 'His characters are like watches with dial-plates of transparent crystal; they show you the hour like others, and the inward mechanism also is all visible.'

The seeing eye! It is this that discloses the inner harmony of things; what Nature meant, what musical idea Nature has wrapped-up in these often rough embodiments. Something she did mean. To the seeing eye that something were discernible. Are they base, miserable things? You can laugh over them, you can weep over them; you can in some way or other genially relate yourself to them;—you can, at lowest, hold your peace about them, turn away your own and others' face from them, till the hour come for practically exterminating and extinguishing them! At bottom, it is the Poet's first gift, as it is all men's, that he have intellect enough. He will be a Poet if he have: a Poet in word; or failing that, perhaps still better, a Poet in act. Whether he write at all; and if so, whether in prose or in verse, will depend on accidents: who knows on what extremely trivial accidents,—perhaps on his having had a singing-master, on his being taught to sing in his boyhood! But the faculty which enables him to discern the inner heart of things, and the harmony that dwells there (for whatsoever exists has a harmony in the heart of it, or it would not hold together and exist), is not the result of habits or accidents, but the gift of Nature herself; the primary outfit for a Heroic Man in what sort soever. To the Poet, as to every other, we say first of all, *See*. If you cannot do that, it is of no use to keep stringing rhymes together, jingling sensibilities against each other, and *name* yourself a Poet; there is no hope for you. If you can, there is, in prose or verse, in action or speculation, all manner of hope. The crabbed old Schoolmaster used to ask, when they brought him a new pupil, 'But are ye sure he 's *not a dunce*?' Why, really one might ask the same thing, in regard to every man proposed for whatsoever function; and consider it as the one inquiry needful: Are ye sure he 's not a dunce? There is, in this world, no other entirely fatal person.

For, in fact, I say the degree of vision that dwells in a man is a correct measure of the man. If called to define Shakespeare's faculty, I should say superiority of Intellect, and think I had included all under that. What indeed are faculties? We talk of faculties as if they were distinct, things separable; as if a man had intellect, imagination, fancy, etc., as he has hands, feet and arms. That is a capital error. Then again, we hear of a man's 'intellectual nature,' and of his 'moral nature,' as if these again were divisible, and existed apart. Necessities of language do perhaps prescribe such forms of utterance; we must speak, I am aware, in that way, if we are to speak at all. But words ought not to harden into things for us. It seems to me, our apprehension of this matter is, for the most part, radically falsified thereby. We ought to know withal, and to keep for ever in mind, that these divisions are at bottom but *names*; that man's spiritual nature, the vital Force which dwells in him, is essentially one and indivisible; that what we call imagination, fancy, understanding, and so forth, are but different figures of the same Power of Insight, all indissolubly connected with each other, physiognomically related; that if we knew one of them, we might know all of them. Morality itself, what we call the moral quality of a man, what is this but another *side* of the one vital Force whereby he is and works? All that a man does is physiognomical of him. You may see how a man would fight, by the way in which he sings; his courage, or want of courage, is visible in the word he utters, in the opinion he has formed, no less than in the stroke he strikes. He is *one*; and preaches the same Self abroad in all these ways.

Without hands a man might have feet, and could still walk: but, consider it,—without morality, intellect were impossible for him; a thoroughly immoral *man* could not know anything at all! To know a thing, what we can call knowing, a man must first *love* the thing, sympathise with it: that is, be *virtuously* related to it. If he have not the justice to put down his own selfishness at every turn, the courage to stand by the dangerous-true at every turn, how shall he know? His virtues, all of them, will lie recorded in his knowledge. Nature, with her truth, remains to the bad, to the selfish and the pusillanimous forever a sealed book: what such can know of Nature is mean, superficial, small; for the uses of the day merely.—But does not the very Fox know something of Nature? Exactly so: it knows where the geese lodge! The human Reynard, very frequent everywhere in the world, what more does he know but this and the like of this? Nay, it should be considered, too, that if the Fox had not a certain vulpine *morality*, he could not even know where the geese were, or get at the geese! If he spent his time in splenetic atrabiliar reflections on his own misery, his ill usage by Nature, Fortune and other Foxes, and so forth; and had not courage, promptitude, practicality, and other suitable vulpine gifts and graces, he would catch no geese. We may say of the Fox too, that his morality and insight are of the same dimensions; different faces of the same internal unity of vulpine life!—These things are worth stating; for the contrary of them acts with manifold very baleful perversion, in this time: what limitations, modifications they require, your own candour will supply.

If I say, therefore, that Shakespeare is the greatest of Intellects, I have said all concerning him. But there is more in Shakespeare's intellect than we have yet seen. It is what I call an unconscious intellect: there is more virtue in it than he himself is aware of. Novalis beautifully remarks of him, that those Dramas of his are Products of Nature too, deep as Nature herself. I find a great truth in this saying. Shakespeare's Art is not Artifice; the noblest worth of it is not there by plan or precontrivance. It grows-up from the deeps of Nature, through this noble sincere soul, who is a voice of Nature. The latest generations of men will find new meanings in Shakespeare, new elucidations of their own human being; 'new harmonies with the infinite structure of the Universe; concurrences with later ideas, affinities with the higher powers and senses of man.' This well deserves meditating. It is Nature's highest reward to a true simple great soul, that he get thus to be *a part of herself*. Such a man's works, whatsoever he with utmost conscious exertion and forethought shall accomplish, grow up withal *un*consciously, from the unknown deeps in him;—as the oak-tree grows from the Earth's bosom, as the mountains and waters shape themselves; with a symmetry grounded on Nature's own laws, conformable to all Truth whatsoever. How much in Shakespeare lies hid; his sorrows, his silent struggles known to himself; much that was not known at all, not speakable at all; like *roots*, like sap and forces working underground! Speech is great; but Silence is greater.

Withal the joyful tranquillity of this man is notable. I will not blame Dante for his misery; it is as battle without victory; but true battle,—the first, indispensable thing. Yet I call Shakespeare greater than Dante, in that he fought truly, and did conquer. Doubt it not, he had his own sorrows: those *Sonnets* of his will even testify expressly in what deep waters he had waded, and swum struggling for his life;—as what man like him ever failed to have to do? It seems to me a heedless notion, our common one, that he sat like a bird on the bough; and sang forth, free and offhand, never knowing the troubles of other men. Not so; with no man is it so. How could a man travel forward from rustic deer-poaching to such tragedy-writing, and not fall-in with sorrows by the way? Or, still better, how could a man delineate a Hamlet, a Coriolanus, a Macbeth, so many suffering heroic hearts, if his own heroic heart had never suffered?—And now, in contrast with all this, observe his mirthfulness, his genuine overflowing love of laughter! You would say, in no point does he *exaggerate* but only in laughter. Fiery objurgations, words that pierce and burn, are to be found in Shakespeare: yet he is always in measure here; never what Johnson would remark as a specially 'good hater.' But his laughter seems to pour from him in floods; he heaps all manner of ridiculous nicknames on the butt he is bantering, tumbles and tosses him in all sorts of horse-play; you would say, with his whole heart laughs. And then, if not always the finest, it is always a genial laughter. Not at mere weakness, at misery or poverty; never. No man who *can* laugh, what we call laughing, will laugh at these things. It is some poor character only *desiring* to laugh, and have the credit of wit, that does so. Laughter means sympathy; good laughter is not 'the crackling of thorns under the pot.' Even at stupidity and pretension this Shakespeare does not laugh otherwise than genially. Dogberry and Verges tickle our very hearts; and we dismiss them covered with explosions of laughter: but we like the poor fellows only the better for our laughing; and hope they will get on well there, and continue Presidents of the City-watch. Such laughter, like sunshine on the deep sea, is very beautiful to me.

We have no room to speak of Shakespeare's individual works; though perhaps there is much still waiting to be said on that head. Had we, for instance, all his plays reviewed as *Hamlet*, in *Wilhelm Meister*, is! A thing which might, one day, be done. August Wilhelm Schlegel has a remark on his Historical Plays, *Henry Fifth* and the others, which is worth remembering. He calls them a kind of National Epic.

Marlborough, you recollect, said, he knew no English History but what he had learned from Shakespeare. There are really, if we look to it, few as memorable Histories. The great salient points are admirably seized; all rounds itself off, into a kind of rhythmic coherence; it is, as Schlegel says, *epic*;—as indeed all delineation by a great thinker will be. There are right beautiful things in those Pieces, which indeed together form one beautiful thing. That battle of Agincourt strikes me as one of the most perfect things, in its sort, we anywhere have of Shakespeare's. The description of the two hosts: the worn-out, jaded English; the dread hour, big with destiny, when the battle shall begin; and then that deathless valour: 'Ye good yeomen, whose limbs were made in England!' There is a noble Patriotism in it,—far other than the 'indifference' you sometimes hear ascribed to Shakespeare. A true English heart breathes, calm and strong, through the whole business; not boisterous, protrusive; all the better for that. There is a sound in it like the ring of steel. This man too had a right stroke in him, had it come to that!

But I will say, of Shakespeare's works generally, that we have no full impress of him there; even as full as we have of many men. His works are so many windows, through which we see a glimpse of the world that was in him. All his works seem, comparatively speaking, cursory, imperfect, written under cramping circumstances; giving only here and there a note of the full utterance of the man. Passages there are that come upon you like splendour out of Heaven; bursts of radiance, illuminating the very heart of the thing: you say, 'That is *true*, spoken once and forever; wheresoever and whensoever there is an open human soul, that will be recognised as true!' Such bursts, however, make us feel that the surrounding matter is not radiant; that it is, in part, temporary, conventional. Alas, Shakespeare had to write for the Globe Play-house: his great soul had to crush itself, as it could, into that and no other mould. It was with him, then, as it is with us all. No man works save under conditions. The sculptor cannot set his own free Thought before us; but his Thought as he could translate it into the stone that was given, with the tools that were given. *Disjecta membra* are all that we find of any Poet, or of any man.

Whoever looks intelligently at this Shakespeare may recognise that he too was a *Prophet*, in his way; of an insight analogous to the Prophetic, though he took it up in another strain. Nature seemed to this man also divine; *un*speakable, deep as Tophet, high as Heaven: 'We are such stuff as Dreams are made of!' That scroll in Westminster Abbey, which few read with understanding, is of the depth of any seer. But the man sang; did not preach, except musically. We called Dante the melodious Priest of Middle-Age Catholicism. May we not call Shakespeare the still more melodious Priest of a *true* Catholicism, the 'Universal Church' of the Future and of all times? No narrow superstition, harsh asceticism, intolerance, fanatical fierceness or perversion: a Revelation, so far as it goes, that such a thousandfold hidden beauty and divineness dwells in all Nature; which let all men worship as they can! We may say without offence, that there rises a kind of universal Psalm out of this Shakespeare too; not unfit to make itself heard among the still more sacred Psalms. Not in disharmony with these, if we understood them, but in harmony!—I cannot call this Shakespeare a 'Sceptic,' as some do; his indifference to the creeds and theological quarrels of his time misleading them. No: neither unpatriotic, though he says little about his Patriotism; nor sceptic, though he says little about his Faith. Such 'indifference' was the fruit of his greatness withal: his whole heart was in his own grand sphere of worship (we may call it such): these other controversies, vitally important to other men, were not vital to him.

But call it worship, call it what you will, is it not a

right glorious thing, and set of things, this that Shakespeare has brought us? For myself, I feel that there is actually a kind of sacredness in the fact of such a man being sent into this Earth. Is he not an eye to us all; a blessed heaven-sent Bringer of Light?—And, at bottom, was it not perhaps far better that this Shakespeare, everyway an unconscious man, was *conscious* of no Heavenly message? He did not feel, like Mahomet, because he saw into those internal Splendours, that he specially was the 'Prophet of God': and was he not greater than Mahomet in that? Greater; and also, if we compute strictly, as we did in Dante's case, more successful. It was intrinsically an error that notion of Mahomet's, of his supreme Prophethood: and has come down to us inextricably involved in error to this day; dragging along with it such a coil of fables, impurities, intolerances, as makes it a questionable step for me here and now to say, as I have done, that Mahomet was a true Speaker at all, and not rather an ambitious charlatan, perversity and simulacrum; no Speaker, but a Babbler! Even in Arabia, as I compute, Mahomet will have exhausted himself and become obsolete, while this Shakespeare, this Dante may still be young;—while this Shakespeare may still pretend to be a Priest of Mankind, of Arabia as of other places, for unlimited periods to come!

Compared with any speaker or singer one knows, even with Æschylus or Homer, why should he not, for veracity and universality, last like them? He is *sincere* as they; reaches deep down like them, to the universal and perennial. But as for Mahomet, I think it had been better for him *not* to be so conscious! Alas, poor Mahomet; all that he was *conscious* of was a mere error; a futility and triviality,—as indeed such ever is. The truly great in him too was the unconscious: that he was a wild Arab lion of the desert, and did speak-out with that great thunder-voice of his, not by words which he *thought* to be great, but by actions, by feelings, by a history which *were* great! His Koran has become a stupid piece of prolix absurdity; we do not believe, like him, that God wrote that! The Great Man here too, as always, is a Force of Nature: whatsoever is truly great in him springs-up from the *in*articulate deeps.

Well: this is our poor Warwickshire Peasant, who rose to be Manager of a Playhouse, so that he could live without begging; whom the Earl of Southampton cast some kind glances on; whom Sir Thomas Lucy, many thanks to him, was for sending to the Treadmill! We did not account him a god, like Odin, while he dwelt with us;—on which point there were much to be said. But I will say rather, or repeat: In spite of the sad state Hero-worship now lies in, consider what this Shakespeare has actually become among us. Which Englishman we ever made, in this land of ours, which million of Englishmen, would we not give-up rather than the Stratford Peasant? There is no regiment of highest Dignitaries that we would sell him for. He is the grandest thing we have yet done. For our honour among foreign nations, as an ornament to our English Household, what item is there that we would not surrender rather than him? Consider now, if they asked us, Will you give-up your Indian Empire or your Shakespeare, you English; never have had any Indian Empire, or never have had any Shakespeare? Really it were a grave question. Official persons would answer doubtless in official language; but we, for our part too, should not we be forced to answer: Indian Empire, or no Indian Empire; we cannot do without Shakespeare! Indian Empire will go, at any rate, some day; but this Shakespeare does not go, he lasts forever with us; we cannot give-up our Shakespeare!

Nay, apart from spiritualities; and considering him merely as a real, marketable, tangibly-useful possession. England, before long, this Island of ours, will hold but a small fraction of the English: in America, in New Holland, east and west to the very Antipodes.

there will be a Saxondom covering great spaces of the Globe. And now, what is it that can keep all these together into virtually one Nation, so that they do not fall-out and fight, but live at peace, in brotherlike intercourse, helping one another? This is justly regarded as the greatest practical problem, the thing all manner of sovereignties and governments are here to accomplish: what is it that will accomplish this? Acts of Parliament, administrative prime-ministers cannot. America is parted from us, so far as Parliament could part it. Call it not fantastic, for there is much reality in it: Here, I say, is an English King, whom no time or chance, Parliament or combination of Parliaments, can dethrone! This King Shakespeare, does not he shine, in crowned sovereignty, over us all, as the noblest, gentlest, yet strongest of rallying-signs; *in*destructible; really more valuable in that point of view than any other means or appliance whatsoever? We can fancy him as radiant aloft over all the Nations of Englishmen, a thousand years hence. From Paramatta, from New York, wheresoever, under what sort of Parish-Constable soever, English men and women are, they will say to one another: 'Yes, this Shakespeare is ours; we produced him, we speak and think by him; we are of one blood and kind with him.' The most common-sense politician, too, if he pleases, may think of that.

Yes, truly, it is a great thing for a Nation that it get an articulate voice; that it produce a man who will speak-forth melodiously what the heart of it means! Italy, for example, poor Italy lies dismembered, scattered asunder, not appearing in any protocol or treaty as a unity at all; yet the noble Italy is actually *one*: Italy produced its Dante; Italy can speak! The Czar of all the Russias he is strong, with so many bayonets, Cossacks and cannons; and does a great feat in keeping such a tract of Earth politically together; but he cannot yet speak. Something great in him, but it is a dumb greatness. He has had no voice of genius, to be heard of all men and times. He must learn to speak. He is a great dumb monster hitherto. His cannons and Cossacks will all have rusted into non-entity, while that Dante's voice is still audible. The Nation that has a Dante is bound together as no dumb Russia can be.—We must here end what we had to say of the *Hero-Poet.*

LORD MACAULAY

1800–1859

OLIVER GOLDSMITH

OLIVER GOLDSMITH, one of the most pleasing English writers of the eighteenth century. He was of a Protestant and Saxon family which had been long settled in Ireland, and which had, like most other Protestant and Saxon families, been, in troubled times, harassed and put in fear by the native population. His father, Charles Goldsmith, studied in the reign of Queen Anne at the diocesan school at Elphin, became attached to the daughter of the schoolmaster, married her, took orders, and settled at a place called Pallas, in the county of Longford. There he with difficulty supported his wife and children on what he could earn, partly as a curate and partly as a farmer.

At Pallas Oliver Goldsmith was born in November 1728. That spot was then, for all practical purposes, almost as remote from the busy and splendid capital in which his later years were passed, as any clearing in Upper Canada or any sheep-walk in Australasia now is. Even at this day those enthusiasts who venture to make a pilgrimage to the birthplace of the poet are forced to perform the latter part of their journey on foot. The hamlet lies far from any highroad on a dreary plain which in wet weather is often a lake. The lanes would break any jaunting-car to pieces; and there are ruts and sloughs through which the most strongly-built wheels cannot be dragged.

While Oliver was still a child, his father was presented to a living worth about £200 a year, in the county of West Meath. The family accordingly quitted their cottage in the wilderness for a spacious house on a frequented road, near the village of Lissoy. Here the boy was taught his letters by a maid-servant, and was sent in his seventh year to a village school kept by an old quarter-master on half-pay, who professed to teach nothing but reading, writing, and arithmetic, but who had an inexhaustible fund of stories about ghosts, banshees, and fairies, about the great Rapparee chiefs, Baldearg O'Donnell and galloping Hogan, and about the exploits of Peterborough and Stanhope, the surprise of Monjuich, and the glorious disaster of Briheuga. This man must have been of the Protestant religion; but he was of the aboriginal race, and not only spoke the Irish language, but could pour forth unpremeditated Irish verses. Oliver early became, and through life continued to be, a passionate admirer of the Irish music, and especially of the compositions of Carolan, some of the last notes of whose harp he heard. It ought to be added that Oliver, though by birth one of the Englishry, and though connected by numerous ties with the Established Church, never showed the least sign of that contemptuous antipathy with which, in his days, the ruling minority in Ireland too generally regarded the subject majority. So far indeed was he from sharing the opinions and feelings of the caste to which he belonged, that he conceived an aversion to the Glorious and Immortal Memory, and, even when George the Third was on the throne, maintained that nothing but the restoration of the banished dynasty could save the country.

From the humble academy kept by the old soldier Goldsmith was removed in his ninth year. He went to several grammar-schools, and acquired some knowledge of the ancient languages. His life at this time seems to have been far from happy. He had, as appears from the admirable portrait of him at Knowle, features harsh even to ugliness. The small-pox had set its mark on him with more than usual severity. His stature was small, and his limbs ill put together. Among boys little tenderness is shown to personal defects; and the ridicule excited by poor Oliver's appearance was heightened by a peculiar simplicity and a disposition to blunder which he retained to the last. He became the common butt of boys and masters, was pointed at as a fright in the playground, and flogged as a dunce in the schoolroom. When he had risen to eminence, those who had once derided him ransacked their memory for the events of his early years, and recited repartees and couplets which had dropped from him, and which, though little noticed at the time, were supposed a quarter of a century later, to indicate the powers which produced the *Vicar of Wakefield* and the *Deserted Village*.

In his seventeenth year Oliver went up to Trinity College, Dublin, as a sizar. The sizars paid nothing for food and tuition, and very little for lodging; but they had to perform some menial services from which they have long been relieved. They swept the court: they carried up the dinner to the fellows' table, and changed the plates and poured out the ale of the rulers of the society. Goldsmith was quartered, not alone, in a garret, on the window of which his name, scrawled by himself, is still read with interest.[1] From such garrets many men of less parts than his have made their way to the woolsack or to the episcopal bench. But Goldsmith, while he suffered all the humiliations, threw away all the advantages of his situation. He neglected the studies of the place, stood low at the examinations, was turned down to the bottom of his class for playing the buffoon in the lecture-room, was severely reprimanded for pumping on a constable, and was caned by a brutal tutor for giving a ball in the attic story of the college to some gay youths and damsels from the city.

While Oliver was leading at Dublin a life divided between squalid distress and squalid dissipation, his

[1] The glass on which the name is written has, as we are informed by a writer in *Notes and Queries* (2nd S. ix. p. 91), been enclosed in a frame deposited in the Manuscript Room of the College Library, where it is still to be seen.

father died, leaving a mere pittance. The youth obtained his bachelor's degree, and left the University. During some time the humble dwelling to which his widowed mother had retired was his home. He was now in his twenty-first year; it was necessary that he should do something; and his education seemed to have fitted him to do nothing but to dress himself in gaudy colours, of which he was as fond as a magpie, to take a hand at cards, to sing Irish airs, to play the flute, to angle in summer, and to tell ghost stories by the fire in winter. He tried five or six professions in turn without success. He applied for ordination; but, as he applied in scarlet clothes, he was speedily turned out of the episcopal palace. He then became tutor in an opulent family, but soon quitted his situation in consequence of a dispute about play. Then he determined to emigrate to America. His relations, with much satisfaction, saw him set out for Cork on a good horse, with thirty pounds in his pocket. But in six weeks he came back on a miserable hack, without a penny, and informed his mother that the ship in which he had taken his passage, having got a fair wind while he was at a party of pleasure, had sailed without him. Then he resolved to study the law. A generous kinsman advanced fifty pounds. With this sum Goldsmith went to Dublin, was enticed into a gaming-house, and lost every shilling. He then thought of medicine. A small purse was made up: and in his twenty-fourth year he was sent to Edinburgh. At Edinburgh he passed eighteen months in nominal attendance on lectures, and picked up some superficial information about chemistry and natural history. Thence he went to Leyden, still pretending to study physic. He left that celebrated university, the third university at which he had resided, in his twenty-seventh year, without a degree, with the merest smattering of medical knowledge, and with no property but his clothes and his flute. His flute, however, proved a useful friend. He rambled on foot through Flanders,

France, and Switzerland, playing tunes which everywhere set the peasantry dancing, and which often procured for him a supper and a bed. He wandered as far as Italy. His musical performances, indeed, were not to the taste of the Italians, but he contrived to live on the alms which he obtained at the gates of convents. It should, however, be observed that the stories which he told about this part of his life ought to be received with great caution; for strict veracity was never one of his virtues; and a man who is ordinarily inaccurate in narration is likely to be more than ordinarily inaccurate when he talks about his own travels. Goldsmith, indeed, was so regardless of truth as to assert in print that he was present at a most interesting conversation between Voltaire and Fontenelle, and that this conversation took place at Paris. Now it is certain that Voltaire never was within a hundred leagues of Paris during the whole time which Goldsmith passed on the Continent.

In 1756 the wanderer landed at Dover, without a shilling, without a friend, and without a calling. He had, indeed, if his own unsupported evidence may be trusted, obtained from the University of Padua a doctor's degree; but this dignity proved utterly useless to him. In England his flute was not in request; there were no convents; and he was forced to have recourse to a series of desperate expedients. He turned strolling player; but his face and figure were ill suited to the boards even of the humblest theatre. He pounded drugs and ran about London with phials for charitable chemists. He joined a swarm of beggars, which made its nest in Axe Yard. He was for a time usher of a school, and felt the miseries and humiliations of this situation so keenly that he thought it a promotion to be permitted to earn his bread as a bookseller's hack; but he soon found the new yoke more galling than the old one, and was glad to become an usher again. He obtained a medical appointment in the service of the East India Company: but the appointment was speedily revoked. Why it was revoked we are not told. The subject was one on which he never liked to talk. It is probable that he was incompetent to perform the duties of the place. Then he presented himself at Surgeons' Hall for examination, as mate to a naval hospital. Even to so humble a post he was found unequal. By this time the schoolmaster whom he had served for a morsel of food and the third part of a bed was no more. Nothing remained but to return to the lowest drudgery of literature. Goldsmith took a garret in a miserable court, to which he had to climb from the brink of Fleet Ditch by a dizzy ladder of flagstones called Breakneck Steps. The court and the ascent have long disappeared; but old Londoners will remember both. Here, at thirty, the unlucky adventurer sat down to toil like a galley slave.

In the succeeding six years he sent to the press some things which have survived and many which have perished. He produced articles for reviews, magazines, and newspapers; children's books which, bound in gilt paper and adorned with hideous woodcuts, appeared in the window of the once far-famed shop at the corner of Saint Paul's Churchyard; *An Enquiry into the State of Polite Learning in Europe*, which, though of little or no value, is still reprinted among his works; a *Life of Beau Nash*, which is not reprinted, though it well deserves to be so; a superficial and incorrect, but very readable, *History of England*, in a series of letters purporting to be addressed by a nobleman to his son; and some lively and amusing *Sketches of London Society*, in a series of letters purporting to be addressed by a Chinese traveller to his friends. All these works were anonymous; but some of them were well known to be Goldsmith's; and he gradually rose in the estimation of the booksellers for whom he drudged. He was, indeed, emphatically a popular writer. For accurate research or grave disquisition he was not well qualified by nature or by education. He knew nothing accurately: his reading had been desultory; nor had he meditated deeply on what he had read. He had seen much of the world; but he had noticed and retained little more of what he had seen than some grotesque incidents and characters which had happened to strike his fancy. But, though his mind was very scantily stored with materials, he used what materials he had in such a way as to produce a wonderful effect. There have been many greater writers; but perhaps no writer was ever more uniformly agreeable. His style was always pure and easy, and, on proper occasions, pointed and energetic. His narratives were always amusing, his descriptions always picturesque, his humour rich and joyous, yet not without an occasional tinge of amiable sadness. About everything that he wrote, serious or sportive, there was a certain natural grace and decorum, hardly to be expected from a man a great part of whose life had been passed among thieves and beggars, street-walkers, and merry-andrews, in those squalid dens which are the reproach of great capitals.

As his name gradually became known, the circle of his acquaintance widened. He was introduced to Johnson, who was then considered as the first of living English writers; to Reynolds, the first of English painters; and to Burke, who had not yet entered Parliament, but who had distinguished himself greatly by his writings and by the eloquence of his conversation. With these eminent men Goldsmith became intimate. In 1763 he was one of the nine original members of that celebrated fraternity which has sometimes been called the Literary Club, but which has always disclaimed that epithet, and still glories in the simple name of The Club.

By this time Goldsmith had quitted his miserable dwelling at the top of Breakneck Steps, and had taken chambers in the more civilised region of the Inns of Court. But he was still often reduced to pitiable shifts. Towards the close of 1764 his rent was so long in arrear that his landlady one morning called in the help of a sheriff's officer. The debtor, in great perplexity, dispatched a messenger to Johnson; and Johnson, always friendly, though often surly, sent back the messenger with a guinea, and promised to follow speedily. He came, and found that Goldsmith had changed the guinea, and was railing at the landlady over a bottle of Madeira. Johnson put the cork into the bottle, and entreated his friend to consider calmly how money was to be procured. Goldsmith said that he had a novel ready for the press. Johnson glanced at the manuscript, saw that there were good things in it, took it to a bookseller, sold it for £60, and soon returned with the money. The rent was paid; and the sheriff's officer withdrew. According to one story, Goldsmith gave his landlady a sharp reprimand for her treatment of him: according to another he insisted on her joining him in a bowl of punch. Both stories are probably true. The novel which was thus ushered into the world was the *Vicar of Wakefield*.

But, before the *Vicar of Wakefield* appeared in print, came the great crisis of Goldsmith's literary life. In Christmas week, 1764, he published a poem entitled the *Traveller*. It was the first work to which he had put his name; and it at once raised him to the rank of a legitimate English classic. The opinion of the most skilful critics was, that nothing finer had appeared in verse since the fourth book of the *Dunciad*. In one respect the *Traveller* differs from all Goldsmith's other writings. In general his designs were bad, and his execution good. In the *Traveller*, the execution, though deserving of much praise, is far inferior to the design. No philosophical poem, ancient or modern, has a plan so noble, and at the same time so simple. An English wanderer, seated on a crag among the Alps, near the point where three great countries meet, looks down on the boundless prospect, reviews his long pilgrimage, recalls the varieties of scenery, of climate, of government, of religion, of national character, which he has observed, and comes to the conclusion, just or unjust, that our happiness depends little on political institutions, and much on the temper and regulation of our own minds.

While the fourth edition of the *Traveller* was on the counters of the booksellers, the *Vicar of Wakefield* appeared, and rapidly obtained a popularity which has lasted down to our own time, and which is likely to last as long as our language. The fable is indeed one of the worst that ever was constructed. It wants, not merely that probability which ought to be found in a tale of common English life, but that consistency which ought to be found even in the wildest fiction about witches, giants, and fairies. But the earlier chapters have all the sweetness of pastoral poetry, together with all the vivacity of comedy. Moses and his spectacles, the vicar and his monogamy, the sharper and his cosmogony, the squire proving from Aristotle that relatives are related, Olivia preparing herself for the arduous task of converting a rakish lover by studying the controversy between Robinson Crusoe and Friday, the great ladies with their scandal about Sir Tomkyn's amours and Dr. Burdock's verses, and Mr. Burchell with his 'Fudge,' have caused as much harmless mirth as has ever been caused by matter packed into so small a number of pages. The latter part of the tale is unworthy of the beginning. As we approach the catastrophe, the absurdities lie thicker and thicker; and the gleams of pleasantry become rarer and rarer.

The success which had attended Goldsmith as a novelist emboldened him to try his fortune as a dramatist. He wrote the *Goodnatured Man*, a piece which had a worse fate than it deserved. Garrick refused to produce it at Drury Lane. It was acted at Covent Garden in 1768, but was coldly received. The author, however, cleared by his benefit nights, and by the sale of the copyright, no less than £500, five times as much as he had made by the *Traveller* and the *Vicar of Wakefield* together. The plot of the *Good-natured Man* is, like almost all Goldsmith's plots, very ill constructed. But some passages are exquisitely ludicrous; much more ludicrous, indeed, than suited the taste of the town at that time. A canting, mawkish play, entitled *False Delicacy*, had just had an immense run. Sentimentality was all the mode. During some years, more tears were shed at comedies than at tragedies; and a pleasantry which moved the audience to anything more than a grave smile was reprobated as low. It is not strange, therefore, that the very best scene in the *Goodnatured Man*, that in which Miss Richland finds her lover attended by the bailiff and the bailiff's follower in full court dresses, should have been mercilessly hissed, and should have been omitted after the first night.

In 1770 appeared the *Deserted Village*. In mere diction and versification this celebrated poem is fully equal, perhaps superior, to the *Traveller*, and it is generally preferred to the *Traveller* by that large class of readers who think, with Bayes in the *Rehearsal*, that the only use of a plan is to bring in fine things. More discerning judges, however, while they admire the beauty of the details, are shocked by one unpardonable fault which pervades the whole. The fault we mean is not that theory about wealth and luxury which has so often been censured by political economists. The theory is indeed false; but the poem, considered merely as a poem, is not necessarily the worse on that account. The finest poem in the Latin language, indeed the finest didactic poem in any language, was written in defence of the silliest and meanest of all systems of natural and moral philosophy. A poet may easily be pardoned for reasoning ill; but he cannot be pardoned for describing ill, for observing the world in which he lives so carelessly that his portraits bear no resemblance to the originals, for exhibiting as copies from real life monstrous combinations of things which never were and never could be found together. What would be thought of a painter who should mix August and January in one landscape, who should introduce a frozen river into a harvest scene? Would it be a sufficient defence of such a picture to say that every part was exquisitely coloured, that the green hedges, the apple-trees loaded with fruit, the wagons reeling under the yellow sheaves, and the sunburned reapers wiping their foreheads, were very fine, and that the ice and the boys sliding were also very fine? To such a picture the *Deserted Village* bears a great resemblance. It is made up of incongruous parts. The village in its happy days is a true English village. The village in its decay is an Irish village. The felicity and the misery which Goldsmith has brought close together belong to two different countries, and to two different stages in the progress of society. He had assuredly never seen in his native island such a rural paradise, such a seat of plenty, content, and tranquillity, as his 'Auburn.' He had assuredly never seen in England all the inhabitants of such a paradise turned out of their homes in one day and forced to emigrate in a body to America. The hamlet he had probably seen in Kent; the ejectment he had probably seen in Munster; but, by joining the two, he has produced something which never was and never will be seen in any part of the world.

In 1773 Goldsmith tried his chance at Covent Garden with a second play, *She Stoops to Conquer.* The manager was not without great difficulty induced to bring this piece out. The sentimental comedy still reigned; and Goldsmith's comedies were not sentimental. The *Goodnatured Man* had been too funny to succeed; yet the mirth of the *Goodnatured Man* was sober when compared with the rich drollery of *She Stoops to Conquer*, which is, in truth, an incomparable farce in five acts. On this occasion, however, genius triumphed. Pit, boxes, and galleries were in a constant roar of laughter. If any bigoted admirer of

Kelly and Cumberland ventured to hiss or groan, he was speedily silenced by a general cry of 'Turn him out,' or 'Throw him over.' Two generations have since confirmed the verdict which was pronounced on that night.

While Goldsmith was writing the *Deserted Village* and *She Stoops to Conquer*, he was employed in works of a very different kind, works from which he derived little reputation but much profit. He compiled for the use of schools a *History of Rome*, by which he made £300; a *History of England*, by which he made £600; a *History of Greece*, for which he received £250; a *Natural History*, for which the booksellers covenanted to pay him 800 guineas. These works he produced without any elaborate research, by merely selecting, abridging, and translating into his own clear, pure, and flowing language what he found in books well known to the world, but too bulky or too dry for boys and girls. He committed some strange blunders; for he knew nothing with accuracy. Thus in his *History of England* he tells us that Naseby is in Yorkshire; nor did he correct this mistake when the book was reprinted. He was very nearly hoaxed into putting into the *History of Greece* an account of a battle between Alexander the Great and Montezuma. In his *Animated Nature* he relates, with faith and with perfect gravity, all the most absurd lies which he could find in books of travels about gigantic Patagonians, monkeys that preach sermons, nightingales that repeat long conversations. 'If he can tell a horse from a cow,' said Johnson, 'that is the extent of his knowledge of zoology.' How little Goldsmith was qualified to write about the physical sciences is sufficiently proved by two anecdotes. He on one occasion denied that the sun is longer in the northern than in the southern signs. It was in vain to cite the authority of Maupertuis. 'Maupertuis!' he cried; 'I understand those matters better than Maupertuis.' On another occasion he, in defiance of the evidence of his own senses, maintained obstinately, and even angrily, that he chewed his dinner by moving his upper jaw.

Yet, ignorant as Goldsmith was, few writers have done more to make the first steps in the laborious road to knowledge easy and pleasant. His compilations are widely distinguished from the compilations of ordinary bookmakers. He was a great, perhaps an unequalled, master of the arts of selection and condensation. In these respects his histories of Rome and of England, and still more his own abridgments of these histories, well deserve to be studied. In general nothing is less attractive than an epitome; but the epitomes of Goldsmith, even when most concise, are always amusing; and to read them is considered by intelligent children, not as a task, but as a pleasure.

Goldsmith might now be considered as a prosperous man. He had the means of living in comfort, and even in what to one who had so often slept in barns and on bulks must have been luxury. His fame was great and was constantly rising. He lived in what was intellectually far the best society of the kingdom, in a society in which no talent or accomplishment was wanting, and in which the art of conversation was cultivated with splendid success. There probably were never four talkers more admirable in four different ways than Johnson, Burke, Beauclerk, and Garrick; and Goldsmith was on terms of intimacy with all the four. He aspired to share in their colloquial renown; but never was ambition more unfortunate. It may seem strange that a man who wrote with so much perspicuity, vivacity, and grace should have been, whenever he took a part in conversation, an empty, noisy, blundering rattle. But on this point the evidence is overwhelming. So extraordinary was the contrast between Goldsmith's published works and the silly things which he said, that Horace Walpole described him as an inspired idiot.

'Noll,' said Garrick, 'wrote like an angel, and talked like poor Poll.' Chamier declared that it was a hard exercise of faith to believe that so foolish a chatterer could have really written the *Traveller*. Even Boswell could say, with contemptuous compassion, that he liked very well to hear honest Goldsmith run on. 'Yes, sir,' said Johnson; 'but he should not like to hear himself.' Minds differ as rivers differ. There are transparent and sparkling rivers from which it is delightful to drink as they flow; to such rivers the minds of such men as Burke and Johnson may be compared. But there are rivers of which the water when first drawn is turbid and noisome, but becomes pellucid as crystal, and delicious to the taste, if it be suffered to stand till it has deposited a sediment; and such a river is a type of the mind of Goldsmith. His first thoughts on every subject were confused even to absurdity; but they required only a little time to work themselves clear. When he wrote they had that time; and therefore his readers pronounced him a man of genius; but when he talked he talked nonsense, and made himself the laughing-stock of his hearers. He was painfully sensible of his inferiority in conversation; he felt every failure keenly; yet he had not sufficient judgment and self-command to hold his tongue. His animal spirits and vanity were always impelling him to try to do the one thing which he could not do. After every attempt he felt he had exposed himself, and writhed with shame and vexation; yet the next moment he began again.

His associates seem to have regarded him with kindness, which, in spite of their admiration of his writings, was not unmixed with contempt. In truth, there was in his character much to love, but very little to respect. His heart was soft, even to weakness: he was so generous that he quite forgot to be just: he forgave injuries so readily that he might be said to invite them: and was so liberal to beggars that he had nothing left for his tailor and his butcher. He was vain, sensual, frivolous, profuse, improvident. One vice of a darker shade was imputed to him, envy. But there is not the least reason to believe that this bad passion, though it sometimes made him wince and utter fretful exclamations, ever impelled him to injure by wicked arts the reputation of any of his rivals. The truth probably is, that he was not more envious, but merely less prudent than his neighbours. His heart was on his lips. All those small jealousies, which are but too common among men of letters, but which a man of letters who is also a man of the world does his best to conceal, Goldsmith avowed with the simplicity of a child. When he was envious instead of affecting indifference, instead of damning with faint praise, instead of doing injuries slily and in the dark, he told everybody that he was envious. 'Do not, pray, do not talk of Johnson in such terms,' he said to Boswell; 'you harrow up my very soul.' George Steevens and Cumberland were men far too cunning to say such a thing. They would have echoed the praises of the man they envied, and then have sent to the newspapers anonymous libels upon him. Both what was good and what was bad in Goldsmith's character was to his associates a perfect security that he would never commit such villainy. He was neither ill-natured enough, nor long-headed enough to be guilty of any malicious act which required contrivance and disguise.

Goldsmith has sometimes been represented as a man of genius, cruelly treated by the world, and doomed to struggle with difficulties which at last broke his heart. But no representation can be more remote from the truth. He did, indeed, go through much sharp misery before he had done anything considerable in literature. But, after his name had appeared on the title-page of the *Traveller*, he had none to blame but himself for his distresses. His average income during the last seven years of his life certainly exceeded £400 a year; and £400 a year ranked, among the incomes of that day, at least as high as £800 a year would rank at present. A single man living in the Temple with £400 a year might then be called opulent. Not one in ten of the young gentlemen of good families who were studying the law there had so much. But all the wealth which Lord Clive had brought from Bengal, and Sir Lawrence Dundas from Germany, joined together would not have sufficed for Goldsmith. He spent twice as much as he had. He wore fine clothes, gave dinners of several courses, paid court to venal beauties. He had also, it should be remembered, to the honour of his heart, though not of his head, a guinea, or five, or ten, according to the state of his purse, ready for any tale of distress, true or false. But it was not in dress or feasting, in promiscuous amours or promiscuous charities, that his chief expense lay. He had been from boyhood a gambler, and at once the most sanguine and the most unskilful of gamblers. For a time he put off the day of inevitable ruin by temporary expedients. He obtained advances from booksellers, by promising to execute works which he never began. But at length this source of supply failed. He owed more than £2000; and he saw no hope of extrication from his embarrassments. His spirits and health gave way. He was attacked by a nervous fever, which he thought himself competent to treat. It would have been happy for him if his medical skill had been appreciated as justly by himself as by others. Notwithstanding the degree which he pretended to have received at Padua, he could procure no patients. 'I do not practise,' he once said; 'I make it a rule to prescribe only for my friends.' 'Pray, dear Doctor,' said Beauclerk, 'alter your rule, and prescribe only for your enemies.' Goldsmith now, in spite of this excellent advice, prescribed for himself. The remedy aggravated the malady. The sick man was induced to call in real physicians; and they at one time imagined that they had cured the disease. Still his weakness and restlessness continued. He could get no sleep, he could take no food. 'You are worse,' said one of his medical attendants, 'than you should be from the degree of fever which you have. Is your mind at ease?' 'No, it is not,' were the last recorded words of Oliver Goldsmith. He died on the 3rd of April 1774, in his forty-sixth year. He was laid in the churchyard of the Temple; but the spot was not marked by any inscription, and is now forgotten. The coffin was followed by Burke and Reynolds. Both these great men were sincere mourners. Burke, when he heard of Goldsmith's death, had burst into a flood of tears. Reynolds had been so much moved by the news that he had flung aside his brush and palette for the day.

A short time after Goldsmith's death, a little poem appeared, which will, as long as our language lasts, associate the names of his two illustrious friends with his own. It has already been mentioned that he sometimes felt keenly the sarcasm which his wild blundering talk brought upon him. He was, not long before his last illness, provoked into retaliating. He wisely betook himself to his pen; and at that weapon he proved himself a match for all his assailants together. Within a small compass he drew with a singularly easy and vigorous pencil the characters of nine or ten of his intimate associates. Though this little work did not receive his last touches, it must always be regarded as a masterpiece. It is impossible, however, not to wish that four or five likenesses which have no interest for posterity were wanting to that noble gallery, and that their places were supplied by sketches of Johnson and Gibbon, as happy and vivid as the sketches of Burke and Garrick.

Some of Goldsmith's friends and admirers honoured him with a cenotaph in Westminster Abbey. Nollekens was the sculptor; and Johnson wrote the inscription. It is much to be lamented that Johnson did not leave to posterity a more durable and a more valuable memorial of his friend. A life of Goldsmith would have been an inestimable addition to the Lives of the Poets. No man appreciated Goldsmith's writings more justly than Johnson: no man was better acquainted with Goldsmith's character and habits: and no man was more competent to delineate with truth and spirit the peculiarities of a mind in which great powers were found in company with great weaknesses. But the list of poets to whose works Johnson was requested by the booksellers to furnish prefaces ended with Lyttelton, who died in 1773. The line seems to have been drawn expressly for the purpose of excluding the person whose portrait would have most fitly closed the series. Goldsmith, however, has been fortunate in his biographers. Within a few years his life has been written by Mr. Prior, by Mr. Washington Irving, and by Mr. Forster. The diligence of Mr. Prior deserves great praise; the style of Mr. Washington Irving is always pleasing; but the highest place must, in justice, be assigned to the eminently interesting work of Mr. Forster.

DR. JOHN BROWN

1810–1882

RAB AND HIS FRIENDS

FOUR-AND-THIRTY years ago, Bob Ainslie and I were coming up Infirmary Street from the High School, our heads together, and our arms intertwisted, as only lovers and boys know how, or why.

When we got to the top of the street, and turned north, we espied a crowd at the Tron Church. 'A dog-fight!' shouted Bob, and was off; and so was I, both of us all but praying that it might not be over before we got up! And is not this boy-nature? and human nature too? and don't we all wish a house on fire not to be out before we see it? Dogs like fighting; old Isaac says they 'delight' in it, and for the best of all reasons; and boys are not cruel because they like to see the fight. They see three of the great cardinal virtues of dog or man—courage, endurance, and skill—in intense action. This is very different from a love of making dogs fight, and enjoying, and aggravating, and making gain by their pluck. A boy, be he ever so fond himself of fighting—if he be a good boy, hates and despises all this, but he would have run off with Bob and me fast enough: it is a natural, and a not wicked interest, that all boys and men have in witnessing intense energy in action.

Does any curious and finely-ignorant woman wish to know how Bob's eye at a glance announced a dog-fight to his brain? He did not, he could not see the dogs fighting; it was a flash of inference, a rapid induction. The crowd round a couple of dogs fighting is a crowd masculine mainly, with an occasional active, compassionate woman, fluttering wildly round the outside, and using her tongue and her hands freely upon the men, as so many 'brutes'; it is a crowd annular, compact, and mobile; a crowd centripetal, having its eyes and its heads all bent downwards and inwards, to one common focus.

Well, Bob and I are up, and find it is not over: a small thoroughbred, white bull-terrier is busy throttling a large shepherd's dog, unaccustomed to war, but not to be trifled with. They are hard at it; the scientific little fellow doing his work in great style, his pastoral enemy fighting wildly, but with the sharpest of teeth and a great courage. Science and breeding, however, soon had their own; the Game Chicken, as the premature Bob called him, working his way up, took his final grip of poor Yarrow's throat, and he lay gasping and done for. His master, a brown, handsome, big young shepherd from Tweedsmuir, would have liked to have knocked down any man, would 'drink up Esil, or eat a crocodile,' for that part, if he had a chance: it was no use kicking the little dog; that would only make him hold the closer. Many were the means shouted out in mouthfuls, of the best possible ways of ending it. 'Water!' but there was none near, and many cried for it who might have got it from the well at Blackfriars Wynd. 'Bite the tail!' and a large, vague, benevolent, middle-aged man, more desirous than wise, with some struggle got the bushy end of *Yarrow's* tail into his ample mouth, and bit it with all his might. This was more than enough for the much-enduring, much-perspiring shepherd, who, with a gleam of joy over his broad visage, delivered a terrific facer upon our large, vague, benevolent, middle-aged friend, who went down like a shot.

Still the Chicken holds; death not far off. 'Snuff! a pinch of snuff!' observed a calm, highly-dressed young buck, with an eye-glass in his eye. 'Snuff, indeed!' growled the angry crowd, affronted and glaring. 'Snuff! a pinch of snuff!' again observes the buck, but with more urgency; whereon were produced several open boxes, and from a mull which may have been at Culloden, he took a pinch, knelt down, and presented it to the nose of the Chicken. The laws of physiology and of snuff take their course; the Chicken sneezes, and Yarrow is free!

The young pastoral giant stalks off with Yarrow in his arms, comforting him.

But the bull-terrier's blood is up, and his soul unsatisfied; he grips the first dog he meets, and discovering she is not a dog, in Homeric phrase, he makes a brief sort of *amende*, and is off. The boys, with Bob and me at their head, are after him: down Niddry Street he goes, bent on mischief; up the Cowgate like an arrow—Bob and I, and our small men, panting behind.

There, under the single arch of the South Bridge, is a huge mastiff, sauntering down the middle of the causeway, as if with his hands in his pockets; he is old, grey, brindled, as big as a little Highland bull, and has the Shakespearian dewlaps shaking as he goes.

The Chicken makes straight at him, and fastens on his throat. To our astonishment, the great creature does nothing but stand still, hold himself up, and roar—yes, roar; a long, serious, remonstrative roar. How is this? Bob and I are up to them. *He is muzzled!* The bailies had proclaimed a general muzzling, and his master, studying strength and economy mainly, had encompassed his huge jaws in a home-made apparatus, constructed out of the leather of some ancient *breechin.* His mouth was open as far as it could; his lips curled up in rage—a sort of terrible grin; his teeth gleaming, ready, from out the darkness; the strap across his mouth tense as a bowstring; his whole frame stiff with indignation and surprise; his roar asking us all round, 'Did you ever see the like of this?' He looked a statue of anger and astonishment, done in Aberdeen granite.

We soon had a crowd: the Chicken held on. 'A knife!' cried Bob; and a cobbler gave him his knife; you know the kind of knife, worn away obliquely to a point, and always keen. I put its edge to the tense leather; it ran before it; and then!—one sudden jerk of that enormous head, a sort of dirty mist about his mouth, no noise,—and the bright and fierce little fellow is dropped, limp and dead. A solemn pause: this was more than any of us had bargained for. I turned the little fellow over, and saw he was quite dead; the mastiff had taken him by the small of the back like a rat, and broken it.

He looked down at his victim appeased, ashamed, and amazed; snuffed him all over, stared at him, and taking a sudden thought, turned round and trotted off. Bob took the dead dog up, and said, 'John, we'll bury him after tea.' 'Yes,' said I, and was off after the mastiff. He made up the Cowgate at a rapid swing; he had forgotten some engagement. He turned up the Candlemaker Row, and stopped at the Harrow Inn.

There was a carrier's cart ready to start, and a keen, thin, impatient, black-a-vised little man, his hand at his grey horse's head, looking about angrily for something. 'Rab, ye thief!' said he, aiming a kick at my great friend, who drew cringing up, and avoiding the heavy shoe with more agility than dignity, and watching his master's eye, slunk dismayed under the cart, his ears down, and as much as he had of tail down too.

What a man this must be, thought I, to whom my tremendous hero turns tail! The carrier saw the muzzle hanging, cut and useless, from his neck, and I eagerly told him the story, which Bob and I always thought, and still think, Homer, or King David, or Sir Walter alone were worthy to rehearse. The severe little man was mitigated, and condescended to say, 'Rab, ma man, puir Rabbie,'—whereupon the stump of a tail rose up, the ears were cocked, the eyes filled, and were comforted; the two friends were reconciled. 'Hupp!' and a stroke of the whip was given to Jess; and off went the three.

Bob and I buried the Game Chicken that night (we had not much of a tea) in the backgreen of his house, in Melville Street, No. 17, with considerable gravity and silence; and being at the time in the *Iliad*, and, like all boys, Trojans, we called him Hector of course.

Six years have passed,—a long time for a boy and a dog; Bob Ainslie is off to the wars; I am a medical student, and clerk at Minto House Hospital.

Rab I saw almost every week, on the Wednesday; and we had much pleasant intimacy. I found the way to his heart by frequent scratching of his huge head, and an occasional bone. When I did not notice him he would plant himself straight before me, and stand wagging that bud of a tail, and looking up, with his head a little to the one side. His master I occasionally saw; he used to call me 'Maister John,' but was laconic as any Spartan.

One fine October afternoon, I was leaving the hospital, when I saw the large gate open, and in walked Rab, with that great and easy saunter of his. He looked as if taking general possession of the place; like the Duke of Wellington entering a subdued city, satiated with victory and peace. After him came Jess, now white from age, with her cart; and in it a woman, carefully wrapped up,—the carrier leading the horse anxiously, and looking back. When he saw me, James (for his name was James Noble) made a curt and grotesque 'boo,' and said 'Maister John, this is the mistress; she 's got a trouble in her breest—some kind o' an income, we're thinkin'.'

By this time I saw the woman's face; she was sitting on a sack filled with straw, her husband's plaid round her, and his big-coat, with its large white metal buttons, over her feet.

I never saw a more unforgettable face—pale, serious, *lonely*,[1] delicate, sweet, without being at all what we call fine. She looked sixty, and had on a mutch, white

[1] It is not easy giving this look by one word; it was expressive of her being so much of her life alone.

as snow, with its black ribbon; her silvery, smooth hair setting off her dark-grey eyes—eyes such as one sees only twice or thrice in a lifetime, full of suffering, full also of the overcoming of it: her eyebrows black and delicate, and her mouth firm, patient, and contented, which few mouths ever are.

As I have said, I never saw a more beautiful countenance, or one more subdued to settled quiet. 'Ailie,' said James, 'this is Maister John, the young doctor; Rab's freend, ye ken. We often speak aboot you, doctor.' She smiled, and made a movement, but said nothing; and prepared to come down, putting her plaid aside and rising. Had Solomon in all his glory been handing down the Queen of Sheba at his palace gate, he could not have done it more daintily, more tenderly, more like a gentleman, than did James the Howgate carrier, when he lifted down Ailie his wife. The contrast of his small, swarthy, weather-beaten, keen, worldly face to hers—pale, subdued, and beautiful—was something wonderful. Rab looked on concerned and puzzled, but ready for anything that might turn up, were it to strangle the nurse, the porter, or even me. Ailie and he seemed great friends.

'As I was sayin', she 's got a kind o' trouble in her breest, doctor; wull ye tak' a look at it?' We walked into the consulting-room, all four; Rab grim and comic, willing to be happy and confidential if cause could be shown, willing also to be the reverse, on the same terms. Ailie sat down, undid her open gown and her lawn handkerchief round her neck, and, without a word, showed me her right breast. I looked at and examined it carefully, she and James watching me, and Rab eyeing all three. What could I say? there it was, that had once been so soft, so shapely, so white, so gracious and bountiful, so 'full of all blessed conditions,'—hard as a stone, a centre of horrid pain, making that pale face, with its grey, lucid, reasonable eyes, and its sweet resolved mouth, express the full measure of suffering overcome. Why was that gentle, modest, sweet woman, clean and lovable, condemned by God to bear such a burden?

I got her away to bed. 'May Rab and me bide?' said James. '*You* may; and Rab, if he will behave himself.' 'I'se warrant he 's do that, doctor'; and in slunk the faithful beast. I wish you could have seen him. There are no such dogs now. He belonged to a lost tribe. As I have said, he was brindled, and grey like Rubislaw granite; his hair short, hard, and close, like a lion's; his body thickset, like a little bull—a sort of compressed Hercules of a dog. He must have been ninety pounds' weight, at the least; he had a large blunt head; his muzzle black as night, his mouth blacker than any night, a tooth or two—being all he had—gleaming out of his jaws of darkness. His head was scarred with the records of old wounds, a sort of series of fields of battle all over it; one eye out, one ear cropped as close as was Archbishop Leighton's father's; the remaining eye had the power of two; and above it, and in constant communication with it, was a tattered rag of an ear, which was for ever unfurling itself, like an old flag; and then that bud of a tail, about one inch long, if it could in any sense be said to be long, being as broad as long—the mobility, the instantaneousness of that bud were very funny and surprising, and its expressive twinklings and winkings, the intercommunications between the eye, the ear and it, were of the oddest and swiftest.

Rab had the dignity and simplicity of great size; and having fought his way all along the road to absolute supremacy, he was as mighty in his own line as Julius Cæsar or the Duke of Wellington, and had the gravity[1] of all great fighters.

You must have often observed the likeness of certain men to certain animals, and of certain dogs to men.

[1] A Highland gamekeeper, when asked why a certain terrier, of singular pluck, was so much more solemn than the other dogs, said, 'Oh, sir, life 's full o' sairiousness to him—he just never can get enuff o' fechtin'.'

Now, I never looked at Rab without thinking of the great Baptist preacher, Andrew Fuller.[1] The same large, heavy, menacing, combative, sombre, honest countenance, the same deep inevitable eye, the same look,—as of thunder asleep, but ready,—neither a dog nor a man to be trifled with.

Next day my master, the surgeon, examined Ailie. There was no doubt it must kill her, and soon. It could be removed—it might never return—it would give her speedy relief—she should have it done. She curtsied, looked at James, and said, 'When?' 'To-morrow,' said the kind surgeon—a man of few words. She and James and Rab and I retired. I noticed that he and she spoke little, but seemed to anticipate everything in each other. The following day, at noon, the students came in, hurrying up the great stair. At the first landing-place, on a small well-known black board, was a bit of paper fastened by wafers, and many remains of old wafers beside it. On the paper were the words—'An operation to-day. J. B. *Clerk.*'

Up ran the youths, eager to secure good places: in they crowded, full of interest and talk. 'What's the case?' 'Which side is it?'

Don't think them heartless; they are neither better nor worse than you or I: they get over their professional horrors, and into their proper work; and in

[1] Fuller was, in early life, when a farmer lad at Soham, famous as a boxer; not quarrelsome, but not without 'the stern delight' a man of strength and courage feels in their exercise. Dr. Charles Stewart, of Dunearn, whose rare gifts and graces as a physician, a divine, a scholar, and a gentleman, live only in the memory of those few who knew and survive him, liked to tell how Mr. Fuller used to say, that when he was in the pulpit, and saw a *buirdly* man come along the passage, he would instinctively draw himself up, measure his imaginary antagonist, and forecast how he would deal with him, his hands meanwhile condensing into fists, and tending to 'square.' He must have been a hard hitter if he boxed as he preached—what 'The Fancy' would call 'an ugly customer.'

them pity—as an *emotion*, ending in itself, or at best in tears and a long-drawn breath, lessens, while pity as a *motive* is quickened, and gains power and purpose. It is well for poor human nature that it is so.

The operating theatre is crowded; much talk and fun, and all the cordiality and stir of youth. The surgeon with his staff of assistants is there. In comes Ailie: one look at her quiets and abates the eager students. That beautiful old woman is too much for them; they sit down, and are dumb, and gaze at her. These rough boys feel the power of her presence. She walks in quickly, but without haste; dressed in her mutch, her neckerchief, her white dimity short-gown, her black bombazeen petticoat, showing her white worsted stockings and her carpet-shoes. Behind her was James with Rab. James sat down in the distance, and took that huge and noble head between his knees. Rab looked perplexed and dangerous; for ever cocking his ear and dropping it as fast.

Ailie stepped up on a seat, and laid herself on the table, as her friend the surgeon told her; arranged herself, gave a rapid look at James, shut her eyes, rested herself on me, and took my hand. The operation was at once begun; it was necessarily slow; and chloroform—one of God's best gifts to his suffering children—was then unknown. The surgeon did his work. The pale face showed its pain, but was still and silent. Rab's soul was working within him; he saw that something strange was going on,—blood flowing from his mistress, and she suffering; his ragged ear was up, and importunate; he growled and gave now and then a sharp impatient yelp; he would have liked to have done something to that man. But James had him firm, and gave him a *glower* from time to time, and an intimation of a possible kick;—all the better for James, it kept his eye and his mind off Ailie.

It is over; she is dressed, steps gently and decently down from the table, looks for James; then, turning to the surgeon and the students, she curtsies, and in a low, clear voice, begs their pardon if she has behaved ill. The students—all of us—wept like children; the surgeon happed her up carefully, and, resting on James and me, Ailie went to her room, Rab following. We put her to bed. James took off his heavy shoes, crammed with tackets, heel-capt and toe-capt, and put them carefully under the table, saying, 'Maister John, I'm for nane o' yer strynge nurse bodies for Ailie. I'll be her nurse, and I'll gang aboot on my stockin' soles as canny as pussy.' And so he did; and handy and clever, and swift and tender as any woman, was that horny-handed, snell, peremptory little man. Everything she got he gave her: he seldom slept; and often I saw his small shrewd eyes out of the darkness, fixed on her. As before they spoke little.

Rab behaved well, never moving, showing us how meek and gentle he could be, and occasionally, in his sleep, letting us know that he was demolishing some adversary. He took a walk with me every day, generally to the Candlemaker Row; but he was sombre and mild; declined doing battle, though some fit cases offered, and indeed submitted to sundry indignities; and was always very ready to turn, and came faster back, and trotted up the stair with much lightness, and went straight to that door.

Jess, the mare, had been sent, with her weather-worn cart, to Howgate, and had doubtless her own dim and placid meditations and confusions, on the absence of her master and Rab, and her unnatural freedom from the road and her cart.

For some days Ailie did well. The wound healed 'by the first intention'; for as James said, 'Oor Ailie's skin 's ower clean to beil.' The students came in quiet and anxious, and surrounded her bed. She said she liked to see their young, honest faces. The surgeon dressed her, and spoke to her in his own short kind way, pitying her through his eyes, Rab and James outside the circle,—Rab being now reconciled, and even cordial, and having made up his mind that as yet nobody required worrying, but as you may suppose, *semper paratus*.

So far well: but, four days after the operation, my patient had a sudden and long shivering, a 'groosin',' as she called it. I saw her soon after; her eyes were too bright, her cheek coloured: she was restless, and ashamed of being so; the balance was lost; mischief had begun. On looking at the wound, a blush of red told the secret: her pulse was rapid, her breathing anxious and quick, she wasn't herself, as she said, and was vexed at her restlessness. We tried what we could. James did everything, was everything; never in the way, never out of it; Rab subsided under the table into a dark place, and was motionless, all but his eye, which followed every one. Ailie got worse; began to wander in her mind, gently; was more demonstrative in her ways to James, rapid in her questions, and sharp at times. He was vexed, and said, 'She was never that way afore; no, never.' For a time she knew her head was wrong, and was always asking our pardon—the dear, gentle old woman: then delirium set in strong, without pause. Her brain gave way, and then came that terrible spectacle,

> The intellectual power, through words and things,
> Went sounding on its dim and perilous way;

she sang bits of old songs and Psalms, stopping suddenly, mingling the Psalms of David, and the diviner words of his Son and Lord, with homely odds and ends and scraps of ballads.

Nothing more touching, or in a sense more strangely beautiful, did I ever witness. Her tremulous, rapid, affectionate, eager, Scotch voice,—the swift, aimless, bewildered mind, the baffled utterance, the bright and perilous eye; some wild words, some household cares, something for James, the names of the dead, Rab called rapidly and in a 'fremyt' voice, and he starting up, surprised, and slinking off as if he were to blame somehow, or had been dreaming he heard. Many eager questions and beseechings which James and I could make nothing of, and on which she seemed to set her all, and then sink back ununderstood. It was very sad, but better than many things that are not called sad. James hovered about, put out and miserable, but active and exact as ever; read to her, when there was a lull, short bits from the Psalms, prose and metre, chanting the latter in his own rude and serious way, showing great knowledge of the fit words, bearing up like a man, and doating over her as his 'ain Ailie.' 'Ailie, ma woman!' 'Ma ain bonnie wee dawtie!'

The end was drawing on: the golden bowl was breaking; the silver cord was fast being loosed—that *animula blandula, vagula, hospes, comesque*, was about to flee. The body and the soul—companions for sixty years—were being sundered, and taking leave. She was walking, alone, through the valley of that shadow, into which one day we must all enter—and yet she was not alone, for we know whose rod and staff were comforting her.

One night she had fallen quiet, and as we hoped, asleep; her eyes were shut. We put down the gas, and sat watching her. Suddenly she sat up in bed, and taking a bedgown which was lying on it rolled up, she held it eagerly to her breast,—to the right side. We could see her eyes bright with a surprising tenderness and joy, bending over this bundle of clothes. She held it as a woman holds her sucking child; opening out her nightgown impatiently, and holding it close, and brooding over it, and murmuring foolish little words, as over one whom his mother comforteth, and who sucks and is satisfied. It was pitiful and strange to see her wasted dying look, keen and yet vague—her immense love.

'Preserve me!' groaned James, giving way. And then she rocked back and forward, as if to make it sleep, hushing it, and wasting on it her infinite fondness. 'Wae 's me, doctor; I declare she 's thinkin' it 's that bairn.' 'What bairn?' 'The only bairn we ever had; our wee Mysie, and she 's in the Kingdom, forty years and mair.' It was plainly true: the pain in the breast, telling its urgent story to a bewildered, ruined brain, was misread and mistaken; it suggested to her the uneasiness of a breast full of milk, and then the child; and so again once more they were together, and she had her ain wee Mysie in her bosom.

This was the close. She sank rapidly: the delirium left her; but, as she whispered, she was 'clean silly'; it was the lightening before the final darkness. After having for some time lain still—her eyes shut, she said 'James!' He came close to her, and lifting up her calm, clear, beautiful eyes, she gave him a long look, turned to me kindly but shortly, looked for Rab but could not see him, then turned to her husband again, as if she would never leave off looking, shut her eyes, and composed herself. She lay for some time breathing quick, and passed away so gently, that when we thought she was gone, James, in his old-fashioned way, held the mirror to her face. After a long pause, one small spot of dimness was breathed out; it vanished away, and never returned, leaving the blank clear darkness of the mirror without a stain. 'What is our life? it is even a vapour, which appeareth for a little time, and then vanisheth away.'

Rab all this time had been full awake and motionless: he came forward beside us: Ailie's hand, which James had held, was hanging down; it was soaked with his tears; Rab licked it all over carefully, looked at her, and returned to his place under the table.

James and I sat, I don't know how long, but for some time,—saying nothing: he started up abruptly, and with some noise went to the table, and putting his right fore and middle fingers each into a shoe, pulled them out, and put them on, breaking one of the leather latchets, and muttering in anger, 'I never did the like o' that afore!'

I believe he never did; nor after either. 'Rab!' he said roughly, and pointing with his thumb to the bottom of the bed. Rab leapt up, and settled himself; his head and eye to the dead face. 'Maister John, ye'll wait for me,' said the carrier; and disappeared in the darkness, thundering downstairs in his heavy shoes. I ran to a front window: there he was, already round the house, and out at the gate, fleeing like a shadow.

I was afraid about him, and yet not afraid; so I sat down beside Rab, and being wearied, fell asleep. I awoke from a sudden noise outside. It was November, and there had been a heavy fall of snow. Rab was *in statu quo*; he heard the noise too, and plainly knew it, but never moved. I looked out; and there, at the gate, in the dim morning—for the sun was not up, was Jess and the cart,—a cloud of steam rising from the old mare. I did not see James; he was already at the door, and came up the stairs, and met me. It was less than three hours since he left, and he must have posted out—who knows how?—to Howgate, full nine miles off; yoked Jess, and driven her astonished into town. He had an armful of blankets, and was streaming with perspiration. He nodded to me, spread out on the floor two pairs of clean old blankets having at their corners, 'A. G., 1796,' in large letters in red worsted. These were the initials of Alison Græme, and James may have looked in at her from without—himself unseen but not unthought of—when he was 'wat, wat, and weary,' and after having walked many a mile over the hills, may have seen her sitting, while 'a' the lave were sleepin' '; and by the firelight working her name on the blankets, for her ain James's bed.

He motioned Rab down, and taking his wife in his arms, laid her in the blankets, and happed her carefully and firmly up, leaving the face uncovered; and then lifting her, he nodded again sharply to me, and with a resolved but utterly miserable face, strode along the passage, and downstairs, followed by Rab.

I followed with a light; but he didn't need it. I went out, holding stupidly the candle in my hand in the calm frosty air; we were soon at the gate. I could have helped him, but I saw he was not to be meddled with, and he was strong, and did not need it. He laid her down as tenderly, as safely, as he had lifted her out ten days before—as tenderly as when he had her first in his arms when she was only 'A. G.,'—sorted her, leaving that beautiful sealed face open to the heavens; and then taking Jess by the head, he moved away. He did not notice me, neither did Rab, who presided behind the cart.

I stood till they passed through the long shadow of the College, and turned up Nicolson Street. I heard the solitary cart sound through the streets and die away and come again; and I returned, thinking of that company going up Liberton Brae, then along Roslin Muir, the morning light touching the Pentlands and making them like on-looking ghosts; then down the hill through Auchindinny woods, past 'haunted Woodhouselee'; and as daybreak came sweeping up the bleak Lammermuirs, and fell on his own door, the company would stop, and James would take the key and lift Ailie up again, laying her on her own bed, and, having put Jess up, would return with Rab and shut the door.

James buried his wife, with his neighbours mourning, Rab inspecting the solemnity from a distance. It was snow, and that black ragged hole would look strange in the midst of the swelling, spotless cushion of white. James looked after everything; then rather suddenly fell ill and took to bed; was insensible when the doctor came, and soon died. A sort of low fever was prevailing in the village, and his want of sleep, his exhaustion, and his misery, made him apt to take it. The grave was not difficult to re-open. A fresh fall of snow had again made all things white and smooth; Rab once more looked on, and slunk home to the stable.

And what of Rab? I asked for him next week at the new carrier who got the goodwill of James's business, and was now master of Jess and her cart. 'How's Rab?' He put me off, and said rather rudely, 'What's *your* business wi' the dowg?' I was not to be so put off. 'Where's Rab?' He, getting confused and red, and intermeddling with his hair, said, ''Deed, sir, Rab 's deid.' 'Dead! what did he die of?' 'Weel, sir,' said he, getting redder, 'he didna exactly dee; he was killed. I had to brain him wi' a rack-pin; there was nae doin' wi' him. He lay in the treviss wi' the mear, and wadna come oot. I tempit him wi' kail and meat, but he wad tak naething, and keepit me frae feedin' the beast, and he was aye gur gurrin', and grup gruppin' me by the legs. I was laith to make awa wi' the auld dowg, his like wasna atween this and Thornhill,—but, 'deed, sir, I could dae naething else.' I believed him. Fit end for Rab, quick and complete. His teeth and his friends gone, why should he keep the peace and be civil?

He was buried in the braeface, near the burn, the children of the village, his companions, who used to make very free with him and sit on his ample stomach, as he lay half asleep at the door in the sun—watching the solemnity.

Horae Subsecivae, Second Series, 1859.

WILLIAM MAKEPEACE THACKERAY

1811–1863

ON A LAZY IDLE BOY

I HAD occasion to pass a week in the autumn in the little old town of Coire or Chur, in the Grisons, where lies buried that very ancient British king, saint, and martyr, Lucius,[1] who founded the Church of St. Peter, on Cornhill. Few people note the church nowadays, and fewer ever heard of the saint. In the cathedral at Chur, his statue appears surrounded by other sainted persons of his family. With tight red breeches, a Roman habit, a curly brown beard, and a neat little gilt crown and sceptre, he stands, a very comely and cheerful image: and from what I may call his peculiar position with regard to Cornhill, I beheld this figure of St. Lucius with more interest than I should have bestowed upon personages who, hierarchically, are, I daresay, his superiors.

The pretty little city stands, so to speak, at the end of the world—of the world of to-day, the world of rapid motion, and rushing railways, and the commerce and intercourse of men. From the northern gate, the iron road stretches away to Zürich, to Basle, to Paris, to home. From the old southern barriers, before which a little river rushes, and around which stretch the crumbling battlements of the ancient town, the road bears the slow diligence or lagging vetturino

[1] Stow quotes the inscription still extant 'from the table fast chained in St. Peter's Church, Cornhill'; and says, 'he was after some chronicle buried at London, and after some chronicle buried at Glowcester'—but, oh! these incorrect chroniclers! when Alban Butler, in the *Lives of the Saints*, v. 12, and Murray's *Handbook*, and the Sacristan at Chur, all say Lucius was killed there, and I saw his tomb with my own eyes.

by the shallow Rhine, through the awful gorges of the Via Mala, and presently over the Splügen to the shores of Como.

I have seldom seen a place more quaint, pretty, calm, and pastoral, than this remote little Chur. What need have the inhabitants for walls and ramparts, except to build summer-houses, to trail vines, and hang clothes to dry on them? No enemies approach the great mouldering gates: only at morn and even the cows come lowing past them, the village maidens chatter merrily round the fountains, and babble like the ever-voluble stream that flows under the old walls. The schoolboys, with book and satchel, in smart uniforms, march up to the gymnasium, and return thence at their stated time. There is one coffee-house in the town, and I see one old gentleman goes to it. There are shops with no customers seemingly, and the lazy tradesmen look out of their little windows at the single stranger sauntering by. There is a stall with baskets of queer little black grapes and apples, and a pretty brisk trade with half-a-dozen urchins standing round. But, beyond this, there is scarce any talk or movement in the street. There's nobody at the book-shop. 'If you will have the goodness to come again in an hour,' says the banker, with his mouth full of dinner at one o'clock, 'you can have the money.' There is nobody at the hotel, save the good landlady, the kind waiters, the brisk young cook who ministers to you. Nobody is in the Protestant church—(oh! strange sight, the two confessions are here at peace!) —nobody in the Catholic church: until the sacristan, from his snug abode in the cathedral close, espies the traveller eyeing the monsters and pillars before the old shark-toothed arch of his cathedral, and comes out (with a view to remuneration possibly) and opens the gate, and shows you the venerable church, and the queer old relics in the sacristy, and the ancient vestments (a black velvet cope, amongst other robes, as fresh as yesterday, and presented by that notorious 'pervert,' Henry of Navarre and France), and the statue of St. Lucius who built St. Peter's Church, on Cornhill.

What a quiet, kind, quaint, pleasant, pretty old town! Has it been asleep these hundreds and hundreds of years, and is the brisk young Prince of the Sidereal Realms in his screaming car drawn by his snorting steel elephant coming to waken it? Time was when there must have been life and bustle and commerce here. Those vast, venerable walls were not made to keep out cows, but men-at-arms, led by fierce captains, who prowled about the gates, and robbed the traders as they passed in and out with their bales, their goods, their pack-horses, and their wains. Is the place so dead that even the clergy of the different denominations can't quarrel? Why, seven or eight, or a dozen, or fifteen hundred years ago (they haven't the register at St. Peter's up to that remote period. I daresay it was burnt in the fire of London)—a dozen hundred years ago, when there was some life in the town, St. Lucius was stoned here on account of theological differences, after founding our church in Cornhill.

There was a sweet pretty river walk we used to take in the evening and mark the mountains round glooming with a deeper purple; the shades creeping up the golden walls; the river brawling, the cattle calling, the maids and chatterboxes round the fountains babbling and bawling; and several times in the course of our sober walks we overtook a lazy slouching boy, or hobbledehoy, with a rusty coat, and trousers not too long, and big feet trailing lazily one after the other, and large lazy hands dawdling from out the tight sleeves, and in the lazy hands a little book, which my lad held up to his face, and which I daresay so charmed and ravished him, that he was blind to the beautiful sights around him; unmindful, I would venture to lay any wager, of the lessons he had to learn for to-morrow; forgetful of mother waiting supper, and father preparing a scolding;—absorbed utterly and entirely in his book.

What was it that so fascinated the young student, as he stood by the river shore? Not the *Pons Asinorum.* What book so delighted him, and blinded him to all the rest of the world, so that he did not care to see the apple-woman with her fruit, or (more tempting still to sons of Eve) the pretty girls with their apple-cheeks, who laughed and prattled round the fountain! What was the book? Do you suppose it was Livy, or the Greek grammar? No; it was a NOVEL that you were reading, you lazy, not very clean, good-for-nothing, sensible boy! It was D'Artagnan locking up General Monk in a box, or almost succeeding in keeping Charles the First's head on. It was the prisoner of the Château d'If cutting himself out of the sack fifty feet under water (I mention the novels I like best myself—novels without love or talking, or any of that sort of nonsense, but containing plenty of fighting, escaping, robbery, and rescuing)—cutting himself out of the sack, and swimming to the island of Monte Cristo. O Dumas! O thou brave, kind, gallant old Alexandre! I hereby offer thee homage, and give thee thanks for many pleasant hours. I have read thee (being sick in bed) for thirteen hours of a happy day, and had the ladies of the house fighting for the volumes. Be assured that lazy boy was reading Dumas (or I will go so far as to let the reader here pronounce the eulogium, or insert the name of his favourite author); and as for the anger, or it may be, the reverberations of his schoolmaster, or the remonstrances of his father, or the tender pleadings of his mother that he should not let the supper grow cold—I don't believe the scape-grace cared one fig. No! figs are sweet, but fictions are sweeter.

Have you ever seen a score of white-bearded, white-robed warriors, or grave seniors of the city, seated at the gate of Jaffa or Beyrout, and listening to the story-teller reciting his marvels out of *Antar* or the

Arabian Nights? I was once present when a young gentleman at table put a tart away from him, and said to his neighbour, the Younger Son (with rather a fatuous air), 'I never eat sweets.'

'Not eat sweets! and do you know why?' says T.

'Because I am past that kind of thing,' says the young gentleman.

'Because you are a glutton and a sot!' cries the Elder (and Juvenis winces a little). 'All people who have natural, healthy appetites, love sweets; all children, all women, all Eastern people, whose tastes are not corrupted by gluttony and strong drink.' And a plateful of raspberries and cream disappeared before the philosopher.

You take the allegory? Novels are sweets. All people with healthy literary appetites love them—almost all women;—a vast number of clever, hard-headed men. Why, one of the most learned physicians in England said to me only yesterday, 'I have just read *So-and-So* for the second time' (naming one of Jones's exquisite fictions). Judges, bishops, chancellors, mathematicians, are notorious novel-readers; as well as young boys and sweet girls, and their kind tender mothers. Who has not read about Eldon, and how he cried over novels every night when he was not at whist?

As for that lazy naughty boy at Chur, I doubt whether *he* will like novels when he is thirty years of age. He is taking too great a glut of them now. He is eating jelly until he will be sick. He will know most plots by the time he is twenty, so that *he* will never be surprised when the Stranger turns out to be the rightful earl,—when the old Waterman, throwing off his beggarly gabardine, shows his stars and the collars of his various orders, and clasping Antonia to his bosom, proves himself to be the prince, her long-lost father. He will recognise the novelist's same characters, though they appear in red-heeled pumps and *ailes-de-pigeon*, or the garb of the nineteenth century. He will get weary of sweets, as boys of private schools grow (or used to grow, for I have done growing some little time myself, and the practice may have ended too)—as private schoolboys used to grow tired of the pudding before their mutton at dinner.

And pray what is the moral of this apologue? The moral I take to be this: the appetite for novels extending to the end of the world; far away in the frozen deep, the sailors reading them to one another during the endless night;—far away under the Syrian stars, the solemn sheiks and elders hearkening to the poet as he recites his tales; far away in the Indian camps, where the soldiers listen to ——'s tales, or ——'s, after the hot day's march; far away in little Chur yonder where the lazy boy pores over the fond volume, and drinks it in with all his eyes:—the demand being what we know it is, the merchant must supply it, as he will supply saddles and pale ale for Bombay or Calcutta.

But as surely as the cadet drinks too much pale ale, it will disagree with him; and so surely, dear youth, will too much novels cloy on thee. I wonder, do novel-writers themselves read many novels? If you go into Gunter's you don't see those charming young ladies (to whom I present my most respectful compliments) eating tarts and ices, but at the proper eventide they have good plain wholesome tea and bread and butter. Can anybody tell me does the author of the *Tale of Two Cities* read novels? does the author of the *Tower of London* devour romances? does the dashing *Harry Lorrequer* delight in *Plain or Ringlets* or *Spunge's Sporting Tour*? Does the veteran, from whose flowing pen we had the books which delighted our young days, *Darnley*, and *Richelieu*, and *Delorme*,[1] relish the

[1] By the way, what a strange fate is that which befell the veteran novelist! He was appointed her Majesty's Consul-General in Venice, the only city in Europe where the famous 'Two Cavaliers' cannot by any possibility be seen riding together.

works of Alexandre the Great, and thrill over the *Three Musqueteers*? Does the accomplished author of *The Caxtons* read the other tales in *Blackwood*? (For example, that ghost-story printed last August, and which for my part, though I read it in the public reading-room at the 'Pavilion Hotel' at Folkestone, I protest frightened me so that I scarce dared look over my shoulder.) Does *Uncle Tom* admire *Adam Bede*; and does the author of the *Vicar of Wrexhill* laugh over *The Warden* and the *Three Clerks*? Dear youth of ingenuous countenance and ingenuous pudor! I make no doubt that the eminent parties above named all partake of novels in moderation—eat jellies—but mainly nourish themselves upon wholesome roast and boiled.

Here, dear youth aforesaid! our *Cornhill Magazine* owners strive to provide thee with facts as well as fiction; and though it does not become them to brag of their Ordinary, at least they invite thee to a table where thou shalt sit in good company. That story of the *Fox*[1] was written by one of the gallant seamen who sought for poor Franklin under the awful Arctic Night: that account of China[2] is told by the man of all the empire most likely to know of what he speaks: those pages regarding Volunteers[3] come from an honoured hand that has borne the sword in a hundred famous fields, and pointed the British guns in the greatest siege in all the world.

Shall we point out others? We are fellow-travellers, and shall make acquaintance as the voyage proceeds. In the Atlantic steamers, on the first day out (and on high and holy-days subsequently), the jellies set down on table are richly ornamented; *medioque in fonte leporum* rise the American and British flags nobly

[1] *The Search for Sir John Franklin.* (From the Private Journal of an Officer of the *Fox*.)

[2] *The Chinese and the Outer Barbarians.* By Sir John Bowring.

[3] *Our Volunteers.* By Sir John Burgoyne.

emblazoned in tin. As the passengers remark this pleasing phenomenon, the Captain no doubt improves the occasion by expressing a hope, to his right and left, that the flag of Mr. Bull and his younger Brother may always float side by side in friendly emulation. Novels having been previously compared to jellies—here are two (one perhaps not entirely saccharine, and flavoured with an *amari aliquid* very distasteful to some palates)—two novels[1] under two flags, the one that ancient ensign which has hung before the well-known booth of *Vanity Fair*; the other that fresh and handsome standard which has lately been hoisted on *Barchester Towers*. Pray, sir, or madam, to which dish will you be helped?

So have I seen my friends Captain Lang and Captain Comstock press their guests to partake of the fare on that memorable 'First day out,' when there is no man, I think, who sits down but asks a blessing on his voyage, and the good ship dips over the bar, and bounds away into the blue water.

NOTES OF A WEEK'S HOLIDAY

Most of us tell old stories in our families. The wife and children laugh for the hundredth time at the joke. The old servants (though old servants are fewer every day) nod and smile a recognition at the well-known anecdote. 'Don't tell that story of Grouse in the gun-room,' says Diggory to Mr. Hardcastle in the play, 'or I must laugh.' As we twaddle, and grow old and forgetful, we may tell an old story; or, out of mere benevolence, and a wish to amuse a friend when conversation is flagging, disinter a Joe Miller now and then; but the practice is not quite honest, and entails a certain necessity of hypocrisy on story hearers and tellers. It is a sad thing to think that a man with what you call a fund of anecdote is a

[1] *Lovel the Widower* and *Framley Parsonage*.

humbug, more or less amiable and pleasant. What right have I to tell my 'Grouse in the gun-room' over and over in the presence of my wife, mother, mother-in-law, sons, daughters, old footman or parlour-maid, confidential clerk, curate, or what not? I smirk and go through the history, giving my admirable imitations of the characters introduced: I mimic Jones's grin, Hobbs's squint, Brown's stammer, Grady's brogue, Sandy's Scotch accent, to the best of my power: and the family part of my audience laughs good-humouredly. Perhaps the stranger, for whose amusement the performance is given, is amused by it, and laughs too. But this practice continued is not moral. This self-indulgence on your part, my dear Paterfamilias, is weak, vain—not to say culpable. I can imagine many a worthy man, who begins unguardedly to read this page, and comes to the present sentence, lying back in his chair thinking of that story which he has told innocently for fifty years, and rather piteously owning to himself, 'Well, well, it *is* wrong; I have no right to call on my poor wife to laugh, my daughters to affect to be amused, by that old, old jest of mine. And they would have gone on laughing, and they would have pretended to be amused, to their dying day, if this man had not flung his damper over our hilarity.' . . . I lay down the pen, and think, 'Are there any old stories which I still tell myself in the bosom of my family? Have I any "Grouse in my gun-room"?' If there are such, it is because my memory fails; not because I want applause, and wantonly repeat myself. You see, men with the so-called fund of anecdote will not repeat the same story to the same individual; but they do think that, on a new party, the repetition of a joke ever so old may be honourably tried. I meet men walking the London street, bearing the best reputation, men of anecdotal powers:—I know such, who very likely will read this, and say, 'Hang the fellow, he means *me*!' And so I do. No—no man ought to tell an anecdote more than thrice, let us say, unless he is sure he is speaking only to give pleasure to his hearers—unless he feels that it is not a mere desire for praise which makes him open his jaws.

And is it not with writers as with *raconteurs*? Ought they not to have their ingenuous modesty? May authors tell old stories, and how many times over? When I come to look at a place which I have visited any time these twenty or thirty years, I recall not the place merely, but the sensations I had at first seeing it, and which are quite different to my feelings to-day. That first day at Calais; the voices of the women crying out at night, as the vessel came alongside the pier; the supper at Quillacq's and the flavour of the cutlets and wine; the red-calico canopy under which I slept; the tiled floor, and the fresh smell of the sheets; the wonderful postilion in his jack-boots and pigtail;—all return with perfect clearness to my mind, and I am seeing them, and not the objects which are actually under my eyes. Here is Calais. Yonder is that commissioner I have known this score of years. Here are the women screaming and bustling over the baggage; the people at the passport-barrier who take your papers. My good people, I hardly see you. You no more interest me than a dozen orange-women in Covent Garden, or a shop book-keeper in Oxford Street. But you make me think of a time when you were indeed wonderful to behold—when the little French soldiers wore white cockades in their shakos—when the diligence was forty hours going to Paris; and the great-booted postilion, as surveyed by youthful eyes from the coupé, with his *jurons*, his ends of rope for the harness, and his clubbed pigtail, was a wonderful being, and productive of endless amusement. You young folks don't remember the apple-girls who used to follow the diligence up the hill beyond Boulogne, and the delights of the jolly road? In making continental journeys with young folks, an oldster may be very quiet, and, to outward appearance, melancholy;

but really he has gone back to the days of his youth, and he is seventeen or eighteen years of age (as the case may be), and is amusing himself with all his might. He is noting the horses as they come squealing out of the post-house yard at midnight; he is enjoying the delicious meals at Beauvais and Amiens, and quaffing *ad libitum* the rich table-d'hôte wine; he is hail-fellow with the conductor, and alive to all the incidents of the road. A man can be alive in 1860 and 1830 at the same time, don't you see? Bodily, I may be in 1860, inert, silent, torpid; but in the spirit I am walking about in 1828, let us say;—in a blue dress-coat and brass-buttons, a sweet-figured silk waistcoat (which I button round a slim waist with perfect ease), looking at beautiful things with gigot sleeves and tea-tray hats under the golden chesnuts of the Tuileries, or round the Place Vendôme, where the *drapeau blanc* is floating from the statueless column. Shall we go and dine at 'Bombarda's,' near the 'Hôtel Breteuil,' or at the 'Café Virginie'?—Away! 'Bombarda's' and the 'Hôtel Breteuil' have been pulled down ever so long. They knocked down the poor old Virginia Coffee-house last year. My spirit goes and dines there. My body, perhaps, is seated with ever so many people in a railway-carriage, and no wonder my companions find me dull and silent. Have you read Mr. Dale Owen's *Footfalls on the Boundary of Another World*?—(My dear sir, it will make your hair stand quite refreshingly on end.) In that work you will read that when gentlemen's or ladies' spirits travel off a few score or thousand miles to visit a friend, their bodies lie quiet and in a torpid state in their beds or in their arm-chairs at home. So in this way, I am absent. My soul whisks away thirty years back into the past. I am looking out anxiously for a beard. I am getting past the age of loving Byron's poems, and pretend that I like Wordsworth and Shelley much better. Nothing I eat or drink (in reason) disagrees with me; and I know whom I think to be the most lovely creature in the world. Ah, dear maid (of that remote but well-remembered period), are you a wife or widow now?—are you dead?—are you thin and withered and old?—or are you grown much stouter, with a false front? and so forth.

O Eliza, Eliza!—Stay, *was* she Eliza? Well, I protest I have forgotten what your Christian name was. You know I only met you for two days, but your sweet face is before me now, and the roses blooming on it are as fresh as in that time of May. Ah, dear Miss X——, my timid youth and ingenuous modesty would never have allowed me, even in my private thoughts, to address you otherwise than by your paternal name, but *that* (though I conceal it) I remember perfectly well, and that your dear and respected father was a brewer.

Carillon.—I was awakened this morning with the chime which Antwerp cathedral clock plays at half-hours. The tune has been haunting me ever since, as tunes will. You dress, eat, drink, walk, and talk to yourself to their tune: their inaudible jingle accompanies you all day: you read the sentences of the paper to their rhythm. I tried uncouthly to imitate the tune to the ladies of the family at breakfast, and they say it is 'the shadow dance of *Dinorah*.' It may be so. I dimly remember that my body was once present during the performance of that opera, whilst my eyes were closed, and my intellectual faculties dormant at the back of the box; howbeit, I have learned that shadow dance from hearing it pealing up ever so high in the air, at night, morn, noon.

How pleasant to lie awake and listen to the cheery peal! whilst the old city is asleep at midnight, or waking up rosy at sunrise, or basking in noon, or swept by the scudding rain which drives in gusts over the broad places, and the great shining river; or sparkling in snow which dresses up a hundred thousand masts, peaks, and towers; or wrapt round with thunder-cloud canopies, before which the white gables shine whiter; day and night the kind little carillon plays its fantastic melodies overhead. The bells go on ringing. *Quot vivos vocant*, *mortuos plangunt*, *fulgura frangunt*; so on to the past and future tenses, and for how many nights, days, and years! whilst the French were pitching their *fulgura* into Chassé's citadel, the bells went on ringing quite cheerfully. Whilst the scaffolds were up and guarded by Alva's soldiery, and regiments of penitents, blue, black, and grey, poured out of churches and convents, droning their dirges, and marching to the place of the Hôtel de Ville, where heretics and rebels were to meet their doom, the bells up yonder were chanting at their appointed half-hours and quarters, and rang the *mauvais quart d'heure* for many a poor soul. This bell can see as far away as the towers and dykes of Rotterdam. That one can call a greeting to St. Ursula's at Brussels, and toss a recognition to that one at the town-hall of Oudenarde, and remember how after a great struggle there a hundred and fifty years ago the whole plain was covered with the flying French cavalry—Burgundy, and Berri, and the Chevalier of St. George flying like the rest. 'What is your clamour about Oudenarde?' says another bell (Bob major *this* one must be). 'Be still, thou querulous old clapper! *I* can see over to Hougoumont and St. John. And about forty-five years since, I rang all through one Sunday in June, when there was such a battle going on in the corn-fields there, as none of you others ever heard tolled of. Yes, from morning service until after vespers, the French and English were all at it, ding-dong.' And then calls of business intervening, the bells have to give up their private jangle, resume their professional duty, and sing their hourly chorus out of *Dinorah*.

What a prodigious distance those bells can be heard! I was awakened this morning to their tune, I say. I have been hearing it constantly ever since. And this house whence I write, Murray says, is two hundred and ten miles from Antwerp. And it is a week off; and there is the bell still jangling its shadow dance out of *Dinorah*. An audible shadow you understand, and an invisible sound, but quite distinct; and a plague take the tune!

UNDER THE BELLS.—Who has not seen the church under the Bells? Those lofty aisles, those twilight chapels, that cumbersome pulpit with its huge carvings, that wide grey pavement flecked with various light from the jewelled windows, those famous pictures between the voluminous columns over the altars, which twinkle with their ornaments, their votive little silver hearts, legs, limbs, their little guttering tapers, cups of sham roses, and what not? I saw two regiments of little scholars creeping in and forming square, each in its appointed place, under the vast roof; and teachers presently coming to them. A stream of light from the jewelled windows beams slanting down upon each little squad of children, and the tall background of the church retires into a greyer gloom. Pattering little feet of laggards arriving echo through the great nave. They trot in and join their regiments, gathered under the slanting sunbeams. What are they learning? Is it truth? Those two grey ladies with their books in their hands in the midst of these little people have no doubt of the truth of every word they have printed under their eyes. Look, through the windows jewelled all over with saints, the light comes streaming down from the sky, and heaven's own illuminations paint the book! A sweet, touching picture indeed it is, that of the little children assembled in this immense temple which has endured for ages, and grave teachers bending over them. Yes, the picture is very pretty of the children and their teachers, and their book—but the text? Is it the truth, the only truth, nothing but the truth? If I thought so, I would go and sit down on the form *cum parvulis*, and learn the precious lesson with all my heart.

Beadle.—But I submit, an obstacle to conversions is the intrusion and impertinence of that Swiss fellow with the baldric—the officer who answers to the beadle of the British Islands, and is pacing about the church with an eye on the congregation. Now the boast of Catholics is that their churches are open to all; but in certain places and churches there are exceptions. At Rome I have been into St. Peter's at all hours: the doors are always open, the lamps are always burning, the faithful are for ever kneeling at one shrine or the other. But at Antwerp not so. In the afternoon you can go to the church, and be civilly treated; but you must pay a franc at the side gate. In the forenoon the doors are open, to be sure, and there is no one to levy an entrance-fee. I was standing ever so still, looking through the great gates of the choir at the twinkling lights, and listening to the distant chants of the priests performing the service, when a sweet chorus from the organ-loft broke out behind me overhead, and I turned round. My friend the drum-major ecclesiastic was down upon me in a moment. 'Do not turn your back to the altar during divine service,' says he, in very intelligible English. I take the rebuke, and turn a soft right-about face, and listen awhile as the service continues. See it I cannot, nor the altar and its ministrants. We are separated from these by a great screen and closed gates of iron, through which the lamps glitter and the chant comes by gusts only. Seeing a score of children trotting down a side aisle, I think I may follow them. I am tired of looking at that hideous old pulpit with its grotesque monsters and decorations. I slip off to the side aisle: but my friend the drum-major is instantly after me—almost I thought he was going to lay hands on me. 'You mustn't go there,' says he; 'you mustn't disturb the service.' I was moving as quietly as might be, and ten paces off there were twenty children kicking and clattering at their ease. I point them out to the Swiss. 'They come to pray,' says he. '*You* don't come to pray, you——' 'When I come to pay,' says I, 'I am welcome,' and with this withering sarcasm, I walk out of church in a huff. I don't envy the feelings of that beadle after receiving point blank such a stroke of wit.

LEO BELGICUS.—Perhaps you will say after this I am a prejudiced critic. I see the pictures in the cathedral fuming under the rudeness of that beadle, or, at the lawful hours and prices, pestered by a swarm of shabby touters, who come behind me chattering in bad English, and who would have me see the sights through their mean, greedy eyes. Better see Rubens anywhere than in a church. At the Academy, for example, where you may study him at your leisure. But at church?—I would as soon ask Alexandre Dumas for a sermon. Either would paint you a martyrdom very fiercely and picturesquely—writhing muscles, flaming coals, scowling captains and executioners, swarming groups, and light, shade, colour, most dexterously brilliant or dark; but in Rubens I am admiring the performer rather than the piece. With what astonishing rapidity he travels over his canvas; how tellingly the cool lights and warm shadows are made to contrast and relieve each other; how that blazing, blowsy penitent in yellow satin and glittering hair carries down the stream of light across the picture! This is the way to work, my boys, and earn a hundred florins a day. See! I am as sure of my line as a skater of making his figure of eight! and down with a sweep goes a brawny arm or a flowing curl of drapery. The figures arrange themselves as if by magic. The paint-pots are exhausted in furnishing brown shadows. The pupils look wondering on, as the master careers over the canvas. Isabel or Helena, wife No. 1 or No. 2, are sitting by, buxom, exuberant, ready to be painted; and the children are boxing in the corner, waiting till they are wanted to figure as cherubs in the picture. Grave burghers and gentlefolks come in on a visit. There are oysters and Rhenish always ready on yonder table. Was there ever such a painter? He has been an ambassador, an actual Excellency, and what better man could be chosen? He speaks all the languages. He earns a hundred florins a day. Prodigious! Thirty-six thousand five hundred florins a year. Enormous! He rides out to his castle with a score of gentlemen after him, like the Governor. That is his own portrait as St. George. You know he is an English knight? Those are his two wives as the two Maries. He chooses the handsomest wives. He rides the handsomest horses. He paints the handsomest pictures. He gets the handsomest prices for them. That slim young Van Dyck, who was his pupil, has genius too, and is painting all the noble ladies in England, and turning the heads of some of them. And Jordaens—what a droll dog and clever fellow! Have you seen his fat Silenus? The master himself could not paint better. And his altar-piece at St. Bavon's? He can paint you anything, that Jordaens can—a drunken jollification of boors and doxies, or a martyr howling with half his skin off. What a knowledge of anatomy! But there is nothing like the master—nothing. He can paint you his thirty-six thousand five hundred florins' worth a year. Have you heard of what he has done for the French court? Prodigious! I can't look at Rubens' pictures without fancying I see that handsome figure swaggering before the canvas. And Hans Hemmelinck at Bruges? Have you never seen that dear old hospital of St. John, on passing the gate of which you enter into the fifteenth century. I see the wounded soldier still lingering in the house, and tended by the kind grey sisters. His little panel on its easel is placed at the light. He covers his board with the most wondrous, beautiful little figures, in robes as bright as rubies and amethysts. I think he must have a magic glass, in which he catches the reflection of little cherubs with many-coloured wings, very little and bright. Angels, in long crisp robes of white, surrounded with haloes of gold, come and flutter across the mirror, and he draws them. He hears mass every day. He fasts through Lent. No monk is more austere and holy than Hans. Which do you love best to behold, the lamb or the lion? the eagle rushing through the storm, and pouncing mayhap on carrion; or the linnet warbling on the spray?

By much the most delightful of the *Christopher* set of Rubens to my mind (and *ego* is introduced on these occasions, so that the opinion may pass only for my own, at the reader's humble service to be received or declined) is the 'Presentation in the Temple': splendid in colour, in sentiment sweet and tender, finely conveying the story. To be sure, all the others tell their tale unmistakably—witness that coarse 'Salutation,' that magnificent 'Adoration of the Kings' (at the Museum), by the same strong downright hands; that wonderful 'Communion of St. Francis,' which, I think, gives the key to the artist's *faire* better than any of his performances. I have passed hours before that picture in my time, trying and sometimes fancying I could understand by what masses and contrasts the artist arrived at his effect. In many others of the pictures parts of his method are painfully obvious, and you see how grief and agony are produced by blue lips, and eyes rolling blood-shot with dabs of vermilion. There is something simple in the practice. Contort the eyebrow sufficiently, and place the eyeball near it,—by a few lines you have anger or fierceness depicted. Give me a mouth with no special expression, and pop a dab of carmine at each extremity—and there are the lips smiling. This is art if you will, but a very naïve kind of art: and now you know the trick, don't you see how easy it is?

TU QUOQUE.—Now you know the trick, suppose you take a canvas and see whether *you* can do it? There are brushes, palettes, and gallipots full of paint and varnish. Have you tried, my dear sir—you, who set up to be a connoisseur? Have you tried? I have—and many a day. And the end of the day's labour? O dismal conclusion! Is this puerile niggling, this feeble scrawl, this impotent rubbish, all you can produce—you, who but now found Rubens commonplace and vulgar, and were pointing out the tricks of his mystery? Pardon, O great chief, magnificent master and poet! You can *do*. We critics, who sneer and are wise, can but pry, and measure, and doubt, and carp. Look at the lion. Did you ever see such a gross, shaggy, mangy, roaring brute? Look at him eating lumps of raw meat—positively bleeding, and raw and tough—till, faugh! it turns one's stomach to see him—O the coarse wretch! Yes, but he is a lion. Rubens has lifted his great hand, and the mark he has made has endured for two centuries, and we still continue wondering at him, and admiring him. What a strength in that arm! What splendour of will hidden behind that tawny beard, and those honest eyes! Sharpen your pen, my good critic. Shoot a feather into him; hit him, and make him wince. Yes, you may hit him fair, and make him bleed, too; but, for all that, he is a lion—a mighty, conquering, generous, rampagious Leo Belgicus—monarch of his wood. And he is not dead yet, and I will not kick at him.

Sir Antony.—In that 'Pietà' of Van Dyck, in the Museum, have you ever looked at the yellow-robed angel, with the black scarf thrown over her wings and robe? What a charming figure of grief and beauty! What a pretty compassion it inspires! It soothes and pleases me like a sweet rhythmic chant. See how delicately the yellow robe contrasts with the blue sky behind, and the scarf binds the two! If Rubens lacked grace, Van Dyck abounded in it. What a consummate elegance! What a perfect cavalier! No wonder the fine ladies in England admired Sir Antony. Look at——

Here the clock strikes three, and the three gendarmes who keep the Musée cry out, '*Allons! Sortons! Il est trois heures! Allez! Sortez!*' and they skip out of the gallery as happy as boys running from school. And we must go too, for though many stay behind—many Britons with Murray's handbooks in their handsome hands—they have paid a franc for entrance-fee, you see; and we knew nothing about the franc for entrance until those gendarmes with sheathed sabres had driven us out of this Paradise.

But it was good to go and drive on the great quays and see the ships unlading, and by the citadel, and wonder howabouts and whereabouts it was so strong. We expect a citadel to look like Gibraltar or Ehrenbreitstein at least. But in this one there is nothing to see but a flat plain and some ditches, and some trees and mounds of uninteresting green. And then I remember how there was a boy at school, a little dumpy fellow of no personal appearance whatever, who couldn't be overcome except by a much bigger champion, and the immensest quantity of thrashing. A perfect citadel of a boy, with a General Chassé sitting in that bomb-proof casemate, his heart, letting blow after blow come thumping about his head, and never thinking of giving in.

And we go home, and we dine in the company of Britons, at the comfortable Hôtel du Parc, and we have bought a novel apiece for a shilling, and every half-hour the sweet carillon plays the waltz from *Dinorah* in the air. And we have been happy; and it seems about a month since we left London yesterday; and nobody knows where we are, and we defy care and the postman.

Spoorweg.—Vast green flats, speckled by spotted cows, and bound by a grey frontier of windmills; shining canals stretching through the green; odours like those exhaled from the Thames in the dog-days, and a fine pervading smell of cheese; little trim houses with tall roofs, and great windows of many panes; gazebos, or summer-houses, hanging over pea-green canals; kind-looking, dumpling-faced farmers' women, with laced caps and golden frontlets and ear-rings; about the houses and towns which we pass a great air of comfort and neatness; a queer feeling of wonder that you can't understand what your fellow-passengers are saying, the tone of whose voices, and a certain comfortable dowdiness of dress, are so like our own; whilst we are remarking on these sights, sounds, smells, the little railway journey from Rotterdam to the Hague comes to an end. I speak to the railway porters and hackney coachmen in English, and they reply in their own language, and it seems somehow as if we understood each other perfectly. The carriage drives to the handsome, comfortable, cheerful hotel. We sit down a score at the table; and there is one foreigner and his wife,—I mean every other man and woman at dinner are English. As we are close to the sea, and in the midst of endless canals, we have no fish. We are reminded of dear England by the noble prices which we pay for wines. I confess I lost my temper yesterday at Rotterdam, where I had to pay a florin for a bottle of ale (the water not being drinkable, and country or Bavarian beer not being genteel enough for the hotel);—I confess, I say, that my fine temper was ruffled, when the bottle of pale ale turned out to be a pint bottle; and I meekly told the waiter that I had bought beer at Jerusalem at a less price. But then Rotterdam is eighteen hours from London, and the steamer with the passengers and beer comes up to the hotel windows; whilst to Jerusalem they have to carry the ale on camels' backs from Beyrout or Jaffa, and through hordes of marauding Arabs, who evidently don't care for pale ale, though I am told it is not forbidden in the Koran. Mine would have been very good, but I choked with rage whilst drinking it. A florin for a bottle, and that bottle having the words 'imperial pint,' in bold relief, on the surface! It was too much. I intended not to say anything about it; but I *must* speak. A florin a bottle, and that bottle a pint! Oh, for shame! for shame! I can't cork down my indignation; I froth up with fury; I am pale with wrath, and bitter with scorn.

As we drove through the old city at night, how it swarmed and hummed with life! What a special clatter, crowd, and outcry there was in the Jewish quarter, where myriads of young ones were trotting about the fishy streets! Why don't they have lamps? We passed by canals seeming so full that a pailful of water more would overflow the place. The *laquais-de-place* calls out the names of the buildings: the town-hall, the cathedral, the arsenal, the synagogue, the statue of Erasmus. Get along! *We* know the statue of Erasmus well enough. We pass over drawbridges by canals where thousands of barges are at roost. At roost—at rest! Shall *we* have rest in those bedrooms, those ancient lofty bedrooms, in that inn where we have to pay a florin for a pint of pa—psha! at the 'New Bath Hotel' on the Boompjes? If this dreary edifice is the 'New Bath,' what must the Old Bath be like? As I feared to go to bed, I sat in the coffee-room as long as I might; but three young men were imparting their private adventures to each other with such freedom and liveliness that I felt I ought not to listen to their artless prattle. As I put the light out, and felt the bed-clothes and darkness overwhelm me, it was with an awful sense of terror—that sort of sensation which I should think going down in a diving-bell would give. Suppose the apparatus goes wrong, and they don't understand your signal to mount? Suppose your matches miss fire when you wake; when you *want* them, when you will have to rise in half-an-hour, and do battle with the horrid enemy who crawls on you in the darkness? I protest I never was more surprised than when I awoke and beheld the light of dawn. Indian birds and strange trees were visible on the ancient gilt hangings of the lofty chamber, and through the windows the Boompjes and the ships along the quay. We have all read of deserters being brought out, and made to kneel, with their eyes bandaged, and hearing the word to 'Fire' given! I declare I underwent all the terrors of execution that night, and wonder how I ever escaped unwounded.

But if ever I go to the 'Bath Hotel,' Rotterdam, again, I am a Dutchman. A guilder for a bottle of pale ale, and that bottle a pint! Ah! for shame—for shame!

MINE EASE IN MINE INN.—Do you object to talk about inns? It always seems to me to be very good talk. Walter Scott is full of inns. In *Don Quixote* and *Gil Blas* there is plenty of inn-talk. Sterne, Fielding, and Smollett constantly speak about them; and, in their travels, the last two tot up the bill, and describe the dinner quite honestly; whilst Mr. Sterne becomes sentimental over a cab, and weeps generous tears over a donkey.

How I admire and wonder at the information in Murray's Handbooks—wonder how it is got, and admire the travellers who get it. For instance, you read: Amiens (please select your towns), 60,000 inhabitants. Hotels, etc.—'Lion d'Or,' good and clean. 'Le Lion d'Argent,' so-so. 'Le Lion Noir,' bad, dirty, and dear. Now say, there are three travellers—three inn-inspectors, who are sent forth by Mr. Murray on a great commission, and who stop at every inn in the world. The eldest goes to the 'Lion d'Or'—capital house, good table-d'hôte, excellent wine, moderate charges. The second commissioner tries the 'Silver Lion'—tolerable house, bed, dinner, bill, and so forth. But fancy Commissioner No. 3—the poor fag, doubtless, and boots of the party. He has to go to the 'Lion Noir.' He knows he is to have a bad dinner—he eats it uncomplainingly. He is to have bad wine. He swallows it, grinding his wretched teeth, and aware that he will be unwell in consequence. He knows he is to have a dirty bed, and what he is to expect there. He pops out the candle. He sinks into those dingy sheets. He delivers over his body to the nightly tormentors, he pays an exorbitant bill, and he writes down, 'Lion Noir, bad, dirty, dear.' Next day the commission sets out for Arras, we will say, and they begin again: 'Le Cochon d'Or,' 'Le Cochon d'Argent,' 'Le Cochon Noir'—and that is poor Boots's inn, of course. What a life that poor man must lead! What horrors of dinners he has to go through! What a hide he must have! And yet not impervious; for unless he is bitten, how is he to be able to warn others? No; on second thoughts, you will perceive that he ought to have a very delicate skin. The monsters ought to troop to him eagerly, and bite him instantaneously and freely, so that he may be able to warn all future handbook buyers of their danger. I fancy this man devoting himself to danger, to dirt, to bad dinners, to sour wine, to damp beds, to midnight agonies, to extortionate bills. I admire him, I thank him. Think of this champion, who devotes his body for us—this dauntless gladiator going to do battle alone in the darkness, with no other armour than a light helmet of cotton, and a *lorica* of calico. I pity and honour him. Go, Spartacus! Go, devoted man—to bleed, to groan, to suffer—and smile in silence as the wild beasts assail thee!

How did I come into this talk? I protest it was the word inn set me off—and here is one, the 'Hôtel de Belle Vue,' at the Hague, as comfortable, as handsome, as cheerful, as any I ever took mine ease in. And the Bavarian beer, my dear friend, how good and brisk and light it is! Take another glass—it refreshes and does not stupefy—and then we will sally out, and see the town and the park and the pictures.

The prettiest little brick city, the pleasantest little park to ride in, the neatest comfortable people walking about, the canals not unsweet, and busy and picturesque with old-world life. Rows upon rows of houses, built with the neatest little bricks, with windows fresh painted, and tall doors polished and carved to a nicety. What a pleasant spacious garden our inn has, all sparkling with autumn flowers, and bedizened with statues! At the end is a row of trees, and a summer-house, over the canal, where you might go and smoke a pipe with Mynheer van Dunck, and quite cheerfully catch the ague. Yesterday, as we passed, they were making hay, and stacking it in a barge which was lying by the meadow, handy. Round about Kensington Palace there are houses, roofs, chimneys, and bricks like these. I feel that a Dutchman is a man and a brother. It is very funny to read the newspaper, one can understand it somehow. Sure it is the neatest, gayest little city—scores and hundreds of mansions looking like Cheyne Walk, or the ladies' schools about Chiswick and Hackney.

LE GROS LOT.—To a few lucky men the chance befalls of reaching fame at once, and (if it is of any profit *morituro*) retaining the admiration of the world. Did poor Oliver, when he was at Leyden yonder, ever think that he should paint a little picture which should secure him the applause and pity of all Europe for a century after? He and Sterne drew the twenty-thousand pound prize of fame. The latter had splendid instalments during his lifetime. The ladies pressed round him; the wits admired him; the fashion hailed the successor of Rabelais. Goldsmith's little gem was hardly so valued until later days. Their works still form the wonder and delight of the lovers of English art; and the pictures of the Vicar and Uncle Toby are among the masterpieces of our English school. Here in the Hague Gallery is Paul Potter's pale, eager face, and yonder is the magnificent work by which the young fellow achieved his fame. How did you, so young, come to paint so well? What hidden power lay in that weakly lad that enabled him to achieve such a wonderful victory? Could little Mozart, when he was five years old, tell you how he came to play those wonderful sonatas? Potter was gone out of the world before he was thirty, but left this prodigy (and I know not how many more specimens of his genius and skill) behind him. The details of this admirable picture are as curious as the effect is admirable and complete. The weather being unsettled, and clouds and sunshine in the gusty sky, we saw in our little tour numberless Paul Potters—the meadows streaked with sunshine and spotted with cattle, the city twinkling in the distance, the thunder-clouds glooming overhead. Napoleon carried off the picture (*vide* Murray) amongst the spoils of his bow and spear to decorate his triumph of the Louvre. If I were a conquering prince, I would have this picture certainly, and the Raphael 'Madonna' from Dresden, and the Titian 'Assumption' from Venice, and that matchless Rembrandt of the 'Dissection.' The prostrate nations would howl with rage as my gendarmes took off the pictures, nicely packed, and addressed to 'Mr. the Director of my Imperial Palace of the Louvre, at Paris. This side uppermost.' The Austrians, Prussians, Saxons, Italians, etc., should be free to come and visit my capital, and bleat with tears before the pictures torn from their native cities. Their ambassadors would meekly remonstrate, and with faded grins make allusions to the feeling of despair occasioned by the absence of the beloved works of art. Bah! I would offer them a pinch of snuff out of my box as I walked along my gallery, with their Excellencies cringing after me. Zenobia was a fine woman and a queen, but she had to walk in Aurelian's triumph. The *procédé* was *peu délicat*? *En usez-vous, mon cher monsieur!* (The marquis says the 'Macaba' is delicious.) What a splendour of colour there is in that cloud! What a richness, what a freedom of handling, and what a marvellous precision! I trod upon your Excellency's corn?—a thousand pardons. His Excellency grins and declares he rather likes to have his corns trodden on.

Were you ever very angry with Soult—about that Murillo which we have bought? The veteran loved that picture because it saved the life of a fellow-creature—the fellow-creature who hid it, and whom the Duke intended to hang unless the picture was forthcoming.

We gave several thousand pounds for it—how many thousand? About its merit is a question of taste which we will not here argue. If you choose to place Murillo in the first class of painters, founding his claim upon these Virgin altarpieces, I am your humble servant. Tom Moore painted altarpieces as well as Milton, and warbled Sacred Songs and Loves of the Angels after his fashion. I wonder did Watteau ever try historical subjects? And as for Greuze, you know that his heads will fetch £1000, £1500, £2000 —as much as a Sèvres 'cabaret' of Rose du Barri. If cost price is to be your criterion of worth, what shall we say to that little receipt for £10 for the copyright of *Paradise Lost* which used to hang in old Mr. Rogers' room? When living painters, as frequently happens in our days, see their pictures sold at auctions for four or five times the sums which they originally received, are they enraged or elated? A hundred years ago the state of the picture-market was different: that dreary old Italian stock was much higher than at present; Rembrandt himself, a close man, was known to be in difficulties. If ghosts are fond of money still, what a wrath his must be at the present value of his works?

The Hague Rembrandt is the greatest and grandest of all his pieces to my mind. Some of the heads are as sweetly and lightly painted as Gainsborough; the faces not ugly, but delicate and high-bred; the exquisite grey tones are charming to mark and study; the heads not plastered, but painted with a free, liquid brush; the result, one of the great victories won by this consummate chief, and left for the wonder and delight of succeeding ages.

The humblest volunteer in the ranks of art, who has served a campaign or two ever so ingloriously, has at least this good fortune of understanding, or fancying he is able to understand, how the battle has been fought, and how the engaged general won it. This is the Rhinelander's most brilliant achievement—victory along the whole line. The 'Night-watch' at Amsterdam is magnificent in parts, but on the side to the spectator's right, smoky and dim. The 'Five Masters of the Drapers' is wonderful for depth, strength, brightness, massive power. What words are these to express a picture! to describe a description! I once saw a moon riding in the sky serenely, attended by her sparkling maids of honour, and a little lady said, with an air of great satisfaction, '*I must sketch it.*' Ah, my dear lady, if with an H.B., a Bristol board, and a bit of india-rubber, you can sketch the starry firmament on high, and the moon in her glory, I make you my compliment! I can't sketch 'The Five Drapers' with any ink or pen at present at command—but can look with all my eyes and be thankful to have seen such a masterpiece.

They say he was a moody, ill-conditioned man, the old tenant of the mill. What does he think of the 'Van der Helst' which hangs opposite his 'Night-watch,' and which is one of the great pictures of the world? It is not painted by so great a man as Rembrandt; but there it is—to see it is an event of your life. Having beheld it you have lived in the year 1648, and celebrated the treaty of Munster. You have shaken the hands of the Dutch Guardsmen, eaten from their platters, drunk their Rhenish, heard their jokes as they wagged their jolly beards. The Amsterdam Catalogue discourses thus about it:—a model catalogue: it gives you the prices paid, the signatures of the painters, a succinct description of the work.

'This masterpiece represents a banquet of the civic guard, which took place on the 18th June 1648, in the great hall of the St. Joris Doele, on the Singel at

Amsterdam, to celebrate the conclusion of the Peace at Munster. The thirty-five figures composing the picture are all portraits.

'"The Captain WITSE" is placed at the head of the table, and attracts our attention first. He is dressed in black velvet, his breast covered with a cuirass, on his head a broad-brimmed black hat with white plumes. He is comfortably seated on a chair of black oak, with a velvet cushion, and holds in his left hand, supported on his knee, a magnificent drinking-horn, surrounded by a St. George destroying the dragon, and ornamented with olive-leaves. The captain's features express cordiality and good-humour; he is grasping the hand of "Lieutenant VAN WAVERN" seated near him, in a habit of dark grey, with lace and buttons of gold, lace-collar and wrist-bands, his feet crossed, with boots of yellow leather, with large tops, and gold spurs, on his head a black hat and dark-brown plumes. Behind him, at the centre of the picture, is the standard-bearer, "JACOB BANNING," in an easy martial attitude, hat in hand, his right hand on his chair, his right leg on his left knee. He holds the flag of blue silk, in which the Virgin is embroidered (such a silk! such a flag! such a piece of painting!) emblematic of the town of Amsterdam. The banner covers his shoulder, and he looks towards the spectator frankly and complacently.

'The man behind him is probably one of the sergeants. His head is bare. He wears a cuirass, and yellow gloves, grey stockings, and boots with large tops, and kneecaps of cloth. He has a napkin on his knees, and in his hand a piece of ham, a slice of bread, and a knife. The old man behind is probably "WILLIAM THE DRUMMER." He has his hat in his right hand, and in his left a gold-footed wineglass, filled with white wine. He wears a red scarf, and a black satin doublet, with little slashes of yellow silk. Behind the drummer, two matchlock-men are seated at the end of the table. One in a large black habit, a napkin on his knee, a *hausse-col* of iron, and a linen scarf and collar. He is eating with his knife. The other holds a long glass of white wine. Four musketeers, with different shaped hats, are behind these, one holding a glass, three others with their guns on their shoulders. Other guests are placed between the personage who is giving the toast and the standard-bearer. One with his hat off, and his hand uplifted, is talking to another. The second is carving a fowl. A third holds a silver plate; and another, in the background, a silver flagon, from which he fills a cup. The corner behind the captain is filled by two seated personages, one of whom is peeling an orange. Two others are standing, armed with halberts, of whom one holds a plumed hat. Behind him are other three individuals, one of them holding a pewter pot, on which the name "Poock," the landlord of the "Hôtel Doele," is engraved. At the back, a maid-servant is coming in with a pasty, crowned with a turkey. Most of the guests are listening to the captain. From an open window in the distance, the façades of two houses are seen, surrounded by stone figures of sheep.'

There, now you know all about it: now you can go home and paint just such another. If you do, do pray remember to paint the hands of the figures as they are here depicted; they are as wonderful portraits as the faces. None of your slim Van Dyck elegancies, which have done duty at the cuffs of so many doublets; but each man with a hand for himself, as with a face for himself. I blushed for the coarseness of one of the chiefs in this great company, that fellow behind 'WILLIAM THE DRUMMER,' splendidly attired, sitting full in the face of the public; and holding a pork bone in his hand. Suppose the *Saturday Review* critic were to come suddenly on this picture? Ah! what a shock it would give that noble nature! Why is that knuckle of pork not painted out? at any rate, why is not a little fringe of lace painted round it? or a cut pink paper? or couldn't a smelling-bottle be painted in instead, with a crest and a gold top, or a cambric pocket-handkerchief, in lieu of the horrid pig, with a pink coronet in the corner? or suppose you covered the man's hand (which is very coarse and strong), and gave him the decency of a kid glove? But a piece of pork in a naked hand? O nerves and eau de Cologne, hide it, hide it!

In spite of this lamentable coarseness, my noble sergeant, give me thy hand as nature made it! A great, and famous, and noble handiwork I have seen here. Not the greatest picture in the world—not a work of the highest genius—but a performance so great, various, and admirable, so shrewd of humour, so wise of observation, so honest and complete of expression, that to have seen it has been a delight, and to remember it will be a pleasure for days to come. Well done, Bartholomeus van der Helst! Brave, meritorious, victorious, happy Bartholomew, to whom it has been given to produce a masterpiece!

May I take off my hat and pay a respectful compliment to Jan Steen, Esq.? He is a glorious composer. His humour is as frank as Fielding's. Look at his own figure sitting in the window-sill yonder, and roaring with laughter! What a twinkle in the eyes! what a mouth it is for a song, or a joke, or a noggin! I think the composition in some of Jan's pictures amounts to the sublime, and look at them with the same delight and admiration which I have felt before works of the very highest style. This gallery is admirable—and the city in which the gallery is, is perhaps even more wonderful and curious to behold than the gallery.

The first landing at Calais (or, I suppose, on any foreign shore)—the first sight of an Eastern city—the first view of Venice—and this of Amsterdam, are among the delightful shocks which I have had as a traveller. Amsterdam is as good as Venice, with a superadded humour and grotesqueness, which gives the sightseer the most singular zest and pleasure. A run through Pekin I could hardly fancy to be more odd, strange, and yet familiar. This rush, and crowd, and prodigious vitality; this immense swarm of life; these busy waters, crowding barges, swinging draw-bridges, piled ancient gables, spacious markets teeming with people; that ever-wonderful Jews' quarter; that dear old world of painting and the past, yet alive, and throbbing, and palpable—actual, and yet passing before you swiftly and strangely as a dream. Of the many journeys of this Roundabout life, that drive through Amsterdam is to be specially and gratefully remembered. You have never seen the palace of Amsterdam, my dear sir? Why, there's a marble hall in that palace that will frighten you as much as any hall in *Vathek*, or a nightmare. At one end of that old, cold, glassy, glittering, ghostly marble hall there stands a throne, on which a white marble king ought to sit with his white legs gleaming down into the white marble below, and his white eyes looking at a great white marble Atlas, who bears on his icy shoulders a blue globe as big as a full moon. If he were not a genie, and enchanted, and with a strength altogether hyperatlantean, he would drop the moon with a shriek on to the white marble floor, and it would splitter into perdition. And the palace would rock, and heave, and tumble; and the waters would rise, rise, rise; and the gables sink, sink, sink; and the barges would rise up to the chimneys; and the water-souchee fishes would flap over the Boompjes, where the pigeons and storks used to perch; and the Amster, and the Rotter, and the Saar, and the Op, and all the dams of Holland would burst, and the Zuyder Zee roll over the dykes: and you would wake out of your dream, and find yourself sitting in your armchair.

Was it a dream? it seems like one. Have we been to Holland? have we heard the chimes at midnight at Antwerp? Were we really away for a week, or have I been sitting up in the room dozing, before this stale old desk? Here's the desk; yes. But if it has been a dream, how could I have learned to hum that tune out of *Dinorah*? Ah, is it that tune, or myself that I am humming? If it was a dream, how comes this yellow NOTICE DES TABLEAUX DU MUSÉE D'AMSTERDAM AVEC FACSIMILE DES MONOGRAMMES before me, and this signature of the gallant

Bartholomeus Van der Helst fecit A°, 1648.

Yes, indeed, it was a delightful little holiday: it lasted a whole week. With the exception of that little pint of *amari aliquid* at Rotterdam, we were all very happy. We might have gone on being happy for whoever knows how many days more? a week more, ten days more: who knows how long that dear teetotum happiness can be made to spin without toppling over?

But one of the party had desired letters to be sent *poste restante*, Amsterdam. The post-office is hard by that awful palace where the Atlas is, and which we really saw.

There was only one letter, you see. Only one chance of finding us. There it was. 'The post has only this moment come in,' says the smirking commissioner. And he hands over the paper, thinking he has done something clever.

Before the letter had been opened, I could read COME BACK as clearly as if it had been painted on the wall. It was all over. The spell was broken. The sprightly little holiday fairy that had frisked and gambolled so kindly beside us for eight days of sunshine—or rain which was as cheerful as sunshine—gave a parting piteous look, and whisked away and vanished. And yonder scuds the postman, and here is the old desk.

Roundabout Papers, 1863.

MATTHEW ARNOLD

1822–1888

THE FRENCH PLAY IN LONDON

ENGLISH opinion concerning France, our neighbour and rival, was formerly full of hostile prejudice, and is still, in general, quite sufficiently disposed to severity. But, from time to time, France or things French become for the solid English public the object of what our neighbours call an *engouement*,—an infatuated interest. Such an *engouement* Wordsworth witnessed in 1802, after the Peace of Amiens, and it disturbed his philosophic mind greatly. Every one was rushing to Paris; every one was in admiration of the First Consul:—

> Lords, lawyers, statesmen, squires of low degree,
> Men known and men unknown, sick, lame, and blind,
> Post forward all like creatures of one kind,
> With first-fruit offerings crowd to bend the knee
> In France, before the new-born majesty.

All measure, all dignity, all real intelligence of the situation, so Wordsworth complained, were lost under the charm of the new attraction:—

> 'Tis ever thus. Ye men of prostrate mind,
> A seemly reverence may be paid to power;
> But that's a loyal virtue, never sown
> In haste, nor springing with a transient shower.
> When truth, when sense, when liberty were flown,
> What hardship had it been to wait an hour?
> Shame on you, feeble heads, to slavery prone!

One or two moralists there may still be found, who comment in a like spirit of impatience upon the extraordinary attraction exercised by the French company of actors which has lately left us. The rush of 'lords, lawyers, statesmen, squires of low degree, men known and men unknown,' of those acquainted with the French language perfectly, of those acquainted with it a little, and of those not acquainted with it at all, to the performances at the Gaiety Theatre,—the universal occupation with the performances and performers, the length and solemnity with which the newspapers chronicled and discussed them, the seriousness with which the whole repertory of the company was taken, the passion for certain pieces and for certain actors, the great ladies who by the acting of Mlle. Sarah Bernhardt were revealed to themselves, and who could not resist the desire of telling her so,—all this has moved, I say, a surviving and aged moralist here and there amongst us to exclaim: 'Shame on you, feeble heads, to slavery prone!' The English public, according to these cynics, have been exhibiting themselves as men of prostrate mind, who pay to power a reverence anything but seemly; we have been conducting ourselves with just that absence of tact, measure, and correct perception, with all that slowness to see when one is making oneself ridiculous, which belongs to the people of our English race.

The nice sense of measure is certainly not one of Nature's gifts to her English children. But then we all of us fail in it, we natives of Great Britain; we have all of us yielded to infatuation at some moment of our lives; we are all in the same boat, and one of us has no right to laugh at the other. I am sure I have not. I remember how in my youth, after a first sight of the divine Rachel at the Edinburgh Theatre, in the part of Hermione, I followed her to Paris, and for two months never missed one of her representations. I, at least, will not cast a stone at the London public for running eagerly after the charming company of actors which has just left us; or at the great ladies who are seeking for soul and have found it in Mlle. Sarah Bernhardt. I will not quarrel with our newspapers for their unremitting attention to these French performances, their copious criticism of them; particularly when the criticism is so interesting and so good as that which the *Times* and the *Daily News* and the *Pall Mall Gazette* have given us. Copious, indeed!—why should not our newspapers be copious on the French play, when they are copious on the Clewer case, and the Mackonochie case, and so many other matters besides, a great deal less important and interesting, all of them, than the *Maison de Molière*?

So I am not going to join the cynics, and to find fault with the *engouement*, the infatuation, shown by the English public in its passion for the French plays and players. A passion of this kind may be salutary, if we will learn the lessons for us with which it is charged. Unfortunately, few people who feel a passion think of learning anything from it. A man feels a passion, he passes through it, and then he goes his way and straightway forgets, as the Apostle says, what manner of man he was. Above all, this is apt to happen with us English, who have, as an eminent German professor is good enough to tell us, 'so much genius, so little method.' The much genius hurries us into infatuations; the little method prevents our learning the right and wholesome lesson from them. Let us join, then, devoutly and with contrition, in the prayer of the German professor's great countryman, Goethe, a prayer which is more needful, one may surely say, for us than for him: 'God help us, and enlighten us for the time to come! that we may not stand in our own way so much, but may have clear notions of the consequences of things!'

To get a clear notion of the consequences which do in reason follow from what we have been seeing and admiring at the Gaiety Theatre, to get a clear notion of them, and frankly to draw them, is the object which I propose to myself here. I am not going to criticise one by one the French actors and actresses who have been giving us so much pleasure. For a foreigner this must always be a task, as it seems to me, of some peril. Perilous or not, it has been abundantly attempted; and to attempt it yet again, now that the performances are over and the performers gone back to Paris, would be neither timely nor interesting. One remark I will make, a remark suggested by the inevitable comparison of Mlle. Sarah Bernhardt with Rachel. One talks vaguely of genius, but I had never till now comprehended how much of Rachel's superiority was purely in intellectual power, how eminently this power counts in the actor's art as in all art, how just is the instinct which led the Greeks to mark with a high and severe stamp the Muses. Temperament and quick intelligence, passion, nervous mobility, grace, smile, voice, charm, poetry,—Mlle. Sarah Bernhardt has them all. One watches her with pleasure, with admiration,—and yet not without a secret disquietude. Something is wanting, or, at least, not present in sufficient force; something which alone can secure and fix her administration of all the charming gifts which she has, can alone keep them fresh, keep them sincere, save them from perils by caprice, perils by mannerism. That something is high intellectual power. It was here that Rachel was so great; she began, one says to oneself as one recalls her image and dwells upon it,—she began almost where Mlle. Sarah Bernhardt ends.

But I return to my object,—the lessons to be learnt by us from the immense attraction which the French company has exercised, the consequences to be drawn from it. Certainly we have something to learn from it, and something to unlearn. What have we to unlearn? Are we to unlearn our old estimate of serious French poetry and drama? For every lover of poetry and of the drama, this is a very interesting question. In the great and serious kinds of poetry, we used to think that the French genius, admirable as in so many other ways it is, showed radical weakness. But there is a new generation growing up amongst us,—and to this young and stirring generation who of us would not gladly belong, even at the price of having to catch some of its illusions and to pass through them?—a new generation which takes French poetry and drama as seriously as Greek, and for which M. Victor Hugo is a great poet of the race and lineage of Shakespeare.

M. Victor Hugo is a great romance-writer. There are people who are disposed to class all imaginative producers together, and to call them all by the name of poet. Then a great romance-writer will be a great poet. Above all are the French inclined to give this wide extension to the name poet, and the inclination is very characteristic of them. It betrays that very defect which we have mentioned, the inadequacy of their genius in the higher regions of poetry. If they were more at home in those regions, they would feel the essential difference between imaginative production in verse, and imaginative production in prose, too strongly, to be ever inclined to call both by the common name of poetry. They would perceive with us, that M. Victor Hugo, for instance, or Sir Walter Scott, may be a great romance-writer, and may yet be by no means a great poet.

Poetry is simply the most delightful and perfect form of utterance that human words can reach. Its rhythm and measure, elevated to a regularity, certainty, and force very different from that of the rhythm and measure which can pervade prose, are a part of its perfection. The more of genius that a nation has for high poetry, the more will the rhythm and measure which its poetical utterance adopts be distinguished by adequacy and beauty. That is why M. Henry Cochin's remark on Shakespeare, which I have elsewhere quoted, is so good: 'Shakespeare is not only,' says M. Henry Cochin, 'the king of the realm of thought, he is also the king of poetic rhythm and style. Shakespeare has succeeded in giving us the most varied, the most harmonious verse, which has ever sounded upon the human ear since the verse of the Greeks.'

Let us have a line or two of Shakespeare's verse before us, just to supply the mind with a standard of reverence in the discussion of this matter. We may take the lines from him almost at random:

> Five hundred poor I have in yearly pay,
> Who twice a day their wither'd hands hold up
> Toward heaven, to pardon blood; and I have built
> Two chantries, where the sad and solemn priests
> Sing still for Richard's soul.

Yes, there indeed is the verse of Shakespeare, the verse of the highest English poetry; there is what M. Henry Cochin calls 'the majestic English iambic!' We will not inflict Greek upon our readers, but every one who knows Greek will remember that the iambic of the Attic tragedians is a rhythm of the same high and splendid quality.

Which of us doubts that imaginative production, uttering itself in such a form as this, is altogether another and a higher thing from imaginative production uttering itself in any of the forms of prose? And if we find a nation doubting whether there is any great difference between imaginative and eloquent production in verse, and imaginative and eloquent production in prose, and inclined to call all imaginative producers by the common name of poets, then we may be sure of one thing: namely, that this nation has never yet succeeded in finding the highest and most adequate form for poetry. Because, if it had, it could never have doubted of the essential superiority of this form to all prose forms of utterance. And if a nation has never succeeded in creating this high and adequate form for its poetry, then we may conclude that it is not gifted with the genius for high poetry; since the genius for high poetry calls forth the high and adequate form, and is inseparable from it. So that, on the one hand, from the absence of conspicuous genius in a people for poetry, we may predict the absence of an adequate poetical form; and on the other hand, again, from the want of an adequate poetical form, we may infer the want of conspicuous national genius for poetry.

And we may proceed, supposing that our estimate of a nation's success in poetry is said to be much too low, and is called in question, in either of two ways. If we are said to underrate, for instance, the production of Corneille and Racine in poetry, we may compare this production in power, in penetrativeness, in criticism of life, in ability to call forth our energy and joy, with the production of Homer and Shakespeare. M. Victor Hugo is said to be a poet of the race and lineage of Shakespeare, and I hear astonishment expressed at my not ranking him much above Wordsworth. Well, then, compare their production, in cases where it lends itself to a comparison. Compare the poetry of the moonlight scene in *Hernani*, really the most poetical scene in that play, with the poetry of the moonlight scene in the *Merchant of Venice.* Compare

> . . . Sur nous, tout en dormant,
> La nature à demi veille amoureusement—

with

> Sit, Jessica; look how the floor of heaven
> Is thick inlaid with patines of bright gold!

Compare the laudation of their own country, an inspiring but also a trying theme for a poet, by Shakespeare and Wordsworth on the one hand, and by M. Victor Hugo on the other. Compare Shakespeare's

> This precious stone set in the silver sea,
> This blessed plot, this earth, this realm, this England—

or compare Wordsworth's

> We must be free or die, who speak the tongue
> Which Shakespeare spake, the faith and morals hold
> Which Milton held . . .

with M. Victor Hugo's

> Non, France, l'univers a besoin que tu vives!
> Je le redis, la France est un besoin des hommes.

Who does not recognise the difference of spirit here? And the difference is, that the English lines have the distinctive spirit of high poetry, and the French lines have not.

Here we have been seeking to attend chiefly to the contents and spirit of the verses chosen. Let us now attend, so far as we can, to form only, and the result will be the same. We will confine ourselves, since our subject is the French play in London, to dramatic verse. We require an adequate form of verse for high poetic drama. The accepted form with the French is the rhymed Alexandrine. Let us keep the iambic of the Greeks or of Shakespeare, let us keep such verse as

> This precious stone set in the silver sea

present to our minds. Then let us take such verse as this from *Hernani*:

> Le comte d'Onate, qui l'aime aussi, la garde
> Et comme un majordome et comme un amoureux.
> Quelque reître, une nuit, *gardien peu langoureux*,
> Pourrait bien, etc., etc.

or as this, from the same:

> Quant à lutter ensemble
> Sur le terrain d'amour, *beau champ qui toujours tremble*.
> De fadaises, mon cher, je sais mal faire assaut.

The words in italics will suffice to give us, I think, the sense of what constitutes the fatal fault of the rhyming Alexandrine of French tragedy,—its incurable artificiality, its want of the fluidity, the naturalness, the rapid forward movement of true dramatic verse. M. Victor Hugo is said to be a cunning and mighty artist in Alexandrines, and so unquestionably he is; but he is an artist in a form radically inadequate and inferior, and in which a drama like that of Sophocles or Shakespeare is impossible.

It happens that in our own language we have an example of the employment of an inadequate form in tragedy and in elevated poetry, and can see the result of it. The rhymed ten-syllable couplet, the heroic couplet as it is often called, is such a form. In the earlier work of Shakespeare, work adopted or adapted by him even if not altogether his own work, we find this form often employed:

> Alas! what joy shall noble Talbot have
> To bid his young son welcome to his grave?
> Away! vexation almost stops my breath
> That sundered friends greet in the hour of death.
> Lucy, farewell; no more my future can
> But curse the cause I cannot aid the man.
> Maine, Blois, Poitiers and Tours are won away
> 'Long all of Somerset and his delay.

Traces of this form remain in Shakespeare's work to the last, in the rhyming of final couplets. But because he had so great a genius for true tragic poetry, Shakespeare dropped this necessarily inadequate form and took a better. We find the rhymed couplet again in Dryden's tragedies. But this vigorous rhetorical poet had no real genius for true tragic poetry, and his form is itself a proof of it. True tragic poetry is impossible with this inadequate form. Again, all through the eighteenth century this form was dominant as the main form for high efforts in English poetry; and our serious poetry of that century, accordingly, has something inevitably defective and unsatisfactory. When it rises out of this, it at the same time adopts instinctively a truer form, as Gray does in the *Elegy*. The just and perfect use of the ten-syllable couplet is to be seen in Chaucer. As a form for tragedy, and for poetry of the most serious and elevated kind, it is defective. It makes real adequacy in poetry of this kind impossible; and its prevalence, for poetry of this kind, proves that those amongst whom it prevails have for poetry of this kind no signal gift.

The case of the great Molière himself will illustrate the truth of what I say. Molière is by far the chief name in French poetry; he is one of the very greatest names in all literature. He has admirable and delightful power, penetrativeness, insight; a masterly criticism of life. But he is a comic poet. Why? Had he no seriousness and depth of nature? He had profound seriousness. And would not a dramatic poet with this depth of nature be a tragedian if he could? Of course he would. For only by breasting in full the storm and cloud of life, breasting it and passing through it and above it, can the dramatist who feels the weight of mortal things liberate himself from the pressure, and rise, as we all seek to rise, to content and joy. Tragedy breasts the pressure of life. Comedy eludes it, half liberates itself from it by irony. But the tragedian, if he has the sterner labour, has also the higher prize. Shakespeare has more joy than Molière, more assurance and peace. *Othello*, with all its passion and terror, is on the whole a work animating and fortifying; more so a thousand times than *George Dandin*, which is mournfully depressing. Molière, if he could, would have given us Othellos instead of George Dandins; let us not doubt it. If he did not give Othellos to us, it was because the highest sort of poetic power was wanting to him. And if the highest sort of poetic power had been not wanting to him but present, he would have found no adequate form of dramatic verse for conveying it, he would have had to create one. For such tasks Molière had not power; and this is only another way of saying that for the highest tasks in poetry the genius of his nation appears to have not power. But serious spirit and great poet that he was, Molière had far too sound an instinct to attempt so earnest a matter as tragic drama with inadequate means. It would have been a heart-breaking business for him. He did not attempt it, therefore, but confined himself to comedy.

The *Misanthrope* and the *Tartufe* are comedy, but they are comedy in verse, poetic comedy. They employ the established verse of French dramatic poetry, the Alexandrine. Immense power has gone to the making of them; a world of vigorous sense, piercing observation, pathetic meditation, profound criticism of life. Molière had also one great advantage as a dramatist over Shakespeare; he wrote for a more developed theatre, a more developed society. Moreover he was at the same time, probably, by nature a better *theatre-poet* than Shakespeare; he had a keener sense for theatrical situation. Shakespeare is not rightly to be called, as Goethe calls him, an epitomator rather than a dramatist; but he may rightly be called rather a dramatist than a theatre-poet. Molière,—and here his French nature stood him in good stead,—was a theatre-poet of the very first order. Comedy, too, escapes, as has been already said, the test of entire seriousness; it remains, by the law of its being, in a region of comparative lightness and of irony. What is artificial can pass in comedy more easily. In spite of all these advantages, the *Misanthrope* and the *Tartufe* have, and have by reason of their poetic form, an artificiality which makes itself too much felt, and which provokes weariness. The freshness and power of Molière are best felt when he uses prose, in pieces such as the *Avare*, or the *Fourberies de Scapin*, or *George Dandin*. How entirely the contrary is the case with Shakespeare; how undoubtedly is it his verse which shows his power most! But so inadequate a vehicle for dramatic poetry is the French Alexandrine, that its sway hindered Molière, one may think, from being a tragic poet at all, in spite of his having gifts for this highest form of dramatic poetry which are immeasurably superior to those of any other French poet. And in comedy, where Molière thought he could use the Alexandrine, and where he did use it with splendid power, it yet in a considerable degree hampered and lamed him, so that this true and great poet is actually most satisfactory in his prose.

If Molière cannot make us insensible to the inherent defects of French dramatic poetry, still less can Corneille and Racine. Corneille has energy and nobility, Racine an often Virgilian sweetness and pathos. But while Molière, in depth, penetrativeness, and powerful criticism of life, belongs to the same family as Sophocles and Shakespeare, Corneille and Racine are quite of another order. We must not be misled by the excessive estimate of them among their own countrymen. I remember an answer of M. Sainte-Beuve, who always treated me with great kindness, and to whom I once ventured to say that I could not think Lamartine a poet of very high importance. 'He was important to *us*,' answered M. Sainte-Beuve. In a far higher degree can a Frenchman say of Corneille and Racine: 'They were important to *us*.' Voltaire pronounces of them: 'These men taught our nation to think, to feel, and to express itself' (*Ces hommes enseignèrent à la nation à penser, à sentir et à s'exprimer*). They were thus the instructors and formers of a society in many respects the most civilised and consummate that the world has ever seen, and which certainly has not been inclined to underrate its own advantages. How natural, then, that it should feel grateful to its formers, and should extol them! 'Tell your brother Rodolphe,' writes Joseph de Maistre from Russia to his daughter at home, 'to get on with his French poets; let him have them by heart,—the inimitable Racine above all; never mind whether he understands him or not. I did not understand him, when my mother used to come and sit on my bed, and repeat from him, and put me to sleep with her beautiful voice to the sound of this incomparable music. I knew hundreds of lines of him before I could read; and this is why my ears, having drunk in this ambrosia betimes, have never been able to endure common stuff since.' What a spell must such early use have had for riveting the affections; and how civilising are such affections, how honourable to the society which can be imbued with them, to the literature which can inspire them! Pope was in a similar way, though not at all in the same degree, a forming and civilising influence to our grandfathers, and limited their literary taste while he stimulated and formed it. So, too, the Greek boy was fed by his mother and nurse with Homer; but then in this case it was Homer!

We English had Shakespeare waiting to open our eyes, whensoever a favourable moment came, to the insufficiencies of Pope. But the French had no Shakespeare to open their eyes to the insufficiencies of Corneille and Racine. Great artists like Talma and Rachel, whose power, as actors, was far superior to the power, as poets, of the dramatists whose work they were rendering, filled out with their own life and warmth the parts into which they threw themselves, gave body to what was meagre, fire to what was cold, and themselves supported the poetry of the French classic drama rather than were supported by it. It was easier to think the poetry of Racine inimitable, when Talma or Rachel were seen producing in it such inimitable effects. Indeed French acting is so good, that there are few pieces, excepting always those of Molière, in the repertory of a company such as that which we have just seen, where the actors do not show themselves to be superior to the pieces they render, and to be worthy of pieces which are better. *Phèdre* is a work of much beauty, yet certainly one felt this in seeing Rachel in the part of Phèdre. I am not sure that one feels it in seeing Mlle. Sarah Bernhardt as Phèdre, but I am sure that one feels it in seeing her as Doña Sol.

The tragedy of M. Victor Hugo has always, indeed, stirring events in plenty; and so long as the human nerves are what they are, so long will things like the sounding of the horn, in the famous fifth act of *Hernani*, produce a thrill in us. But so will Werner's *Twenty-fourth of February*, or Scott's *House of Aspen.* A thrill of this sort may be raised in us, and yet our poetic sense may remain profoundly dissatisfied. So it remains in *Hernani.* M. Sarcey, a critic always acute and intelligent, and whom one reads with profit and pleasure, says that we English are fatigued by the long speeches in *Hernani*, and that we do not appreciate what delights French people in it, the splendour of the verse, the wondrous beauty of the style, the poetry. Here recurs the question as to the adequacy of the French Alexandrine as tragic verse. If this form is vitally inadequate for tragedy, then to speak absolutely of splendour of verse and wondrous beauty of style in it when employed for tragedy, is misleading. Beyond doubt M. Victor Hugo has an admirable gift for versification. So had Pope. But to speak absolutely of the splendour of verse and wondrous beauty of style of the *Essay on Man* would be misleading. Such terms can be properly used only of verse and style of an altogether higher and more adequate kind, a verse and style like that of Dante, Shakespeare, or Milton. Pope's brilliant gift for versification is exercised within the limits of a form inadequate for true philosophic poetry, and by its very presence excluding it. M. Victor Hugo's brilliant gift for versification is exercised within the limits of a form inadequate for true tragic poetry, and by its very presence excluding it.

But, if we are called upon to prove this from the poetry itself, instead of inferring it from the form, our task, in the case of *Hernani*, is really only too easy. What is the poetical value of this famous fifth act of *Hernani*? What poetical truth, or verisimilitude, or possibility has Ruy Gomez, this chivalrous old Spanish grandee, this venerable nobleman, who, because he cannot marry his niece, presents himself to her and her husband upon their wedding night, and insists on the husband performing an old promise to commit suicide if summoned by Ruy Gomez to do so? Naturally the poor young couple raise difficulties, and the venerable nobleman keeps plying them with: *Bois! Allons! Le sépulcre est ouvert, et je ne puis attendre! J'ai hâte! Il faut mourir!* This is a mere character of Surrey melodrama. And Hernani, who, when he is reminded that it is by his father's head that he has sworn to commit suicide, exclaims:

Mon père! mon père!—Ah! j'en perdrai la raison!

and who, when Doña Sol gets the poison away from him, entreats her to return it:

Par pitié, ce poison,
Rends-le-moi! Par l'amour, par notre âme immortelle!

because

Le duc a ma parole, et mon père est là-haut!

The *poetry*! says M. Sarcey;—and one thinks of the poetry of *Lear*! M. Sarcey must pardon me for saying, that in

Le duc a ma parole, et mon père est là-haut!

we are not in the world of poetry at all, hardly even in the world of literature, unless it be the literature of *Bombastes Furioso.*

Our sense, then, for what is poetry and what is not, the attractiveness of the French plays and players must not make us unlearn. We may and must retain our old conviction of the fundamental insufficiency, both in substance and in form, of the rhymed tragedy of the French. We are to keep, too, what in the main has always been the English estimate of Molière: that he is a man of creative and splendid power, a dramatist whose work is truly delightful, is edifying and immortal; but that even Molière in poetic drama is hampered and has not full swing, and, in consequence, leaves us somewhat dissatisfied. Finally, we poor old people should pluck up courage to stand out yet, for the few years of life which yet remain to us, against that passing illusion of the confident young generation who are newly come out on the war-path, that M. Victor Hugo is a poet of the race and lineage of Shakespeare.

What, now, are we to say of the prose drama of modern life, the drama of which the *Sphinx* and the *Étrangère* and the *Demi-Monde* are types, and which was the most strongly attractive part, probably, of the feast offered to us by the French company? The first thing to be said of these pieces is that they are admirably acted. But then constantly, as I have already said, one has the feeling that the French actors are better than the pieces which they play. What are we to think of this modern prose drama in itself, the drama of M. Octave Feuillet, and M. Alexandre Dumas the younger, and M. Augier? Some of the pieces composing it are better constructed and written than others, and much more effective. But this whole drama has one character common to it all. It may be best described as the theatre of the *homme sensuel moyen*, the average sensual man, whose country is France, and whose city is Paris, and whose ideal is the free, gay, pleasurable life of Paris,—an ideal which our young literary generation, now out on the war-path here in England, seek to adopt from France, and which they busily preach and work for. Of course there is in Paris much life of another sort too, as there are in France many men of another type than that of the *homme sensuel moyen*. But for many reasons, which I need not enumerate here, the life of the free, confident, harmonious development of the senses, all round, has been able to establish itself among the French and at Paris, as it has established itself nowhere else: and the ideal life of Paris is this sort of life triumphant. And of this ideal the modern French drama, works like the *Sphinx* and the *Étrangère* and the *Demi-Monde*, are the expression. It is the drama, I say, this drama now in question, of the *homme sensuel moyen*, the average sensual man. It represents the life of the senses developing themselves all round without misgiving; a life confident, fair and free, with fireworks of fine emotions, grand passions, and devotedness,—or rather, perhaps, we should say *dévouement*,—lighting it up when necessary.

We in England have no modern drama at all. We have our Elizabethan drama. We have a drama of the last century and of the latter part of the century preceding, a drama which may be called our drama of *the town*, when *the town* was an entity powerful enough, because homogeneous enough, to evoke a drama embodying its notions of life. But we have no modern drama. Our vast society is not at present homogeneous enough for this,—not sufficiently united, even any large portion of it, in a common view of life, a common ideal, capable of serving as basis for a modern English drama. We have apparitions of poetic and romantic drama (as the French, too, have their charming *Gringoire*), which are always possible, because man has always in his nature the poetical fibre. Then we have numberless imitations and adaptations from the French. All of these are at the bottom fantastic. We may truly say of them, that 'truth and sense and liberty are flown.' And the reason is evident. They are pages out of a life which the ideal of the *homme sensuel moyen* rules, transferred to a life where this ideal, notwithstanding the fervid adhesion to it of our young generation, does not reign. For the attentive observer the result is a sense of incurable falsity in the piece as adapted. Let me give an example. Everybody remembers *Pink Dominoes*. The piece turns upon an incident possible and natural enough in the life of Paris. Transferred to the life of London the incident is altogether unreal, and its unreality makes the whole piece, in its English form, fantastic and absurd.

Still that does not prevent such pieces, and the theatre generally, from now exercising upon us a great attraction. For we are at the end of a period, and have to deal with the facts and symptoms of a new period on which we are entering; and prominent among these fresh facts and symptoms is the irresistibility of the theatre. We know how the Elizabethan theatre had its cause in an ardent zest for life and living, a bold and large curiosity, a desire for a fuller, richer existence, pervading this nation at large, as they pervaded other nations, after the long mediæval time of obstruction and restraint. But we know, too, how the great middle class of this nation, alarmed at grave symptoms which showed themselves in the new movement, drew back; made choice for its spirit to live at one point, instead of living, or trying to live, at many; entered, as I have so often said, the prison of Puritanism, and had the key turned upon its spirit there for two hundred years. Our middle class forsook the theatre. The English theatre reflected no more the aspiration of a great community for a fuller and richer sense of human existence.

This theatre came afterwards, however, to reflect the aspirations of 'the town.' It developed a drama to suit these aspirations; while it also brought back and re-exhibited the Elizabethan drama, so far as 'the town' wanted it and liked it. Finally, as even 'the town' ceased to be homogeneous, the theatre ceased to develop anything expressive. It still repeated what was old with more or less of talent. But the mass of our English community, the mass of the middle class, kept aloof from the whole thing.

I remember how, happening to be at Shrewsbury, twenty years ago, and finding the whole Haymarket company acting there, I went to the theatre. Never was there such a scene of desolation. Scattered at very distant intervals through the boxes were about half-a-dozen chance comers like myself; there were some soldiers and their friends in the pit, and a good many riff-raff in the upper gallery. The real townspeople, the people who carried forward the business and life of Shrewsbury, and who filled its churches and chapels on Sundays, were entirely absent. I pitied the excellent Haymarket company; it must have been like acting to oneself upon an iceberg. Here one had a good example,—as I thought at the time, and I have often thought since,—of the complete estrangement of the British middle class from the theatre.

What is certain is, that a signal change is coming over us, and that it has already made great progress. It is said that there are now forty theatres in London. Even in Edinburgh, where in old times a single theatre maintained itself under protest, there are now, I believe, over half-a-dozen. The change is not due only to an increased liking in the upper class and in the working class for the theatre. Their liking for it has certainly increased, but this is not enough to account for the change. The attraction of the theatre begins to be felt again, after a long interval of insensibility, by the middle class also. Our French friends would say that this class, long petrified in a narrow Protestantism and in a perpetual reading of the Bible, is beginning at last to grow conscious of the horrible unnaturalness and *ennui* of its life, and is seeking to escape from it. Undoubtedly the type of religion to which the British middle class has sacrificed the theatre, as it has sacrificed so much besides, is defective. But I prefer to say that this great class, having had the discipline of its religion, is now awakening to the sure truth that the human spirit cannot live aright if it lives at one point only, that it can and ought to live at several points at the same time. The human spirit has a vital need, as we say, for conduct and religion; but it has the need also for expansion, for intellect and knowledge, for beauty, for social life and manners. The revelation of these additional needs brings the middle class to the theatre.

The revelation was indispensable, the needs are real, the theatre is one of the mightiest means of satisfying them, and the theatre, therefore, is irresistible. That conclusion, at any rate, we may take for certain. We have to unlearn, therefore, our long disregard of the theatre; we have to own that the theatre is irresistible.

But I see our community turning to the theatre with eagerness, and finding the English theatre without organization, or purpose, or dignity, and no modern English drama at all except a fantastical one. And then I see the French company from the chief theatre of Paris showing themselves to us in London, —a society of actors admirable in organisation, purpose, and dignity, with a modern drama not fantastic at all, but corresponding with fidelity to a very palpable and powerful ideal, the ideal of the life of the *homme sensuel moyen* in Paris, his beautiful city. I see in England a materialised upper class, sensible of the nullity of our own modern drama, impatient of the state of false constraint and of blank to which the Puritanism of our middle class has brought our stage and much of our life, delighting in such drama as the modern drama of Paris. I see the emancipated youth of both sexes delighting in it; the new and clever newspapers, which push on the work of emancipation and serve as devoted missionaries of the gospel of the life of Paris and of the ideal of the average sensual man, delighting in it. And in this condition of affairs I see the middle class beginning to arrive at the theatre again after an abstention of two centuries and more; arriving eager and curious, but a little bewildered.

Now, lest at this critical moment such drama as the *Sphinx* and the *Étrangère* and the *Demi-Monde*, positive as it is, and powerful as it is, and pushed as it is, and played with such prodigious care and talent, should too much rule the situation, let us take heart of grace and say, that as the right conclusion from the unparalleled success of the French company was not that we should reverse our old notions about the tragedy of M. Victor Hugo, or about French classic tragedy, or even about the poetic drama of the great Molière, so neither is it the right conclusion from this success that we should be converted and become believers in the legitimacy of the life-ideal of the *homme sensuel moyen*, and in the sufficiency of his drama. This is not the occasion to deliver a moral discourse. It is enough to revert to what has been already said, and to remark that the French ideal and its theatre have the defect of leaving out too much of life, of treating the soul as if it lived at one point or group of points only, of ignoring other points, or groups of points, at which it must live as well. And herein the conception of life shown in this French ideal and in its drama really resembles, different as in other ways they are, the conception of life prevalent with the British middle class, and has the like kind of defect. Both conceptions of life are too narrow. Sooner or later, if we adopt either, our soul and spirit are starved, and go amiss, and suffer.

What then, finally, *are* we to learn from the marvellous success and attractiveness of the performances at the Gaiety Theatre? What *is* the consequence which it is right and rational for us to draw? Surely it is this: 'The theatre is irresistible; *organise the theatre*. Surely, if we wish to stand less in our own way, and to have clear notions of the consequences of things, it is to this conclusion that we should come.

The performances of the French company show us plainly, I think, what is gained,—the theatre being admitted to be an irresistible need for civilised communities,—by organising the theatre. Some of the drama played by this company is, as we have seen, questionable. But, in the absence of an organisation such as that of this company, it would be played even yet more; it would, with a still lower drama to accompany it, almost if not altogether reign; it would have far less correction and relief by better things. An older and better drama, containing many things of high merit, some things of surpassing merit, is kept before the public by means of this company, is given frequently, is given to perfection. Pieces of truth and beauty, which emerge here and there among the questionable pieces of the modern drama, get the benefit of this company's skill, and are given to perfection. The questionable pieces themselves lose something of their unprofitableness and vice in their hands; the acting carries us into the world of correct and pleasing art, if the piece does not. And the type of perfection fixed by these fine actors influences for good every actor in France.

Moreover, the French company shows us not only what is gained by organising the theatre, but what is meant by organising it. The organisation in the example before us is simple and rational. We have a society of good actors, with a grant from the State on condition of their giving with frequency the famous and classic stage-plays of their nation, and with a commissioner of the State attached to the society and taking part in council with it. But the society is to all intents and purposes self-governing. And in connection with the society is the school of dramatic elocution of the *Conservatoire*, a school with the names of Regnier, Monrose, Got and Delaunay on its roll of professors.

The Society of the French Theatre dates from Louis the Fourteenth and from France's great century. It has, therefore, traditions, effect, consistency, and a place in the public esteem, which are not to be won in a day. But its organisation is such as a judicious man, desiring the results which in France have been by this time won, would naturally have devised; and it is such as a judicious man, desiring in another country to secure like results, would naturally imitate.

We have in England everything to make us dissatisfied with the chaotic and ineffective condition into which our theatre has fallen. We have the remembrance of better things in the past, and the elements for better things in the future. We have a splendid national drama of the Elizabethan age, and a later drama of 'the town' which has no lack of pieces conspicuous by their stage-qualities, their vivacity and their talent, and interesting by their pictures of manners. We have had great actors. We have good actors not a few at the present moment. But we have been unlucky, as we so often are, in the work of organisation. In the essay at organisation which in the patent theatres, with their exclusive privilege of acting Shakespeare, we formerly had, we find by no means an example, such as we have in the constitution of the French Theatre, of what a judicious man, seeking the good of the drama and of the public, would naturally devise. We find rather such a machinery as might be devised by a man prone to stand in his own way, a man devoid of clear notions, of the consequences of things. It was inevitable that the patent theatres should provoke discontent and attack. They were attacked, and their privilege fell. Still, to this essay, however imperfect, of a public organisation for the English theatre, our stage owes the days of power and greatness which it has enjoyed. So far as we have had a school of great actors, so far as our stage has had tradition, effect, consistency, and a hold on public esteem, it had them under the system of the privileged theatres. The system had its faults, and was abandoned; but then, instead of devising a better plan of public organisation for the English theatre, we gladly took refuge in our favourite doctrines of the mischief of State interference, of the blessedness of leaving every man free to do as he likes, of the impertinence of presuming to check any man's natural taste for the bathos, and pressing him to relish the sublime. We left the English theatre to take its chance. Its present impotence is the result.

It seems to me that every one of us is concerned to find a remedy for this melancholy state of things; and that the pleasure we have had in the visit of the French company is barren, unless it leaves us with the impulse to mend the condition of our theatre, and with the lesson how alone it can be rationally attempted. 'Forget,'—can we not hear these fine artists saying in an undertone to us, amidst their graceful compliments of adieu?—'forget your clap-trap, and believe that the State, the nation in its collective and corporate character, does well to concern itself about an influence so important to national life and manners as the theatre. Form a company out of the materials ready to your hand in your many good actors or actors of promise. Give them a theatre at the West End. Let them have a grant from your Science and Art Department; let some intelligent and accomplished man, like our friend Mr. Pigott, your present Examiner of Plays, be joined to them as Commissioner from the Department, to see that the conditions of the grant are observed. Let the conditions of the grant be that a repertory is agreed upon, taken out of the works of Shakespeare and out of the volumes of the *Modern British Drama*, and that pieces from this repertory are played a certain number of times in each season; as to new pieces, let your company use its discretion. Let a school of dramatic elocution and declamation be instituted in connection with your company. It may surprise you to hear that elocution and declamation are things to be taught and learnt, and do not come by nature; but it is so. Your best and most serious actors' (this is added with a smile) 'would have been better if in their youth they had learnt elocution. These recommendations, you may think, are not very much; but, as your divine William says, they are enough; they will serve. Try them. When your institution in the West of London has become a success, plant a second of like kind in the East. The people *will* have the theatre; then make it a good one. Let your two or three provincial towns institute, with municipal subsidy and co-operation, theatres such as you institute in the metropolis with State subsidy and co-operation. So you will restore the English theatre. And then a modern drama of your own will also, probably, spring up amongst you, and you will not have to come to us for pieces like *Pink Dominoes*.'

No, and we will hope, too, that the modern English drama, when it comes, may be something different from even the *Sphinx* and the *Demi-Monde*. For my part, I have all confidence, that if it ever does come, it will be different and better. But let us not say a word to wound the feelings of those who have given us so much pleasure, and who leave to us as a parting legacy such excellent advice. For excellent advice it is, and everything we saw these artists say and do upon the Gaiety stage inculcates it for us, whether they exactly formulated it in words or no. And still, even now that they are gone, when I pass along the Strand and come opposite to the Gaiety Theatre, I see a fugitive vision of delicate features under a shower of hair and a cloud of lace, and hear the voice of Mlle. Sarah Bernhardt saying in its most caressing terms to the Londoners: 'The theatre is irresistible; *organise the theatre!*'

Irish Essays, 1882.

JOHN ADDINGTON SYMONDS

1840–1893

A VENETIAN MEDLEY

I. FIRST IMPRESSIONS AND FAMILIARITY

IT is easy to feel and to say something obvious about Venice. The influence of this sea-city is unique, immediate, and unmistakable. But to express the sober truth of those impressions which remain when the first astonishment of the Venetian revelation has subsided, when the spirit of the place has been harmonised through familiarity with our habitual mood, is difficult.

Venice inspires at first an almost Corybantic rapture. From our earliest visits, if these have been measured by days rather than weeks, we carry away with us the memory of sunsets emblazoned in gold and crimson upon cloud and water; of violet domes and bell-towers etched against the orange of a western sky; of moonlight silvering breeze-rippled breadths of liquid blue; of distant islands shimmering in sunlitten haze; of music and black gliding boats; of labyrinthine darkness made for mysteries of love and crime; of statue-fretted palace fronts; of brazen clangour and a moving crowd; of pictures by earth's proudest painters, cased in gold on walls of council chambers where Venice sat enthroned a queen, where nobles swept the floors with robes of Tyrian brocade. These reminiscences will be attended by an ever-present sense of loneliness and silence in the world around; the sadness of a limitless horizon, the solemnity of an unbroken arch of heaven, the calm and greyness of evening on the lagoons, the pathos of a marble city crumbling to its grave in mud and brine.

These first impressions of Venice are true. Indeed

they are inevitable. They abide, and form a glowing background for all subsequent pictures, toned more austerely, and painted in more lasting hues of truth upon the brain. Those have never felt Venice at all who have not known this primal rapture, or who perhaps expected more of colour, more of melodrama, from a scene which nature and the art of man have made the richest in these qualities. Yet the mood engendered by this first experience is not destined to be permanent. It contains an element of unrest and unreality which vanishes upon familiarity. From the blare of that triumphal bourdon of brass instruments emerge the delicate voices of violin and clarinet. To the contrasted passions of our earliest love succeed a multitude of sweet and fanciful emotions. It is my present purpose to recapture some of the impressions made by Venice in more tranquil moods. Memory might be compared to a kaleidoscope. Far away from Venice I raise the wonder-working tube, allow the glittering fragments to settle as they please, and with words attempt to render something of the patterns I behold.

II. A LODGING IN SAN VIO

I have escaped from the hotels with their bustle of tourists and crowded *tables d'hôte*. My garden stretches down to the Grand Canal, closed at the end with a pavilion, where I lounge and smoke and watch the cornice of the Prefettura fretted with gold in sunset light. My sitting-room and bedroom face the southern sun. There is a canal below, crowded with gondolas, and across its bridge the good folk of San Vio come and go the whole day long—men in blue shirts with enormous hats, and jackets slung on their left shoulder; women in kerchiefs of orange and crimson. Bare-legged boys sit upon the parapet dangling their feet above the rising tide. A hawker passes, balancing a basket full of live and crawling crabs. Barges filled with Brenta water or Mirano wine take up their station at the neighbouring steps, and then ensues a mighty splashing and hurrying to and fro of men with tubs upon their heads. The brawny fellows in the wine-barge are red from brows to breast with drippings of the vat. And now there is a bustle in the quarter. A *barca* has arrived from St. Erasmo, the island of the market gardens. It is piled with gourds and pumpkins, cabbages and tomatoes, pomegranates and pears —a pyramid of gold and green and scarlet. Brown men lift the fruit aloft, and women bending from the pathway bargain for it. A clatter of chaffering tongues, a ring of coppers, a Babel of hoarse sea-voices, proclaim the sharpness of the struggle. When the quarter has been served, the boat sheers off diminished in its burden. Boys and girls are left seasoning their polenta with a slice of *zucca*, while the mothers of a score of families go pattering up yonder courtyard, with the material for their husbands' supper in their handkerchiefs. Across the canal, or more correctly the *Rio*, opens a wide grass-grown court. It is lined on the right hand by a row of poor dwellings, swarming with goldoliers' children. A garden wall runs along the other side, over which I can see pomegranate trees in fruit and pergolas of vines. Far beyond are more low houses, and then the sky, swept with sea-breezes, and the masts of an ocean-going ship against the dome and turrets of Palladio's Redentore.

This is my home. By day it is as lively as a scene in *Masaniello*. By night, after nine o'clock, the whole stir of the quarter has subsided. Far away I hear the bell of some church tell the hours. But no noise disturbs my rest, unless perhaps belated gondolier moors his boat beneath the window. My one maid, Catina, sings at her work the whole day through. My gondolier, Francesco, acts as valet. He wakes me in the morning, opens the shutters, brings sea-water for my bath, and takes his orders for the day. 'Will it do for Chioggia, Francesco?' 'Sissignore! The Signorino has set off in his *sandolo* already with

Antonio. The Signora is to go with us in the gondola.' 'Then get three more men, Francesco, and see that all of them can sing.'

III. TO CHIOGGIA WITH OAR AND SAIL

The *sandolo* is a boat shaped like the gondola, but smaller and lighter, without benches, and without the high steel prow or ferro which distinguishes the gondola. The gunwale is only just raised above the water, over which the little craft skims with a rapid bounding motion, affording an agreeable variation from the stately swan-like movement of the gondola. In one of these boats—called by him the *Fisolo* or *Seamew*—my friend Eustace had started with Antonio, intending to row the whole way to Chioggia, or, if the breeze favoured, to hoist a sail and help himself along. After breakfast, when the crew for my gondola had been assembled, Francesco and I followed with the Signora. It was one of those perfect mornings which occur as a respite from broken weather, when the air is windless and the light falls soft through haze on the horizon. As we broke into the lagoon behind the Redentore, the islands in front of us, St. Spirito, Poveglia, Malamocco, seemed as though they were just lifted from the sea-line. The Euganeans, far away to westward, were bathed in mist, and almost blent with the blue sky. Our four rowers put their backs into their work; and soon we reached the port of Malamocco, where a breeze from the Adriatic caught us sideways for a while. This is the largest of the breaches in the Lidi, or raised sand-reefs, which protect Venice from the sea: it affords an entrance to vessels of draught like the steamers of the Peninsular and Oriental Company. We crossed the dancing wavelets of the port; but when we passed under the lee of Pelestrina, the breeze failed, and the lagoon was once again a sheet of undulating glass. At St. Pietro on this island a halt was made to give the oarsmen wine, and here we saw the women at their cottage doorways making lace. The old lace industry of Venice has recently been revived. From Burano and Pelestrina cargoes of hand-made imitations of the ancient fabrics are sent at intervals to Jesurun's magazine at St. Marco. He is the chief *impresario* of the trade, employing hundreds of hands, and speculating for a handsome profit in the foreign market on the price he gives his workwomen.

Now we are well lost in the lagoons—Venice no longer visible behind; the Alps and Euganeans shrouded in a noonday haze; the lowlands at the mouth of Brenta marked by clumps of trees ephemerally faint in silver silhouette against the filmy, shimmering horizon. Form and colour have disappeared in light irradiated vapour of an opal hue. And yet instinctively we know that we are not at sea; the different quality of the water, the piles emerging here and there above the surface, the suggestion of coastlines scarcely felt in this infinity of lustre, all remind us that our voyage is confined to the charmed limits of an inland lake. At length the jutting headland of Palestrina was reached. We broke across the Porto di Chioggia, and saw Chioggia itself ahead—a huddled mass of houses low upon the water. One by one, as we rowed steadily, the fishing-boats passed by, emerging from their harbour for a twelve hours' cruise upon the open sea. In a long line they came, with variegated sails of orange, red, and saffron, curiously chequered at the corners, and cantled with devices in contrasted tints. A little land-breeze carried them forward. The lagoon reflected their deep colours till they reached the port. Then, slightly swerving eastward on their course, but still in single file, they took the sea and scattered, like beautiful bright-plumaged birds, who from a streamlet float into a lake, and find their way at large according as each wills.

The Signorino and Antonio, though want of wind obliged them to row the whole way from Venice, had reached Chioggia an hour before, and stood waiting to receive us on the quay. It is a quaint town this Chioggia, which has always lived a separate life from that of Venice. Language and race and customs have held the two populations apart from those distant years when Genoa and the Republic of St. Mark fought their duel to the death out in the Chioggian harbours, down to these days, when your Venetian gondolier will tell you that the Chioggoto loves his pipe more than his *donna* or his wife. The main canal is lined with substantial palaces, attesting to old wealth and comfort. But from Chioggia, even more than from Venice, the tide of modern luxury and traffic has retreated. The place is left to fishing folk and builders of the fishing craft, whose wharves still form the liveliest quarter. Wandering about its wide deserted courts and *calli*, we feel the spirit of the decadent Venetian nobility. Passages from Goldoni's and Casanova's *Memoirs* occur to our memory. It seems easy to realise what they wrote about the dishevelled gaiety and lawless license of Chioggia in the days of powder, sword-knot, and *soprani.* Baffo walks beside us in hypocritical composure of bag-wig and senatorial dignity, whispering unmentionable sonnets in his dialect of *Xe* and *Ga.* Somehow or another that last dotage of St. Mark's decrepitude is more recoverable by our fancy than the heroism of Pisani in the fourteenth century. From his prison in blockaded Venice the great admiral was sent forth on a forlorn hope, and blocked victorious Doria here with boats on which the nobles of the Golden Book had spent their fortunes. Pietro Doria boasted that with his own hands he would bridle the bronze horses of St. Mark. But now he found himself between the navy of Carlo Zeno in the Adriatic and the flotilla led by Vittore Pisani across the lagoon. It was in vain that the Republic of St. George strained every nerve to send him succour from the Ligurian sea; in vain that the lords of Padua kept opening communications with him from the mainland. From the 1st of January 1380 till the 21st of June the Venetians pressed the blockade ever closer, grappling their foemen in a grip that if relaxed one moment would have hurled him at their throats. The long and breathless struggle ended in the capitulation at Chioggia of what remained of Doria's forty-eight galleys and 14,000 men.

These great deeds are far away and hazy. The brief sentences of mediæval annalists bring them less near to us than the *chroniques scandaleuses* of good-for-nothing scoundrels, whose vulgar adventures might be revived at the present hour with scarce a change of setting. Such is the force of *intimité* in literature. And yet Baffo and Casanova are as much of the past as Doria and Pisani. It is only perhaps that the survival of decadence in all we see around us, forms a fitting framework for our recollections of their vividly described corruption.

Not far from the landing-place a balustraded bridge of ample breadth and large bravura manner spans the main canal. Like everything at Chioggia, it is dirty and has fallen from its first estate. Yet neither time nor injury can obliterate style or wholly degrade marble. Hard by the bridge there are two rival inns. At one of these we ordered a sea-dinner—crabs, cuttle-fishes, soles, and turbots—which we ate at a table in the open air. Nothing divided us from the street except a row of Japanese privet-bushes in hooped tubs. Our banquet soon assumed a somewhat unpleasant similitude to that of Dives; for the Chioggoti, in all stages of decrepitude and squalor, crowded round to beg for scraps—indescribable old women, enveloped in their own petticoats thrown over their heads; girls hooded with sombre black mantles; old men wrinkled beyond recognition by their nearest relatives; jabbering, half-naked boys; slow, slouching fishermen with clay pipes in their mouths and philosophical acceptance on their sober foreheads.

That afternoon the gondola and sandolo were lashed

together side by side. Two sails were raised, and in this lazy fashion we stole homewards, faster or slower according as the breeze freshened or slackened, landing now and then on islands, sauntering along the sea walls which bulwark Venice from the Adriatic, and singing—those at least of us who had the power to sing. Four of our Venetians had trained voices and memories of inexhaustible music. Over the level water, with the ripple plashing at our keel, their songs went abroad, and mingled with the failing day. The barcaroles and serenades peculiar to Venice were, of course, in harmony with the occasion. But some transcripts from classical operas were even more attractive through the dignity with which these men invested them. By the peculiarity of their treatment the *recitativo* of the stage assumed a solemn movement, marked in rhythm, which removed it from the commonplace into antiquity, and made me understand how cultivated music may pass back by natural, unconscious transition into the realm of popular melody.

The sun sank, not splendidly, but quietly in banks of clouds above the Alps. Stars came out, uncertainly at first, and then in strength, reflected on the sea. The men of the Dogana watch-boat challenged us and let us pass. Madonna's lamp was twinkling from her shrine upon the harbour-pile. The city grew before us. Stealing into Venice in that calm—stealing silently and shadowlike, with scarce a ruffle of the water, the masses of the town emerging out of darkness into twilight, till San Giorgio's gun boomed with a flash athwart our stern, and the gas-lamps of the Piazzetta swam into sight; all this was like a long enchanted chapter of romance. And now the music of our men had sunk to one faint whistling from Eustace of tunes in harmony with whispers at the prow.

Then came the steps of the Palazzo Venier and the deep-scented darkness of the garden. As we passed through to supper, I plucked a spray of yellow Banksia rose, and put it in my buttonhole. The dew was on its burnished leaves, and evening had drawn forth its perfume.

IV. MORNING RAMBLES

A story is told of Poussin, the French painter, that when he was asked why he would not stay in Venice, he replied, 'If I stay here, I shall become a colourist!' A somewhat similar tale is reported of a fashionable English decorator. While on a visit to friends in Venice, he avoided every building which contains a Tintoretto, averring that the sight of Tintoretto's pictures would injure his carefully trained taste. It is probable that neither anecdote is strictly true. Yet there is a certain epigrammatic point in both; and I have often speculated whether even Venice could have so warped the genius of Poussin as to shed one ray of splendour on his canvases, or whether even Tintoretto could have so sublimed the prophet of Queen Anne as to make him add dramatic passion to a London drawing-room. Anyhow, it is exceedingly difficult to escape from colour in the air of Venice, or from Tintoretto in her buildings. Long, delightful mornings may be spent in the enjoyment of the one and the pursuit of the other by folk who have no classical or pseudo-mediæval theories to oppress them.

Tintoretto's house, though changed, can still be visited. It formed part of the Fondamenta di Mori, so called from having been the quarter assigned to Moorish traders in Venice. A spirited carving of a turbaned Moor leading a camel charged with merchandise remains above the water-line of a neighbouring building; and all about the crumbling walls sprout flowering weeds—samphire and snapdragon and the spiked sampanula, which shoots a spire of sea-blue stars from chinks of Istrian stone.

The house stands opposite the Church of Santa Maria dell' Orto, where Tintoretto was buried, and where four of his chief masterpieces are to be seen. This church, swept and garnished, is a triumph of modern Italian restoration. They have contrived to make it as commonplace as human ingenuity could manage. Yet no malice of ignorant industry can obscure the treasures it contains—the pictures of Cima, Gian Bellini, Palma, and the four Tintorettos, which form its crowning glory. Here the master may be studied in four of his chief moods: as the painter of tragic passion and movement, in the huge 'Last Judgment'; as the painter of impossibilities, in the 'Vision of Moses upon Sinai'; as the painter of purity and tranquil pathos, in the 'Miracle of St. Agnes'; as the painter of Biblical history brought home to daily life, in the 'Presentation of the Virgin.' Without leaving the Madonna dell' Orto, a student can explore his genius in all its depth and breadth; comprehend the enthusiasm he excites in those who seek, as the essentials of art, imaginative boldness and sincerity; understand what is meant by adversaries who maintain that, after all, Tintoretto was but an inspired Gustave Doré. Between that quiet canvas of the 'Presentation,' so modest in its cool greys and subdued gold, and the tumult of flying, running, ascending figures in the 'Judgment,' what an interval there is! How strangely the white lamb-like maiden, kneeling beside her lamb in the picture of St. Agnes, contrasts with the dusky gorgeousness of the Hebrew women despoiling themselves of jewels for the golden calf! Comparing these several manifestations of creative power, we feel ourselves in the grasp of a painter who was essentially a poet, one for whom his art was the medium for expressing before all things thought and passion. Each picture is executed in the manner suited to its tone of feeling, the key of its conception.

Elsewhere than in the Madonna dell' Orto there are more distinguished single examples of Tintoretto's realising faculty. 'The Last Supper' in San Giorgio, for instance, and the 'Adoration of the Shepherds' in the Scuola di San Rocco, illustrate his unique power of presenting sacred history in a novel, romantic framework of familiar things. The commonplace circumstances of ordinary life have been employed to pourtray in the one case a lyric of mysterious splendour; in the other an idyll of infinite sweetness. Divinity shines through the rafters of that upper chamber, where round a low large table the Apostles are assembled in a group translated from the social customs of the painter's days. Divinity is shed upon the straw-spread manger, where Christ lies sleeping in the loft, with shepherds crowding through the room beneath.

A studied contrast between the simplicity and repose of the central figure and the tumult of passions in the multitude around, may be observed in the 'Miracle of St. Agnes.' It is this which gives dramatic vigour to the composition. But the same effect is carried to its highest fulfilment, with even a loftier beauty, in the episode of Christ before the judgment-seat of Pilate, at San Rocco. Of all Tintoretto's religious pictures, that is the most profoundly felt, the most majestic. No other artist succeeded as he has here succeeded in presenting to us God incarnate. For this Christ is not merely the just man, innocent, silent before his accusers. The stationary, white-draped figure, raised high above the agitated crowd, with tranquil forehead slightly bent, facing his perplexed and fussy judge, is more than man. We cannot say perhaps precisely why he is divine. But Tintoretto has made us feel that he is. In other words, his treatment of the high theme chosen by him has been adequate.

We must seek the Scuola di San Rocco for examples of Tintoretto's liveliest imagination. Without ceasing to be Italian in his attention to harmony and grace, he far exceeded the masters of his nation in the power of suggesting what is weird, mysterious, upon the borderland of the grotesque. And of this quality there are three remarkable instances in the Scuola.

No one but Tintoretto could have evoked the fiend in his 'Temptation of Christ.' It is an indescribable hermaphroditic genius, the genius of carnal fascination, with outspread downy rose-plumed wings and flaming bracelets on the full but sinewy arms, who kneels and lifts aloft great stones, smiling entreatingly to the sad, grey Christ seated beneath a rugged penthouse of the desert. No one again but Tintoretto could have dashed the hot lights of that fiery sunset in such quivering flakes upon the golden flesh of Eve, half hidden among laurels, as she stretches forth the fruit of the Fall to shrinking Adam. No one but Tintoretto, till we come to Blake, could have imagined yonder Jonah, summoned by the beck of God from the whale's belly. The monstrous fish rolls over in the ocean, blowing portentous vapour from his trump-shaped nostril. The prophet's beard descends upon his naked breast in hoary ringlets to the girdle. He has forgotten the past peril of the deep, although the whale's jaws yawned around him. Between him and the outstretched finger of Jehovah calling him again to life, there runs a spark of unseen spiritual electricity.

To comprehend Tintoretto's touch upon the pastoral idyll we must turn our steps to San Giorgio again, and pace those meadows by the running river in company with his 'Manna-Gatherers.' Or we may seek the Accademia, and notice how he here has varied the 'Temptation of Adam by Eve,' choosing a less tragic motive of seduction than the one so powerfully rendered at San Rocco. Or in the Ducal Palace we may take our station, hour by hour, before the 'Marriage of Bacchus and Ariadne.' It is well to leave the very highest achievements of art untouched by criticism, undescribed. And in this picture we have the most perfect of all modern attempts to realise an antique myth—more perfect than Raphael's 'Galatea,' or Titian's 'Meeting of Bacchus with Ariadne,' or Botticelli's 'Birth of Venus from the Sea.' It may suffice to marvel at the slight effect which melodies so powerful and so direct as these produce upon the ordinary public. Sitting, as is my wont, one Sunday morning, opposite the 'Bacchus,' four Germans with a cicerone sauntered by. The subject was explained to them. They waited an appreciable space of time. Then the youngest opened his lips and spake: '*Bacchus war der Wein-Gott.*' And they all moved heavily away. *Bos locutus est.* 'Bacchus was the wine-god.' This, apparently, is what a picture tells to one man. To another it presents divine harmonies, perceptible indeed in nature, but here by the painter-poet for the first time brought together and cadenced in a work of art. For another it is perhaps the hieroglyph of pent-up passions and desired impossibilities. For yet another it may only mean the unapproachable inimitable triumph of consummate craft.

Tintoretto, to be rightly understood, must be sought all over Venice—in the church as well as the Scuola di San Rocco; in the 'Temptation of St. Anthony at St. Trovaso no less than in the Temptations of Eve and Christ; in the decorative pomp of the Sala del Senato, and in the Paradisal vision of the Sala del Gran Consiglio. Yet, after all, there is one of his most characteristic moods, to appreciate which fully we return to the Madonna dell' Orto. I have called him 'the painter of impossibilities.' At rare moments he rendered them possible by sheer imaginative force. If we wish to realise this phase of his creative power, and to measure our own subordination to his genius in its most hazardous enterprise, we must spend much time in the choir of this church. Lovers of art who mistrust this play of the audacious fancy—aiming at sublimity in supersensual regions, sometimes attaining to it by stupendous effort or authentic revelation, not seldom shrinking to the verge of bathos, and demanding the assistance of interpretative sympathy in the spectator—such men will not take the point of view required of them by Tintoretto in his boldest flights, in the 'Worship of the Golden Calf' and in the 'Destruction of the World by Water.' It is for them to ponder well the flying archangel with the scales of judgment in his hand, and the seraph-charioted Jehovah enveloping Moses upon Sinai in lightnings.

The gondola has had a long rest. Were Francesco but a little more impatient, he might be wondering what had become of the padrone. I bid him turn, and we are soon gliding into the Sacca della Misericordia. This is a protected float, where the wood which comes from Cadore and the hills of the Ampezzo is stored in spring. Yonder square white house standing out to sea, fronting Murano and the Alps, they call the Casa degli Spiriti. No one cares to inhabit it; for here, in old days, it was the wont of the Venetians to lay their dead for a night's rest before their final journey to the graveyard of San Michele. So many generations of dead folk had made that house their inn, that it is now no fitting home for living men. San Michele is the island close before Murano, where the Lombardi built one of their most romantically graceful churches of pale Istrian stone, and where the Campo Santo has for centuries received the dead into its oozy clay. The cemetery is at present undergoing restoration. Its state of squalor and abandonment to cynical disorder makes one feel how fitting for Italians would be the custom of cremation. An island in the lagoons devoted to funeral pyres is a solemn and ennobling conception. This graveyard, with its ruinous walls, its mangy riot of unwholesome weeds, its corpses festering in slime beneath neglected slabs in hollow chambers, and the mephitic wash of poisoned waters that surround it, inspires the horror of disgust.

The morning has not lost its freshness. Antelao and Tofana, guarding the vale above Cortina, show faint streaks of snow upon their amethyst. Little clouds hang in the still autumn sky. There are men dredging for shrimps and crabs through shoals uncovered by the ebb. Nothing can be lovelier, more resting to eyes tired with pictures, than this tranquil, sunny expanse of the lagoon. As we round the point of the Bersaglio, new landscapes of island and Alp and low-lying mainland move into sight at every slow stroke of the oar. A luggage-train comes lumbering along the railway-bridge, puffing white smoke into the placid blue. Then we strike down Cannaregio, and I muse upon processions of kings and generals and noble strangers, entering Venice by this waterpath from Mestre, before the Austrians built their causeway for the trains. Some of the rare scraps of fresco upon house fronts, still to be seen in Venice, are left in Cannaregio. They are chiaroscuro allegories in a bold bravura-manner of the sixteenth century. From these and from a few rosy fragments on the Fondaco dei Tedeschi, the Fabbriche Nuove, and precious fading figures in a certain courtyard near San Stefano, we form some notion how Venice looked when all her palaces were painted. Pictures by Gentile Bellini, Mansueti, and Carpaccio help the fancy in this work of restoration. And here and there, in back canals, we come across coloured sections of old buildings, capped by true Venetian chimneys, which for a moment seem to realise our dream.

A morning with Tintoretto might well be followed by a morning with Carpaccio or Bellini. But space is wanting in these pages. Nor would it suit the manner of this medley to hunt the Lombardi through palaces and churches, pointing out their singularities of violet and yellow panellings in marble, the dignity of their wide-opened arches, or the delicacy of their shallow chiselled traceries in cream-white Istrian stone. It is enough to indicate the goal of many a pleasant pilgrimage: warrior angels of Vivarini and Bassaiti hidden in a dark chapel of the Frari; Fra Francesco's fantastic orchard of fruits and flowers in distant St. Francesco della Vigna; the golden Gian Bellini in St. Zaccaria; Palma's majestic St. Barbara in St. Maria Formosa; San Giobbe's wealth of sculptured frieze and floral scroll; the Ponte di Paradiso, with its Gothic arch; the painted plates in the Museo Civico; and palace after palace, loved for some quaint piece of tracery, some moulding of mediæval symbolism, some fierce impossible Renaissance freak of fancy.

Rather than prolong this list, I will tell a story which drew me one day past the Public Gardens to the Metropolitan Church of Venice, San Pietro di Castello. The novella is related by Bandello. It has, as will be noticed, points of similarity to that of *Romeo and Juliet.*

V. A VENETIAN NOVELLA

At the time when Carpaccio and Gentile Bellini were painting those handsome youths in tight jackets, parti-coloured hose, and little round caps placed awry upon their shocks of well-combed hair, there lived in Venice two noblemen, Messer Pietro and Messer Paolo, whose palaces fronted each other on the Grand Canal. Messer Paolo was a widower, with one married daughter, and an only son of twenty years or thereabouts, named Gerado. Messer Pietro's wife was still living; and this couple had but one child, a daughter, called Elena, of exceeding beauty, aged fourteen. Gerado, as is the wont of gallants, was paying his addresses to a certain lady, and nearly every day he had to cross the Grand Canal in his gondola, and to pass beneath the house of Elena on his way to visit his Dulcinea; for this lady lived some distance up a little canal on which the western side of Messer Pietro's palace looked.

Now it so happened that at the very time when the story opens, Messer Pietro's wife fell ill and died, and Elena was left alone at home with her father and her old nurse. Across the little canal of which I spoke there dwelt another nobleman with four daughters, between the years of seventeen and twenty-one. Messer Pietro, desiring to provide amusement for poor little Elena, besought this gentleman that his daughters might come on feast-days to play with her. For you must know that, except on festivals of the Church, the custom of Venice required that gentlewomen should remain closely shut within the private apartments of their dwellings. His request was readily granted; and on the next feast-day the five girls began to play at ball together for forfeits in the great saloon, which opened with its row of Gothic arches and balustraded balcony upon the Grand Canal. The four sisters, meanwhile, had other thoughts than for the game. One or other of them, and sometimes three together, would let the ball drop, and run to the balcony to gaze upon their gallants, passing up and down in gondolas below; and then they would drop flowers or ribands for tokens. Which negligence of theirs annoyed Elena much; for she thought only of the game. Wherefore she scolded them in childish wise, and one of them made answer, 'Elená, if you only knew how pleasant it is to play as we are playing on this balcony, you would not care so much for ball and forfeits!'

On one of those feast-days, the four sisters were prevented from keeping their little friend company. Elena, with nothing to do, and feeling melancholy, leaned upon the window-sill which overlooked the narrow canal. And it chanced that just then Gerado, on his way to Dulcinea, went by; and Elena looked down at him, as she had seen those sisters look at passers-by. Gerado caught her eye, and glances passed between them, and Gerado's gondolier, bending from the poop, said to his master, 'O master! methinks that gentle maiden is better worth your wooing than Dulcinea.' Gerado pretended to pay no heed to these words; but after rowing a little way, he bade the man turn, and they went slowly back beneath the window. This time, Elena, thinking to play the game which her four friends had played, took from her hair a clove carnation and let it fall close to Gerado on the cushion of the gondola. He raised the flower and put it to his lips, acknowledging the courtesy with a grave bow. But the perfume of the clove and the beauty of Elena in that moment took possession of his heart together, and straightway he forgot Dulcinea.

As yet he knew not who Elena was. Nor is this wonderful; for the daughters of Venetian nobles were but rarely seen or spoken of. But the thought of her haunted him awake and sleeping; and every feast-day when there was the chance of seeing her, he rowed his gondola beneath her windows. And there she appeared to him in company with her four friends; the five girls clustering together like sister roses beneath the pointed windows of the Gothic balcony. Elena, on her side, had no thought of love; for of love she had heard no one speak. But she took pleasure in the game those friends had taught her, of leaning from the balcony to watch Gerado. He meanwhile grew love-sick and impatient, wondering how he might declare his passion. Until one day it happened that, walking through a lane or *calle* which skirted Messer Pietro's palace, he caught sight of Elena's nurse, who was knocking at the door, returning from some shopping she had made. This nurse had been his own nurse in childhood; therefore he remembered her, and cried aloud, 'Nurse, nurse!' But the old woman did not hear him, and passed into the house and shut the door behind her. Whereupon Gerado, greatly moved, still called to her, and when he reached the door began to knock upon it violently. And whether it was the agitation of finding himself at last so near the wish of his heart, or whether the pains of waiting for his love had weakened him, I know not; but, while he knocked, his senses left him, and he fell fainting in the doorway. Then the nurse recognised the youth to whom she had given suck, and brought him into the courtyard by the help of handmaidens, and Elena came down and gazed upon him. The house was now full of bustle, and Messer Pietro heard the noise, and seeing the son of his neighbour in so piteous a plight, he caused Gerado to be laid upon a bed. But for all they could do with him, he recovered not from his swoon. And after a while force was that they should place him in a gondola and ferry him across to his father's house. The nurse went with him, and informed Messer Paolo of what had happened. Doctors were sent for, and the whole family gathered round Gerado's bed. After a while he revived a little; and thinking himself still upon the doorstep of Pietro's palace, called again, 'Nurse, nurse!' She was near at hand, and would have spoken to him. But while he summoned his senses to his aid, he became gradually aware of his own kinsfolks, and dissembled the secret of his grief. They beholding him in better cheer, departed on their several ways, and the nurse still sat alone beside him. Then he explained to her what he had at heart, and how he was in love with a maiden whom he had seen on feast-days in the house of Messer Pietro. But still he knew not Elena's name; and she, thinking it impossible that such a child had inspired this passion, began to marvel which of the four sisters it was Gerado loved. Then they appointed the next Sunday, when all the five girls should be together, for Gerado, by some sign, as he passed beneath the window, to make known to the old nurse his lady.

Elena, meanwhile, who had watched Gerado lying still and pale in swoon beneath her on the pavement of the palace, felt the stirring of a new unknown emotion in her soul. When Sunday came, she devised excuses for keeping her four friends away, bethinking her that she might see him once again alone, and not betray the agitation which she dreaded. This ill suited the schemes of the nurse, who nevertheless was forced to be content. But after dinner, seeing how restless was the girl, and how she came and went, and ran a thousand times to the balcony, the nurse began to wonder whether Elena herself were not in love with some one. So she feigned to sleep, but placed herself within sight of the window. And soon Gerado came by in his gondola; and Elena, who was prepared, threw to him her nosegay. The watchful nurse had risen, and peeping behind the girl's shoulder, saw at a glance how matters stood. Thereupon she began to scold her charge, and say, 'Is this a fair and comely thing to stand all day at balconies and throw flowers at passers-by? Woe to you if your father should come to know of this! He would make you wish yourself among the dead!' Elena, sore troubled at her nurse's rebuke, turned and threw her arms about her neck, and called her 'Nanna!' as the wont is of Venetian children. Then she told the old woman how she had learned that game from the four sisters, and how she thought it was not different, but far more pleasant, than the game of forfeits; whereupon her nurse spoke gravely, explaining what love is, and how that love should lead to marriage, and bidding her search her own heart if haply she could choose Gerado for her husband. There was no reason, as she knew, why Messer Paolo's son should not mate with Messer Pietro's daughter. But being a romantic creature, as many women are, she resolved to bring the match about in secret.

Elena took little time to reflect, but told her nurse that she was willing, if Gerado willed it too, to have him for her husband. Then went the nurse and made the young man know how matters stood, and arranged with him a day, when Messer Pietro should be in the Council of the Pregadi, and the servants of the palace otherwise employed, for him to come and meet his Elena. A glad man was Gerado, nor did he wait to think how better it would be to ask the hand of Elena in marriage from her father. But when the day arrived he sought the nurse, and she took him to a chamber in the palace, where there stood an image of the blessed Virgin. Elena was there, pale and timid; and when the lovers clasped hands, neither found many words to say. But the nurse bade them take heart, and leading them before Our Lady, joined their hands, and made Gerado place his ring on his bride's finger. After this fashion were Gerado and Elena wedded. And for some while, by the assistance of the nurse, they dwelt together in much love and solace, meeting often as occasion offered.

Messer Paolo, who knew nothing of these things, took thought meanwhile for his son's career. It was the season when the Signiory of Venice sends a fleet of galleys to Beirut with merchandise; and the noblemen may bid for the hiring of a ship, and charge it with wares, and send whomsoever they list as factor in their interest. One of these galleys, then, Messer Paolo engaged, and told his son that he had appointed him to journey with it and increase their wealth. 'On thy return, my son,' he said, 'we will bethink us of a wife for thee.' Gerado, when he heard these words, was sore troubled, and first he told his father roundly that he would not go, and flew off in the twilight to pour out his perplexities to Elena. But she, who was prudent and of gentle soul, besought him to obey his father in this thing, to the end, moreover, that, having done his will and increased his wealth, he might afterwards unfold the story of their secret marriage. To these good counsels, though loth, Gerado consented. His father was overjoyed at his son's repentance. The galley was straightway laden with merchandise, and Gerado set forth on his voyage.

The trip to Beirut and back lasted usually six months or at the most seven. Now when Gerado had been some six months away, Messer Pietro, noticing how fair his daughter was, and how she had grown into womanhood, looked about him for a husband for her. When he had found a youth suitable in birth and wealth and years, he called for Elena, and told her that the day had been appointed for her marriage. She, alas! knew not what to answer. She feared to tell her father that she was already married, for she knew not whether this would please Gerado. For the same reason she dreaded to throw herself upon the kindness of Messer Paolo. Nor was her nurse of any help in counsel; for the old woman repented her of what she had done, and had good cause to believe that, even if the marriage with Gerado were accepted by the two fathers, they would punish her for her own part in the affair. Therefore she bade Elena wait on fortune, and hinted to her that, if the worst came to the worst, no one need know she had been wedded with the ring to Gerado. Such weddings, you must know, were binding; but till they had been blessed by the Church they had not taken the force of a religious sacrament. And this is still the case in Italy among the common folk, who will say of a man, '*Si, è ammogliato; ma il matrimonio non è stato benedetto*' ('Yes, he has taken a wife, but the marriage has not yet been blessed').

So the days flew by in doubt and sore distress for Elena. Then on the night before her wedding, she felt that she could bear this life no longer. But having no poison, and being afraid to pierce her bosom with a knife, she lay down on her bed alone, and tried to die by holding in her breath. A mortal swoon came over her; her senses fled; the life in her remained suspended. And when her nurse came next morning to call her, she found poor Elena cold as a corpse. Messer Pietro and all the household rushed at the nurse's cries into the room, and they all saw Elena stretched dead upon her bed undressed. Physicians were called, who made theories to explain the cause of death. But all believed that she was really dead, beyond all help of art or medicine. Nothing remained but to carry her to church for burial instead of marriage. Therefore, that very evening, a funeral procession was formed, which moved by torchlight up the Grand Canal, along the Riva, past the blank walls of the Arsenal, to the Campo before San Pietro in Castello. Elena lay beneath the black felze in one gondola, with a priest beside her praying, and other boats followed bearing mourners. Then they laid her in a marble chest outside the church, and all departed, still with torches burning, to their homes.

Now it so fell out that upon that very evening Gerado's galley had returned from Syria, and was anchoring within the port of Lido, which looks across to the island of Castello. It was the gentle custom of Venice at that time that, when a ship arrived from sea, the friends of those on board at once came out to welcome them, and take and give the news. Therefore many noble youths and other citizens were on the deck of Gerado's galley, making merry with him over the safe conduct of his voyage. Of one of these he asked, 'Whose is yonder funeral procession returning from San Pietro?' The young man made answer, 'Alas, for poor Elena, Messer Pietro's daughter! She should have been married this day. But death took her, and to-night they buried her in the marble monument outside the church.' A woeful man was Gerado, hearing suddenly this news, and knowing what his dear wife must have suffered ere she died. Yet he restrained himself, daring not to disclose his anguish, and waited till his friends had left the galley. Then he called to him the captain of the oarsmen, who was his friend, and unfolded to him all the story of his love and sorrow, and said that he must go that night and see his wife once more, if even he should have to break her tomb. The captain tried to dissuade him, but in vain. Seeing him so obstinate, he resolved not to desert Gerado. The two men took one of the galley's boats, and rowed together toward San Pietro. It was past midnight when they reached the Campo and broke the marble sepulchre asunder. Pushing back its lid, Gerado descended into the grave and abandoned himself upon the body of his Elena. One who had seen them at that moment could not have said which of the two was dead and which was living—Elena or her husband. Meantime the captain of the oarsmen, fearing lest the watch (set by the Masters of the Night to keep the peace of Venice) might arrive, was calling on Gerado to come back. Gerado heeded him no whit. But at the last, compelled by his entreaties, and as it were astonied, he arose, bearing his wife's corpse in his arms, and carried her clasped against his bosom to the boat, and laid her therein, and sat down by her side and kissed her frequently, and suffered not his friend's remonstrances. Force was for the captain, having brought himself into this scrape, that he should now seek refuge by the nearest way from justice. Therefore he hoved gently from the bank, and plied his oar, and brought the gondola apace into the open waters. Gerado still clasped Elena, dying husband by dead wife. But the sea-breeze freshened towards daybreak; and the captain looking down upon that pair, and bringing to their faces the light of his boat's lantern, judged their case not desperate at all. On Elena's cheek there was a flush of life less deadly even than the pallor of Gerado's forehead. Thereupon the good man called aloud, and Gerado started from his grief; and both together they chafed the hands and feet of Elena; and, the sea-breeze aiding with its saltness, they awoke in her the spark of life.

Dimly burned the spark. But Gerado, being aware of it, became a man again. Then, having taken counsel with the captain, both resolved to bear her to that brave man's mother's house. A bed was soon made ready, and food was brought; and after due time, she lifted up her face and knew Gerado. The peril of the grave was past, but thought had now to be taken for the future. Therefore Gerado, leaving his wife to the captain's mother, rowed back to the galley and prepared to meet his father. With good store of merchandise and with great gains from his traffic, he arrived in that old palace on the Grand Canal. Then having opened to Messer Paolo the matters of his journey, and shown him how he had fared, and set before him tables of disbursements and receipts, he seized the moment of his father's gladness. 'Father,' he said, and as he spoke he knelt upon his knees, 'Father, I bring you not good store of merchandise and bags of gold alone; I bring you also a wedded wife, whom I have saved this night from death.' And when the old man's surprise was quieted, he told him the whole story. Now Messer Paolo, desiring no better than that his son should wed the heiress of his neighbour, and knowing well that Messer Pietro would make great joy receiving back his daughter from the grave, bade Gerado in haste take rich apparel and clothe Elena therewith, and fetch her home. These things were swiftly done; and after evenfall Messer Pietro was bidden to grave business in his neighbour's palace. With heavy heart he came, from a house of mourning to a house of gladness. But there, at the banquet-table's head, he saw his dead child Elena alive, and at her side a husband. And when the whole truth had been declared, he not only kissed and embraced the pair who knelt before him, but of his goodness forgave the nurse, who in her turn came trembling to his feet. Then fell there joy and bliss in overmeasure that night upon both palaces of the Canal Grande. And with the morrow the Church blessed the spousals which long since had been on both sides vowed and consummated.

VI. ON THE LAGOONS

The mornings are spent in study, sometimes among pictures, sometimes in the Marcian Library, or again in those vast convent chambers of the Frari, where the archives of Venice load innumerable shelves. The afternoons invite us to a further flight upon the water. Both sandolo and gondola await our choice, and we may sail or row, according as the wind and inclination tempt us.

Yonder lies San Luzzaro, with the neat red buildings of the Armenian convent. The last oleander blossoms shine rosy pink above its walls against the pure blue sky as we glide into the little harbour. Boats piled with coal-black grapes block the landing-place, for the Padri are gathering their vintage from the Lido. and their presses run with new wine. Eustace and I have not come to revive memories of Byron—that curious patron-saint of the Armenian colony—or to inspect the printing-press, which issues books of little value for our studies. It is enough to pace the terrace, and linger half an hour beneath the low broad arches of the alleys pleached with vines, through which the domes and towers of Venice rise more beautiful by distance.

Malamocco lies considerably farther, and needs a full hour of stout rowing to reach it. Alighting there, we cross the narrow strip of land, and find ourselves upon the huge sea-wall—block piled on block—of Istrian stone in tiers and ranks, with cunning breathing-places for the waves to wreak their fury on and foam their force away in fretful waste. The very existence of Venice may be said to depend sometimes on these *murazzi*, which were finished at an immense cost by the Republic in the days of its decadence. The enormous monoliths which compose them had to be brought across the Adriatic in sailing vessels. Of all the Lidi, that of Malamocco is the weakest; and here, if anywhere, the sea might effect an entrance into the lagoon. Our gondoliers told us of some places where the *murazzi* were broken in a gale, or *sciroccale*, not very long ago. Lying awake in Venice, when the wind blows hard, one hears the sea thundering upon its sandy barrier, and blesses God for the *murazzi*. On such a night it happened once to me to dream a dream of Venice overwhelmed by water. I saw the billows roll across the smooth lagoon like a gigantic Eager. The Ducal Palace crumbled, and San Marco's domes went down. The Campanile rocked and shivered like a reed. And all along the Grand Canal the palaces swayed helpless, tottering to their fall, while boats piled high with men and women strove to stem the tide, and save themselves from those impending ruins. It was a mad dream, born of the sea's roar and Tintoretto's painting. But this afternoon no such visions are suggested. The sea sleeps, and in the moist autumn air we break tall branches of the seeded yellowing samphire from hollows of the rocks, and bear them homeward in a wayward bouquet mixed with cobs of Indian-corn.

Fusina is another point for these excursions. It lies at the mouth of the Canal di Brenta, where the mainland ends in marsh and meadows, intersected by broad renes. In spring the ditches bloom with fleurs-de-lys; in autumn they take sober colouring from lilac daises and the delicate sea-lavender. Scores of tiny plants are turning scarlet on the brown moist earth; and when the sun goes down behind the Euganean hills, his crimson canopy of cloud, reflected on these shallows, muddy shoals, and wilderness of matted weeds, converts the common earth into a fairy-land of fabulous dyes. Purple, violet, and rose are spread around us. In front stretches the lagoon, tinted with a pale light from the east, and beyond this pallid mirror shines Venice—a long low broken line, touched with the softest roseate flush. Ere we reach the Giudecca on our homeward way, sunset has faded. The western skies have clad themselves in green, barred with dark fire-rimmed clouds. The Euganean hills stand like stupendous pyramids, Egyptian, solemn, against a lemon space on the horizon. The far reaches of the lagoons, the Alps, and islands assume those tones of glowing lilac which are the supreme beauty of Venetian evening. Then, at last, we see the first lamps glitter on the Zattere. The quiet of the night has come.

Words cannot be formed to express the endless varieties of Venetian sunset. The most magnificent follow after wet stormy days, when the west breaks suddenly into a labyrinth of fire, when chasms of clear turquoise heavens emerge, and horns of flame are flashed to the zenith, and unexpected splendours scale the fretted clouds, step over step, stealing along the purple caverns till the whole dome throbs. Or, again, after a fair day, a change of weather approaches, and high, infinitely high, the skies are woven over with a web of half-transparent cirrus-clouds. These in the afterglow blush crimson, and through their rifts the depth of heaven is of a hard and gemlike blue, and all the water turns to rose beneath them. I remember one such evening on the way back from Torcello. We were well out at sea between Mazzorbo and Murano. The ruddy arches overhead were reflected without interruption in the waveless ruddy lake below. Our black boat was the only dark spot in this sphere of splendour. We seemed to hang suspended; and such as this, I fancied, must be the feeling of an insect caught in the heart of a fiery-petalled rose. Yet not these melodramatic sunsets alone are beautiful. Even more exquisite, perhaps, are the lagoons, painted in monochrome of greys, with just one touch of pink upon a western cloud, scattered in ripples here and there on the waves below, reminding us that day has passed and evening come. And beautiful again are the calm settings of fair weather, when sea and sky alike are cheerful, and the topmost blades of the lagoon grass, peeping from the shallows, glance like emeralds upon the surface. There is no deep stirring of the spirit in a symphony of light and colour; but purity, peace, and freshness make their way into our hearts.

VII. AT THE LIDO

Of all these afternoon excursions, that to the Lido is most frequent. It has two points for approach. The more distant is the little station of San Nicoletto, at the mouth of the Porto. With an ebb-tide, the water of the lagoon runs past the mulberry gardens of this hamlet like a river. There is here a grove of acacia-trees, shadowy and dreamy, above deep grass, which even in Italian summer does not wither. The Riva is fairly broad, forming a promenade, where one may conjure up the personages of a century ago. For San Nicoletto used to be a fashionable resort before the other points of Lido had been occupied by pleasure-seekers. An artist even now will select its old-world quiet, leafy shade, and prospect through the islands of Vignole and Sant' Erasmo to snow-touched peaks of Antelao and Tofana, rather than the glare and bustle and extended view of Venice which its rival Sant' Elisabetta offers.

But when we want a plunge into the Adriatic, or a stroll along smooth sands, or a breath of genuine sea-breeze, or a handful of horned poppies from the dunes, or a lazy half-hour's contemplation of a limitless horizon flecked with russet sails, then we seek Sant' Elisabetta. Our boat is left at the landing-place. We saunter across the island and back again. Antonio and Francesco wait and order wine, which we drink with them in the shade of the little *osteria's* wall.

A certain afternoon in May I well remember, for this visit to the Lido was marked by one of those apparitions which are as rare as they are welcome to the artist's soul. I have always held that in our modern life the only real equivalent for the antique mythopœic sense—that sense which enabled the Hellenic race to figure for themselves the powers of earth and air, streams and forests, and the presiding genii of places, under the forms of living human beings, is supplied by the appearance at some felicitous moment of a man or woman who impersonates for our imagination the essence of the beauty that environs us. It seems, at such a fortunate moment, as though we had been waiting for this revelation, although perchance the want of it had not been previously felt. Our sensations and perceptions test themselves at the touchstone of this living individuality. The keynote of the whole music dimly sounding in our ears is struck. A melody emerges, clear in form and excellent in rhythm. The landscapes we have painted on our brain no longer lack their central figure. The life proper to the complex conditions we have studied is discovered, and every detail, judged by this standard of vitality, falls into its right relations.

I had been musing long that day and earnestly upon the mystery of the lagoons, their opaline transparencies of air and water, their fretful risings and sudden subsidence into calm, the treacherousness of their shoals, the sparkle and the splendour of their sunlight. I had asked myself how would a Greek sculptor have personified the elementary deity of these salt-water lakes, so different in quality from the Ægean or Ionian sea? What would he find distinctive of their spirit? The Tritons of these shallows must be of other form and lineage than the fierce-eyed youth who blows his conch upon the curled crest of a wave, crying aloud to his comrades, as he bears the nymph away to caverns where the billows plunge in tideless instability.

We had picked up shells and looked for sea-horses on the Adriatic shore. Then we returned to give our boatmen wine beneath the vine-clad *pergola*. Four other men were there, drinking, and eating from a dish of fried fish set upon the coarse white linen cloth. Two of them soon rose and went away. Of the two who stayed, one was a large, middle-aged man; the other was still young. He was tall and sinewy, but slender, for these Venetians are rarely massive in their strength. Each limb is equally developed by the exercise of rowing upright, bending all the muscles to their stroke. Their bodies are elastically supple, with free sway from the hips and a mercurial poise upon the ankle. Stefano showed these qualities almost in exaggeration. The type in him was refined to its artistic perfection. Moreover, he was rarely in repose, but moved with a singular brusque grace. A black broad-brimmed hat was thrown back upon his matted *zazzera* of dark hair tipped with dusky brown. This shock of hair, cut in flakes, and falling wilfully, reminded me of the lagoon grass when it darkens in autumn upon uncovered shoals, and sunset gilds its sombre edges. Fiery grey eyes beneath it gazed intensely, with compulsive effluence of electricity. It was the wild glance of a Triton. Short blonde moustache, dazzling teeth, skin bronzed, but showing white and healthful through open front and sleeves of lilac shirt. The dashing sparkle of this animate splendour, who looked to me as though the sea-waves and the sun had made him in some hour of secret and unquiet rapture, was somehow emphasised by a curious dint dividing his square chin—a cleft that harmonised with smile on lip and steady flame in eyes. I hardly know what effect it would have upon a reader to compare eyes to opals. Yet Stefano's eyes, as they met mine, had the vitreous intensity of opals, as though the colour of Venetian waters were vitalised in them. This noticeable being had a rough, hoarse voice, which, to develop the parallel with a sea-god, might have screamed in storm or whispered raucous messages from crests of tossing billows.

I felt, as I looked, that here, for me at least, the mythopoem of the lagoons was humanised; the spirit of the salt-water lakes had appeared to me; the final touch of life emergent from nature had been given; I was satisfied; for I had seen a poem.

Then we rose, and wandered through the Jews' cemetery. It is a quiet place, where the flat gravestones, inscribed in Hebrew and Italian, lie deep in Lido sand, waved over with wild grass and poppies. I would fain believe that no neglect, but rather the fashion of this folk, had left the monuments of generations to be thus resumed by nature. Yet, knowing nothing of the history of this burial-ground, I dare not affirm so much. There is one outlying piece of the cemetery which seems to contradict my charitable interpretation. It is not far from San Nicoletto. No enclosure marks it from the unconsecrated dunes. Acacia-trees sprout amid the monuments, and break the tablets with their thorny shoots upthrusting from the soil. Where patriarchs and rabbis sleep for centuries, the fishers of the sea now wander, and defile these habitations of the dead:

> Corruption most abhorred
> Mingling itself with their renowned ashes.

Some of the gravestones have been used to fence the towing path; and one I saw, well carved with letters legible of Hebrew on fair Istrian marble, which roofed an open drain leading from the stable of a Christian dog.

VIII. A VENETIAN RESTAURANT

At the end of a long glorious day, unhappy is that mortal whom the Hermes of a cosmopolitan hotel, white-chokered and white-waistcoated, marshals to the Hades of the *table d'hôte*. The world has often been compared to an inn; but on my way down to this common meal I have, not unfrequently, felt fain to reverse the simile. From their separate stations, at the appointed hour, the guests like ghosts flit to a gloomy gas-lit chamber. They are of various speech and race, preoccupied with divers interests and cares. Necessity and the waiter drive them all to a sepulchral syssition, whereof the cook too frequently deserves that old Greek comic epithet—ᾅδου μάγειρος—cook of the Inferno. And just as we are told that in Charon's boat we shall not be allowed to pick our society, so here we must accept what fellowship the fates provide. An English spinster retailing paradoxes culled to-day from Ruskin's handbooks; an American citizen describing his jaunt in a gondola from the railway station; a German shopkeeper descanting in one breath on Baur's Bock and the beauties of Marcusplatz; an intelligent æsthete bent on working into clearness his own views of Carpaccio's genius; all these in turn, or all together, must be suffered gladly through well-nigh two long hours. Uncomforted in soul we rise from the expensive banquet; and how often rise from it unfed!

Far other be the doom of my own friends—of pious bards and genial companions, lovers of natural and lovely things! Nor for these do I desire a seat at Florian's marble tables, or a perch in Quadri's window, though the former supply dainty food, and the latter command a bird's-eye view of the Piazza. Rather would I lead them to a certain humble tavern on the Zattere. It is a quaint, low-built, unpretending little place, near a bridge, with a garden hard by which sends a cataract of honeysuckles sunward over a too-jealous wall. In front lies a Mediterranean steamer, which all day long has been discharging cargo. Gazing westward up Giudecca, masts and funnels bar the sun-set and the Paduan hills; and from a little front room of the *trattoria* the view is so marine that one keeps fancying oneself in some ship's cabin. Sea-captains sit and smoke beside their glass of grog in the pavilion and the *caffé*. But we do not seek their company at dinner-time. Our way lies under yonder arch, and up the narrow alley into a paved court. Here are oleanders in pots, and plants of Japanese spindle-wood in tubs; and from the walls beneath the window hang cages of all sorts of birds—a talking parrot, a whistling blackbird, goldfinches, canaries, linnets. Athos, the fat dog, who goes to market daily in a *barchetta* with his master, snuffs around. 'Where are Porthos and Aramis, my friend?' Athos does not take the joke; he only wags his stump of tail and pokes his nose into my hand. What a Tartufe's nose it is! Its bridge displays the full parade of leather-bound brass-nailed muzzle. But beneath, this muzzle is a patent sham. The frame does not even pretend to close on Athos' jaw, and the wise dog wears it like a decoration. A little further we meet that ancient grey cat, who has no discoverable name, but is famous for the sprightliness and grace with which she bears her eighteen years. Not far from the cat one is sure to find Carlo—the bird-like, bright-faced, close-cropped Venetian urchin, whose duty it is to trot backwards and forwards between the cellar and the dining-tables. At the end of the court we walk into the kitchen, where the black-capped little *padrone* and the gigantic white-capped *chef* are in close consultation. Here we have the privilege of inspecting the larder—fish of various sorts, meat, vegetables, several kinds of birds, pigeons, tordi, beccafichi, geese, wild ducks, chickens, woodcock, etc., according to the season. We select our dinner, and retire to eat it either in the court among the birds beneath the vines, or in the low dark room which occupies one side of it. Artists of many nationalities and divers ages frequent this house; and the talk arising from the several little tables, turns upon points of interest and beauty in the life and landscape of Venice. There can be no difference of opinion about the excellence of the *cuisine*, or about the reasonable charges of this *trattoria*. A soup of lentils, followed by boiled turbot or fried soles, beefsteak or mutton cutlets, tordi or beccafichi, with a salad, the whole enlivened with good red wine or Florio's Sicilian Marsala from the cask, costs about four francs. Gas is unknown in the establishment. There is no noise, no bustle, no brutality of waiters, no *ahurissement* of tourists. And when dinner is done, we can sit awhile over our cigarette and coffee, talking until the night invites us to a stroll along the Zattere or a *giro* in the gondola.

IX. NIGHT IN VENICE

Night in Venice! Night is nowhere else so wonderful, unless it be in winter among the high Alps. But the nights of Venice and the nights of the mountains are too different in kind to be compared.

There is the ever-recurring miracle of the full moon rising, before day is dead, behind San Giorgio, spreading a path of gold on the lagoon, which black boats traverse with the glow-worm lamp upon their prow; ascending the cloudless sky and silvering the domes of the Salute; pouring vitreous sheen upon the red lights of the Piazzetta; flooding the Grand Canal, and lifting the Rialto higher in ethereal whiteness; piercing but penetrating not the murky labyrinth of *rio* linked with *rio*, through which we wind in light and shadow, to reach once more the level glories and the luminous expanse of heaven beyond Misericordia.

This is the melodrama of Venetian moonlight; and if a single impression of the night has to be retained from one visit to Venice, those are fortunate who chance upon a full moon of fair weather. Yet I know not whether some quieter and soberer effects are not more thrilling. To-night, for example, the waning moon will rise late through veils of *scirocco*. Over the bridges of San Cristofore and San Gregorio, through the deserted Calle di Mezzo, my friend and I walk in darkness, pass the marble basements of the Salute, and push our way along its Riva to the point of the Dogana. We are out at sea alone, between the Canalozzo and the Giudecca. A moist wind ruffles the water and cools our forehead. It is so dark that we can only see San Giorgio by the light reflected on it from the Piazzetta. The same light climbs the Campanile of St. Mark, and shows the golden angel in a mystery of gloom. The only noise that reaches us is a confused hum from the Piazza. Sitting and musing there, the blackness of the water whispers in our ears a tale of death. And now we hear a splash of oars, and gliding through the darkness comes a single boat. One man leaps upon the landing-place without a word and disappears. There is another wrapped in a military cloak asleep. I see his face beneath me, pale and quiet. The *barcaruolo* turns the point in silence. From the darkness they came; into the darkness they have gone. It is only an ordinary incident of coast-guard service. But the spirit of the night has made a poem of it.

Even tempestuous and rainy weather, though melancholy enough, is never sordid here. There is no noise from carriage traffic in Venice, and the sea-wind preserves the purity and transparency of the atmosphere. It had been raining all day, but at evening came a partial clearing. I went down to the Molo, where the large reach of the lagoon was all moon-silvered, and San Giorgio Maggiore dark against the bluish sky, and Santa Maria della Salute domed with moon-irradiated pearl, and the wet slabs of the Riva shimmering in moonlight, the whole misty sky, with its clouds and stellar spaces, drenched in moonlight, nothing but moonlight sensible except the tawny flare of gas-lamps and the orange lights of gondolas afloat upon the waters. On such a night the very spirit of Venice is abroad. We feel why she is called Bride of the Sea.

Take another night. There had been a representation of Verdi's *Forza del Destino* at the Teatro Malibran. After midnight we walked homeward through the Merceria, crossed the Piazza, and dived into the narrow *calle* which leads to the *traghetto* of the Salute. It was a warm moist starless night, and there seemed no air to breathe in those narrow alleys. The gondolier was half asleep. Eustace called him as we jumped into his boat, and rang our *soldi* on the gunwale. Then he arose and turned the *ferro* round, and stood across towards the Salute. Silently, insensibly, from the oppression of confinement in the airless streets to the liberty and immensity of the water and the night we passed. It was but two minutes ere we touched the shore and said good-night, and went our way and left the ferryman. But in that brief passage he had opened our souls to everlasting things—the freshness, and the darkness, and the kindness of the brooding, all-enfolding night above the sea.

Italian Byways, 1883.

RICHARD JEFFERIES

1848–1887

MEADOW THOUGHTS

THE old house stood by the silent country road, secluded by many a long, long mile, and yet again secluded within the great walls of the garden. Often and often I rambled up to the milestone which stood under an oak, to look at the chipped inscription low down—'To London, 79 miles.' So far away, you see, that the very inscription was cut at the foot of the stone, since no man would be likely to want that information. It was half hidden by docks and nettles, despised and unnoticed. A broad land this seventy-nine miles—how many meadows and cornfields, hedges and woods, in that distance?—wide enough to seclude any house, to hide it like an acorn in the grass. Those who have lived all their lives in remote places do not feel the remoteness. No one else seemed to be conscious of the breadth that separated the place from the great centre, but it was, perhaps, that consciousness which deepened the solitude to me. It made the silence more still; the shadows of the oaks yet slower in their movement; everything more earnest. To convey a full impression of the intense concentration of Nature in the meadows is very difficult—everything is so utterly oblivious of man's thought and man's heart. The oaks stand—quiet, still—so still that the lichen loves them. At their feet the grass grows, and heeds nothing. Among it the squirrels leap, and their little hearts are as far away from you or me as the very wood of the oaks. The sunshine settles itself in the valley by the brook, and abides there whether we come or not. Glance through the gap in the hedge by the oak, and see how concentrated it is—all of it, every blade of grass, and leaf, and flower, and living creature, finch or squirrel. It is mesmerised upon itself. Then I used to feel that it really was seventy-nine miles to London, and not an hour or two only by rail, really all those miles. A great, broad province of green furrow and ploughed furrow between the old house and the city of the world. Such solace and solitude seventy-nine miles thick cannot be painted; the trees cannot be placed far enough away in perspective. It is necessary to stay in it like the oaks to know it.

Lime-tree branches overhung the corner of the garden-wall, whence a view was easy of the silent and dusty road, till over-arching oaks concealed it. The white dust heated by the sunshine, the green hedges, and the heavily massed trees, white clouds rolled together in the sky, a footpath opposite lost in the fields, as you might thrust a stick into the grass, tender lime leaves caressing the cheek, and silence. That is, the silence of the fields. If a breeze rustled the boughs, if a greenfinch called, if the cart-mare in the meadow shook herself, making the earth and air tremble by her with the convulsion of her mighty muscles, these were not sounds, they were the silence itself. So sensitive to it as I was, in its turn it held me firmly, like the fabled spells of old time. The mere touch of a leaf was a talisman to bring me under the enchantment, so that I seemed to feel and know all that was proceeding among the grass-blades and in the bushes. Among the lime-trees along the wall the birds never built, though so close and sheltered. They built everywhere but there. To the broad coping-stones of the wall under the lime boughs speckled thrushes came almost hourly, sometimes to peer out and reconnoitre if it was safe to visit the garden, sometimes to see if a snail had climbed up the ivy. Then they dropped quietly down into the long strawberry patch immediately under. The cover of strawberries is the constant resource of all creeping things; the thrushes looked round every plant and under every leaf and runner. One toad always resided there, often two, and as you gathered a ripe strawberry you might catch sight of his black eye watching you take the fruit he had saved for you.

Down the road skims an eave-swallow, swift as an arrow, his white back making the sun-dried dust dull and dingy; he is seeking a pool for mortar, and will waver to and fro by the brook below till he finds a convenient place to alight. Thence back to the eave here, where for forty years he and his ancestors built in safety. Two white butterflies fluttering round each other rise over the limes, once more up over the house, and soar on till their white shows no longer against the illumined air. A grasshopper calls on the sward by the strawberries, and immediately fillips himself over seven leagues of grass blades. Yonder a line of men and women file across the field, seen for a moment as they pass a gateway, and the hay changes from hay-colour to green behind them as they turn the under but still sappy side upwards. They are working hard, but it looks easy, slow, and sunny. Finches fly out from the hedgerow to the overturned hay. Another butterfly, a brown one, floats along the dusty road—the only traveller yet. The white clouds are slowly passing behind the oaks, large puffed clouds, like deliberate loads of hay, leaving little wisps and flecks behind them caught in the sky. How pleasant it would be to read in the shadow! There is a broad shadow on the sward by the strawberries cast by a tall and fine-grown American crab tree. The very place for a book; and although I know it is useless, yet I go and fetch one and dispose myself on the grass.

I can never read in summer out of doors. Though in shadow the bright light fills it, summer shadows are broadest daylight. The page is so white and hard, the letters so very black, the meaning and drift not quite intelligible, because neither eye nor mind will dwell upon it. Human thoughts and imaginings written down are pale and feeble in bright summer light. The eye wanders away, and rests more lovingly on greensward and green lime leaves. The mind wanders yet deeper and farther into the dreamy mystery of the azure sky. Once now and then, determined to write down that mystery and delicious sense while actually in it, I have brought out table and ink and paper, and sat there in the midst of the summer day. Three words, and where is the thought? Gone. The paper is so obviously paper, the ink so evidently ink, the pen so stiff; all so inadequate. You want colour, flexibility, light, sweet low sound—all these to paint it and play it in music, at the same time you want something that will answer to and record in one touch the strong throb of life and the thought or feeling, or whatever it is that goes out into the earth and sky and space, endless as a beam of light. The very shade of the pen on the paper tells you how utterly hopeless it is to express these things. There is the shade and the brilliant gleaming whiteness; now tell me in plain written words the simple contrast of the two. Not in twenty pages, for the bright light shows the paper in its common fibre-ground, coarse aspect, in its reality, not as a mind-tablet.

The delicacy and beauty of thought or feeling is so extreme that it cannot be inked in; it is like the green and blue of field and sky, of veronica flower and grass blade, which in their own existence throw light and beauty on each other, but in artificial colours repel. Take the table indoors again, and the book: the thoughts and imaginings of others are vain, and of your own too deep to be written. For the mind is filled with the exceeding beauty of these things, and their great wondrousness and marvel. Never yet have I been able to write what I felt about the sunlight only. Colour and form and light are as magic to me. It is a trance. It requires a language of ideas to convey it. It is ten years since I last reclined on that grass plot, and yet I have been writing of it as if it was yesterday, and every blade of grass is as visible and as real to me now as then. They were greener towards the house, and more brown tinted on the margin of the strawberry bed, because towards the house the shadow rested longest. By the strawberries the fierce sunlight burned them.

The sunlight put out the books I brought into it just as it put out the fire on the hearth indoors. The tawny flames floating upwards could not bite the crackling sticks when the full beams came pouring on them. Such extravagance of light overcame the little fire till it was screened from the power of the heavens. So here in the shadow of the American crab tree the light of the sky put out the written pages. For this beautiful and wonderful light excited a sense of some likewise beautiful and wonderful truth, some unknown but grand thought hovering as a swallow above. The swallows hovered and did not alight, but they were there. An inexpressible thought quivered in the azure overhead; it could not be fully grasped, but there was a sense and feeling of its presence. Before that mere sense of its presence the weak and feeble pages, the small fires of human knowledge, dwindled and lost meaning. There was something here that was not in the books. In all the philosophies and searches of mind there was nothing that could be brought to face it, to say, This is what it intends, this is the explanation of the dream. The very grass-blades confounded the wisest, the tender lime leaf put them to shame, the grasshopper derided them, the sparrow on the wall chirped his scorn. The books were put out, unless a screen were placed between them and the light of the sky—that is, an assumption, so as to make an artificial mental darkness. Grant some assumptions—that is, screen off the light—and in that darkness everything was easily arranged, this thing here and that yonder. But Nature grants no assumptions, and the books were put out. There is something beyond the philosophies in the light, in the grass-blades, the leaf, the grasshopper, the sparrow on the wall. Some day the great and beautiful thought which hovers on the confines of the mind will at last alight. In that is hope, the whole sky is full of abounding hope. Something beyond the books, that is consolation.

The little lawn beside the strawberry bed, burned brown there, and green towards the house shadow, holds how many myriad grass-blades? Here they are all matted together, long and dragging each other down. Part them, and beneath them are still more, overhung and hidden. The fibres are intertangled, woven in an endless basket work and chaos of green and dried threads. A blamable profusion this; a fifth as many would be enough; altogether a wilful waste here. As for these insects that spring out of it as I press the grass, a hundredth part of them would suffice. The American crab tree is a snowy mount in spring; the flakes of bloom, when they fall, cover the grass with a film—a bushel of bloom, which the wind takes and scatters afar. The extravagance is sublime. The two little cherry trees are as wasteful; they throw away handfuls of flower: but in the meadows the careless, spendthrift ways of grass and flower and all things are not to be expressed. Seeds by the hundred million float with absolute indifference on the air. The oak has a hundred thousand more leaves than necessary, and never hides a single acorn. Nothing utilitarian—everything on a scale of splendid waste. Such noble, broadcast, open-armed waste is delicious to behold. Never was there such a lying proverb as 'Enough is as good as a feast.' Give me the feast; give me squandered millions of seeds, luxurious carpets of petals, green mountains of oak leaves. The greater the waste, the greater the enjoyment—the nearer the approach to real life. Casuistry is of no avail; the fact is obvious; Nature flings treasures abroad, puffs them with open lips along on every breeze, piles up lavish layers of them in the free open air, packs countless numbers together in the needles of a fir tree. Prodigality and superfluity are stamped on everything she does. The ear of wheat returns a hundredfold the grain from which it grew. The surface of the earth offers to us far more than we can consume—the grains, the seeds, the fruits, the animals, the abounding products are beyond the power of all the human race to devour. They can, too, be multiplied a thousandfold. There is no natural lack. Whenever there is lack among us it is from artificial causes, which intelligence should remove.

From the littleness, and meanness, and niggardliness forced upon us by circumstances, what a relief to turn aside to the exceeding plenty of Nature! There are no bounds to it, there is no comparison to parallel it, so great is this generosity. No physical reason exists why every human being should not have sufficient, at least, of necessities. For any human being to starve, or even to be in trouble about the procuring of simple food, appears, indeed, a strange and unaccountable thing, quite upside down, and contrary to sense, if you do but consider a moment the enormous profusion the earth throws at our feet. In the slow process of time, as the human heart grows larger, such provision, I sincerely trust, will be made that no one need ever feel anxiety about mere subsistence. Then, too, let there be some imitation of this open-handed generosity and divine waste. Let the generations to come feast free of care, like my finches on the seeds of the mowing-grass, from which no voice drives them. If I could but give away as freely as the earth does!

The white-backed eave-swallow has returned many, many times from the shallow drinking-place by the brook to his half-built nest. Sometimes the pair of them cling to the mortar they have fixed under the eave, and twitter to each other about the progress of the work. They dive downwards with such velocity when they quit hold that it seems as if they must strike the ground, but they shoot up again, over the wall and the lime trees. A thrush has been to the arbour yonder twenty times; it is made of crossed laths, and overgrown with 'tea-plant,' and the nest is inside the lath-work. A sparrow has visited the rose tree by the wall—the buds are covered with aphides. A brown tree-creeper has been to the limes, then to the cherries, and even to a stout lilac stem. No matter how small the tree, he tries all that are in his way. The bright colours of a bullfinch were visible a moment just now, as he passed across the shadows farther down the garden under the damson trees and into the bushes. The grasshopper has gone past and along the garden-path, his voice is not heard now; but there is another coming. While I have been dreaming, all these and hundreds out in the meadow have been intensely happy. So concentrated on their little work in the sunshine, so intent on the tiny egg, on the insect captured, on the grass-tip to be carried to the eager fledglings, so joyful in listening to the song poured out for them or in pouring it forth, quite oblivious of all else. It is in this intense concentration that they are so happy. If they could only live longer! but a few such seasons for them—I wish they could live a hundred years just to feast on the seeds and sing and be utterly happy and oblivious of everything but the moment they are passing. A black line has rushed up from the espalier apple yonder to the housetop thirty times at least. The starlings fly so swiftly and so straight that they seem to leave a black line along the air. They have a nest in the roof, they are to and fro it and the meadow the entire day, from dawn till eve. The espalier apple, like a screen, hides the meadow from me, so that the descending starlings appear to dive into a space behind it. Sloping downwards the meadow makes a valley; I cannot see it, but know that it is golden with buttercups, and that a brook runs in the groove of it.

Afar yonder I can see a summit beyond where the grass swells upwards to a higher level than this spot. There are bushes and elms whose height is decreased by distance on the summit, horses in the shadow of the trees, and a small flock of sheep crowded, as is their wont, in the hot and sunny gateway. By the side of the summit is a deep green trench, so it looks from here, in the hill-side: it is really the course of a streamlet worn deep in the earth. I can see nothing between the top of the espalier screen and the horses under the elms on the hill. But the starlings go up and down into the hollow space, which is aglow with golden buttercups, and, indeed, I am looking over a hundred finches eagerly searching, sweetly calling, happy as the summer day. A thousand thousand grasshoppers are leaping, thrushes are labouring, filled with love and tenderness, doves cooing—there is as much joy as there are leaves on the hedges. Faster than the starling's flight my mind runs up to the streamlet in the deep green trench beside the hill.

Pleasant it was to trace it upwards, narrowing at every ascending step, till the thin stream, thinner than fragile glass, did but merely slip over the stones. A little less and it could not have run at all, water could not stretch out to greater tenuity. It smoothed the brown growth on the stones, stroking it softly. It filled up tiny basins of sand and ran out at the edges between minute rocks of flint. Beneath it went under thickest brooklime, blue flowered, and serrated water-parsnips, lost like many a mighty river for awhile among a forest of leaves. Higher up masses of bramble and projecting thorn stopped the explorer, who must wind round the grassy mound. Pausing to look back a moment there were meads under the hill with the shortest and greenest herbage, perpetually watered, and without one single buttercup, a strip of pure green among yellow flowers and yellowing corn. A few hollow oaks on whose boughs the cuckoos stayed to call, two or three peewits coursing up and down, larks singing, and for all else silence. Between the wheat and the grassy mound the path was almost closed, burdocks and brambles thrust the adventurer outward to brush against the wheat-ears. Upwards till suddenly it turned, and led by steep notches in the bank, as it seemed, down to the roots of the elm trees. The clump of elms grew right over a deep and rugged hollow; their branches reached out across it, roofing in the cave.

Here was the spring, at the foot of a perpendicular rock, moss-grown low down, and overrun with creeping ivy higher. Green thorn bushes filled the chinks and made a wall to the well, and the long narrow hart's-tongue streaked the face of the cliff. Behind the thick thorns hid the course of the streamlet, in front rose the solid rock, upon the right hand the sward came to the edge—it shook every now and then as the horses in the shade of the elms stamped their feet—on the left hand the ears of wheat peered over the verge. A rocky cell in concentrated silence of green things. Now and again a finch, a starling, or a sparrow would come meaning to drink—athirst from the meadow or the cornfield—and start and almost entangle their wings in the bushes, so completely astonished that any one should be there. The spring rises in a hollow under the rock imperceptibly, and without bubble or sound. The fine sand of the shallow basin is undisturbed—no tiny water-volcano pushes up a dome of particles. Nor is there any crevice in the stone, but the basin is always full and always running over. As it slips from the brim a gleam of sunshine falls through the boughs and meets it. To this cell I used to come once now and then on a summer's day, tempted, perhaps, like the finches, by the sweet cool water, but drawn also by a feeling that could not be analysed. Stooping, I lifted the water in the hollow of my hand—carefully, lest the sand might be disturbed—and the sunlight gleamed on it as it slipped through my fingers. Alone in the green-roofed cave, alone with the sunlight and the pure water, there was a sense of something more than these. The water was more to me than water, and the sun than sun. The gleaming rays on the water in my palm held me for a moment, the touch of the water gave me something from itself. A moment, and the gleam was gone, the water flowing away, but I had had them. Beside the physical water and physical light I had received from them their beauty; they had communicated to me this silent mystery. The pure and beautiful water, the pure, clear, and beautiful light, each had given me something of their truth.

So many times I came to it, toiling up the long and shadowless hill in the burning sunshine, often carrying a vessel to take some of it home with me. There was a brook, indeed; but this was different, it was the spring; it was taken home as a beautiful flower might be brought. It is not the physical water, it is the sense of feeling that it conveys. Nor is it the physical sunshine; it is the sense of inexpressible beauty which it brings with it. Of such I still drink, and hope to do so still deeper.

The Life of the Fields, 1884.

ROBERT LOUIS STEVENSON

1850–1894

WALKING TOURS

IT must not be imagined that a walking tour, as some would have us fancy, is merely a better or worse way of seeing the country. There are many ways of seeing landscape quite as good; and none more vivid, in spite of canting dilettantes, than from a railway train. But landscape on a walking tour is quite accessory. He who is indeed of the brotherhood does not voyage in quest of the picturesque, but of certain jolly humours—of the hope and spirit with which the march begins at morning, and the peace and spiritual repletion of the evening's rest. He cannot tell whether he puts his knapsack on, or takes it off, with more delight. The excitement of the departure puts him in key for that of the arrival. Whatever he does is not only a reward in itself, but will be further rewarded in the sequel; and so pleasure leads on to pleasure in an endless chain. It is this that so few can understand; they will either be always lounging or always at five miles an hour; they do not play off the one against the other, prepare all day for the evening, and all evening for the next day. And, above all, it is here that your overwalker fails of comprehension. His heart rises against those who drink their curaçoa in liqueur glasses, when he himself can swill it in a brown john. He will not believe that the flavour is more delicate in the smaller dose. He will not believe that to walk this unconscionable distance is merely to stupefy and brutalise himself, and come to his inn, at night, with a sort of frost on his five wits, and a starless night of darkness in his spirit. Not for him the mild luminous evening of the temperate walker! He has nothing left of man but a physical need for bedtime and a double nightcap; and even his pipe, if he be a smoker, will be savourless and disenchanted. It is the fate of such an one to take twice as much trouble as is needed to obtain happiness, and miss the happiness in the end; he is the man of the proverb, in short, who goes further and fares worse.

Now, to be properly enjoyed, a walking tour should be gone upon alone. If you go in a company, or even in pairs, it is no longer a walking tour in anything but name; it is something else and more in the nature of a picnic. A walking tour should be gone upon alone, because freedom is of the essence: because you should be able to stop and go on, and follow this way or that, as the freak takes you; and because you must have your own pace and neither trot alongside a champion walker, nor mince in time with a girl. And then you must be open to all impressions and let your thoughts take colour from what you see. You should be as a pipe for any wind to play upon. 'I cannot see the wit,' says Hazlitt, 'of walking and talking at the same time. When I am in the country, I wish to vegetate like the country,' which is the gist of all that can be said upon the matter. There should be no cackle of voices at your elbow, to jar on the meditative silence of the morning. And so long as a man is reasoning he cannot surrender himself to that fine intoxication that comes of much motion in the open air, that begins in a sort of dazzle and sluggishness of the brain, and ends in a peace that passes comprehension.

During the first day or so of any tour there are moments of bitterness, when the traveller feels more than coldly towards his knapsack, when he is half in a mind to throw it bodily over the hedge and, like Christian on a similar occasion, 'give three leaps and go on singing.' And yet it soon acquires a property of easiness. It becomes magnetic; the spirit of the journey enters into it. And no sooner have you passed the straps over your shoulder than the lees of sleep are cleared from you, you pull yourself together with a shake, and fall at once into your stride. And surely, of all possible moods, this, in which a man takes the road, is the best. Of course, if he *will* keep thinking of his anxieties, if he *will* open the merchant Abudah's chest and walk arm in arm with the hag—why, wherever he is, and whether he walk fast or slow, the chances are that he will not be happy. And so much the more shame to himself! There are perhaps thirty men setting forth at that same hour, and I would lay a large wager there is not another dull face among the thirty. It would be a fine thing to follow, in a coat of darkness, one after another of these wayfarers, some summer morning, for the first few miles upon the road. This one, who walks fast, with a keen look in his eyes, is all concentrated in his own mind; he is up at his loom, weaving and weaving, to set the landscape to words. This one peers about, as he goes, among the grasses; he waits by the canal to watch the dragon-flies; he leans on the gate of the pasture, and cannot look enough upon the complacent kine. And here comes another talking, laughing, and gesticulating to himself. His face changes from time to time, as indignation flashes from his eyes or anger clouds his forehead. He is composing articles, delivering orations, and conducting the most impassioned interviews, by the way. A little farther on, and it is as like as not he will begin to sing. And well for him, supposing him to be no great master in that art, if he stumble across no stolid peasant at a corner; for on such an occasion, I scarcely know which is the more troubled, or whether it is worse to suffer the confusion of your troubadour or the unfeigned alarm of your clown. A sedentary population, accustomed, besides, to the strange mechanical bearing of the common tramp, can in no wise explain to itself the gaiety of these passers-by. I knew one man who was arrested as a runaway lunatic because, although a full-grown person with a red beard, he skipped as he went like a child. And you would be astonished if I were to tell you all the grave and learned heads who have confessed to me that, when on walking tours, they sang—and sang very ill—and had a pair of red ears when, as described above, the inauspicious peasant plumped into their arms from round a corner. And here, lest you should think I am exaggerating, is Hazlitt's own confession, from his essay *On going a Journey*, which is so good that there should be a tax levied on all who have not read it:—

'Give me the clear blue sky over my head,' says he, 'and the green turf beneath my feet, a winding road before me, and a three hours' march to dinner—and then to thinking! It is hard if I cannot start some game on these lone heaths. I laugh, I run, I leap, I sing for joy.'

Bravo! After that adventure of my friend with the policeman, you would not have cared, would you, to publish that in the first person? But we have no bravery nowadays, and, even in books, must all pretend to be as dull and foolish as our neighbours. It was not so with Hazlitt. And notice how learned he is (as, indeed, throughout the essay) in the theory of walking tours. He is none of your athletic men in purple stockings, who walk their fifty miles a day: three hours' march is his ideal. And then he must have a winding road, the epicure!

Yet there is one thing I object to in these words of his, one thing in the great master's practice that seems to me not wholly wise. I do not approve of that leaping and running. Both of these hurry the respiration; they both shake up the brain out of its glorious open-air confusion; and they both break the pace. Uneven walking is not so agreeable to the body, and it distracts and irritates the mind. Whereas, when once you have fallen into an equable stride, it requires no conscious thought from you to keep it up, and yet it prevents you from thinking earnestly of anything else. Like knitting, like the work of a copying clerk, it gradually neutralises and sets to sleep the serious activity of the mind. We can think of this or that, lightly and laughingly, as a child thinks, or as we think in a morning doze; we can make puns or puzzle out acrostics, and trifle in a thousand ways with words and rhymes; but when it comes to honest work, when we come to gather ourselves together for an effort, we may sound the trumpet as loud and long as we please; the great barons of the mind will not rally to the standard, but sit, each one, at home, warming his hands over his own fire and brooding on his own private thought!

In the course of a day's walk, you see, there is much variance in the mood. From the exhilaration of the start, to the happy phlegm of the arrival, the change is certainly great. As the day goes on, the traveller moves from the one extreme towards the other. He becomes more and more incorporated with the material landscape, and the open-air drunkenness grows upon him with great strides, until he posts along the road, and sees everything about him, as in a cheerful dream. The first is certainly brighter, but the second stage is the more peaceful. A man does not make so many articles towards the end, nor does he laugh aloud; but the purely animal pleasures, the sense of physical wellbeing, the delight of every inhalation, of every time the muscles tighten down the thigh, console him for the absence of the others, and bring him to his destination still content.

Nor must I forget to say a word on bivouacs. You come to a milestone on a hill, or some place where deep ways meet under trees; and off goes the knapsack, and down you sit to smoke a pipe in the shade. You sink into yourself, and the birds come round and look at you, and your smoke dissipates upon the afternoon under the blue dome of heaven; and the sun lies warm upon your feet, and the cool air visits your neck and turns aside your open shirt. If you are not happy, you must have an evil conscience. You may dally as long as you like by the roadside. It is almost as if the millennium were arrived, when we shall throw our clocks and watches over the housetop, and remember time and seasons no more. Not to keep hours for a lifetime is, I was going to say, to live for ever. You have no idea, unless you have tried it, how endlessly long is a summer's day, that you measure out only by hunger, and bring to an end only when you are drowsy. I know a village where there are hardly any clocks, where no one knows more of the days of the week than by a sort of instinct for the *fête* on Sundays, and where only one person can tell you the day of the month, and she is generally wrong; and if people were aware how slow Time journeyed in that village, and what armfuls of spare hours he gives, over and above the bargain, to its wise inhabitants, I believe there would be a stampede out of London, Liverpool, Paris, and a variety of large towns, where the clocks lose their heads, and shake the hours out each one faster than the other, as though they were all in a wager. And all these foolish pilgrims would each bring his own misery along with him, in a watch-pocket! It is to be noticed, there were no clocks and watches in the much-vaunted days before the flood. It follows, of course, there were no appointments, and punctuality was not yet thought upon. 'Though ye take from a covetous man all his treasure,' says Milton, 'he has yet one jewel left; ye cannot deprive him of his covetousness.' And so I would say of a modern man of business, you may do what you will for him, put him in Eden, give him the elixir of life—he has still a flaw at heart, he still has his business habits. Now, there is no time when business habits are more mitigated than on a walking tour. And so during these halts, as I say, you will feel almost free.

But it is at night, and after dinner, that the best hour comes. There are no such pipes to be smoked as those that follow a good day's march; the flavour of the tobacco is a thing to be remembered, it is so dry and aromatic, so full and so fine. If you wind up the evening with grog, you will own there was never such grog; at every sip a jocund tranquillity spreads about your limbs, and sits easily in your heart. If you read a book—and you will never do so save by fits and starts—you find the language strangely racy and harmonious; words take a new meaning; single sentences possess the ear for half an hour together; and the writer endears himself to you, at every page, by the nicest coincidence of sentiment. It seems as if it were a book you had written yourself in a dream. To all we have read on such occasions we look back with special favour. 'It was on the 10th of April 1798,' says Hazlitt, with amorous precision, 'that I sat down to a volume of the new *Heloïse*, at the Inn at Llangollen, over a bottle of sherry and a cold chicken.' I should wish to quote more, for though we are mighty fine fellows nowadays, we cannot write like Hazlitt. And, talking of that, a volume of Hazlitt's essays would be a capital pocket-book on such a journey; so would a volume of Heine's songs; and for *Tristram Shandy* I can pledge a fair experience.

If the evening be fine and warm, there is nothing better in life than to lounge before the inn door in the sunset, or lean over the parapet of the bridge, to watch the weeds and the quick fishes. It is then, if ever, that you taste joviality to the full significance of that audacious word. Your muscles are so agreeably slack, you feel so clean and so strong and so idle, that whether you move or sit still, whatever you do is done with pride and a kingly sort of pleasure. You fall in talk with any one, wise or foolish, drunk or sober. And it seems as if a hot walk purged you, more than of anything else, of all narrowness and pride, and left curiosity to play its part freely, as in a child or a man of science. You lay aside all your own hobbies to watch provincial humours develop themselves before you, now as a laughable farce, and now grave and beautiful like an old tale.

Or perhaps you are left to your own company for the night, and surly weather imprisons you by the fire. You may remember how Burns, numbering past pleasures, dwells upon the hours when he has been 'happy thinking.' It is a phrase that may well perplex a poor modern girt about on every side by clocks and chimes, and haunted, even at night, by flaming dial-plates. For we are all so busy, and have so many far-off projects to realise, and castles in the fire to turn into solid, habitable mansions on a gravel soil, that we can find no time for pleasure trips into the Land of Thought and among the Hills of Vanity. Changed times, indeed, when we must sit all night, beside the fire, with folded hands; and a changed world for most of us, when we find we can pass the hours without discontent, and be happy thinking. We are in such haste to be doing, to be writing, to be gathering gear, to make our voice audible a moment in the derisive silence of eternity, that we forget that one thing, of which these are but the parts—namely to live. We fall in love, we drink hard, we run to and fro upon the earth like frightened sheep. And now you are to ask yourself if, when all is done, you would not have been better to sit by the fire at home, and be happy thinking. To sit still and contemplate,—to remember the faces of women without desire, to be pleased by the great deeds of men without envy, to be everything and everywhere in sympathy, and yet content to remain where and what you are—is not this to know both wisdom and virtue, and to dwell with happiness? After all, it is not they who carry flags, but they who look upon it from a private chamber, who have the fun of the procession. And once you are at that, you are in the very humour of all social heresy. It is no time for shuffling, or for big empty words. If you ask yourself what you mean by fame, riches, or learning, the answer is far to seek;

and you go back into that kingdom of light imaginations, which seem so vain in the eyes of Philistines perspiring after wealth, and so momentous to those who are stricken with the disproportions of the world, and, in the face of the gigantic stars, cannot stop to split differences between two degrees of the infinitesimally small, such as a tobacco pipe or the Roman Empire, a million of money or a fiddlestick's end.

You lean from the window, your last pipe reeking whitely into the darkness, your body full of delicious pains, your mind enthroned in the seventh circle of content; when suddenly the mood changes, the weather-cock goes about, and you ask yourself one question more: whether, for the interval, you have been the wisest philosopher or the most egregious of donkeys? Human experience is not yet able to reply; but at least you have had a fine moment, and looked down upon all the kingdoms of the earth. And whether it was wise or foolish, to-morrow's travel will carry you, body and mind, into some different parish of the infinite.

Virginibus Puerisque, 1880.

PRINTED IN GREAT BRITAIN
AT THE UNIVERSITY PRESS, OXFORD
BY VIVIAN RIDLER
PRINTER TO THE UNIVERSITY